Agapanthus

Agapanthus

A REVISION OF THE GENUS

Wim Snoeijer, F.L.S.

TIMBER PRESS
Portland · Cambridge

In association with the Royal Boskoop Horticultural Society

Published in 2004 by
Timber Press, Inc.
The Haseltine Building
133 S.W. Second Avenue, Suite 450
Portland, Oregon 97204, U.S.A.

Timber Press
2 Station Road
Swavesey, Cambridge CB4 5QJ, U.K.

www.timberpress.com

Printed in China

Library of Congress Cataloging-in-Publication Data

Snoeijer, W. (Wim)
    Agapanthus : a revision of the genus / Wim Snoeijer.
        p.   cm.
Includes bibliographical references (p.   ).
    ISBN 0-88192-631-0 (hardback)
    1. Agapanthus—Identification. 2. Agapanthus—Classification. I. Royal Boskoop
Horticultural Society. II. Title.
    QK495.L72 S66 2004
    584'.34—dc22

2003017447

A Catalogue record for this book is also available from the British Library.

Contents

Color plates follow page 160

Foreword

Is there an important standard work of cultivated *Agapanthus*? With this book, the question has been settled, and the answer, finally, is a resounding "yes." How very satisfying that this enormous lack in horticultural knowledge has been filled for now! Not only does this book offer extensive coverage of preferable names and synonyms of species and cultivars and their detailed descriptions, but it is also up-to-date. Traditional classification methods based on evolutionary relationships are in the main unsatisfactory for highly cultivated crops; the modern classification of *Agapanthus* cultivars into groups, as presented in this book, has a high practical value in horticulture.

Likewise satisfying is that this book is the first in a new series to be published under the auspices of the Royal Boskoop Horticultural Society, a series that will consist of several books on specific genera which are too huge and too detailed to be published as articles in *Dendroflora*.

It remains only for me to compliment Wim Snoeijer for the incredible amount of work he has performed here, with a skill and enthusiasm that were equally high.

Marco Hoffman
Taxonomist and chief editor, *Dendroflora*
Royal Boskoop Horticultural Society

Preface

The popularity of *Agapanthus* continues to rise. The amount of cultivars introduced in recent years is amazing, and some cultivars are grown in enormous numbers. Yet hardly any material concerning the plants is offered to the gardening public. This is very strange because the popularity of a genus is usually linked with the information available, whether via scientific publications, monographs, popular books, articles, sales sheets, or television.

I have always been interested in monocotyledons (my main interest, both professionally and as a hobby, is *Clematis*). In the early 1990s, as a member of the Oranjerievereniging (Dutch Orangery Society), I noted the interest in *Agapanthus* of several members and their complaints that information was hard to find. I started to collect references about *Agapanthus* in early 1995 at the library of our National Herbarium, Leiden University Branch. I also collected catalogues and started correspondence. I visited several collections during the flowering period in 1995 and ended my research at the library of the KAVB (Koninklijke Algemeene Vereeniging voor Bloembollencultuur = Royal General Bulb Growers' Association). I then wrote an article for *De Parel*, the Dutch Orangery Society's journal, and privately published the full results of my research as a book in 1998, with much success.

In 1996 I began to collect Dutch *Agapanthus* cultivars at work, Division of Pharmacognosy, Leiden/Amsterdam Center for Drug Research. Rob Verpoorte, head of our division, had proposed a project on flower colours, and *Agapanthus* fit the project perfectly. Accordingly I started a newsletter for those interested in Dutch *Agapanthus* cultivars. The collection, now part of the NPC (Nederlandse Planten Collectie = Dutch Plant Collection) under the umbrella of the KVBC (Koninklijke Vereniging voor Boskoopse Culturen = Royal Boskoop Horticultural Society), contained 68 Dutch cultivars in summer 2003.

In August 2001, I contacted the KVBC; yes, the Society was interested in publishing my 1998 manuscript, augmented with much more information, many more names, some conclusions and, most importantly, a modern cultivar classification and a revision of the species. In this book, six species are accepted, instead of the normal ten. Most of the approximately 625 cultivar names in this book are accompanied with some information, and many will have a full description. Valid names appear in **boldface** type.

Acknowledgments

Kees Duivenvoorde, a breeder and grower of *Agapanthus* in Holland and a real agapanthus friend of mine, provided me with many records, concerning not only his own cultivars but also those of other Dutch cultivars, and supplied many plants to the NPC. His assistance, both at the NPC presentation at the Floriade 2002 in Holland and in reading the manuscript, was invaluable. His wife, Catharina, and daughter too were closely involved, attending open days in Leiden and helping at the Floriade.

I am indebted to Gary Dunlop of Ballyrogan Nurseries, Northern Ireland, UK, with whom I have had an extensive correspondence, especially for notes on raisers and details concerning his own plants, which appear throughout the book. Dick Fulcher of Pine Cottage Plants, UK, too provided many records from his NCCPG (National Council for the Conservation of Plants and Gardens) collection; Ignace van Doorslaer of Melle-Gontrode, Belgium, checked descriptions and sent me additional information.

The KAVB library is an incredible, amazing, and surprising collection. Thanks to the devoted librarians they had in the past and to the present librarian and registrar, Johan van Scheepen. The library holds many old catalogues, such as those produced by Krelage, Leichtlin, Lemoine, von Siebold, and van Tubergen. Johan also sent me several photocopies of journal notes and articles on *Agapanthus*. Thank you, Johan.

The library of the National Herbarium, Leiden University Branch, was another invaluable source of references. I would like to say a sincere thank-you for all the help I received during the years from the librarian and his staff.

It is a real honour to have gained permission, from the present editor of the *South African Journal of Botany*, professor J. van Staden, with help of the former editor professor J.N. Eloff, to reproduce some of the plates from Mrs Leighton's 1965 article. I am also grateful to Brian Mathew, editor of *Curtis's Botanical Magazine*, who gave permission to reproduce the plate of *Agapanthus* 'Weillighii'. All these plates are of great historic and botanical interest and are the treasures in this book. The cooperation of both editors is highly appreciated.

Thanks also to Hanneke van Dijk, author of many plant and garden books, with whom I discussed many things, including editorial matters, on many occasions accompanied by her husband, George. Thank you, Hanneke and George.

I would also like to thank Wim van der Poel of the Publication Committee for the Royal Boskoop Horticultural Society, and, of course, the other Committee members. Without their efforts, this book would not have been published. Thanks also to Marco Hoffman, editor of *Dendroflora*, Journal of the Royal Boskoop Horticultural Society, who not only provided the foreword but also read the manuscript and gave some very constructive criticism, including the proposal for a new cultivar group; and to the members of the KVBC and the Society's board, for their trust and the opportunity to make this book possible.

Finally, thanks to all those around the world who were willing to take my phonecalls, answer my letters, send information, or host me on visits. A publication like this would be impossible without such people, mentioned above and below, who provide the necessary link to the living plants. Thank you very much indeed for your enthusiastic help, care, and attention! I sincerely apologize to anyone I have forgotten.

Australia
Trevor Nottle, Walnut Hill, Crafers, South Australia.

The Netherlands
Library of the Proefstation voor de Bloemisterij (Experimental Station for Floristry), Aalsmeer; V.K.C. Vaste Keurings Commissie, Wilbert Hetterscheid, Aalsmeer; van Beek, Hillegom; Wim van Dam, Gouda; George Otter, IJsselstein; Cor van Eijk, Nootdorp; Martin Fontein, Haarlem; Jan Fopma, Hilversum; Pauline de Graaf, Leiden; Griffioen, Wassenaar; Karel Hooijman, Amstelveen; Coen Jansen, Dalfsen; Luc Klinkhamer, Lisse; Hans Kramer, De Hessenhof, Ede; Dik and Frenk Maas, Maas & van Stein, De Zilk; Arno Rijnbeek, Rijnbeek en Zoon B.V., Boskoop; Nico van Os, Bergschenhoek; J.M.A. Reintjes, Veulen; Els Schlatmann, Oegstgeest; Mrs and Mr Snoeijer, Gouda; Gerard van Tol, Boskoop; L. van der Valk, Zoeterwoude; Jan van Zoest, Boskoop; Ben Zonneveld, Leiden.

France
Bulbes d'Opale, Buysscheure; Lesley and David Sleigh, B&T World Seeds, Olonzac.

Germany
Dr Josef Sieber, Internationale Stauden-Union, Freising.

Japan
Mr Y. Aihara, Tokyo; Mr H. Hayakawa, Izumi-cho; Mr S. Komoriya, Chiba-city; Mrs S. Kuriyama, Ichimiya Shi Aichi.

New Zealand
Lady Anne Berry, Hackfalls Arboretum, Gisborne; Peter Diack, Diack Nurseries Ltd, Invercargill; Sandra Simpson, Multiflora, Newmarket, Auckland; Lucie Wenmakers, Mill House Nursery, Akaroa.

South Africa
Biofleur, Cape Seed & Bulb at Rosarium Nursery, Lynedoch, Stellenbosch; Harry Molteno Library, Nat. Botanical Institute, Claremont; Malanseuns, Plesier Plante/ Pleasure Plants.

United Kingdom
Edwin Aldridge, Asterby & Chalkcroft Nurseries, Blunham, Bedfordshire; Apple Court, Hordle, Lymington; Beeches Nursery, Village Centre, Ashdon, Saffron Walden; J.D. Bond, The Crown Estate, The Great Park, Windsor; Rod Casey, Lodge Lane Nursery, Dutton, Cheshire; Mrs B. Chatto, The Beth Chatto Gardens, Elmstead Market; David Clark, Nottcuts Nurseries, Woodbridge; J.M. Gardiner and Kate Haywood, RHS Wisley; I.C. Greenfield, Raveningham Gardens, Norwich; Dr John Howells MD, Higham, Colchester; Peter Manfield, The Village Nurseries, Pulborough, West Sussex; Victoria Matthews, *Clematis* Registrar for the RHS; Judith Read, Read's Nursery, Lodden; Joe Sharman, Monksilver Nursery, Cottenham; Olly Spencer, Webbs of Wychbold Nursery; David Way, Hunton, Maidstone.

United States
Myrna Ougland, Heronswood Nursery, Kingston, Washington; Wendy Proud, Monrovia; Wayside Gardens, Hodges, South Carolina.

Chapter 1

Introduction

The first mention in The Netherlands of a cultivated *Agapanthus* is a description by Jacob Breyne (Breynius) in 1680, of a flowering plant in the garden of Hieronymus van Beverningk in Warmond, The Netherlands, in 1679. This makes sense: in 1652 a Dutch camp had been set up at the Cape of Good Hope in South Africa by the Verenigde Oostindische Compagnie, and ever since, many plants from South Africa were brought to The Netherlands. Breynius published the plant as *Hyacinthus Africanus Tuberosus, Flore caeruleo umbellato*. In 1687, the plant was published in Hermann's Catalogue as *Hyacintho affinis Africana Tuberosa radice umbella caerulea inodora*, from a plant grown at the Hortus Botanicus Leiden, The Netherlands, and *Agapanthus africanus* was cultivated at the Hortus Medicus of Amsterdam, according to the Moninckx Atlas of 1698 (a reproduction of Jan Monincks drawing of *A. africanus* appears in Wijnands 1983).

The first known plant cultivated in England is mentioned in a 1692 publication of L. Plukenet, of a flowering plant at Hampton Court Palace named *Hyacintho affinis, tuberosa radice, Africana, umbella caerulea inodora*. Plukenet included a line drawing (a photograph of which is published in Leighton 1965). Very little imagination is required to speculate that the Hampton Court Palace plant could have been derived from the Dutch plant (shades of William and Mary!).

Linnaeus published the name as *Crinum africanum* in 1753. The next figure that appeared was by Phillip Miller in his Gardener's Dictionary (1760).

L'Héritier, director of the Jardin des Plantes in Paris, changed the name, in 1789, to *Agapanthus*, with the invalid species denomination *umbellatus*. This should have been *africanus* from Linnaeus's name. This mistake is the basis for the confusion of nomenclature within this genus. The correct name, *A. africanus*, was published by Hoffmannsegg in 1824.

The first taxonomic monograph on the genus was written by Frances M. (Mrs Isaac) Leighton (at that time an assistant in the Bolus Herbarium of the University of Cape Town) in her spare time and published in the Journal of South African Bot-

13

any, Suppl. Vol. IV, January 1965. Her study depended on borrowed herbarium specimens from overseas (including the National Herbarium, Leiden University Branch) and a collection of living plants at Kirstenbosch National Botanical Garden, most of which came from wild locations.

Herb or Poisonous?

Agapanthus rootstocks contain saponin. According to Hegnauer (1963, 1986) the sapogen was isolated, 4 g from 1 kg of rootstock. It is usually accompanied by yucca-genin. Saponin is also found in the seeds of *A. caulescens* and *A. praecox.*

Chewed leaves cause severe pain in the mouth. When leaves are crushed on the skin, the skin becomes irritated, sometimes for only a few minutes, sometimes longer, turning the skin red. Eyes are irritated by the cell sap.

Batten and Bokelmann (1966) give the best information about native uses for *Agapanthus praecox*: "The roots are much sought after by native herbalists. A young Xhosa bride always wears a necklace of the roots; if not a number of roots, then one or two added to a beaded necklace, as they are considered to promote an abundance of children and easy childbirth. A young mother with her first child constantly wears the necklace, in order that both mother and child may find health and happiness. Often, if necessary, the roots are ground up and used as medicine by the mother." They also refer to *A. comptonii*, whose root "is used by the Xhosa to make a paste for the treatment of swollen legs."

Pearse (1978) refers to some native and similar uses: "The Zulus make an infusion from the roots to sprinkle their yards and huts with, as a protection against thunderstorms. It is also used to *phalaza* [an old Zulu custom: an infusion of herbs or roots is mixed with hot or cold water; the Zulu drinks this, takes up a kneeling position, and tickles his throat to induce vomiting, which supposedly cleanses the stomach]. Sometimes a lotion is made from the flowers [and applied to] newly-born babies, in the belief that it will make them strong. Xhosas use the roots to make a paste for the treatment of swollen legs."

The Bantash used *Agapanthus* for both medical and magic purposes (Doutt 1994). Maliehe (1997) refers to *A. campanulatus* as "a medicinal plant, usually sold at market stalls. The roots are crushed and administered to infants as a general tonic. It is also used to heal body rash. The same mixture is used to alleviate menstrual pains in women." Van Wyk (2000) refers to *A. praecox* thus: "In traditional medicine a decoction of the rhizome and roots, or water in which a plant was grown, are widely used by women before and after childbirth. Crude extracts of the plant have a proven effect on the contraction of the uterus wall."

The most recent publication on *Agapanthus* as a medical plant is probably by van Wyk, van Oudtshoorn, and Gericke (2000). They included several paragraphs on the medicinal uses, active ingredients, and pharmacological effects of the species, including preparation and dosage. The information is similar to what is offered in the aforementioned references, but they add that the saponin has a biological activity and biochemical effect, "including anti-flammatory, anti-oedema, antitussive, and immunoregulatory properties."

Anthocyanin

The violet-blue-purple colouring is caused by anthocyanin. White-flowering plants can be divided into two groups: plants having green buds and pure white flowers (probably derived from *Agapanthus praecox*) and plants having purple buds and white flowers with a purple tint (probably derived from, or interbreeding with, *A. campanulatus* and *A. caulescens*). In the first group, anthocyanin is not present; in the last, the purple colouring is caused by anthocyanin.

The degree of anthocyanin visible on a plant is dependent on the amount of sunlight it receives. Plants growing in full sun all day, and showing distinct anthocyanin in their peduncle, pedicel, and flower, may have much less anthocyanin colouring in the shade. The easiest way to check whether the plant contains anthocyanin is the leafbase. This will be either green, or, when anthocyanin is present, will have some purple colouring, even when growing in the shade. This characteristic is also known in *Clivia*, in which seedlings with an purple leafbase colouring will flower orange or red, while with green leafbase colouring, the flower will be yellow (photographs of this feature are published in Duncan 1999 and Koopowitz 2002, which last book includes a very good chapter about colour that makes worthwhile reading). The relation between leafbase colour and flower colour, however, does not exist in *Agapanthus*. Plants with white flowers and a purple tint may have a green leafbase colouring.

Trials

Wisley trial

From 1971 to 1977 an *Agapanthus* trial was held at the RHS Garden Wisley, UK. The first 58 entries, 34 of which came from the collection of the Hon. Lewis Palmer, were planted in 1971. In subsequent years more plants were planted at the Portsmouth Field, with the result that 71 different plants were on trial, 60 of which came from Palmer. The trial was inspected by a sub-committee consisting of members of Floral A and Floral B Committees. At the last meeting, 30 August 1977, awards were given based on all previous inspections. This trial gave rise to the interest in and popularity of *Agapanthus*, which can be attributed mostly to Palmer. Details of the plants and awards were published by the Royal Horticultural Society in their Journal in 1977, and a report was written by J. Bond (1978).

Unfortunately, after the trial the fields were cleared, and it is unknown what happened to the plants. At Battleston Hill, however, many *Agapanthus* grow, and it seems likely that those plants were originally from the trial. These plants are not labelled, and if they are from the trial it will be hard, if not impossible, to identify them. The plants indeed looked about 20 years old when I visited Wisley in 1995.

In the Wisley guides published by the RHS, nothing refers to the origin of the *Agapanthus* on Battleston Hill. Only Rix (1989) comes close: "The climate, soil and aspect proved ideal for hardy *Agapanthus*, and large clumps lined many paths. There was a trial of *Agapanthus*, held in around 1973, so that Wisley has an especially good collection of hardy species and cultivars."

Research to identify these cultivars would have been welcome. Unfortunately, since 1998, most plants have been removed; only a few remain (see remarks under 'Weillighii'). However many new cultivars are planted at Battleston Hill, it is a great loss that these original Palmer plants were expelled.

Aalsmeer trial

In 1978, an *Agapanthus* trial was held at the Proefstation voor de Bloemisterij (Experimental Station for Florestry), Aalsmeer, The Netherlands. This student research project was a cooperative venture between the Proefstation and the Vakgroep Taxonomy van Cultuurgewassen of the Landbouwhogeschool (Division of Taxonomy of Crops of the Agricultural Highschool [today University]), Wageningen, also in The Netherlands. That year, 58 different plants were collected and planted at the trial fields of the Experimental Station. Most were named cultivars, but several were unnamed plants that had only a number. Many of the English cultivars came from Wisley.

A study of the trial was published by A.J.M. Gillissen in 1979; unfortunately, this report is not well known and, perhaps even worse, written in Dutch, but I have included much of the very detailed information in this work. Gillissen also published a classification of the cultivars (the first known) and a thorough study of the inflorescence, which was missed by taxonomists like Dahlgren, Clifford, and Yeo (1985) and Fay and Chase (1996).

Awards

Several cultivars have received awards over the years. Many were presented during the Wisley trial in 1977; these awards are of interest as they were given after some years of examination. Other awards are given during flower shows and are just an impression at the moment of judging; such awards do not give any idea about the plant's ornamental value or its value as a cut flower. Although these awards are of less interest than those given in 1977, they are still mentioned in this book, in chapter 5, at the cultivar involved. Awards have also been given to species, but these awards are not noted here. As species are so enormously variable, the award has nothing to say about the species as a whole and was usually presented to one cultivated plant only.

Abbreviations of the awards are as follows:

The Netherlands
GI = Getuigschrift Eerste Klas (First Class Certificate)
GV = Getuigschrift van Verdienste (Certificate of Merit)

United Kindgom
AGM = Award of Garden Merit
AM = Award of Merit
C = Commended
FCC = First Class Certificate

HC = Highly Commended
PC = Certificate of Preliminary Commendation

The GV is equal to the AGM.

Recent Developments

After my 1995 journal article, I began to correspond with many people around the world, including famous plantsmen like Gary Dunlop in Northern Ireland and Dick Fulcher in England. New cultivars were introduced in New Zealand, the United States, Japan, and South Africa. Closer to home, Kees Duivenvoorde was and still is busy breeding new cultivars; he shows them every year at the KAVB show in Lisse, The Netherlands. Some other Dutch nurseries, of which Maas & van Stein is probably the most well known, introduced new cultivars. Stock is grown outside; when in flower the inflorescences are cut to be traded as cut flowers. Later, in winter, the plants are sold for the perennial trade. For strictly cut flower purposes, several growers breed their own selections under glass. Most famous of these growers is Cor van Eijk, who has raised several cultivars that are used as year-round cut flowers. In Belgium a few collections and nurseries offer a couple of cultivars; the best known is the collection of Ignace van Doorslaer, many of whose 100 cultivars are available for retail sale. Most cultivars raised by the Dutch breeder Duivenvoorde can be obtained via van Doorslaer.

Well known for his knowledge on *Agapanthus*, Graham Duncan of South Africa published a booklet at the National Botanical Institute, Kirstenbosch, in 1998. Another two articles soon followed (Dunlop 2000, Fulcher 2000). Gary Dunlop raised and introduced *Agapanthus* cultivars, and Dick Fulcher is holder of the NCCPG's *Agapanthus* collection, housed at his nursery Pine Cottage Plants, Fourways, Eggesford, Devon. This collection was started principally by Neil Lucas at Bicton College, Devon, and was taken over by Fulcher in 1988. Since 1997 the collection is based at holder's nursery. The collection contains up to 200 cultivars and several species. Fulcher too bred new cultivars, including several of the Tubular Group.

Scientific publications are still hard to find. One of the most recent is a study, in Dutch, on how to force *Agapanthus* for late flowering (van de Wiel 2001). Although this report does contain valuable information for wholesale growers, hardly any information from it is used in this book. The last scientific publication used as a reference in this book (Allemand and Pionnat 2001) contains essentially the same information as my 1998 book but with added information for growers and nurseries and on pests and diseases; unfortunately, this publication is in French.

In early 2001 a guide about the NPC, written by Hanneke van Dijk and myself as second author, was published by the Royal Boskoop Horticultural Society. Of course the *Agapanthus* collection was included, together with 69 other plant collections. Unique in the guide are the lists of all plants grown in the collections.

A highlight of my years maintaining the Dutch *Agapanthus* cultivars was a presentation of the collection at the Floriade 2002. With the help of the Duivenvoordes and many others, I managed to show 56 Dutch cultivars, each in one pot, perhaps the most diverse collection ever seen. I sent out my seventh newsletter in November 2002 (the last since financial cuts at Leiden University halted the activities of our Division of Pharmacognosy), and that autumn the collection moved to a new holder, Stichting het Geldersch Landschap, which foundation runs several estates in the Gelderland province in The Netherlands. The NPC is housed at Castle Rosendael, near Arnhem, and its 68 Dutch cultivars (summer 2003) are now on permanent display during their normal open hours.

Also in 2002 I contacted Ben Zonneveld, a retired scientist who still works at Leiden University. He too was interested in *Agapanthus* and so did a study on the DNA contents of nearly all the plants I grew. He was also able to convince growers outside Holland to send material, including the famous and mysterious *A. africanus*. Results of this research (see chapter 2) will no doubt be the base for further studies. Conclusions in relation with my cultivar groups and keys are very interesting; I leave it to readers to come to their own!

Our human society is marked by rumours; one very strong rumour is that somewhere on this planet a pink-flowering cultivar exists, and some murmurs even concern a red one. The origins of such plants are as mysterious as their colour—some say New Zealand, others talk about South Africa, others believe the plants grow in California. Personally I have not come across a good pink cultivar, but for trading purposes, "pink" sells well. We are usually dealing with white-flowering plants, which contain a lot of anthocyanin, given the purplish colouring. A good pink should be possible to breed, and doubtless this will be achieved in a few years, with reference to genera like *Hyacinthus* and *Scilla*.

Also new is that cultivars are introduced as being fragrant. Again, this sounds nice for trading purposes, but fragrance is subjective, and a great deal depends on the personal experience of each person who sticks his or her nose in the inflorescence. Other conditions too play a part (time of the day, age of the flowers, temperature, humidity). Still, a good scent is important for any cut flower, and when your car is loaded with *Agapanthus* cut flowers, the fragrance is distinct.

On New Zealand's South Island a program has been set up to get rid of escaped *Agapanthus* and *Agapanthus* seedlings on wild locations, which is good news for the local flora (and in future, perhaps, *Agapanthus* will not be allowed to be cultivated in New Zealand). As similar situations appear in nearly all warm or Mediterranean climates, it is high time breeders start breeding true sterile cultivars.

Many new introductions are sold in the ornamental trade as dwarf. This is nice for the seasoned gardener, but not for the customer who buys a plant impulsively at a garden centre or DIY chain, for to maintain such a plant is quite difficult—expect a one-year ornamental on the terrace, at best. The plant collector who wants to have something different searches the world for the new introductions and is usually interested in the taller cultivars. I have seen new breedings, in large stock, with short leaves and straight upright peduncles, in wonderful colours, but these will not be introduced as ornamentals, for several reasons. One is that plants are normally traded on small trailers, and only one layer of such tall plants can be displayed thus. Add an 80 cm tall peduncle to a 20 cm high pot, and some space above the plant to boot, and there is no room left to add another shelf, for a second layer of plants, on the same trailer. Not surprising, then, that the trader is hardly interested in tall *Agapanthus* cultivars. Rather, the trade focuses on the shorter ones, so that two- or three-shelf trailers can display three or four layers of plants. And so these wonderfull tall cultivars are withheld from the gardener. Those gardeners who continue their dogged search for tall cultivars contribute to the enormous popularity of 'Loch Hope' and 'Purple Cloud'.

Finally, I am still surprised to find that, even in South Africa, cultivars are mainly traded or linked to *Agapanthus africanus*. In nearly all cases, these plants have nothing to do with this species; almost all are selections or hybrids from *A. praecox*. Even so close to the natural habitat, it seems impossible to get rid of this confusion, but I hope this book is of help.

The following valuable chapter is by Ben Zonneveld, based on his DNA research. It is a very good scientific start to understanding the genus *Agapanthus* before reading and studying the rest of this book, which I based on morphological studies. Fortunately for me, Ben's results coincide with my findings. Of course, a cultivar group classification does not prove the relation between the cultivars, but because Ben's DNA research does prove the relations between the plants involved, I have accepted his proposals for some changes in taxonomy.

Chapter 2

Genome Size in Species and Cultivars of *Agapanthus* L'Hér. (Agapanthaceae)

Ben J.M. Zonneveld
Institute of Biology, Clusius Laboratory, Leiden University
Wassenaarseweg 64, 2333 AL Leiden, The Netherlands
e-mail: zonneveld@rulbim.leidenuniv.nl
tel: + 31 71 527 5054

Summary

Nuclear DNA content (2C) and pollen vitality and color are used as new criteria to investigate all species and nearly 130 cultivars of the genus *Agapanthus*. All taxa have the same chromosome number (2n = 2x = 30), with the exception of four triploid species. The nuclear DNA content of the diploids, as measured by flow cytometry with propidium iodide, is demonstrated to range from 22.1 to 31.6 pg (picogram). This implies that the largest genome contains roughly 10^{10} more base pairs than the smallest. The species have been divided in two sections based on pollen color: section Lilacinipollini, with lilac pollen, containing *A. campanulatus*, *A. caulescens* and *A. coddii*; and section Ochraceipollini, with yellow-brownish pollen, containing *A. praecox*, *A. inapertus* and *A. africanus*. Four other taxa recognized by Leighton (1965) are treated as follows: *A. comptonii* is considered a synonym of *A. praecox* subsp. *minimus*. *A. walshii* is renamed as a subspecies of *A. africanus*. *A. dyeri* is considered synonymous with *A. inapertus* subsp. *intermedius*. *A. nutans* is considered synonymous with *A. caulescens*.

Based on nuclear DNA content and shape of the flowers, four groups can be clearly recognized among the cultivars. All plants with salver-shaped flowers range from 21.9 to 22.8 pg, suggesting that they are all derived from *A. campanulatus* or resulted from repeated backcrosses and selection for salver-shaped flowers. The evergreen-leaved plants can be separated as being nearly all in the highest range, with amounts of DNA ranging from 24.4 to 25.3 pg. This suggests that they are derived from *A. praecox*. Plants of the third group fall in between these DNA values, ranging from 22.9 to 24.4 pg, and have mainly trumpet-shaped flowers. The fourth group would be formed by *A. inapertus* with tubular flowers. Results from some crosses seem to indicate that trumpet-shaped flowers are genetically intermediate between salver/funnel- and tubular-shaped flowers. Nuclear DNA content as measured by flow cytometry is a relevant trait to throw light on the relationships between *Agapanthus* species and cultivars.

Introduction

Agapanthus (Agapanthaceae) is a perennial, endemic in southern Africa. There are, according to Leighton (1965), three evergreen species, occurring mainly in the southern parts of South Africa and seven deciduous species from the northern parts. They range from the Cape Peninsula to the mountain ranges just south of the Limpopo River (Duncan 1998). The altitude range for the genus, but also for species like *A. africanus*, starts at sea level rising to about 2000 m. *A. africanus* was the first species to be described in 1679. Although the name is still often encountered in the ornamental plant trade, it rarely if ever is this species as it is very difficult to grow, requiring very dry and hot conditions. *Agapanthus* is gaining more and more horticultural interest, and large numbers of new cultivars are being introduced (Duncan 1985, 1998; Snoeijer 1998). All plants measured have the same chromosome number, $2n = 2x = 30$ (Riley and Mukerjee 1960). *Agapanthus* taxonomy is generally considered difficult as there are few unique characters and these vary considerably depending on growing circumstances and geographical areas. Leighton (1965) states that there are very few characters, which are restricted to a certain species. So it is not surprising that others suggest there is actually only one species (McNeil 1972).

Genome size Cx (Greilhuber 1979) and C-value (C) are receiving more attention (Bennett 1972, Ohri 1998). Flow cytometry was successfully used to investigate the genera *Hosta* (Zonneveld and van Iren 2001), *Helleborus* (Zonneveld 2001), and *Galanthus* (Zonneveld et al. 2003). When all species in a genus have the same chromosome number, as in *Agapanthus*, differences in nuclear DNA content have proven to be very effective in delimiting infrageneric divisions in a number of taxa (Ohri 1998). Moreover it is shown (Greilhuber 1998) that species vary less than often assumed and the so-called fluid genome seems not very well founded. In this study the total amount of nuclear DNA, pollen color, and pollen vitality were introduced as novel criteria in *Agapanthus*. Based on our earlier results for the species of *Agapanthus* (Zonneveld and Duncan 2003), it is concluded that there are six species: *A. campanulatus*, *A. caulescens*, *A. coddii*, *A. praecox*, *A. inapertus*, and *A. africanus*. The other four taxa recognized by Leighton (1965) as species (i.e., *A. comptonii*, *A. walshii*, *A. dyeri*, and *A. nutans*) are given a status below species rank (Zonneveld and Duncan 2003).

The cultivars are, at least in The Netherlands, mainly of the deciduous type (Snoeijer 1998). Mainly two species seem to be involved in selection: the deciduous *A. campanulatus* with small, few-flowered umbels and salver-shaped flowers and the evergreen *A. praecox* with large, multiflowered umbels with funnel-shaped flowers.

In addition to the results obtained earlier with the species (Zonneveld and Duncan 2003) I have determined, in a large number of cultivars, the range of nuclear DNA involved.

Materials and Methods

Plant material

Plants were obtained from the holder of the Dutch Plant Collection of *Agapanthus*, Wim Snoeijer of Leiden University, The Netherlands. These plants are listed alphabetically in Table 2b; also given is the nursery from which the plant originally was obtained, except when Dunlop is listed as the origin. This material came from Gary Dunlop of Ballyrogan Nurseries, Newtownards, Northern Ireland. The species were mainly obtained from Graham Duncan, Kirstenbosch National Botanical Garden, Cape Town, South Africa. Most Dutch cultivars are maintained today as a living collection at Castle Rosendael, The Netherlands; these are documented with slides and some with vouchers. These vouchers are in Leiden Herbarium. Vouchers of the species are in the Compton Herbarium, South Africa.

Flow cytometric measurement of nuclear DNA content

For the isolation of nuclei, about 0.5 cm^2 of adult leaf was chopped together with a piece of *Agave americana* L. as internal standard. The nuclear DNA content (2C-value) of *A. americana* was measured as 15.9 pg per nucleus with human leucocytes (= 7 pg, Tiersch et al. 1989) as the standard. The chopping was done with a new razor blade in a Petri dish in 0.25 ml nuclei-isolation buffer as described by Johnston et al. (1999). After adding 2 ml Propidium Iodide (PI) solution (50 mg PI/l in isolation buffer) the suspension with nuclei was filtered through a 30 μm nylon filter. The fluorescence of the nuclei was measured, half an hour and one hour after addition of PI, using a Partec CA-II flow cytometer. The more DNA is present in a nucleus, the higher the intensity of the fluorescence is. The 2C DNA content of the sample was calculated as the sample peak mean, divided by the *Agave* peak mean, and multiplied with the amount of DNA of the *Agave* standard. In most cases, two different samples, and at least 5000 nuclei, were measured twice for each clone. *Agapanthus* turned out to be favorable material for flow cytometry. Most histograms revealed a CV of less than 5% and the figures could be read +/- 1%.

Results and Discussion

DNA content and pollen color of the species

Table 1 shows the results of the nuclear DNA measurements of all species of *Agapanthus*. These were earlier classified as species, based on their morphology and geography (Leighton 1965). The results presented are a summary of the more extensive measurements based on 81 taxa (Zonneveld and Duncan 2003). Despite the fact that all diploid taxa have the same chromosome number (2n = 2x = 30), the nuclear DNA content ranges from 22.1 to 31.6 pg. The pollen vitality of the species ranged from 90 to 100% (Zonneveld and Duncan 2003). The pollen vitality of the hybrids is rather high, between 60 and 85%. Further, a new important character was the fact that three deciduous species had clear lilac pollen coinciding with the three species with a lower DNA content of 22.3 to 24.0 pg. These species, *A. campanulatus*, *A. caulescens* and *A. coddii*, were placed in section Lilacinipollini. Further, three species (one deciduous, the other two evergreen) had yellow-brownish pollen coinciding with the three species with a higher DNA content of 25.2 to 31.6 pg. These were placed in section Ochraceipollini. These species are *A. inapertus*, *A. praecox*, and *A. africanus*. The lilac pollen color also coincided with a purple base to the leaf. The exception is *A. inapertus*, which, although having yellow-brownish pollen, also has light purple leafbases.

Four other taxa recognized by Leighton (1965) are treated as follows: *A. comptonii* is considered a synonym of *A. praecox* subsp. *minimus*. *A. walshii* is renamed as *A. africanus* subsp. *walshii*. *A. dyeri*, including the plants from Mozambique, is

Table 1. Species of *Agapanthus* with average nuclear DNA content (2C), pollen color, and number of taxa measured

	Average DNA (2C) in pg	Pollen colour	No. of taxa measured	Origin
Section Lilacinipollini				
A. campanulatus	22.3	lilac	6	Kirstenbosch RSA
A. caulescens	23.2	lilac	4	Kirstenbosch RSA
A. caulescens (syn. A. nutans)	23.4	lilac	1	Kirstenbosch RSA
A. coddii	24.0	lilac	6	Kirstenbosch RSA
Section Ochraceipollini				
A. inapertus	25.2	ochre	9	Kirstenbosch RSA
A. inapertus subsp. intermedius (syn. A. dyeri)	25.1	ochre	5	Kirstenbosch RSA
A. praecox	25.5	ochre	17	Kirstenbosch RSA
A. praecox subsp. minimus (syn. A. comptonii)	25.5	ochre	3	Kirstenbosch RSA
A. africanus	31.6	ochre	5	Kirstenbosch RSA
A. africanus subsp. walshii	31.6	ochre	2	Kirstenbosch RSA

considered synonymous with *A. inapertus* subsp. *intermedius*. *A. nutans* is considered synonymous with *A. caulescens*. It is clear that the DNA content of these four taxa, already renamed in Table 1, coincide with other DNA values. These four taxa occupy small territories close to the larger areas of the species recognized here (Palmer 1967). In the 81 mainly wild-collected plants, we found four plants with 50% more DNA that are presumed to be triploids: three taxa of *A. inapertus* and one of *A. africanus* (Zonneveld and Duncan 2003). Therefore it is remarkable that in the 130 cultivars of *Agapanthus* investigated here, not a single polyploid was found (Tables 2a and 2b).

Flowershape and DNA content of the cultivars

The nuclear DNA amount was also determined in 130 *Agapanthus* cultivars. The *Agapanthus* cultivars have been arranged according to increasing 2C DNA content (Table 2a). Based also on our earlier results with other plants, it is not illogical to assume that related cultivars have similar amounts of DNA, but the reverse is not always true. Table 2a shows that genome size in the investigated cultivars varies between 21.9 and 25.6 pg. This suggests that *Agapanthus* cultivars have been hybridised and selected from a few related species. By combining the DNA results obtained with the species with the flowershapes and leaf types of the cultivars as provided by Wim Snoeijer, it was possible to make sense of this gradual increase in the nuclear DNA amounts of the cultivars. They can be divided in four groups based on DNA content, leaf type, and flowershape (Gillissen 1980, Snoeijer 1998). These categories coincide largely. The following divisions can be made. The first is a deciduous group with salver-shaped flowers around *A. campanulatus*. These all fall in the lowest DNA group and vice versa, with 21.9 to 22.8 pg of DNA per nucleus. This suggests that they all are derived from *A. campanulatus* or are at least F_2 or later backcrosses, as an F_1 plant with *A. praecox/inapertus* would result in a higher amount of DNA. Crossing *A. campanulatus* with 22.2 pg with *A. praecox* with 25.4 pg will result in a hybrid with 23.8 pg ([22.2 + 25.4] / 2 = 23.8 pg). Plants with salver-shaped flowers will reappear only in the F_2 or later. The fact that hardly any plants with trumpet- or funnel-shaped flowers are in this low DNA group means that plants with trumpet- and funnel-shaped flowers have in general a higher amount of DNA, being closer to *A. praecox/inapertus*.

The second group, with mostly evergreen leaves and funnel-shaped flowers, coincides with the high DNA group, with 24.4 to 25.4 pg of DNA. The total range for plants around *A. praecox*, from 24.6 pg to 25.6 pg, is rather large. The most likely explanation is that those with the lower amounts of DNA show introgression of a species with a lower amount of DNA, most likely *A. campanulatus*. The fact that both funnel- and trumpet-shaped flowers can be found in the Evergreen Group suggests that they are at least partly the result of repeated backcrosses. In backcrosses with *A. praecox* the evergreen habit and funnel-shaped flowers would likely reappear.

The third group is those with trumpet-shaped flowers. These are mainly in the middle DNA group with 23.0 to 24.4 pg of DNA, between the Salver and Evergreen Groups. Plants like *A. campanulatus* 'Albidus' (= **'Franni'**), 'Maximus Albus' (=

'Umbellatus Albus'), and 'Umbellatus Albus' classified as "species" have an intermediate DNA value and are clearly of hybrid origin. Three plants that were supposed to be *A. inapertus* (i.e., *A. i.* ex Guicho Gardens, *A. i.* subsp. *intermedius*, and 'Lydenburg') are clearly lower in their nuclear DNA content than authentic *A. inapertus* (Zonneveld and Duncan 2003) and are considered hybrids. The same can be said of three supposed *A. praecox* plants, *A. p.* 'Giganteus', *A. p.* 'Starburst', and *A. p.* 'Blue Mercury' (Table 2a). Salver- and funnel-shaped flowers have non-overlapping segments that are turned sideways. *A. inapertus* has tubular flowers, and its segments are overlapping. The fact that trumpet-shaped flowers do have overlapping segments and a flower diameter intermediate between salver/funnel and tubular suggests that *A. inapertus* has been in the breeding line. Based on flower length and flowershape, the plants in the group intermediate in DNA, with 22.9 to 24.4 pg, and with mainly trumpet-shaped flowers are probably all hybrids, the result of crossing plants with salver/funnel-shaped flowers with plants with tubular flowers. The fourth group would be formed by *A. inapertus* with tubular flowers.

Two types of white flowers can be found: those with purple-blackish anthers and those with yellow anthers. In both the Salver Group and the Evergreen Group we only find yellow anthers. In the group intermediate in DNA we find that seven out of nine plants have blackish anthers (Table 6). This again shows the relationship among the different cultivars. It is also shown that several plants with the same name but of different origin are indeed identical, e.g., **'Blue Triumphator'** 2x, 'Intermedius' 2x, and **'Blue Giant'** 2x. Some plants suggested earlier to be identical turn out to have the same amount of DNA, e.g., **'Blue Ribbon'**/**'Blauwe Wimpel'**, *A. campanulatus* 'Albidus' (= **'Franni'**)/'Maximus Albus'(= **'Umbellatus Albus'**), and **'Blue Globe'**/'Josephine' (ex Simon). It is also shown that some plants with identical names are different, e.g., 'Josephine' of Simon versus **'Josephine'** of Reintjes and 'Maximus' versus 'Maximus Albus' as already suggested by Snoeijer (1998). *A. africanus*, with a much higher DNA content (Zonneveld and Duncan 2003, Table 1), does not seem to have contributed to the development of the measured *Agapanthus* cultivars. In Table 4 parents and offspring of some crosses are given, with their flowershapes (data provided by Wim Snoeijer). Our working hypothesis is that a single gene with three alleles (for Salver, Funnel, and Tubular) is responsible for flowershape in *Agapanthus*. This is based on the results of crosses (Table 4) and the fact that, despite more than a century of breeding, the flowers can still be attributed to four different, discrete classes. Moreover the Salver Group coincides with the low DNA group. It can then be deduced from the results of the crosses in Table 4 that the resulting flowershape in the F_1 of Salver × Funnel is Funnel. Crossing plants with salver- or funnel-shaped flowers with *A. inapertus*, with tubular flowers with overlapping segments, likely gives rise to trumpet-shaped flowers as in **'Purple Cloud'** (Table 4). The low number of tubular-shaped flowers among the cultivars is probably due to the fact that they are considered less desirable. The deciduous plants with trumpet-shaped flowers, roughly 23 to 24 pg, are then the result of (back)-crosses with the deciduous *A. campanulatus*. The evergreen plants with trumpet-shaped flowers and 24 to 25 pg of DNA are then the result of (back)crosses with *A. praecox*. Table 6 gives all the further details. A cross of Salver × Funnel (S), the latter

Table 2a. *Agapanthus* cultivars arranged by increasing DNA content, with their flowershape and origin

Cultivar	DNA	Group	Origin	Breeder/ introducer	evg	FC
'Premier'	21.9		Dunlop	Dunlop		
'Twilight'	21.9		Dunlop	G. Dunlop		
'Notfred'	21.9	VLG	Dunlop	Notcutts	evg	
'Sapphire'	21.9		Dunlop		evg	
'Wendy'	22.1	Salver	Dunlop	Dunlop		
'Bressingham Blue'	22.2	Salver	Dunlop	Bloom		
'Buckland'	22.2	Salver	Dunlop	Garden House		
'Beth Chatto'	22.2	VLG	Beth Chatto			
'Profusion'	22.2	Salver	Beth Chatto			
'Prinses Marilène'	22.2	Salver	Duivenvoorde	Duivenvoorde		Wy
campanulatus subsp. *patens*	22.3		Dunlop			
'Nottingham'	22.3	Salver	Duivenvoorde	Duivenvoorde		Wy
'Kingston Blue'	22.3	Salver	Dunlop	Miss Raphael		
'Blue Triumphator'	22.4	Salver	van der Valk	ex *caulescens*		
'Blue Triumphator'	22.5	Salver	Maas & van Stein	ex *caulescens*		
'Oxford Blue'	22.5	Salver	Dunlop	Dunlop		
'Patent Blue'	22.5	Salver	Dunlop	Dunlop		
'Helen'	22.5	Salver	Dunlop	Dunlop		
'Midnight Blue'	22.6	Salver	Dunlop	Wood		
'Meibont'	22.7	Salver	Kramer	Kramer		
'Isis'	22.7	Salver	Dunlop	Bloom		
'Blue Cascade'	22.7	Funnel	Dunlop	Dunlop		
'Windsor Castle'	22.7	Trumpet	Dunlop	Crown Estate		
'Violetta'	22.7	Trumpet	Dunlop	G. Dunlop		
'Cobalt Blue'	22.8	Salver	Beth Chatto	Beth Chatto		
'Pinocchio'	22.8	Salver	Maas & van Stein	Maas & van Stein		
'Ardernei'	22.8	Trumpet	Dunlop			
'Buckingham Palace'	22.8	Salver	Dunlop	Crown Estate		
'Intermedius'	22.9	Trumpet	Baltus	van Tubergen		
'Adonis'	22.9	Trumpet	Dunlop	Dunlop		
'Kobold'	23.0	Salver	Maas & van Stein			
'Intermedius'	23.0	Trumpet	Maas & van Stein	van Tubergen		
'Black Beauty'	23.0	Trumpet	Duivenvoorde	Duivenvoorde		
'Duivenbrugge Blue'	23.0	Trumpet	Duivenvoorde	Duivenvoorde		
'Blue Globe'	23.1	Salver	van der Valk	Hoogervorst	(evg)	
'Josephine'	23.1	Salver	Simon	is 'Blue Globe'	(evg)	
'Septemberhemel'	23.1	Funnel	Kramer	Kramer		
'Sylvine'	23.1	Funnel	van Doorslaer	van Doorslaer		

Cultivar	DNA	Group	Origin	Breeder/ introducer	evg	FC
'Blue Companion'	23.1	Trumpet	Dunlop	Dunlop		
'Nyx'	23.1	Salver	Dunlop	Dunlop		
'Midnight Star'	23.2	Trumpet	van Doorslaer	Raveningham Hall		
'Umbellatus Albus'	23.2	Trumpet	RHS Wisley	received as 'Maximus Albus'		
'Umbellatus Albus'	23.3	Trumpet	Fleur			
'Bristol'	23.3	Trumpet	Duivenvoorde	Duivenvoorde		
'Lilac Time'	23.3	Funnel	Dunlop	Dick Fulcher		
'Ballyrogan'	23.3	Salver	Dunlop	Dunlop	evg	
'Goldfinger'	23.4	VLG	Duivenvoorde	Duivenvoorde	evg	
'Blue Moon'	23.4	Trumpet	Dunlop	Smith	(evg)	
'Kew White'	23.4		Dunlop	Kew		
'Columba'	23.6	Trumpet	Duivenvoorde	Duivenvoorde		
'Martine'	23.6	Trumpet	Duivenvoorde	Duivenvoorde		
'Oslo'	23.6	Trumpet	Duivenvoorde	Duivenvoorde		
'Delft'	23.6	Funnel	Dunlop	Palmer		
'Dr Brouwer'	23.7	Trumpet	Duivenvoorde	Duivenvoorde		
'Pinchbeck'	23.7	Funnel	Duivenvoorde	Duivenvoorde		
inapertus ex Guincho	23.5		Dunlop			
inapertus large form	23.6		Dunlop			
'Lydenburg'	23.8	Tubular	Dunlop	Kirstenbosch		
'Franni'	23.8		Dunlop			
'Starburst'	23.9	Funnel	Dunlop	Dunlop	evg	
'Blue Mercury'	23.8	Funnel	Dunlop	Dunlop	evg	
'Loch Hope'	23.6	Funnel	Dunlop			
'Debbie'	23.8	Trumpet	Duivenvoorde	Duivenvoorde		
'Holbeach'	23.8	Funnel	Duivenvoorde	Duivenvoorde		
'Jolanda'	23.8	Trumpet	Duivenvoorde	Duivenvoorde		
'Stephanie Charm'	23.8	Funnel	van Doorslaer	van Doorslaer		Wb
'Sunfield'	23.8	Trumpet	Klinkhamer	Zonneveld		
'Suzan'	23.8	Trumpet	Duivenvoorde	Duivenvoorde		
'Cambridge'	23.9	Funnel	Duivenvoorde	Duivenvoorde		Wb
'Elisabeth'	23.9	Trumpet	Duivenvoorde	Duivenvoorde		
'Glacier Stream'	23.9	Trumpet	Maas & van Stein	Maas & van Stein		Wb
'Rotterdam'	23.9	Funnel	Duivenvoorde	Duivenvoorde		
'Penelope Palmer'	23.9	Funnel	Dunlop	Palmer	(evg)	

(continued)

Table 2a (continued)

Cultivar	DNA	Group	Origin	Breeder/ introducer	evg	FC
'Rosemary'	23.9	Trumpet	Dunlop	Palmer		
'Catharina'	24.0	Trumpet	Duivenvoorde	Duivenvoorde		
'Johanna'	24.0	Trumpet	Duivenvoorde	Duivenvoorde		
'Marianne'	24.0	Trumpet	Duivenvoorde	Duivenvoorde		
'Rhone'	24.0	Trumpet	Maas & van Stein	Maas & van Stein		
'White Beauty'	24.0	Trumpet	Reintjes	Reintjes		Wb
'Aberdeen'	24.2	Funnel	Duivenvoorde	Duivenvoorde		
'Amsterdam'	24.2	Trumpet	Duivenvoorde	Duivenvoorde		
'Tall Boy'	24.2	Tubular	Dunlop	Fulcher		
'Plas Merdyn Blue'	24.2	Trumpet	Dunlop	Dunlop		
'Lady Edith'	24.2	Funnel	Dunlop	Mount Stewart		
'Windsor Grey'	24.2		Dunlop	Crown Estate		
'Winsome'	24.2	Trumpet	Dunlop	G. Dunlop		
'Wolga'	24.3	Trumpet	Duivenvoorde	Schoehuys		
'Raveningham Hall'	24.4	Funnel	Jansen	Raveningham Hall		
'White Smile'	24.4	Funnel	Maas & van Stein	Maas & van Stein		Wb
'Blue Perfection'	24.4	Funnel	Duivenvoorde	Schoehuys	evg	
'Amethyst'	24.5	Trumpet	Reintjes	vd Zwet		
'Ice Lolly'	24.5	Funnel	Maas & van Stein	Maas & van Stein		Wy
'Mariette'	24.5	Trumpet	Duivenvoorde	Duivenvoorde		
'Polar Ice'	24.5	Trumpet	Maas & van Stein	Maas & van Stein		Wy
'Weaver'	24.5	Funnel	Bulbes d'Opale			
'Blue Giant'	24.5	Trumpet	van der Valk		evg	
'Blue Giant'	24.6	Trumpet	Maas & van Stein		evg	
'Dnjepr'	24.6	Trumpet	Maas & van Stein	Schoehuys	evg	
'Josephine'	24.6	Trumpet	Reintjes	vd Zwet		
'Aureovittatus'	24.6	VLG	Acanthus		evg	
'Donau'	24.7	Trumpet	Maas & van Stein	Schoehuys		
'San Gabriel'	24.7	Funnel	Monksilver Nursery	Monksilver Nursery	evg	
'Aphrodite'	24.7	Funnel	Dunlop	Dunlop		
'Blue Ribbon'	24.8	Funnel	Duivenvoorde		evg	
'Argenteus Vittatus'	24.9	VLG	Madeira		evg	

Cultivar	DNA	Group	Origin	Breeder/ introducer	evg	FC
'Blauwe Wimpel'	24.9	Funnel	Reintjes	vd Zwet		
'Maximus'	24.9	Funnel	van Poucke	van Poucke	evg	
'Leicester'	24.9	Funnel	Duivenvoorde	Duivenvoorde		Wb
'Purple Cloud'	24.9	Trumpet	Bulbes d'Opale		evg	
'Cyan'	24.9		Dunlop			
'Mount Stewart'	25.0	Funnel	Dunlop	Dunlop	evg	
'Phantom'	25.0	Funnel	Dunlop	Dunlop	evg	
'Tinkerbell'	25.0	VLG	Bulbes d'Opale		evg	
'Fafner'	25.1	Funnel	Dunlop	Dunlop	evg	
'Magnifico'	25.1	Funnel	Dunlop	Dunlop	evg	
'Titan'	25.1	Funnel	Dunlop	Dunlop	evg	
'Whitney'	25.1	Funnel	v Eijk	v Eijk	evg	Wy
'Blue Formality'	25.2		Dunlop		evg	
'Atlas'	25.2	Funnel	Dunlop	Dunlop	evg	
'Colossus'	25.2		Dunlop		evg	
'Virginia'	25.2	Funnel	Duivenvoorde	Duivenvoorde	evg	Wy
'Rosewarne'	25.2	Trumpet	Dunlop	Rosewarne	evg	
inapertus	25.2		Hortus Amsterdam			
'Bicton Bell'	25.3	Tubular	Dunlop	Fulcher		
'Plas Merdyn White'	25.3	Funnel	Dunlop	Dunlop	evg	
praecox 'Albiflorus'	25.3		Madeira		evg	
'Flore Pleno'	25.4		Dunlop		evg	
praecox	25.4		Zombe plateau, Malawi		evg	
'Supreme'	25.5		Dunlop		evg	
'Bangor Blue'	25.6	Funnel	Dunlop	Dunlop	evg	
'Fasolt'	25.6	Funnel	Dunlop	Dunlop	evg	

evg = evergreen
Wy = white flower, yellow anthers
Wb = white flower, blackish anthers
VLG = Variegated Leaf Group

Table 2b. *Agapanthus* cultivars arranged alphabetically, with their DNA content, flowershape, and origin

Cultivar	DNA	Group	Origin	Breeder/ introducer	evg	FC
'Aberdeen'	24.2	Funnel	Duivenvoorde	Duivenvoorde		
'Adonis'	22.9	Trumpet	Dunlop	Dunlop		
'Amethyst'	24.5	Trumpet	Reintjes	vd Zwet		
'Amsterdam'	24.2	Trumpet	Duivenvoorde	Duivenvoorde		
'Aphrodite'	24.7	Funnel	Dunlop	Dunlop		
'Ardernei'	22.8	Trumpet	Dunlop			
'Argenteus Vittatus'	24.9	VLG	Madeira		evg	
'Atlas'	25.2	Funnel	Dunlop	Dunlop	evg	
'Aureovittatus'	24.6	VLG	Acanthus		evg	
'Ballyrogan'	23.3	Salver	Dunlop	Dunlop	evg	
'Bangor Blue'	25.6	Funnel	Dunlop	Dunlop	evg	
'Beth Chatto'	22.2	VLG	Beth Chatto			
'Bicton Bell'	25.3	Tubular	Dunlop	Fulcher		
'Black Beauty'	23.0	Trumpet	Duivenvoorde	Duivenvoorde		
'Blauwe Wimpel'	24.9	Funnel	Reintjes	vd Zwet		
'Blue Cascade'	22.7	Funnel	Dunlop	Dunlop		
'Blue Companion'	23.1	Trumpet	Dunlop	Dunlop		
'Blue Formality'	25.2		Dunlop		evg	
'Blue Giant'	24.5	Trumpet	van der Valk		evg	
'Blue Giant'	24.6	Trumpet	Maas & van Stein		evg	
'Blue Globe'	23.1	Salver	van der Valk	Hoogervorst	(evg)	
'Blue Mercury'	23.8	Funnel	Dunlop	Dunlop	evg	
'Blue Moon'	23.4	Trumpet	Dunlop	Smith	(evg)	
'Blue Perfection'	24.4	Funnel	Duivenvoorde	Schoehuys	evg	
'Blue Ribbon'	24.8	Funnel	Duivenvoorde		evg	
'Blue Triumphator'	22.4	Salver	van der Valk	ex *caulescens*		
'Blue Triumphator'	22.5	Salver	Maas & van Stein	ex *caulescens*		
'Bressingham Blue'	22.2	Salver	Dunlop	Bloom		
'Bristol'	23.3	Trumpet	Duivenvoorde	Duivenvoorde		
'Buckingham Palace'	22.8	Salver	Dunlop	Crown Estate		
'Buckland'	22.2	Salver	Dunlop	Garden House		
'Cambridge'	23.9	Funnel	Duivenvoorde	Duivenvoorde		Wb
campanulatus subsp. patens	22.3		Dunlop			
'Catharina'	24.0	Trumpet	Duivenvoorde	Duivenvoorde		
'Cobalt Blue'	22.8	Salver	Beth Chatto	Beth Chatto		
'Colossus'	25.2		Dunlop		evg	
'Columba'	23.6	Trumpet	Duivenvoorde	Duivenvoorde		
'Cyan'	24.9		Dunlop			

Cultivar	DNA	Group	Origin	Breeder/ introducer	evg	FC
'Debbie'	23.8	Trumpet	Duivenvoorde	Duivenvoorde		
'Delft'	23.6	Funnel	Dunlop	Palmer		
'Dnjepr'	24.6	Trumpet	Maas & van Stein	Schoehuys	evg	
'Donau'	24.7	Trumpet	Maas & van Stein	Schoehuys		
'Dr Brouwer'	23.7	Trumpet	Duivenvoorde	Duivenvoorde		
'Duivenbrugge Blue'	23.0	Trumpet	Duivenvoorde	Duivenvoorde		
'Elisabeth'	23.9	Trumpet	Duivenvoorde	Duivenvoorde		
'Fafner'	25.1	Funnel	Dunlop	Dunlop	evg	
'Fasolt'	25.6	Funnel	Dunlop	Dunlop	evg	
'Flore Pleno'	25.4		Dunlop		evg	
'Franni'	23.8		Dunlop			
'Glacier Stream'	23.9	Trumpet	Maas & van Stein	Maas & van Stein		Wb
'Goldfinger'	23.4	VLG	Duivenvoorde	Duivenvoorde	evg	
'Helen'	22.5	Salver	Dunlop	Dunlop		
'Holbeach'	23.8	Funnel	Duivenvoorde	Duivenvoorde		
'Ice Lolly'	24.5	Funnel	Maas & van Stein	Maas & van Stein		Wy
inapertus	25.2		Hortus Amsterdam			
inapertus ex Guincho	23.5		Dunlop			
inapertus large form	23.6		Dunlop			
'Intermedius'	23.0	Trumpet	Maas & van Stein	van Tubergen		
'Intermedius'	22.9	Trumpet	Baltus	van Tubergen		
'Isis'	22.7	Salver	Dunlop	Bloom		
'Johanna'	24.0	Trumpet	Duivenvoorde	Duivenvoorde		
'Jolanda'	23.8	Trumpet	Duivenvoorde	Duivenvoorde		
'Josephine'	24.6	Trumpet	Reintjes	vd Zwet		
'Josephine'	23.1	Salver	Simon	is 'Blue Globe'	(evg)	
'Kew White'	23.4		Dunlop	Kew		
'Kingston Blue'	22.3	Salver	Dunlop	Miss Raphael		
'Kobold'	23.0	Salver	Maas & van Stein			
'Lady Edith'	24.2	Funnel	Dunlop	Mount Stewart		
'Leicester'	24.9	Funnel	Duivenvoorde	Duivenvoorde		Wb
'Lilac Time'	23.3	Funnel	Dunlop	Dick Fulcher		
'Loch Hope'	23.6	Funnel	Dunlop			
'Lydenburg'	23.8	Tubular	Dunlop	Kirstenbosch		
'Magnifico'	25.1	Funnel	Dunlop	Dunlop	evg	
'Marianne'	24.0	Trumpet	Duivenvoorde	Duivenvoorde		

(continued)

Table 2b (continued)

Cultivar	DNA	Group	Origin	Breeder/ introducer	evg	FC
'Mariette'	24.5	Trumpet	Duivenvoorde	Duivenvoorde		
'Martine'	23.6	Trumpet	Duivenvoorde	Duivenvoorde		
'Maximus'	24.9	Funnel	van Poucke	van Poucke	evg	
'Meibont'	22.7	Salver	Kramer	Kramer		
'Midnight Blue'	22.6	Salver	Dunlop	Wood		
'Midnight Star'	23.2	Trumpet	van Doorslaer	Raveninham Hall		
'Mount Stewart'	25.0	Funnel	Dunlop	Dunlop	evg	
'Notfred'	21.9	VLG	Dunlop	Notcutts	evg	
'Nottingham'	22.3	Salver	Duivenvoorde	Duivenvoorde		Wy
'Nyx'	23.1	Salver	Dunlop	Dunlop		
'Oslo'	23.6	Trumpet	Duivenvoorde	Duivenvoorde		
'Oxford Blue'	22.5	Salver	Dunlop	Dunlop		
'Patent Blue'	22.5	Salver	Dunlop	Dunlop		
'Penelope Palmer'	23.9	Funnel	Dunlop	Palmer	(evg)	
'Phantom'	25.0	Funnel	Dunlop	Dunlop	evg	
'Pinchbeck'	23.7	Funnel	Duivenvoorde	Duivenvoorde		
'Pinocchio'	22.8	Salver	Maas & van Stein	Maas & van Stein		
'Plas Merdyn Blue'	24.2	Trumpet	Dunlop	Dunlop		
'Plas Merdyn White'	25.3	Funnel	Dunlop	Dunlop	evg	
'Polar Ice'	24.5	Trumpet	Maas & van Stein	Maas & van Stein		Wy
praecox	25.4		Zombe plateau, Malawi		evg	
praecox 'Albiflorus'	25.3		Madeira		evg	
'Premier'	21.9		Dunlop	Dunlop		
'Prinses Marilène'	22.2	Salver	Duivenvoorde	Duivenvoorde		Wy
'Profusion'	22.2	Salver	Beth Chatto			
'Purple Cloud'	24.9	Trumpet	Bulbes d'Opale		evg	
'Raveningham Hall'	24.4	Funnel	Jansen	Raveningham Hall		
'Rhone'	24.0	Trumpet	Maas & van Stein	Maas & van Stein		
'Rosemary'	23.9	Trumpet	Dunlop	Palmer		
'Rosewarne'	25.2	Trumpet	Dunlop	Rosewarne	evg	
'Rotterdam'	23.9	Funnel	Duivenvoorde	Duivenvoorde		
'San Gabriel'	24.7	Funnel	Monksilver Nursery	Monksilver Nursery	evg	

Cultivar	DNA	Group	Origin	Breeder/ introducer	evg	FC
'Sapphire'	21.9		Dunlop		evg	
'Septemberhemel'	23.1	Funnel	Kramer	Kramer		
'Starburst'	23.9	Funnel	Dunlop	Dunlop	evg	
'Stephanie Charm'	23.8	Funnel	van Doorslaer	van Doorslaer		Wb
'Sunfield'	23.8	Trumpet	Klinkhamer	Zonneveld		
'Supreme'	25.5		Dunlop		evg	
'Suzan'	23.8	Trumpet	Duivenvoorde	Duivenvoorde		
'Sylvine'	23.1	Funnel	van Doorslaer	van Doorslaer		
'Tall Boy'	24.2	Tubular	Dunlop	Fulcher		
'Tinkerbell'	25.0	VLG	Bulbes d'Opale		evg	
'Titan'	25.1	Funnel	Dunlop	Dunlop	evg	
'Twilight'	21.9		Dunlop	G. Dunlop		
'Umbellatus Albus'	23.2	Trumpet	RHS Wisley	received as 'Maximus Albus'		
'Umbellatus Albus'	23.3	Trumpet	Fleur			
'Violetta'	22.7	Trumpet	Dunlop	G. Dunlop		
'Virginia'	25.2	Funnel	Duivenvoorde	Duivenvoorde	evg	Wy
'Weaver'	24.5	Funnel	Bulbes d'Opale			
'Wendy'	22.1	Salver	Dunlop	Dunlop		
'White Beauty'	24.0	Trumpet	Reintjes	Reintjes		Wb
'White Smile'	24.4	Funnel	Maas & van Stein	Maas & van Stein		Wb
'Whitney'	25.1	Funnel	v Eijk	v Eijk	evg	Wy
'Windsor Castle'	22.7	Trumpet	Dunlop	Crown Estate		
'Windsor Grey'	24.2		Dunlop	Crown Estate		
'Winsome'	24.2	Trumpet	Dunlop	G. Dunlop		
'Wolga'	24.3	Trumpet	Duivenvoorde	Schoehuys		

evg = evergreen
Wy = white flower, yellow anthers
Wb = white flower, blackish anthers
VLG = Variegated Leaf Group

genetically split (heterozygous) for Salver (an F_1 from Funnel × Salver) might give rise to plants both with salver- and funnel-shaped flowers. That is exactly what is found in the offspring of 'Lilliput' × 'Midnight Star' (Table 4). To say it otherwise: Trumpet could be the genetically intermediate shape between Funnel/Salver and Tubular. Maybe the trumpet-shaped flowers resulting from Salver × Tubular can be separated from the Funnel × Tubular, as was done earlier by Gillissen (1980).

Conclusions

The above conclusions are based on the data collected so far. I am the first to admit that some of my conclusions could be considered as speculative. Still, the DNA contents confirm several relationships that were already suggested by others based on morphological arguments and even revealed some interesting new ones. The results give a firm confirmation to what were earlier mainly educated guesses. In conclusion, it is shown here that flow cytometry can be used, combined with morphological and geographical data, to gain information about the status of the species, the origin of cultivars, and the absence in the investigated cultivars of polyploidy.

Table 3. The number of plants with different flowershapes categorized according to their DNA content

DNA category >	22.2-23.0 pg	23.0-24.5 pg	24.5-25.3 pg	Total no. (evg)
Flowershape				
Salver	12	0	0	12 (0)
Funnel	0	12	15	27 (13)
Tubular	0	1	1	2 (0)
Trumpet	0	27	7	34 (4)

Table 4. Flowershapes of parents and offspring of some *Agapanthus* cultivars

Parents	First generation (F_1)	Flowershapes parents	F_1
A. inapertus × A. praecox	'Purple Cloud'	Tubular × Funnel	Trumpet
'Lilliput' × 'Midnight Star'	'Septemberhemel'	Salver × Funnel	Funnel
'Lilliput' × 'Midnight Star'	'Meibont'	Salver × Funnel	Salver
'Blue Triumphator' × 'Dr Brouwer'	'Oslo'	Salver × Trumpet	Trumpet
'Intermedius' × 'Donau'	'Bristol'	Trumpet × Trumpet	Trumpet
'Intermedius' × 'Columba'	'Pinchbeck'	Trumpet × Trumpet	Funnel

Table 5. Theoretical percentages of flowershapes of *Agapanthus* offspring

Parents	Offspring (F$_1$)
Salver × Salver	100% Salver
Funnel × Funnel	100% Funnel
Tubular × Tubular	100% Tubular
Salver × Funnel	100% Funnel (S)
Salver × Funnel (S)	50% Salver + 50% Funnel
Funnel × Funnel (S)	100% Funnel
Funnel (S) × Funnel (S)	75% Funnel + 25% Salver
Salver × Tubular	Trumpet (S)
Funnel × Tubular	Trumpet (F)
Salver × Trumpet (S)	50% Salver + 50% Trumpet
Salver × Trumpet (F)	50% Funnel + 50% Trumpet
Funnel × Trumpet (S)	50% Funnel + 50% Trumpet
Funnel × Trumpet (F)	50% Funnel + 50% Trumpet
Trumpet (S) × Trumpet (S)	50% Trumpet + 25% Salver + 25% Tubular
Trumpet (F) × Trumpet (F)	50% Trumpet + 25% Funnel + 25% Tubular
Trumpet (S) × Trumpet (F)	50% Trumpet + 25% Funnel + 25% Tubular

Note: (S) or (F) = split (heterozygous) for Salver or Funnel

Table 6. Partition of white flowers over the different categories

Flower/DNA type	Yellow anthers	Black anthers
low DNA (= Salver)	1	0
intermediate DNA	2	7
high DNA (= evergreen)	3	0
Salver	1	0
Trumpet	1	5
Funnel	4	4
Tubular	0	1?

References

M.D. Bennett (1972) Nuclear DNA content and minimum generation time in herbaceous plants. Proc. Roy. Soc. London. 181:109–135.

G.D. Duncan (1985) *Agapanthus* species: their potential, and the introduction of ten selected forms. Veld and Flora 71-4:122–125.

———— (1998) Grow *Agapanthus*. Kirstenbosch Gardening Series. Nat. Bot. Inst., Kirstenbosch, South Africa.

A.J.M. Gillissen (1980) Sortiments onderzoek van het geslacht *Agapanthus* L'Héritier. Thesis, Department of Taxonomy of Cultivated Plants, Wageningen.

J. Greilhuber (1979) Evolutionary changes of DNA and Heterochromatin amounts in the *Scilla bifolia* Group (Liliaceae). Plant Syst. Evol. Suppl 2:263–280.

———— (1998) Intraspecific variation in genome size: a critical reassessment. Ann. Bot. 82: 27–35.

J.S. Johnston, M.D. Bennett, A.L. Rayburn, D.W. Galbraith, and H.J. Price (1999) Reference standards for determination of DNA content of plant nuclei. Amer. J. Bot. 86-5:609–613.

F.M. Leighton (1965) The genus *Agapanthus* L'Héritier. J. South African Bot., Suppl. Vol. IV:1–50.

D. Ohri (1998) Genome size variation and plant systematics. Ann. Bot. 82 (Suppl. A.): 750–812.

G. McNeil (1972) The Katberg *Agapanthus*. J. Roy. Hort. Soc. 97-12:534–536

L. Palmer (1967) Hardy *Agapanthus* as a plant for the outdoor garden. J. Roy. Hort. Soc. 92-8:336–341.

H.P. Riley and D. Mukerjee (1960) Chromosomes in *Agapanthus*. Genetics 45, 1008.

Wim Snoeijer (1998) *Agapanthus*, a review 1-255. (private edition)

T.R. Tiersch, R.W. Chandler, S.S.M. Wachtel, and S. Ellias (1989) Reference standards for flow cytometry and application in comparative studies of nuclear DNA content. Cytometry 10:706–710.

B.J.M. Zonneveld (2001) Nuclear DNA contents of all species of *Helleborus* discriminate between species and sectional divisions. Plant Syst. Evol. 229:125–130.

B.J.M. Zonneveld and F. van Iren (2001) Genome size and pollen viability as taxonomic criteria: application to the genus *Hosta*. Plant Biol. 3:176–185.

B.J.M. Zonneveld, J.M. Grimshaw, and A.P. Davis (2003) The systematic value of nuclear DNA content in *Galanthus*. Plant Syst. Evol. In press.

B.J.M. Zonneveld and G.D. Duncan (2003) Taxonomic implications of genome size and pollen color and vitality for species of *Agapanthus* L'Héritier (Agapanthaceae). Plant Syst. Evol. 241.

Chapter 3

Taxonomy and Nomenclature

Classification of the Family

Agapanthus is a monocotyledon and formally placed within the family Liliaceae sensu lato. Today, the genus is usually placed within the family Alliaceae.

The family Alliaceae sensu lato contains 30 different genera with altogether about 720 different species. The best known genera belonging to this family are *Agapanthus, Allium, Brodiaea, Dichellostemma, Ipheion, Leucocoryne, Nothoscordum,* and *Tulbaghia.* The family can be divided further into subfamilies. To the subfamily Agapanthoideae belong only *Agapanthus* and *Tulbaghia.*

Taxonomists still do not agree in which family *Agapanthus* should be placed. It is also considered to belong to the family Amaryllidaceae. Fortunately, in 1985 a revision of the monocotyledons was published by Dahlgren, Clifford, and Yeo, but, as you can guess, not all that was written is accepted. Although the family Alliaceae is internationally accepted and used, the place of *Agapanthus* in this family remains uncertain.

A family for *Agapanthus* is easily distinguished by the inflorescence, which is a pseudoumbel (or pseudociadium), consisting of a few to many bostryces (this description is mainly from Gillissen 1980 and Mueller-Boblies 1980). In most references, including those references dealing with the taxonomy of the monocotyledons, the inflorescence is referred to as an umbel.

Tulbaghia differs from *Agapanthus* by its inflorescence bearing less flowers, the flower colour being violet, green, brown, or white. The best visible detail is the elongated filaments, which form a kind of corolla. Finally *Tulbaghia* has a distinct onion smell, especially when a part is cut or scratched, which *Agapanthus* lacks.

The term "umbel" is also used to describe the inflorescence for *Tulbaghia.* I have checked many plants of *Tulbaghia,* and to me the inflorescence is similar to that of *Agapanthus.* In some species, true, it is difficult to see whether or not we are dealing with a pseudoumbel, as they flower with only one bostryx; in several species, however, the inflorescence consists of two or more bostryces, and in extreme forms the bostryces themselves are included in their own bract. This results in one inflorescence bearing three kinds of bracts: the bract containing the complete inflorescence, the bract containing one bostryx, and the bract at the base of each pedicel.

On the other hand, *Tulbaghia* is distinguished from *Agapanthus* by its elongated filaments, the difference in the rootstock, and its distinct alliaceous chemistry. Taxonomists tend to put *Tulbaghia* in the Alliaceae because of its onion smell. If a family is based on the smell of its plants, then more plants should change family— *Bulbocodium* (Colchicaceae), for example, in the monocotyledons, and *Alliaria* (Brassicaceae) in the dicotyledons.

Recent studies (Fay and Chase 1996, for one) have split up the family Alliaceae sensu lato, based on corms versus bulbs and hollow versus solid styles. Genera for the Alliaceae will all have the onion smell (alliaceous chemistry): *Allium, Ipheion, Leucocoryne, Nothoscordum, Tristigma*, and *Tulbaghia*. Lacking alliaceous chemistry, genera like *Brodiaea, Dichelostemma*, and *Triteleia* are now placed in the new family Themidaceae, closely allied to Hyacinthaceae.

The simple solution is that when *Tulbaghia* is included in the Alliaceae, *Agapanthus* can be included in the Amaryllidaceae. Fay and Chase (1996) clearly show that *Agapanthus* is actually more closely related to the Amaryllidaceae than to the Alliaceae. But because of the superior ovary in *Agapanthus*, I find it hard to accept, morphologically, that this genus should be included in the Amaryllidaceae, whose members have an inferior ovary.

In 1998 I concluded that *Agapanthus* was best placed in the family **Agapanthaceae**, which conclusion was supported the Angiosperm Phylogeny Group, who published a classification of the families of flowering plants later that same year. Their classification is increasingly accepted worldwide; and so, finally, *Agapanthus* has its own well-established monogeneric family, **Agapanthaceae**.

Key to the Families

1 - style solid, plants with a distinct onion smell = **Alliaceae** J. Agardh (1858) Theoria Syst. Pl.
1 - style hollow, plants without an onion smell = 2

2 from 1
- ovary inferior = **Amaryllidaceae** J. St.-Hil. (1805) Expos. Fam. Nat. 1.
- ovary superior = **Agapanthaceae** Voigt (1850) Pflanzen-Reichs 2.

Sections

Zonneveld and Duncan (2003) proposed two botanical sections for the six species based on the colour of the pollen and the average nuclear DNA content. This botanical classification was published as follows:

Section Lilacinipollini Zonn. & G.D. Duncan (2003) Plant Syst. Evol.
Pollen purple. Leaf usually with purple base, deciduous.

The following species belong to this section:

Agapanthus campanulatus (nuclear DNA content = 22.3 pg)
Agapanthus caulescens (nuclear DNA content = 23.2 pg)
Agapanthus coddii (nuclear DNA content = 24.0 pg)

Section Ochraceipollini Zonn. & G.D. Duncan (2003) Plant Syst. Evol.
Pollen yellow. Leaf usually with a green base or with a purple base, deciduous or evergreen.
The following species belong to this section:

Agapanthus africanus (nuclear DNA content = 31.6 pg)
Agapanthus inapertus (nuclear DNA content = 25.2 pg)
Agapanthus praecox (nuclear DNA content = 25.5 pg)

Key to the Species

The key to the species is a compilation of the keys from Leighton (1965) and the results of Zonneveld and Duncan (2003). For cultivated species, which hybridise so easily, this key is hardly of any help. Species raised from wild-collected seed should be correct; but my own experience is that such offered seed produces a wide range of intermediate forms, and therefore all plants raised from seed should be carefully checked. Even nurseries acknowledge that "wild-collected seed" produces hybrids, or, more precisely: plants raised from so-called wild-collected seed offered as blue flowered white, and vice versa.

1 - pollen yellow = 2
1 - pollen purple = 10

2 from 1
- plants deciduous = *A. inapertus* = 3
- plants evergreen = 6

3 from 2
- perianth segments spreading slightly = *A. inapertus* subsp. *inapertus*
- perianth segments not spreading appreciably = 4
- perianth segments spreading perceptibly = 5

4 from 3
- segments almost as broad as long = *A. inapertus* subsp. *pendulus*
- segments narrow = *A. inapertus* subsp. *parviflorus*

5 from 3
- segments usually as long as the tube = *A. inapertus* subsp. *intermedius*
- segments shorter than the tube = *A. inapertus* subsp. *hollandii*

6 from 2
- perianth open = 7
- perianth tubular = *A. africanus* subsp. *walshii*

7 from 6
- perianth thick in texture, deep blue in colour [rarely white], inflorescence few-
    to many-flowered but not dense = *A. africanus* subsp. *africanus*
- perianth thin in texture, pale to medium blue in colour [rarely white],
    inflorescence few- to many-flowered or dense = *A. praecox* = 8

8 from 7
- leaf up to 2.5 cm wide = *A. praecox* subsp. *minimus*
- leaf wider than 4 cm = 9

9 from 8
- flower up to 5 cm long = *A. praecox* subsp. *orientalis*
- flower longer than 5 cm = *A. praecox* subsp. *praecox*

10 from 1
- perianth segments spreading and recurving = *A. caulescens* = 11
- perianth segments spreading at an angle greater than 90° = 13

11 from 10
- leaves 4 cm wide or more = *A. caulescens* subsp. *caulescens*
- leaves 3 cm wide or less = 12

12 from 11
- leaves flaccid, perianth segments recurving markedly towards the apex =
    A. caulescens subsp. *gracilis*
- leaves stiffly erect or nearly so, perianth segments not recurving markedly =
    A. caulescens subsp. *angustifolius*

13 from 10
- perianth more than 3.5 cm long, plants stout = *A. coddii*
- perianth less than 3.5 cm long, plants slender = *A. campanulatus* = 14

15 from 14
- perianth segments spreading widely to 90° from axis = *A. campanulatus* subsp.
    patens
- perianth segments spreading to c. 45° = *A. campanulatus* subsp. *campanulatus*

Nomenclature

Nomenclature is still confusing, however much Leighton (1965) tried to straighten
up the mess. She concluded that *Agapanthus* is either a genus with many species that
are hardly distinct from each other, or a genus consisting of only a few species with
a large variation (close reading of her publications suggests she leaned towards the
latter possibility). Current views about *Agapanthus* categorize the genus as very
variable, with only a couple of species to be recognized.

Clearly the wild plants of *Agapanthus* are very variable. Because of this variation
it is difficult to recognize species and/or subspecies, as Leighton stated in her monograph. In cultivation too nomenclature is still very confusing, especially given *A.
umbellatus*, an incorrect name that has been used for different species and cultivars.

Chapter 4

Classification of the Cultivars

The classification of the cultivars proposed by Gillissen (1980) in his little-known report is simple and practical, but sadly no later references use it. It is based on the flower shape and whether the plant is evergreen or deciduous. In this book Gillissen's classification is accepted; the only difference is that Gillissen proposed five groups based on the flower shape, while here four groups are accepted. This fifth group was based on intermediate characters between two groups; as such intermediate characters are possible between all the cultivar groups, I decided not to accept this fifth group.

One problem with Gillissen's otherwise great classification is that the names for cultivar groups were based on species names. Even before I published my private book in 1998, I feared that users of this classification—especially those readers with a conservative view—would link the cultivar back to the species whose name was used for the group. So, after careful consideration and several discussions with *Agapanthus* growers, I have decided to maintain the descriptions of the cultivar groups as published in my 1998 book but now with different names. These modern terms were carefully considered; the term "Trumpet" especially might be confusing, but of the several terms available, this seemed the best choice. The classification is still based on flower shape, expanded with the Variegated Leaf Group proposed by Marco Hoffman.

Flowers should be checked carefully before they are assigned to a group; often it is necessary to check the same flower a couple of hours later or next morning. Unfortunately, this is contradictory to the looseness implied by the notion of a group, but if the descriptions are not used literally, the *Agapanthus* cultivar group classification is of no value. All cultivar groups will then merge, and at the end we can only recognize cultivars flowering blue and cultivars flowering white.

International Code of Nomenclature of Cultivated Plants

The rules of nomenclature of wild plants are described in the *International Code of Botanical Nomenclature* (ICBN); the rules of nomenclature for cultivated plants are described in the *International Code of Nomenclature for Cultivated Plants* (ICNCP). A discussion about *Agapanthus campanulatus* is dealt with in the ICBN; a discussion about **'Cobalt Blue'** is dealt with in the ICNCP.

All cultivars included here are accepted under the regulations of the ICNCP-1995. When a cultivar name is invalid according to the ICNCP-1995, a brief note is given under the cultivar name, referencing the appropriate ICNCP-1995 article. Most synonyms can be referred to ICNCP-1995 art. 10.1, which article is not referenced at the cultivar name. Referenced articles are as follows:

10.1.   The accepted cultivar epithet is the earliest one which must be adopted for it under the rules.

17.2.   A cultivar epithet is not to be re-used within the denomination class.

17.9.   To be established, a new cultivar epithet published on or after 1 January 1959 must be a word or words in a modern language.

17.11. To be establised, cultivar epithets may not consist solely of common descriptive words in a modern language.

17.13. To be established on or after 1 January 1959, the botanical, common or vernacular name of any genus or nothogenus . . . may not form a new cultivar epithet.

22.1.   In order to be established, an epithet of a taxon of cultivated plants must . . . be accompanied either by a description or diagnosis, or by reference to a previously published description or diagnosis.

The discussion on how to refer to a cultivar name—either with or without the species name—is ongoing, and the ICNCP-1995 gives several possibilities from which to choose. The best way, when a classification of the cultivars is available, is to refer only to the genus name, the cultivar name, and the cultivar-group name, e.g., *Agapanthus* 'Cobalt Blue' (Salver Group). I realize that people with a conservative view on nomenclature prefer to link the cultivar name to a species name, e.g., *A. campanulatus* 'Cobalt Blue', but in this book—with the exceptions of *A. africanus* 'Albus', *A. inapertus* 'Albus', and *A. praecox* 'Albiflorus'—*Agapanthus* cultivars are no longer linked to a species name.

According to ICNCP-1995 art. 19.3, cultivar groups should be demarcated by round or square brackets (I chose round). The choice of cultivar group for a particular cultivar is either supplied by the contributors mentioned or based on personal observation or on illustrations in combination with other details.

Typography

The ICNCP-1995 also advises on the typography of the cultivar and cultivar-group names in art. 31.1.

31.1.   Cultivar and cultivar-group epithets are distinguished typographically from botanical names in Latin form; for example, they are not printed in italic typeface if the widespread convention of using italics for botanical names is adopted in the work.

In this revision, italics are used for the botanical names, and therefore cultivars and cultivar-group names appear in roman type. Cultivar names that are correct according to the ICNCP-1995 appear in **boldface** type; cultivar names that are invalid appear in the normal-weight type, but this is not described by the ICNCP-1995.

Agapanthus Funnel Group

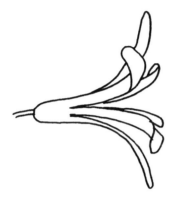 

Flower, Funnel Group

LEAF: usually evergreen.
INFLORESCENCE: bract usually opens on 1 side.
FLOWER: funnel-shaped, upright to horizontal to slightly facing downwards, the diameter can be of the same measurement as the length of the flower but is usually more, the segments are not overlapping.
The following cultivars belong to the Funnel Group:

White flowers

'Accent'	'Blanc Méoni'	'Komos June Bride'
'Albatross'	'Cambridge'	'Leicester'
'Albus Roseus'	**'Garden White'**	'Little White'
'Aphrodite'	**'Getty White'**	**'Maximus Albus'**
'Arctic Star'	'Giganteus Albus'	'Medium White'
'Bianca Perla'	'Ice Lolly'	'Ossato Snow Queen'
'Bianco'	**'Ivory Bells'**	**'Penn's White'**

'Plas Merdyn White'   'Snowy Owl'   'White Classic'
'Sea Spray'   'Stéphanie Charm'   'White Heaven'
'Silver Jubilee'   'Tenshi'   'White Ice'
'Snow Cloud'   'Vans White'   'White Smile'
'Snowdrops'   'Victoria'   'White Superior'
'Snow Queen'   'Virginia'   'Whitney'
'Snowstorm'   'White Christmas'

Violet-blue flowers

'Aalsmeer's Glorie'   'Dorothy Kate'   'Maximus'
'Aberdeen'   'Dwarf Baby Blue'   'Mediterranee'
'Adelaide'   'Dwarf Blue' ex Dobie   'Molly Fenwick'
'Aoisora'   'Elegans'   'Mount Stewart'
'Atlantic Ocean'   'Ellamae'   'Mount Thomas'
'Atlas'   'Emba'   'Nanus'
'Bangor Blue'   'Fafner'   'Pacific Ocean'
'Becky'   'Far Horizon'   'Parijs'
'Big Blue'   'Fasolt'   'Penelope Palmer'
'Black Pantha'   'Floribundus'   'Peter Pan'
'Blauwe Wimpel'   'Formality'   'Phantom'
'Bleu Méoni'   'Garden Blue'   'Pinchbeck'
'Blu'   'Garden King'   'Platinum Pearl'
'Blue Baby'   'Giganteus'   'Platinum Pink'
'Blue Bonnet'   'Glen Avon'   'Politique'
'Blue Brush'   'Goliath'   'Porlock'
'Blue Cascade'   'Guilfoyle'   'Queen Anne'
'Blue Formality'   'Holbeach'   'Raveningham Hall'
'Blue Gown'   'Huntington Blue'   'Rotterdam'
'Blue Heaven'   'Insignis'   'Rotunda'
'Blue Ice'   'Isleworth Blue'   'Royale'
'Blue Mercury'   'Jack's Blue'   'Ruban Bleu'
'Blue Nile'   'Jodie'   'Sarah'
'Blue Perfection'   'Johanna Gärtner'   'Sea Mist'
'Blue Queen'   'Joyce'   'Septemberhemel'
'Blue Ribbon'   'Kirsty'   'Silver Mist'
'Bluestorm'   'Lady Edith'   'Silver Sceptre'
'Carlos Freile'   'Latent Blue'   'Slieve Donard Form'
'Cherry Holley'   'Lena'   'Starburst'
'Christine'   'Lilac Time'   'Stormcloud Mini'
'Colossus'   'Loch Hope'   'Storms River'
'Cool Blue'   'Lost Horizon'   'Superstar' ex NZ
'Dawn Star'   'Luly'   'Supreme'
'Defina's Blush'   'Macho'   'Sylvine'
'Delft'   'Magnifico'   'Titan'
'Diana'   'Margaret Wakehurst'   'Tresco'

'Trudy'   'Violet Tips'
'Twilight'   'Weaver'

Agapanthus Trumpet Group

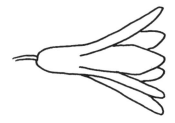

Flower, Trumpet Group

LEAF: evergreen or deciduous.

INFLORESCENCE: bract opens either on 1 or 2 sides.

FLOWER: trumpet-shaped, upright to horizontal to slightly facing downwards, the diameter can be of the same measurement as the length of the flower but is usually less, the segments are usually overlapping at least at the base or rarely not overlapping.

NOTE: in some cultivars the segments are not overlapping but because of the flower diameter, which is less than the length of the flower, the cultivar is placed in the Trumpet Group.

The following cultivars belong to the Trumpet Group:

White flowers

'Albidus'   'Ice Queen'   'Snow Maiden'
'Ardernei'   'Innocence'   'Umbellatus Albus'
'Corinne'   'Polar Ice'   'Washfield'
'Glacier Stream'   'Prolific White'   'White Beauty'

Violet-blue flowers

'Adonis'   'Blue Danube'   'Bristol'
'Amethyst'   'Blue Eyes'   'Catharina'
'Amsterdam'   'Blue Giant'   'Columba'
'Angela'   'Blue Moon'   'Crystal'
'Beatrice'   'Blue Penant'   'Debbie'
'Black Beauty'   'Blue Skies'   'Density'
'Blauwe Valk'   'Blue Velvet'   'Dnjepr'
'Blue Bird' ex Palmer 'Bressingham Bounty'   'Donau'
'Blue Companion'   'Bright Eyes'   'Dr Brouwer'

'Duivenbrugge Blue'   'Lewis Palmer'   'Podge Mill'
'Duná'   'Marcus'   'Purple Cloud'
'Edinburgh'   'Marianne'   'Rhone'
'Elaine'   'Mariètte'   'Rosemary'
'Elisabeth'   'Martine'   'Rosewarne'
'Eve'   'Mercury'   'Streamline'
'Helsinki'   'Midnight Star'   'Sunfield'
'Intermedius'   'Moira'   'Suzan'
'Johanna'   'Molly Howick'   'Sybil Harton'
'Jolanda'   'Mood Indigo'   'Violetta'
'Josephine'   'Mystery'   'Waga'
'June'   'Newa'   'Wholesome'
'Kama'   'Ocean Blue'   'Windsor Castle'
'Kirstenbosch'   'Oslo'   'Windsor Grey'
'Kopenhagen'   'Plas Merdyn Blue'   'Winsome'
'Lavender Girl'   'Plenitude'   'Wolga'
'Leichtlinii'   'Pluto Veil'   'Yves Klein'

Agapanthus Salver Group

Flower, Salver Group

LEAF: usually deciduous.
INFLORESCENCE: bract usually opens on 1 side.
FLOWER: salver-shaped, horizontal but usually slightly facing downwards, the segments are not overlapping or only overlapping at the base.
The following cultivars belong to the Salver Group:

White flowers

'Albus Nanus'   'Nottingham'   'Wendy'
'Alice Gloucester'   'Prinses Marilène'   'White Hope'
'Bressingham White'   'Spalding'   'White Star'
'Duivenbrugge White'   'Stéphanie'   'White Starlet'
'Lady Moore'   'Volendam'   'Yellow Tips'

Violet-blue flowers

'African Moon'
'Anthea'
'Ballyrogan'
'Ben Hope'
'Bleuet'
'Blue Globe'
'Blue Imp'
'Blue Peter'
'Blue Triumphator'
'Bressingham Blue'
'Buckingham Palace'
'Buckland'
'Castle of Mey'
'City of Lincoln'
'Cobalt Blue'
'Dorothy Palmer'
'Dutch Tiles'
'Elizabeth Salisbury'
'Findlay's Blue'
'Fulsome'
'Globosus'
'Hardingsdale'
'Hekiun'

'Helen'
'Hydon Mist'
'Iris'
'Isis'
'Joyful Blue'
'Kingston Blue'
'Kobold'
'Kosui-no-hitomi'
'Lady Grey'
'Lady Wimborne'
'Lilliput'
'Meibont'
'Midnight Blue' ex
    Philip Wood
'Monmid'
'Mooreanus'
'Mori-no-izumi'
'Mori-no-rindou'
'Mori-no-ryozu'
'Murasaki Shikibu'
'Nikki'
'Norman Hadden'
'Nyx'

'Oxbridge'
'Oxford Blue'
'Patent Blue'
'Pinocchio'
'Profusion'
'Prolific Blue'
'Queen Mother'
'Roy'
'Royal Blue' ex UK
'Sandringham'
'Shinkai'
'Sky Star'
'Slieve Donard'
'Small Dark'
'Stockholm'
'Super Star' ex UK
'Ultramarine'
'Wedgwood Blue'
'Windlebrook'
'Wolkberg'
'Zella Thomas'

Agapanthus Tubular Group

Flower, Tubular Group

LEAF: deciduous.
INFLORESCENCE: bract opens on 1 side.
FLOWER: tubular-shaped, hanging downwards, the segments widely overlapping along the whole length.
The following cultivars belong to the Tubular Group:

White flowers

'Weillighii Albus'   'White'

Violet-blue flowers

'Admiral's Cascade'	'Graskop'	'Sky Rocket'
'Bicton Bell'	'Graskopje'	'Tall Boy'
'Blue Steel'	'Inky Tears'	'Weillighii'
'Cambridge Blue'	'Lydenburg'	'Wolkberg'
'Crystal Drop'	'Sky'	
'Cyan'	'Sky Blue'	

Agapanthus Variegated Leaf Group

LEAF: deciduous or evergreen, variegated.
The following cultivars belong to the Variegated Leaf Group:

'Argenteus Vittatus'	'Golden Rule'	'Snoopy'
'Aureovittatus'	'Goldfinger'	'Stripes'
'Beth Chatto'	'Hinag'	'Tigerleaf'
'Early Variegated'	'Jahan'	'Tinkerbell'
'Ed Carman'	'Loch Hope Variegated'	'Variegated Baby Blue'
'Foremost's Variegated Nana'	'Notfred'	'Variegated Wilken'
	'San Gabriel'	'Variegatus Falcatus'
'Geagold'	'Silver Streak'	

Key to the Cultivars

The key to the cultivars is what could be called an "open key": not all ends will refer to a name and more names can be given at those ends that do refer to a name. For one thing, only a few cultivars had enough collected details to be used in a key, and for another, several cultivars are so similar that it is not worth the key's going deeper. What distinguishes these last is more the combination of several details rather than the one or two necessary for a key; thus repetition of every cultivar's complete description in the key is avoided.

Many would ask whether a key should even be attempted for *Agapanthus*. When in a border several blue plants are in flower, it is easy to say, "This one is slightly darker than that one." To put it on paper is another business. Still, I hope what follows gives a clue as to how close the relations between different cultivars are. The various keys also support Ben Zonneveld's conclusions; the relation between and the origin of some cultivars correspond remarkably with Ben's conclusions.

Because this is an "open key," anyone who wants to do so can add more names.

1 - leaves variegated = Table I
1 - leaves not variegated = 2

2 from 1
- flowers main colour white = 3
- flowers very pale to dark violet-blue = 4

3 from 2
- flowers single [6 tepals] = Table II
- flowers (semi-)double [more than 6 tepals] = Table III

4 from 2
- flowers single [6 tepals] = Table IV
- flowers (semi-)double [more than 6 tepals] = Table V

Table I. Plants having variegated leaves
1 - leaves sickle shaped = **'Variegatus Falcatus'**
1 - leaves straight = 2

2 from 1
- flowers white = **'Ed Carman'**
- flowers violet-blue = 3

3 from 2
- summer leaves green with yellow apex = **'Meibont'**
- summer leaves striped variegated = 4

4 from 3
- flowers belonging to the Trumpet Group, plant deciduous = **'Golden Rule'**
- flowers irregular in shape and belonging to the Salver Group, plant deciduous
    = **'Beth Chatto'**
- flowers belonging to the Funnel Group, plant (more or less) evergreen = 5

5 from 4
- leafbase purple = 6
- leafbase white or yellowish to greenish = 7

6 from 5
- leaf up to 20 cm long and 0.9 cm wide, arching to almost flat on the soil =
    'Goldfinger'
- leaf up to 40 cm long and 1.7 cm wide, arching but not flat on the soil =
    'Notfred'

7 from 5
- leaves white variegated = **'Argenteus Vittatus'**
- leaves yellow variegated = 8

8 from 7
- leaves on one plant mixed green, green with yellow stripes and yellow = 'San Gabriel'
- all leaves on one plant rather equally variegated = 9

9 from 8
- leaves green with yellow margin = 'Tigerleaf'
- leaves with yellow margin and the green middle with yellow stripes = 10

10 from 9
- leaves up to 1 cm wide = 'Tinkerbell'
- leaves wider than 2 cm = 'Aureovittatus'

Table II. Plants having green leaves, flowers single [6 tepals] and coloured white

1 - flowers belonging to the Tubular Group = Table IIa
1 - flowers belonging to the Trumpet Group = Table IIb
1 - flowers belonging to the Funnel Group = Table IIc
1 - flowers belonging to the Salver Group = Table IId

Table IIa. Plants having green leaves, flowers single, white, and belonging to the Tubular Group

1 - flowers drooping but not quite vertically =
1 - flowers drooping vertically = 2

2 from 1
- tepal segments at apex hardly spreading, flower up to 1.5 cm across = 'White'
- tepal segments at apex slightly spreading, flower over 2 cm across = 'Crystal Drop'

Table IIb. Plants having green leaves, flowers single, white, and belonging to the Trumpet Group

1 - leafbase green = 2
1 - leafbase with purple or violet = 6

2 from 1
- flowers with purple, which colour is especially visible at the apex of the flowerbud and/or when out of flower = 3
- flowers without any purple colouring = 4

3 from 2
- anthers cream to yellow =
- anthers purple, brown, or black = 'White Beauty'

4 from 2
- anthers cream to yellow = 5
- anthers purple, brown, or black =

5 from 4
- inflorescence 12–18 cm across and many-flowered = **'Polar Ice'**
- inflorescence smaller and with fewer flowers = *A. africanus* **'Albus'**

6 from 1
- flowers with purple, which colour is especially visible at the apex of the flowerbud and/or when out of flower = 7
- flowers without any purple colouring =

7 from 6
- anthers cream to yellow =
- anthers purple, brown, or black = 8

8 from 7
- peduncle round, inflorescence bud opens on 2 sides = **'Umbellatus Albus'**
- peduncle flat, inflorescence bud opens on 1 side = **'Ardernei'**, **'Corinne'**, **'Glacier Stream'**

Table IIc. Plants having green leaves, flowers single, white, and belonging to the Funnel Group

1 - leafbase green = 2
1 - leafbase with purple or violet = 14

2 from 1
- flowers with purple, which colour is especially visible at the apex of the flowerbud and/or when out of flower = 3
- flowers without any purple colouring = 6

3 from 2
- anthers cream to yellow =
- anthers purple, brown, or black = 4

4 from 3
- peduncle round = **'Snowy Owl'**
- peduncle flat = 5

5 from 4
- inflorescence bract remains attached = **'Cambridge'**
- inflorescence bract caducuous = **'Leicester'**, **'White Smile'**

6 from 2
- anthers purple, brown, or black = 7
- anthers cream to yellow = 9

7 from 6
- leaves 4–5 cm wide, inflorescence over 20 cm across = *A. praecox* **'Albiflorus'**
- leaves up to 3 cm wide, inflorescence up to 16 cm across = 8

8 from 7
- pedicel green, stamens exserted = **'Stéphanie Charm'**
- pedicel green with a bit of purple, stamens not exserted = **'Silver Jubilee'**

9 from 6
- inflorescence 16–23 cm across and 30- to many-flowered = 11
- inflorescence smaller and with fewer flowers = 10

10 from 9
- inflorescence up to 15 cm long and with 20–30 flowers = 'Whitney'
- inflorescence smaller and with fewer flowers = *A. africanus* 'Albus'

11 from 9
- most flowers within one inflorescence usually with 8 or 10 tepals = 'White Heaven'
- most flowers within one inflorescence with 6 tepals = 12

12 from 11
- inflorescence open and loose, with 20–50 flowers = 'Albatross'
- inflorescence dense, with usually more than 50 flowers = 13

13 from 12
- leaves deciduous and up to 2.5 cm wide = 'Ice Lolly'
- leaves evergreen and 3–5 cm wide = 'Bianca Perla', 'Ossato Snow Queen', *A. praecox* 'Albiflorus', 'Virginia'

14 from 1
- flowers with purple, this purple colour is especially visible at the apex of the flowerbud and/or when out of flower = 13
- flowers without any purple colouring = 14

13 from 12
- anthers cream to yellow =
- anthers purple, brown, or black = 'Accent'

14 from 12
- anthers cream to yellow =
- anthers purple, brown, or black =

Table IId. Plants having green leaves, flowers single, white, and belonging to the Salver Group
1 - leafbase green = 2
1 - leafbase with purple or violet = 5

2 from 1
- flowers with purple, which colour is especially visible at the apex of the flowerbud and/or when out of flower = 3
- flowers without any purple colouring = 4

3 from 2
- anthers cream to yellow =
- anthers purple, brown, or black =

4 from 2
- anthers cream to yellow = 'Prinses Marilène'
- anthers purple, brown, or black = 'Nottingham'

5 from 1
- flowers with purple, which colour is especially visible at the apex of the flowerbud and/or when out of flower = 6
- flowers without any purple colouring = 9

6 from 5
- anthers cream to yellow =
- anthers purple, brown, or black = 7

7 from 6
- peduncle flat = 'Bressingham White'
- peduncle round = 8

8 from 7
- inflorescence bud opens on 1 side = 'Lady Moore'
- inflorescence bud opens on 2 sides = 'Franni', 'White Star'

9 from 5
- anthers cream to yellow =
- anthers purple, brown, or black =

Table III. Plants having green leaves, flowers (semi-)double [more than 6 tepals] and coloured white

1 - inflorescence 10–11 cm across with 20 flowers = 'Double Diamond'
1 - inflorescence 20–24 cm across with 50–80 flowers = 'White Heaven'

Table IV. Plants having green leaves, flowers single [6 tepals] and coloured very pale to dark violet-blue

- flowers belonging to the Tubular Group = Table IVa
- flowers belonging to the Trumpet Group = Table IVb
- flowers belonging to the Funnel Group = Table IVc
- flowers belonging to the Salver Group = Table IVd

Table IVa. Plants having green leaves, flowers single, violet-blue, and belonging to the Tubular Group

1 - flowers drooping but not quite vertically = 2
1 - flowers drooping vertically = 3

2 from 1
- leaves evergreen = 'Purple Cloud'
- leaves deciduous = 'Bicton Bell', 'Lydenburg'

3 from 1
- leafbase green = 4
- leafbase with purple or violet =

4 from 3
- tepal lobes at apex hardly spreading, flower up to 1.5 cm across = 'Graskop'
- tepal lobes at apex slightly spreading, flower over 2 cm across = 5 (also 'Tall Boy')

5 from 4
- flower tube up to 2 cm long, flower colour outside white with a bit of violet tint = 'Crystal Drop'
- flower tube longer than 2.5 cm, flower colour outside pale violet-blue = 'Sky Rocket'

Table IVb. Plants having green leaves, flowers single, violet-blue, and belonging to the Trumpet Group

1 - leafbase green = 2
1 - leafbase with purple or violet = 8

2 from 1
- peduncle flat = 3
- peduncle round = 4

3 from 2
- flower tube up to 1.3 cm long = 'Amethyst', 'Dnjepr', 'Donau', 'Marcus', 'Mariètte', 'Rhone', 'Sunfield'
- flower tube longer than 1.5 cm = 'Blue Giant', 'Blue Velvet', 'Columba', 'Elisabeth', 'Jolanda', 'Josephine', 'Newa', 'Wolga'

4 from 2
- flower tube longer than 1.5 cm = 5
- flower tube up to 1.3 cm long = 6

5 from 4
- stamens exserted = 'Helsinki'
- stamens not exserted = 'Dr Brouwer', 'Kama'

6 from 4
- peduncle green = 'Blue Moon'
- peduncle green flushed with purple = 7

7 from 6
- inflorescence bud opens on 1 side = 'Johanna'
- inflorescence bud opens on 2 sides = 'Martine'

8 from 1
- peduncle flat = 'Amsterdam', 'Black Beauty', 'Blue Bird', 'Bristol'
- peduncle round = 9

9 from 8
- flower tube up to 1.3 cm long = 10
- flower tube longer than 1.5 cm = 'Purple Cloud'

10 from 9
- peduncle green = 11
- peduncle green flushed with purple = 'Intermedius', '**Midnight Blue**',
  '**Midnight Star**', '**Mood Indigo**', '**Septemberhemel**'

11 from 10
- flower appears violet-blue to dark violet-blue = '**Molly Howick**'
- flower very pale violet-blue = '**Windsor Grey**'

Table IVc. Plants having green leaves, flowers single, violet-blue, and belonging to the Funnel Group

1 - leafbase green = 2
1 - leafbase with purple or violet = 9

2 from 1
- peduncle flat = 3
- peduncle round = 4

3 from 2
- flower tube up to 1.2 cm long = '**Aberdeen**', '**Blue Heaven**', '**Raveningham Hall**', '**Rotterdam**', '**Silver Mist**'
- flower tube 1.5 cm long = '**Blue Perfection**'

4 from 2
- flower tube up to 1.3 cm long = 6
- flower tube longer than 1.5 cm long = 5

5 from 4
- inflorescence 18–22 cm across, stamens exserted = '**Blue Ribbon**' ex Duivenvoorde, 'Floribundus', '**Goliath**', '**Lena**', '**Maximus**'
- inflorescence 16–17 cm across, stamens not exserted = 'Blue Ribbon' ex Beth Chatto, '**Margaret Wakehurst**', '**Marianne**'

6 from 4
- peduncle green = 7
- peduncle green flushed with purple = 8

7 from 6
- peduncle less than 60 cm, inflorescence with 10–25 flowers = '**Peter Pan**', '**Sarah**'
- peduncle over 60 cm, inflorescence with 50 flowers or more = '**Atlantic Ocean**', '**Pacific Ocean**', '**Penelope Palmer**'

8 from 6
- inflorescence globular, flowers horizontal = '**Pinchbeck**'
- inflorescence flat, flowers facing downwards = '**Loch Hope**'

9 from 1
- peduncle flat = '**Blauwe Wimpel**'
- peduncle round = 10

10 from 9
- flower tube up to 1.4 cm long = 11
- flower tube longer than 1.5 cm =

11 from 10
- flower up to 3.5 cm long = 12
- flower longer than 4 cm = 'Delft'

12 from 11
- stamens exserted = 'Emba'
- stamens not exserted = 'Septemberhemel', Sylvine'

Table IVd. Plants having green leaves, flowers single, violet-blue, and belonging to the Salver Group
1 - leafbase green = 2
1 - leafbase with purple or violet = 6

2 from 1
- peduncle flat = 'Blue Globe'
- peduncle round = 3

3 from 2
- peduncle green = 4
- peduncle green flushed with purple = 'Slieve Donard'

4 from 3
- inflorescence 12–15(–19) cm across, 70–120 flowers, globular = 5
- inflorescence 12 cm across, 40 flowers, flat = 'Bressingham Blue', 'Lady Grey'

5 from 4
- flower 2.5–3 cm long (tube 1.1 cm long) and up to 3.5 cm across = 'Blue Triumphator'
- flower larger, up to 3.7 cm long (tube 1.4 cm long) and over 4.2 cm across = 'Stockholm'

6 from 1
- peduncle flat =
- peduncle round = 7

7 from 6
- peduncle green = 14
- peduncle green flushed with purple = 8

8 from 7
- peduncle on average less than 60 cm = 9
- peduncle on average over 60 cm = 13

9 from 8
- inflorescence 15–16 cm across = 'Nikki'
- inflorescence 8–14 cm across = 10

10 from 9
- flower tube 0.7–0.8 cm long = 11
- flower tube 1–1.2 cm long = 12

11 from 10
- stamens exserted = 'Lilliput'
- stamens not exserted = 'Bleuet'

12 from 10
- stamens exserted = 'Castle of Mey'
- stamens not exserted = 'Pinocchio'

13 from 8
- flower tube 0.9 cm long = 'Profusion'
- flower tube 1.2 cm long = 'Cobalt Blue'

14 from 7
- peduncle on average less than 60 cm = 15
- peduncle on average over 60 cm = 'Anthea', 'Blue Imp', 'Buckingham Palace', 'Elizabeth Salisbury', 'Findlay's Blue', 'Hydon Mist', 'Isis', 'Queen Mother', 'Sandringham', 'Super Star', 'Zella Thomas'

15 from 14
- leaf up to 1 cm wide = 'Kingston Blue'
- leaf up to 2 cm wide = 'Ben Hope', 'Royal Blue'

Table V. Plants having green leaves, flowers (semi-)double [more than 6 tepals] and coloured violet-blue
1 - flower with fertile stamens and pistil = 2
1 - flower with tepal-like staminodes and pistillodes = 'Flore Pleno'

2 from 1
- leafbase green = 'Waga'
- leafbase purple = 'Duná'

Chapter 5

Descriptions of the Genus, Species, and Cultivars

The species descriptions are all from Leighton (1965); cultivar descriptions are according to the particular cultivar's registration or are taken from several different gardens and/or nurseries. The critical question—whether these plants were correctly named in the first place!—remains. This is why the origin of the details (referred to in the notes) is so important.

The numbers given for the flower colour refer to the Kleuren Kaart/Colour Chart van Bloemenbureau Holland/Royal Horticultural Society (1986 edition). Some numbers are from Graham Duncan, A.J.M. Gillissen, and like references; Gary Dunlop also sent me details, and many I have checked personally.

The A–Z list of species and cultivars is in strictly alphabetical order, but within a species the botanical order takes precedence over the alphabet:

> *species*
> *species* subsp.
> *species* subsp. 'Cultivar'
> *species* var.
> *species* var. 'Cultivar'
> *species* 'Cultivar'
> 'Cultivar'
> rest of the names

Description of the Genus

Agapanthus L'Hér. (1788) Sert. angl. [6 species, >625 cultivars]

> SYNONYM: *Abumon* Adans. (1763) Fam. II. 54.
> *Mauhlia* Dahl (1787) Obs. Bot. Syst. Linne, 25.
> *Tulbaghia* Heist. non L. (1753) Descr. Nov. Gen. Brunsvig. X.

The name *Agapanthus* is derived from Greek, *agape* meaning "love" and *anthos* meaning "flower." This "flower of love" has many native names, but, in general, African lily will be the best choice. According to Willis ex Shaw (1988), *Agapanthus* is a conserved genus name, as decided at the Botanical Congress of Nomenclature in Vienna, in 1905.

Plants are perennial herbs, glabrous and rich in saponins. Solitary but often forming colonies. Roots almost bulb-like rhizome with many fleshy roots. The leaves grow directly from the rhizome, having sometimes a leek-like stem, deciduous or evergreen, linear, entire, upright to arching or even spreading, normal to dark green to glaucous, dull or shiny, thin fleshy to leathery.

The peduncle is stout, up to 2 m high, always arising from between the leaves, round or flat, which is especially detectable at about ¼ of the peduncle below the inflorescence, in full light upright but in shady places bending over.

The inflorescence is enclosed by a single large bract. This bracts opens on 1 side to release the flowers. In some species and cultivars this bract also splits, giving the inflorescence the appearance of opening on 2 sides. The bract drops or remains attached to the inflorescence.

The inflorescence is a pseudoumbel (or pseudociadium) and consists of a few to many bostryces. To cite Mueller-Boblies (1980), "In fact the *Agapanthus* pseudo-umbel is a compound inflorescence in which cymose partial inflorescences, namely helicoidcymes [= bostryces], are arranged in a racemose order, hence it is a thyrse (thyrsus). A thyrse is an unfortunately little appreciated type of inflorescence which is of very frequent occurrence among the angiosperm families: a racemose main axis bears cymose branches."

According to Gillissen (1980) one bostryx consists of 3–7 flowers; but slicing down an *Agapanthus praecox* quickly reveals bostryces of 8 and even 10 flowers in one inflorescence. These flowers do not open at the same time, they open one by one, giving the complete inflorescence the impression of a long flowering period. A similar inflorescence is also known from *Hemerocallis* (Hemerocallidaceae). In *Agapanthus*, the flowerbuds for next season develop just after the flowering period.

The pedicel is thin, upright to horizontal or bent, at the base one thin bract. This bract can be easily seen throughout the complete inflorescence.

The flower is funnel-shaped, salver-shaped, or tubular/cylindrical, 6 tepals (3 inner and 3 outer) grown together in a tube at the base with free segments, slightly fleshy, blue to violet-blue and with a darker coloured midrib or white. Stamens 6, inserted on the tube, ovary superior. Style canal present. Fruit a triangular capsule, lengthwise opening. Seed flat and winged, usually black.

Distribution

All species grow in South Africa, from the Cape Province to the Limpopo River in the north, from sea level to 2100 m. The deciduous plants grow in areas that are dry in winter with rain only in summer; the evergreen species grow in areas where it rains in winter or in areas with rain all year round.

In cultivation it is sometimes hard to see whether the plant is deciduous or evergreen, especially when all plants are kept indoors in winter or when all plants are

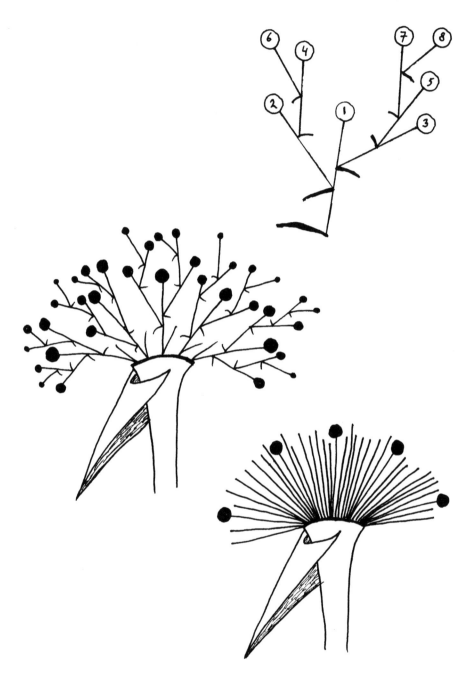

Agapanthus inflorescences (top to bottom): a bostryx with 8 flowers and their bract; an inflorescence showing 5 bostryces with 37 flowers (the thick black line on which the bostryces gather is a reduced thyrse); and a stylized inflorescence, seen as it is in real life.

grown outside in the garden. If, on the other hand, the plant develops new shoots during the flowering period, then the plant is evergreen. The leaves of deciduous plants will turn yellow-brown in autumn.

Plants flower in summer (mainly July and August, but also September into October in the UK and The Netherlands). New introductions are selected for earlier flowering and/or late flowering or reflowering.

In cultivation, evergreen plants are hardy up to zone 10; deciduous plants will survive up to zone 7 when winter protection is given.

Descriptions of the Species and Cultivars

Abumon Adans. = *Agapanthus* L'Hér.

Adans. (1763) Fam. II. 54.

Agapanthus 'Aalsmeer's Glorie' (Funnel Group)

ERROR: 'Aalsmeer Glory'

ORIGIN: (chance seedling of *A. praecox* subsp. *orientalis*) known since 1961 when grown by Fa J. de Jong & Zonen, Aalsmeer, The Netherlands. Probably no longer in cultivation.
LEAF: evergreen.
PEDUNCLE: green.
FLOWER: inside violet-blue with darker midrib (92A).
AWARD: GV in 1961.

Agapanthus 'Aberdeen' (Funnel Group)

ORIGIN: raised by Kees Duivenvoorde, Beverwijk, The Netherlands, introduced in 2001.
NAME: after the city in Scotland.
LEAF: deciduous, up to 40 cm long and 2.2 cm wide, arching, dark green, base green.
PEDUNCLE: 60 cm, green speckled violet, flat.
INFLORESCENCE: 17 cm across, 70 flowers, more or less globular.
PEDICEL: green heavily flushed dull violet.
FLOWERBUD: violet-blue with greenish base, later violet-blue, upright.
FLOWER: inside pale violet-blue (92C) with a bit of purple tint, margin slightly with more purple, midrib darker violet-blue (92AB), outside pale violet-blue (92C) but darker towards apex (92A), midrib slightly darker, small dark violet-blue base (93B), when out of flower purple with violet-blue base, 4 cm long (tube 1 cm long), 3.5–4 cm across, stamens not exserted, anthers black.
NOTE: details from plants grown by Duivenvoorde.
NOTE: nuclear DNA content = 24.2 pg.

Agapanthus 'Accent' (Funnel Group)

ERROR: 'Accebt'

ORIGIN: raised by Griffioen, Wassenaar, The Netherlands, introduced in 1985, and still in cultivation.

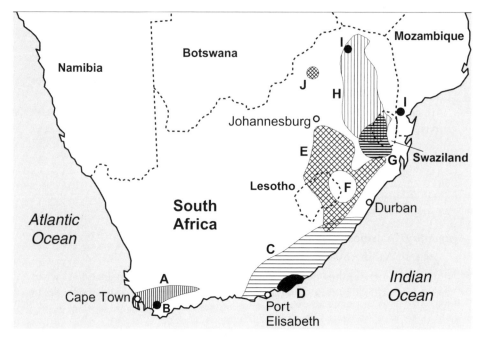

The main localities of the species of *Agapanthus* compiled by Ben Zonneveld after
Palmer (1967). A: *A. africanus.* B: *A. africanus* subsp. *walshii.* C: *A. praecox.*
D: *A. praecox* subsp. *minimus.* E: *A. campanulatus.* F: *A. caulescens.* G: *A. caulescens.*
H: *A. inapertus.* I: *A. inapertus* subsp. *intermedius.* J: *A. coddii.*

LEAF: deciduous, 20–30 cm long and 1 cm wide, pale to normal green, base purple.
PEDUNCLE: up to 50 cm, green, round.
INFLORESCENCE: 14 cm across, 15 flowers, flat.
PEDICEL: dark green and slightly purple towards flower.
FLOWERBUD: white with apex dull greenish-brown-purple, upright.
FLOWER: inside white, midrib transparent, outside white, when out of flower dull
white with apex slightly brownish-purple, horizontal, 3 cm long (tube 1 cm long),
3 cm across, stamens not exserted, anthers first purple changing to brown.
NOTE: details from plants grown by Griffioen.
ILLUSTRATION: photograph, Snoeijer (1998).

Agapanthus 'Adelaide' (Funnel Group)

SYNONYM: *Agapanthus praecox* subsp. *minimus* 'Adelaide'

ORIGIN: (selection of *A. praecox* subsp. *minimus*) from the Adelaide district, eastern
Cape Province. Introduced by Kirstenbosch National Botanical Garden, South
Africa. Known since 1984 and still in cultivation. Also offered as seed.
LEAF: evergreen, very small.

PEDUNCLE: 60–80 cm, dark purple.

INFLORESCENCE: 100 flowers, more or less globular.

PEDICEL: purple.

FLOWER: inside pale violet-blue with thin dark midrib (97A), outside violet-blue with darker base, when out of flower a bit purple, horizontal, stamens slightly exserted, anthers violet.

NOTE: easy grower and best in some shade, very abundant in flowering.

NOTE: seed-propagated and so better to regard this as a group of plants that look similar rather than a proper cultivar.

ILLUSTRATION: drawing, du Plessis and Duncan (1989); photograph, Duncan (1985 as *A. praecox* subsp. *minimus* 'Adelaide', 1998 as *A. praecox* subsp. *minimus* 'Adelaide').

Agapanthus Adelaide Seedlings = *A*. RUBBISH

Agapanthus 'Admiral's Cascade' (Tubular Group)

ORIGIN: (selected from 'Graskop' seedlings) raised by Cape Seed & Bulb, South Africa. Known since 2003 when Plant Variety Right was applied for, commercially available in 2005.

LEAF: deciduous, up to 43 cm long and 4 cm wide.

PEDUNCLE: 90 cm.

INFLORESCENCE: 11 cm across, 30 flowers, bud opens on 1 side.

FLOWER: outside dark blue (103A), hanging downwards, stamens not exserted or just 1–2 slightly exserted, anthers violet-blue with yellow pollen.

NOTE: this is the only *Agapanthus* cultivar I am aware of that has a blue colour (from reference; I have not seen the plant myself). All other "blue" cultivars have colours that read violet-blue on the RHS Colour Chart.

NOTE: details from the Internet [7]; origin details supplied by Biofleur.

Agapanthus 'Adonis' (Trumpet Group)

ORIGIN: raised by Gary Dunlop, Ballyrogan Nurseries, UK, introduced in 2001.

NAME: refers to the mythological Greek youth, loved by Aphrodite and symbol of dying and rising nature.

LEAF: deciduous, 45 cm long and 4 cm wide, upright, normal green, base purple.

PEDUNCLE: 120 cm, green with bronze towards inflorescence.

INFLORESCENCE: 15 cm across, 100 flowers, bud opens on 2 sides.

PEDICEL: purple.

FLOWER: inside white with midrib dark violet-blue (93A), margin violet-blue (93C), outside violet-blue (93C) with dark violet-blue base (93A), horizontal, 3 cm long, 3 cm across.

NOTE: details supplied by Gary Dunlop.

NOTE: invalid name per the ICNCP-1995, art. 17.13.

NOTE: nuclear DNA content = 22.9 pg.

Agapanthus 'African Moon' (Salver Group)

ORIGIN: raised and introduced by Lewis Palmer, known since 1956, and still in cultivation.
LEAF: more or less evergreen, 50 cm long and 2–3.5 cm wide, arching, dark glossy green.
PEDUNCLE: 50–90 cm, normal green.
INFLORESCENCE: 15 cm across, globular.
PEDICEL: pale green flushed with dull purple.
FLOWER: white flushed with pale violet-blue, margin and midrib pale violet-blue (91A), horizontal to slightly facing downwards, 2.5 cm long, 3 cm across, stamens exserted, anthers violet.
ILLUSTRATION: photograph, Warren (1995) and Fulcher (2000).
AWARD: PC in 1958; AM in 1977.

Agapanthus 'African Samba'

ORIGIN: Japan, known since 2001 when offered by Komoriya Nursery Ltd.
PEDUNCLE: 50 cm.
FLOWER: pale violet-blue.
NOTE: details from the Internet [25].

Agapanthus 'African Sky Blue'

ORIGIN: known since 1995, South Africa.
PEDUNCLE: 40–60 cm.
FLOWER: pale violet-blue.

Agapanthus africanus (L.) Hoffmanns. (1824) Verz. Pflanzenkulturen.

DISTRIBUTION: southwestern Cape Province, from sea level up to 1000 m. A very variable species, locally very abundant in mountains with good rainfall, but not always flowering.
LEAF: evergreen, not always developed when flowering, 6–18 per shoot, 10–35(–60) cm long, 0.6–2 cm wide, more or less upright, canaliculate, leathery, apex obtuse to subacute.
INFLORESCENCE: small, 12–30 flowers.
FLOWER: dark violet-blue or rarely paler, violet-blue very rarely, (2–)2.5–5.4 cm long (tube 0.9–3.9 cm long), pollen yellow.
FLOWERING TIME: December into April.
NOTE: nuclear DNA content = 31.55 pg.

Agapanthus africanus subsp. *africanus*

SYNONYM: *Agapanthus africanus* subsp. *minor* (Lodd.) H.R. Wehrh.
Agapanthus africanus subsp. *umbellatus* (Hoffmanns.) H.R. Wehrh. pro parte
Agapanthus africanus var. *minor* Beauverd
Agapanthus africanus 'Minor'
Agapanthus minor Lodd.

Agapanthus tuberosus L. ex P.DC.
Agapanthus umbellatus L'Hér. pro parte
Agapanthus umbellatus Redouté pro parte
Agapanthus umbellatus var. *latifolius* Red.Lil ex Roem. & Schult.
Agapanthus umbellatus var. *minor* DC. ex Redouté
Agapanthus umbellatus 'Minor'
Agapanthus umbelliferus Poir.
Agapanthus variegatus Steud.
Crinum africanum L.
Mauhlia africana Dahl
Mauhlia linearis Thunb.
Mauhlia umbellata Thunb. ex Roem. & Schult.
Polyanthes Mill.
Tulbaghia africana (L.) Kuntze
Tulbaghia africana var. *heisteri* (Fabric.) Kuntze
Tulbaghia africana var. *minor* (Lodd.) Kuntze
Tulbaghia heisteri Fabric.

DISTRIBUTION: southwestern Cape Province; Bredasdorp, Caledon, Cape Peninsula, Paarl, Stellenbosch, and Swellendam, from sea level up to 1000 m. A very variable species, locally very abundant in mountains with good rainfall, but not always flowering.

PEDUNCLE: (25–)30–50(–70) cm, usually purplish and glaucous.

INFLORESCENCE: 12–30 flowers.

FLOWER: dark violet-blue or rarely paler, violet-blue, very rarely white (in cultivation => *A. africanus* 'Albus'), (2–)2.5–3.5 cm long (tube 0.9–1.4 cm long), segments spreading, rather thick in texture, stamens and pistil slightly shorter than the flower, exserted.

FLOWERING TIME: December into April.

NOTE: I am told that *A. africanus* especially flowers after fires; Kidd (1950) and Andrews and Brickell (1999) also refer to this.

NOTE: according to the Department of Nature Conservation (1967), *A. africanus* is a protected species.

NOTE: known in cultivation from 1674, but ever since mixed up with names like *A. umbellatus* and *A. orientalis*.

NOTE: most plants offered under this name, either by nurseries or seed companies, are hybrids. I have never seen a true-to-type plant in the UK or The Netherlands.

NOTE: plants offered under *A. africanus* 'Minor' might belong here.

ILLUSTRATION: drawing, Curtis (1800 as *A. umbellatus*), Edwards (1821 as *A. umbellatus*), Premier (1828 as *A. umbellatus*), Hulme and Hibberd (1907), Krause (1930 as *A. umbellatus*), Kidd (1950), Rice and Compton (1950), Leighton (1965), Department of Nature Conservation (1967), Mallary, Waltermire, and Levin (1986 as *A. umbellatus*), Wijnands (1983), and Kostelijk (1986); photograph, Marloth (1915 as *A. umbellatus* L'Hérit.), van Zyl (1984), Duncan (1998), Andrews and Brickell (1999), and Goldblatt (2000).

Agapanthus africanus subsp. *caulescens* (Sprenger) H.R. Werh. = *A. caulescens* Sprenger
    H.R. Wehrh. (1931) Die Gartenstauden.

Agapanthus africanus subsp. *insignis* (Bull) H.R. Wehrh. = *A. inapertus* Beauv. ex F.M. Leight.
    H.R. Wehrh. (1931) Die Gartenstauden.

Agapanthus africanus subsp. *minor* (Lodd.) H.R. Wehrh. = *type*
    H.R. Wehrh. (1931) Die Gartenstauden.

Agapanthus africanus subsp. *minor* var. *globosus* H.R. Wehrh. = *A.* 'Globosus'
    H.R. Wehrh. (1931) Die Gartenstauden.

Agapanthus africanus subsp. *minor* var. *leichtlinii* H.R. Wehrh. = *A.* 'Leichtlinii'
    H.R. Wehrh. (1931) Die Gartenstauden.

Agapanthus africanus subsp. *minor* var. *mooreanus* H.R. Wehrh. = *A.* 'Mooreanus'
    H.R. Wehrh. (1931) Die Gartenstauden.

Agapanthus africanus subsp. *minor* var. *saintpaulii* H.R. Wehrh. = *A.* 'Saintpaulii'
    H.R. Wehrh. (1931) Die Gartenstauden.

Agapanthus africanus subsp. *praecox* (Willd.) H.R. Wehrh. = *A. praecox* Willd. ex F.M. Leight.
    H.R. Wehrh. (1931) Die Gartenstauden.

Agapanthus africanus subsp. *umbellatus* (Hoffmanns.) H.R. Wehrh. =
    = pro parte = *type*
    = pro parte = *A. praecox* subsp. *orientalis* F.M. Leight.
    H.R. Wehrh. (1931) Die Gartenstauden.

Agapanthus africanus subsp. *umbellatus* var. *albidus* H.R. Wehrh. = *A.* 'Umbellatus Albus'
    H.R. Wehrh. (1931) Die Gartenstauden.

Agapanthus africanus subsp. *umbellatus* var. *atricoeruleus* H.R. Wehrh. = *A.* 'Atrocaeruleus'
    H.R. Wehrh. (1931) Die Gartenstauden.

Agapanthus africanus subsp. *umbellatus* var. *aureus* H.R. Wchrh. =
A. 'Aureovittatus'

H.R. Wehrh. (1931) Die Gartenstauden.

Agapanthus africanus subsp. *umbellatus* var. *giganteus* H.R. Wehrh. =
A. 'Giganteus'

H.R. Wehrh. (1931) Die Gartenstauden.

Agapanthus africanus subsp. *umbellatus* var. *latifolius* H.R. Wehrh. =
A. 'Latifolius'

H.R. Wehrh. (1931) Die Gartenstauden.

Agapanthus africanus subsp. *umbellatus* var. *multifloris* Voss ex H.R. Wehrh. =
A. 'Multiflorus'

H.R. Wehrh. (1931) Die Gartenstauden.

Agapanthus africanus subsp. *umbellatus* var. *pallidus* H.R. Wehrh. =
A. 'Pallidus'

H.R. Wehrh. (1931) Die Gartenstauden.

Agapanthus africanus subsp. *umbellatus* var. *plenus* H.R. Wehrh. = **A. 'Flore
Pleno'**

H.R. Wehrh. (1931) Die Gartenstauden.

Agapanthus africanus subsp. *umbellatus* var. *saundersonianus* H.R. Wehrh. =
A. 'Saundersonianus'

H.R. Wehrh. (1931) Die Gartenstauden.

Agapanthus africanus subsp. *umbellatus* var. *variegatus* H.R. Wehrh. =
A. 'Argenteus Vittatus'

H.R. Wehrh. (1931) Die Gartenstauden.

Agapanthus africanus subsp. *umbellatus* var. *weillighii* H.R. Wehrh. =
A. 'Weillighii'

H.R. Wehrh. (1931) Die Gartenstauden.

Agapanthus africanus subsp. **walshii** (L. Bol.) Zonn. & G.D. Duncan (2003)
Plant Syst. Evol.

synonym: *Agapanthus walshii* L. Bol.

distribution: southwestern Cape Province; Steenbras, Caledon District, at 450–
730 m. According to Rourke (1973), Lewis Palmer tried to collect this plant during
his visit in September 1963 but without luck, or as Rourke writes, "He [Lewis Palmer]
hoped to find *A. walshii* which, at that stage, was regarded by many as almost myth-
ical. But he returned to England empty-handed." Rourke himself found a small

population in 1969 in the western foothills of the Kogelberg Range above the Steenbras reservoir at 730 m. The plate in Rourke (1973) by artist Fay Anderson was from
material collected at the same spot in December 1971.

HABIT: in their native site, plants rarely form large clumps; they are usually found as
single plants or in very small clumps with only a few shoots.

NAME: in honour of A. Walsh, who collected the type specimen at the Steenbras
Railway Station in January 1918.

PEDUNCLE: 30–50(–70) cm.

INFLORESCENCE: 8–14(–19) flowers.

FLOWER: violet-blue or rarely white, segments somewhat spreading, hanging downwards, 3–5.4 cm long (tube 1.6–3.9 cm long), stamens as long as the flowers.

FLOWERING TIME: January and February.

NOTE: discovered in 1918 and since then known in cultivation.

NOTE: Rourke (1973) "From late December until March the inflorescences are produced, often stimulated by a veld fire, although this is apparently not a prerequisite
for flowering. For several years this species has been in cultivation at Kirstenbosch
but had proved rather difficult to flower."

NOTE: the white-flowering form is known since 1977 (Duncan 1983) and was
brought into cultivation at Kirstenbosch National Botanical Garden, South Africa.

NOTE: this subspecies is the only *Agapanthus* referred to by Walter and Gillett
(1998), who list it, as *A. walshii*, as rare. Hilton-Taylor (1996) too, in the Red Data
List of Southern African Plants, lists this subspecies as rare.

ILLUSTRATION: drawing, Leighton (1965 as *A. walshii*) and Rourke (1973 as *A. walshii*); photograph, Duncan (1983 as *A. walshii*, 1998 as *A. walshii*, both blue and
white form), and Allemand and Pionnat (2001 as *A. walshii*).

Agapanthus africanus var. *albus* Philip & Lord = *A. africanus* 'Albus'
  Philip & Lord (1993) The Plant Finder. nom.nud.

Agapanthus africanus var. *atro-caeruleus* Synge = *A.* 'Atrocaeruleus'
  Synge (1986) Dictionary of Gardening. nom.nud.

Agapanthus africanus var. *globosus* (Bull) Bail. ex Boom = *A.* 'Globosus'
  Bail. ex Boom (1950) Flora der gekweekte, kruidachtige gewassen.

Agapanthus africanus var. *leichtlinii* (Baker) Beauverd = *A.* 'Leichtlinii'
  Beauverd (1910) Bull. Soc. Bot. Geneve.

Agapanthus africanus var. *maximus* (Lindl.) Durand & Schinz = *A.* 'Maximus'
  Durand & Schinz (1893) Consp. Fl. Afr.

Agapanthus africanus var. *minimus* (Lindl.) Beauverd = *A. praecox* subsp.
  minimus (Lindl.) F.M. Leight.
  Beauverd (1910) Bull. Soc. Bot. Geneve.

Agapanthus africanus var. *minimus-albus* Boom (1950) Flora der gekweekte, kruidachtige gewassen.

Agapanthus africanus var. *minor* Beauverd = *type*
Beauverd (1910) Bull. Soc. Bot. Geneve.

Agapanthus africanus var. *mooreanus* Nich. ex Boom = *A.* 'Mooreanus'
Boom (1950) Flora der gekweekte, kruidachtige gewassen.

Agapanthus africanus var. *variegatus* Boom = *A.* 'Argenteus Vittatus'
Boom (1950) Flora der gekweekte, kruidachtige gewassen.

Agapanthus africanus 'Alba' => *A. africanus* 'Albus'

Agapanthus africanus 'Albidus' =
= pro parte => *A. campanulatus* 'Albidus' = *A.* 'Franni'
= pro parte = *A.* 'Umbellatus Albus'
NOTE: the name, sensu stricto, is probably nothing more than a simple confusion with *A. campanulatus* 'Albidus'; the plant, however, usually belongs to 'Umbellatus Albus'.

Agapanthus africanus 'Albiflorus' = *A. africanus* 'Albus'
NOTE: invalid name per the ICNCP-1995, art. 17.2, 17.9, and 17.11.

Agapanthus africanus 'Albus' =
= pro parte = *A. africanus* 'Albus'
= pro parte = *A.* 'Umbellatus Albus'
NOTE: the name, sensu stricto, is probably nothing more than a simple confusion with *A. campanulatus* 'Albidus', the plant, however, usually belongs to 'Umbellatus Albus'.

Agapanthus africanus 'Albus'

SYNONYM: *Agapanthus africanus* var. *albus* Philip & Lord
Agapanthus africanus 'Albiflorus'
Agapanthus albus Besant
Agapanthus minor alba
Agapanthus 'Minor Alba'
ERROR: 'Alba'

LEAF: evergreen, rather short and small, upright, pale green, base pale green.
PEDUNCLE: 30–50 cm.
INFLORESCENCE: few-flowered.
FLOWER: white, when out of flower no purple colouring, anthers yellow.
NOTE: Snoeijer (1998) "Most plants offered today under this name, either by nurseries or seed companies, are hybrids and usually belong to 'Umbellatus Albus'. To

be honest, I have actually seen only one plant in The Netherlands which probably was true." Though I still doubt whether this one plant I saw was true to name, I have since come across a few plants in the RHS Garden Wisley labelled as such and perhaps true to name. It seems that this plant is grown by some nurseries in the UK as a clone. This implies, however, that we are not dealing with a true *A. africanus* selection, as this plant is so difficult to cultivate. Most plants offered under this name are, on the other hand, different from the description presented here and are usually doubtful seedlings. Andrews and Brickell (1999) also doubt the existence of this cultivar, referring to the first report of a white-flowering *A. africanus* in 1920 at "a local Wild Flower Show."

NOTE: seed and/or plants offered as *A. minor alba* and 'Minor Alba' might belong here.

NOTE: a company in South Africa offers plants from tissue culture under this name.

Agapanthus africanus 'Albus Nanus' = *A.* 'Albus Nanus'

Agapanthus africanus 'Amethyst' = *A.* **'Amethyst'**

Agapanthus africanus 'Baby Blue' = *A.* **'Blue Baby'**

Agapanthus africanus 'Big Blue' = *A.* 'Big Blue'

Agapanthus africanus 'Blue Giant' = *A.* **'Blue Giant'**

Agapanthus africanus 'Blue Penant' = *A.* **'Blue Penant'**

Agapanthus africanus 'Blue Perfection' = *A.* **'Blue Perfection'**

Agapanthus africanus 'Blue Triumphator' = *A.* **'Blue Triumphator'**

Agapanthus africanus 'Caeruleus' = *A.* 'Caeruleus'

Agapanthus africanus 'Coerulea' = *A.* 'Caeruleus'

Agapanthus africanus 'Coerulea Selection' = *A.* 'Caeruleus Selection'

Agapanthus africanus 'Donau' = *A.* **'Donau'**

Agapanthus africanus 'Dr Brouwer' = *A.* 'Dr Brouwer'

Agapanthus africanus 'Elaine' = *A.* **'Elaine'**

Agapanthus africanus 'Ellamae' = *A.* **'Ellamae'**

Agapanthus africanus 'Flore Pleno' = *A.* **'Flore Pleno'**

Agapanthus africanus 'Getty White' = *A.* **'Getty White'**

Agapanthus africanus 'Hinag' = *A.* **'Hinag'**

Agapanthus africanus 'Intermedius' = *A.* 'Intermedius'

Agapanthus africanus 'Leichtlinii' = *A.* **'Leichtlinii'**

Agapanthus africanus 'Little White' = *A.* 'Little White'

Agapanthus africanus 'Minor' = *type*

Agapanthus africanus 'Mount Stewart' = *A.* **'Mount Stewart'**

Agapanthus africanus 'New Blue' = *A.* RUBBISH

Agapanthus africanus 'Peter Pan' = *A.* **'Peter Pan'**

Agapanthus africanus 'Queen Anne' = *A.* **'Queen Anne'**

Agapanthus africanus 'Rancho Dwarf' = *A.* **'Rancho Dwarf'**

Agapanthus africanus 'Sapphire' = *A.* **'Sapphire'**

Agapanthus africanus 'Streamline' = *A.* **'Streamline'**

Agapanthus africanus 'Sunfield' = *A.* **'Sunfield'**

Agapanthus africanus 'Variegatus' = *A.* **'Argenteus Vittatus'**
    NOTE: invalid name per the ICNCP-1995, art. 17.2, 17.9, and 17.11.

Agapanthus africanus 'Wolga' = *A.* **'Wolga'**

Agapanthus africanus blue
    ORIGIN: offered as seed.

Agapanthus africanus Headbourne Hybrids = *A.* RUBBISH

Agapanthus 'Akinosora'
    ORIGIN: Japan, known since 2001 when offered by Komoriya Nursery Ltd.
    NAME: Japanese, "October sky."
    PEDUNCLE: 50 cm.
    FLOWER: violet-blue with purple tint.
    NOTE: details from the Internet [25].

'Alba' => *Agapanthus africanus* 'Alba'

'Alba' => *Agapanthus campanulatus* 'Alba'

Agapanthus 'Alba Grandiflora'
    ORIGIN: known since 1979, The Netherlands; no further records.
    NOTE: invalid name per the ICNCP-1995, art. 17.9 and 17.11.

Agapanthus 'Alba Roseus' = *A.* 'Albus Roseus'

Agapanthus 'Albatross' (Funnel Group)

SYNONYM: *Agapanthus praecox* subsp. *orientalis* 'Albatross'
Agapanthus praecox subsp. *praecox* 'Albatross'

ORIGIN: (selection of *A. praecox* subsp. *orientalis*) from Oakhurst Nurseries, California, USA. Known since 1976 and still in cultivation.
LEAF: evergreen, 15–40 cm long and 2.5–3.5 cm wide, arching, dark green, base green.
PEDUNCLE: (40–)80–150 cm, green but slightly glaucous, flat.
INFLORESCENCE: 18–25 cm across, 20–50 flowers, more or less globular, bud usually strongly elongated and opens on 1 side.
PEDICEL: green.
FLOWERBUD: cream-white, upright.
FLOWER: inside white with transparent midrib, outside white, when out of flower white, 4–4.5 cm long (tube 1–1.5 cm long), 4–5 cm across, stamens exserted, anthers yellow.
NOTE: details from plants growing at different nurseries.
ILLUSTRATION: *color plate*; photograph, Snoeijer (1999).

Agapanthus albidus L.H. Bailey = *A. praecox* **'Albiflorus'**

L.H. Bailey (1977) Hortus Third.

'Albidus' => *Agapanthus africanus* 'Albidus'

'Albidus' => **Agapanthus campanulatus 'Albidus'**

'Albidus' => *Agapanthus orientalis* 'Albidus'

'Albidus' => *Agapanthus praecox* 'Albidus'

Agapanthus 'Albidus' (Trumpet Group)

ORIGIN: known since 2001, South Africa.
INFLORESCENCE: 50 flowers, globular.
PEDICEL: green.
FLOWERBUD: white with a bit of green, apex slightly cream, base greenish, upright.
FLOWER: inside white, midrib slightly darker to very pale cream, horizontal, anthers yellow.
NOTE: propagated by tissue culture.
NOTE: invalid name per the ICNCP-1995, art. 17.2, 17.9, and 17.11.

Agapanthus albiflorus Erhardt = *A. praecox* **'Albiflorus'**

Erhardt (1995) PPP Index. nom.nud.

'Albiflorus' => *Agapanthus africanus* 'Albiflorus'

'Albiflorus' => *A. praecox* 'Albiflorus'

Agapanthus albo-lilacinus Besant = *A.* 'Albo-lilacinus'
  Besant (1903) Flora and Sylva, 1.

Agapanthus 'Albo-lilacinus'
  SYNONYM: *Agapanthus albo-lilacinus* Besant
  Agapanthus umbellatus var. *albo-lilacinus* Krelage
  ORIGIN: known since 1888 when offered by Krelage, The Netherlands, and still referred to in 1920 but no longer in cultivation.
  PEDUNCLE: "hardly rising above the leaves."
  FLOWER: "white, shaded blue."

Agapanthus 'Albo-monstrosus'
  SYNONYM: *Agapanthus umbellatus* var. *albo-monstrosus* Krelage
  ORIGIN: known since 1888 when offered by Krelage, The Netherlands; no further records.

Agapanthus alboroseus Philip & Lord = *A.* 'Albus Roseus'
  Philip & Lord (1993) The Plant Finder. nom.nud.

'Albovittatus' => *Agapanthus campanulatus* subsp. *campanulatus* 'Albovittatus'

Agapanthus albus Besant = *A. africanus* 'Albus'
  Besant (1903) Flora and Sylva, 1.

'Albus' => *Agapanthus africanus* 'Albus'

'Albus' => *Agapanthus campanulatus* 'Albus'

'Albus' => *Agapanthus gigantea* 'Albus'

'Albus' => *Agapanthus inapertus* 'Albus'

'Albus' => *Agapanthus intermedius* 'Albus'

'Albus' => *Agapanthus maximus* 'Albus'

'Albus' => *Agapanthus nutans* 'Albus'

'Albus' => *Agapanthus praecox* subsp. *orientalis* 'Albus'

'Albus' => *Agapanthus praecox* subsp. *praecox* 'Albus'

'Albus' => *Agapanthus praecox* 'Albus'

Agapanthus 'Albus Nanus'

> SYNONYM: *Agapanthus africanus* 'Albus Nanus'

ORIGIN: introduced from South Africa, known since 1991, UK, and still in cultivation. Also offered as seed.
LEAF: evergreen.
PEDUNCLE: 25 cm.
FLOWER: white.
NOTE: invalid name per the ICNCP-1995, art. 17.9 and 17.11.
ILLUSTRATION: photograph, Vermeulen (1996).

Agapanthus 'Albus Nanus' (Salver Group)

> SYNONYM: *Agapanthus campanulatus* 'Albus Nanus'

ORIGIN: introduced in 1995 by Blounts Court Nurseries, Calne, Wiltshire, UK, which obtained the plant from another UK nursery that is no longer in existence, so the origin can be traced no further back.
LEAF: deciduous.
PEDUNCLE: 45–60 cm.
FLOWER: white.
NOTE: invalid name per the ICNCP-1995, art. 17.2, 17.9, and 17.11.

Agapanthus 'Albus Rosea' = *A.* 'Albus Roseus'

Agapanthus 'Albus Roseus' (Funnel Group)

> SYNONYM: *Agapanthus* 'Alba Roseus'
> *Agapanthus alboroseus* Philip & Lord
> *Agapanthus* 'Albus Rosea'
> *Agapanthus praecox* subsp. *orientalis* 'Albo Roseus'
> *Agapanthus praecox* subsp. *orientalis* 'Albus Roseus'

ORIGIN: introduced in New Zealand, known since 1991, and still in cultivation.
LEAF: evergreen.
PEDUNCLE: 50–75 cm, purplish towards inflorescence.
INFLORESCENCE: 30–50 flowers, more or less flat.
PEDICEL: purplish.
FLOWERBUD: white with pale purple tint, upright.
FLOWER: inside white, outside white with the midrib towards apex purplish, when out of flower slightly pale purple, stamens slightly exserted, anthers purplish with yellow pollen.
NOTE: some details from the Internet [16]: "The closest Australia has to a pink *Agapanthus.*" As the cultivar keys show, several white-flowering cultivars have this purple colouring, so in my view it is overdoing it a bit to call this pink.
NOTE: invalid name per the ICNCP-1995, art. 17.9 and 17.11.
ILLUSTRATION: photograph, CropLink (1997 as *A.* 'Albus Rosea').

Agapanthus 'Albus Roseus Compactus'

ORIGIN: Australia, known since 2001.
NOTE: invalid name per the ICNCP-1995, art. 17.9 and 17.11.

Agapanthus 'Albus Select'

SYNONYM: *Agapanthus orientalis* 'Albus Select'

ORIGIN: introduced by J.N. Giridlian's Oakhurst Gardens, California, USA. Known
since 1962 but may no longer be in cultivation.
INFLORESCENCE: "with extra-large umbels."
FLOWER: white, "large flowering," anthers yellow.
NOTE: invalid name per the ICNCP-1995, art. 17.9.

Agapanthus 'Alice Gloucester' (Salver Group)

ORIGIN: introduced by Lewis Palmer, known since 1973, and still known in 1989.
NAME: after an aristocratic lady.
LEAF: deciduous, up to 45 cm long and 2.5 cm wide, arching, pale green and glaucous.
PEDUNCLE: up to 90 cm, pale to normal green.
INFLORESCENCE: 15–20 cm across, globular.
PEDICEL: green with reddish-brown flush.
FLOWERBUD: purple.
FLOWER: white, more or less upright, 2.5 cm long, 3 cm across.
AWARD: HC in 1977.

Agapanthus 'Amethyst' (Trumpet Group)

SYNONYM: *Agapanthus africanus* 'Amethyst'

ORIGIN: (selection from seedlings) raised by van der Zwet, Roelofarendsveen, The
Netherlands, introduced around 1965, and still in cultivation.
LEAF: more or less evergreen, up to 30 cm long and 3 cm wide, arching, normal to a
bit pale green, base green.
PEDUNCLE: 60 cm, green, flat, usually with a secondary peduncle.
INFLORESCENCE: up to 20 cm across, 40–90 flowers, flat.
PEDICEL: green speckled dark violet.
FLOWERBUD: greyish-green with violet at apex and brownish tip, becoming pale
violet-blue with darker apex and base, upright.
FLOWER: inside very pale violet-blue with a purple tint and slightly darker margin,
midrib violet-blue, outside pale violet-blue with purple tint, base violet-blue, when
out of flower purple, 3.6–4 cm long (tube 1.2 cm long), 3–3.5 cm across, stamens
not exserted, anthers brown.
NOTE: saved from the edge of extinction by cut flower grower J.M.A. Reintjes,
Veulen, The Netherlands, who was left with a couple of rootstocks in the cooler
after selling his whole stock. When he discovered that this cultivar was not repre-
sented in the NPC, he donated a plant in 2001.
NOTE: nuclear DNA content = 24.5 pg.
ILLUSTRATION: *color plate.*

Agapanthus 'Amsterdam' (Trumpet Group)

ORIGIN: ('**Blue Perfection**' × unknown) raised by Kees Duivenvoorde, Beverwijk, The Netherlands, introduced in 1999.

NAME: after the capital of The Netherlands.

LEAF: deciduous, 30–35 cm long and up to 2.4 cm wide, arching, dark green, base dark violet.

PEDUNCLE: 70 cm long, green, flat.

INFLORESCENCE: up to 22 cm across, 60 flowers, globular.

PEDICEL: green flushed purple.

FLOWERBUD: dark violet-blue with darker apex, upright.

FLOWER: inside pale violet-blue (92BC) with purple tint, margin violet-blue (94C) with purple tint especially towards apex, midrib rather wide (0.3 cm) and dark violet-blue (93A), outside violet-blue (92A), midrib slightly darker with purple tint, base dark violet-blue (93A), when out of flower very dark violet-blue with purple towards apex, horizontal to slightly nodding, up to 4.4 cm long (tube 1.5 cm long), 4.2 cm across, stamens just slightly exserted, anthers dark violet becoming black.

NOTE: details from plants grown by Duivenvoorde.

NOTE: flowers tend towards the Funnel Group when fully open.

NOTE: not so good as a cut flower because of bud loss but excellent as a potplant.

NOTE: registered in 1999.

NOTE: nuclear DNA content = 24.2 pg.

Agapanthus 'Andersonii'

ORIGIN: known since 1888, The Netherlands, and still offered by J. Mater & Fils, Leiden, The Netherlands, in 1892 for 70 cents a plant, the midrange. No further records.

Agapanthus 'Angela' (Trumpet Group)

ORIGIN: raised by Dick Fulcher, Pine Cottage Plants, UK, known since 2000, and still in cultivation.

NAME: in honour of the raiser's youngest daughter.

LEAF: evergreen, 55–80 cm long and 2.2–3 cm wide, arching, normal green (137C) but slightly darker towards base (137A), base long caulescent, green.

PEDUNCLE: 120 cm.

INFLORESCENCE: up to 17 cm across, more or less globular.

PEDICEL: normal green (146A).

FLOWERBUD: upright, apex pale violet-blue to cream towards base, base dull violet-blue.

FLOWER: inside violet-blue (96D) with slightly darker tint (96BC), midrib slightly darker, outside pale violet-blue with slightly darker base, horizontal to slightly nodding, up to 3.4 cm long (tube 1.5 cm long), 3.5 cm across, stamens not or just slightly exserted, anthers black.

NOTE: details supplied by Dick Fulcher.

ILLUSTRATION: photograph, Fulcher (2000, 2002).

Agapanthus angustifolius = **A. caulescens** subsp. **angustifolius** F.M. Leight.

Agapanthus 'Anthea' (Salver Group)

ORIGIN: raised and introduced by Lewis Palmer, known since 1974, and still in cultivation.

NAME: after an aristocratic lady.

LEAF: deciduous, 40–60 cm long and up to 2.5 cm wide, arching, normal green and glaucous, base slightly purple.

PEDUNCLE: 80–100 cm, green, round, bending.

INFLORESCENCE: 13 cm across, 20–30 flowers, flat.

PEDICEL: green with purple towards flowers.

FLOWER: inside pale violet-blue (96CD) with white base, margin violet-blue (93B) with purple, midrib violet-blue (93B), outside violet-blue with darker midrib and base, when out of flower more purple, horizontal, 3 cm long (tube 1 cm long), 3.5 cm across, stamens just slightly exserted, anthers dark violet.

NOTE: most details from plants grown at Wisley.

AWARD: FCC in 1977.

Agapanthus 'Aogasumi'

ORIGIN: Japan, known since 2001 when offered by Komoriya Nursery Ltd.

NAME: Japanese, "blue mist."

PEDUNCLE: 80 cm.

INFLORESCENCE: globular.

FLOWER: pale violet-blue.

NOTE: details from the Internet [25].

Agapanthus 'Aoisora' (Funnel Group)

ERROR: 'Aoi Sora'

ORIGIN: raised and introduced in Japan, known since 1998, and still in cultivation.

NAME: Japanese, "blue sky," "blue heaven."

LEAF: evergreen.

PEDUNCLE: 80 cm.

FLOWER: pale violet-blue with purple tint.

NOTE: some details supplied by Y. Aihara and some from the Internet [25].

Agapanthus 'Aoitori'

ORIGIN: Japan, known since 2001 when offered by Komoriya Nursery Ltd.

NAME: Japanese, "blue bird."

LEAF: evergreen.

PEDUNCLE: 40 cm.

FLOWER: violet-blue with purple tint.

NOTE: details from the Internet [25].

Agapanthus 'Aphrodite' (Funnel Group)

ORIGIN: raised and introduced by by Gary Dunlop, Ballyrogan Nurseries, UK, in 2001.
NAME: for the Greek goddess of fertility, love, and beauty.
LEAF: evergreen, 45 cm long and 4 cm wide, upright and arching, yellowish-green, base green.
PEDUNCLE: 90 cm, green.
INFLORESCENCE: 16 cm across, 60 flowers, bud opens on 1 side.
PEDICEL: green flushed bronze towards the flower.
FLOWER: inside white, outside white with cream base and slightly flushed purple, nodding, 5 cm long, 5 cm across.
NOTE: details supplied by Gary Dunlop.
NOTE: nuclear DNA content = 24.7 pg.

Agapanthus 'Apple Court'

ORIGIN: (probably an *A. caulescens* hybrid) introduced by Apple Court nursery, UK, in 1996, and still in cultivation.
LEAF: more or less evergreen.
INFLORESCENCE: "large."
FLOWER: pale violet-blue.

Agapanthus 'Aquamarine'

ORIGIN: probably introduced in the UK, known since 1998 when offered as seed.
LEAF: deciduous.
PEDUNCLE: 40 cm.
FLOWER: "two tones of blue."

Agapanthus 'Arctic Star' (Funnel Group)

ORIGIN: raised by Raveningham Gardens, UK, known since 2000, and still in cultivation.
LEAF: more or less deciduous, glaucous.
PEDUNCLE: 65–100 cm.
INFLORESCENCE: 70–90 flowers, globular.
FLOWER: on both sides white, horizontal, stamens not exserted, anthers brown.
ILLUSTRATION: photograph, Fulcher (2002).

Agapanthus 'Ardernei' (Trumpet Group)

SYNONYM: *Agapanthus* 'Ardernei Hybrid'
Agapanthus Ardernei Hybrids

ORIGIN: (selected from *A. praecox* subsp. *orientalis*, probably with interbreeding of *A. campanulatus*) known since 1966 (the plant was shown at the RHS show in August of that year) and still in cultivation.
LEAF: more or less deciduous, 30–50 cm long and up to 2.5 cm wide, upright to spreading, green and slightly glaucous, base purple.

PEDUNCLE: 60–100 cm, green flushed purple, flat.

INFLORESCENCE: 15 cm across, (20–)30–60(–80) flowers, more or less globular, bud opens on 1 side.

PEDICEL: green heavily flushed dull purple.

FLOWERBUD: white with pale purple apex, upright.

FLOWER: inside white with transparent midrib, outside white with very pale purple apex, when out of flower brownish-white with purple apex at midrib, horizontal, 2.5–3 cm long (tube 1–1.2 cm long), 2.5(–3) cm across, stamens not exserted, anthers black.

NOTE: details from plants grown at RHS Wisley and Beth Chatto Gardens.

NOTE: plants look similar enough to maintain as a cultivar, but as it's been seed-propagated since its introduction, it might be better to regard this name as a group of plants that look similar rather than a proper cultivar.

NOTE: nuclear DNA content = 22.8 pg.

NOTE: Graham Stuart Thomas (1990) blamed the Dutch for naming this plant *A. orientalis albus*, but I have not seen this name at any nursery I visited in Holland. He probably refers to '**Umbellatus Albus**', which is grown widely and usually labelled *A. africanus* 'Albus'.

ILLUSTRATION: photograph, Warren (1995), Dunlop (2000 as *A. praecox* var. *albiflora*), and Fulcher (2000 as *A.* 'Ardernei Hybrid', 2002).

Agapanthus 'Ardernei Hybrid' = *A.* '**Ardernei**'

NOTE: invalid name per the ICNCP-1995, art. 17.16.

Agapanthus Ardernei Hybrids = *A.* '**Ardernei**'

Agapanthus '**Argenteus Vittatus**' (Variegated Leaf Group)

SYNONYM: *Agapanthus africanus* subsp. *umbellatus* var. *variegatus* H.R. Wehrh.
Agapanthus africanus var. *variegatus* Boom
Agapanthus africanus 'Variegatus'
Agapanthus orientalis var. *foliis argenteis vittatis* van Tubergen
Agapanthus orientalis var. *variegatus* Synge
Agapanthus orientalis 'Argenteis Variegatus'
Agapanthus orientalis 'Variegatus'
Agapanthus praecox subsp. *minimus* 'Variegatus'
Agapanthus praecox subsp. *orientalis* 'Argenteus Vittatis'
Agapanthus praecox subsp. *orientalis* 'Variegatus'
Agapanthus praecox subsp. *praecox* 'Argenteus Vittatis'
Agapanthus praecox subsp. *praecox* 'Variegatus'
Agapanthus praecox 'Argenteus Vittatus'
Agapanthus praecox 'Variegatus'
Agapanthus umbellatus var. *argenteus vittatis* van Tubergen
Agapanthus umbellatus var. *foliis albo-vittatis* Lemoine
Agapanthus umbellatus var. *foliis argenteis vittatis* Boom
Agapanthus umbellatus var. *foliis variegatis* Boom

Agapanthus umbellatus var. *variegata* Schauenberg
Agapanthus umbellatus var. *variegatus* G. Nicholson

ORIGIN: known since 1865, UK, 1884, The Netherlands. Still in cultivation but more rarely than '**Aureovittatus**'. Locally quite common because of gardeners' plant exchanges (e.g., in an urban street on Madeira, every house's entrance was flanked by one or more potted plants).

LEAF: evergreen, up to 30 cm long and 3 cm wide but much shorter and less wider when pot grown, first upright but later more arching but not flat on the soil, white with some thin green stripes, apex sub-obtuse.

PEDUNCLE: 30–50 cm, variegated.

INFLORESCENCE: 10–11 cm across, 30–40 flowers.

PEDICEL: variegated.

FLOWER: pale violet-blue with violet-blue midrib, 3 cm long (tube 1.1 cm long), stamens exserted, no fruit.

NOTE: not very free-flowering; a shoot should be well established and several years old before a peduncle emerges, if at all.

NOTE: some plants sold as '**Tinkerbell**' are actually '**Argenteus Vittatus**'.

NOTE: more and more nurseries offer plants under the name '**Variegata**' or '**Variegatus**', but the plant usually is '**Aureovittatus**', not '**Argenteus Vittatus**'.

NOTE: nuclear DNA content = 24.9 pg.

ILLUSTRATION: *color plate*; photograph, Duncan (1998 as *A. praecox* subsp. *minimus*, variegated form), Snoeijer (1998 as *A. praecox* 'Aureovittatus'), and Hirose and Yokoi (2001 as *A. praecox* 'Variegatus').

AWARD: AGM as *A. praecox* 'Variegatus'.

Agapanthus '**Atlantic Ocean**' (Funnel Group)

ORIGIN: raised by C.H.A. van Eijk, Nootdorp, The Netherlands, who applied for European Plant Variety Right in 2003.

LEAF: evergreen, 50–60 cm long and 3–4 cm wide, arching, dark green, base green.

PEDUNCLE: 80–100 cm, glaucous, round.

INFLORESCENCE: 18 cm across, 100–150 flowers, globular, bud opens on 1 side and is rather long acuminate, caducous.

PEDICEL: base green and glaucous, towards the flower with purple speckles.

FLOWERBUD: dark violet-blue with very dark apex.

FLOWER: inside very pale violet-blue to white near the base and with a hint of purple towards apex, margin violet-blue (91A) with purple tint, midrib very dark violet-blue (93A), outside pale violet-blue with purple tint, margin darker coloured with a small white base, midrib very dark violet-blue, base violet-blue, horizontal, up to 4.7 cm long (tube 1 cm long), 6 cm across, slightly reflexed, stamens slightly exserted, anthers dark purple with yellow pollen.

NOTE: the first flowers within an inflorescence tend to have 8 tepals. Selected as a year-round cut flower.

NOTE: details from plants grown by van Eijk.

NOTE: European Plant Variety Right applied for, file no. 2003/0047.

ILLUSTRATION: *color plate*.

Agapanthus 'Atlas' (Funnel Group)

SYNONYM: *Agapanthus praecox* 'Atlas'

ORIGIN: introduced by Gary Dunlop, Ballyrogan Nurseries, UK, known since 1999.
LEAF: evergreen, up to 45 cm long and 5 cm wide, upright and arching like a fan,
apex normal green, base green.
PEDUNCLE: 90 cm, green.
INFLORESCENCE: 25 cm across, 150–200 flowers, globular, bud opens on 2 sides.
PEDICEL: green to bronze near the flower.
FLOWERBUD: pale violet-blue-white with violet-blue apex, first upright but quickly
horizontal to slightly nodding.
FLOWER: inside very pale violet-blue-white with margin towards apex pale violet-
blue, midrib violet-blue (94A) and those of the outer tepals distinctly wider than the
inner, outside very pale violet-blue-white with apex pale violet-blue (94C), midrib
and base pale violet-blue (94C), when out of flower purple, horizontal to slightly
nodding, up to 3.5 cm long, up to 5 cm across, stamens not exserted, anthers violet
with yellow pollen.
NOTE: details supplied by Gary Dunlop.
NOTE: nuclear DNA content = 25.2 pg.

Agapanthus 'ATlblu' = *A.* 'Bluestorm'

Agapanthus atro-coeruleus Besant = *A.* 'Atrocaeruleus'

Besant (1903) Flora and Sylva, 1.

Agapanthus 'Atrocaeruleus'

SYNONYM: *Agapanthus africanus* subsp. *umbellatus* var. *atricoeruleus* H.R. Wehrh.
Agapanthus africanus var. *atro-caeruleus* Synge
Agapanthus atro-coeruleus Besant
Agapanthus umbellatus var. *atricoeruleus* Bonstedt
Agapanthus umbellatus var. *atrocaeruleus* Leichtlin

ORIGIN: (probably a selection of *A. africanus*) known since 1880 when offered by
Leichtlin, Germany, still referred to in 1931, 1965, and 1986, but probably no longer
in cultivation.
FLOWER: "very dark violet-blue."
NOTE: Leighton (1965) refers *A. umbellatus* var. *atrocaeruleus* to *A. inapertus*, but no
publication I could find mentioned drooping flowers.

Agapanthus 'Aureovittatus' (Variegated Leaf Group)

SYNONYM: *Agapanthus africanus* subsp. *umbellatus* var. *aureus* H.R. Wehrh.
Agapanthus aureus Numa Schneider
Agapanthus orientalis var. *aurivittatus* Synge
Agapanthus praecox subsp. *orientalis* 'Aureovittatus'
Agapanthus praecox subsp. *praecox* 'Aureovariegatus'
Agapanthus praecox subsp. *praecox* 'Aureovittatus'

Agapanthus praecox subsp. *praecox* 'Vittatus'
Agapanthus praecox var. *vittatus* Philip & Lord
Agapanthus praecox 'Aureovittatus'
Agapanthus praecox 'Vittatus'
Agapanthus umbellatus var. *aureis vittatus* van Tubergen
Agapanthus umbellatus var. *aureus* G. Nicholson
Agapanthus umbellatus var. *foliis aureis variegatis* Krelage
Agapanthus umbellatus var. *foliis aureo-vittatus* Lemoine
Agapanthus umbellatus var. *maximum* Edwards ex Thomas 'Aureovittatus'

ORIGIN: known since 1875 in The Netherlands, 1885 in England. A flowering plant was shown by Krelage in August 1891 at Artis Zoo, Amsterdam, as *A. umbellatus* var. *foliis aureis variegatis*, with the comment that a flowering variegated plant was rare. Still in cultivation, not really rare; quite common locally because of gardeners' plant exchanges (e.g., in the Pacific Northwest of the USA).

LEAF: evergreen, 40–50 cm long and 2–3.2 cm wide, arching to flat on the soil, yellow margin with green stripes in the middle fading to pale yellow, base yellow.

PEDUNCLE: 60–90 cm, pale green striped cream, round.

INFLORESCENCE: 20 cm across, 50–60 flowers, globular.

PEDICEL: cream flushed green and purple, more purple towards the flower.

FLOWER: inside very pale violet-blue (92CD) and a bit of purple tint, midrib pale violet-blue (92BC), outside very pale violet-blue (92D) and base slightly darker (92A), when out of flower purple, horizontal to slightly nodding, 3.7–4 cm long (tube 1.2 cm long), 3.8 cm across, stamens not exserted, anthers dark brown, not all flowers produce a fruit, fruit yellow or yellow with green, purple at the base.

NOTE: details from a plant grown at the *Agapanthus* NPC, The Netherlands, presented by Bert van Ooijen of Acanthus nursery at Marienwaerdt, Beest. This '**Aureovittatus**' was originally obtained before 1940 by Maria Bultman, who was famous in Holland for her container plant collection, which she stopped maintaining in the 1990s; most of the plants were bought by Acanthus.

NOTE: increasingly nurseries use the (easier?) names 'Variegata' or 'Variegatus' for this cultivar.

NOTE: among the best flowerers, for a variegated plant, but still does not flower regularly.

NOTE: occasionally some flowers have 8 tepals.

NOTE: nuclear DNA content = 24.6 pg.

ILLUSTRATION: *color plate*; photograph, Snoeijer (2000).

Agapanthus aureus Numa Schneider = *A.* '**Aureovittatus**'

Numa Schneider (1911) Revue Horticole.

Agapanthus '**Autumn Mist**' (Funnel Group)

ORIGIN: raised by Dick Fulcher, Pine Cottage Plants, UK, known since 2001.
NAME: refers to the late flowering.
PEDUNCLE: 70–85 cm.

FLOWER: pale violet-blue.
NOTE: details supplied by Dick Fulcher.

Agapanthus 'A. Worsley'

SYNONYM: *Agapanthus umbellatus* 'A. Worsley'

ORIGIN: introduced by van Tubergen, The Netherlands, offered only in 1937.
NAME: for Arthington Worsley (d. 1943), "a mining engineer who travelled extensively in South America and became a specialist in bulbous plants on his retirement in Middlesex" (Brickell and Sharman 1986). Worsley wrote an article on *Agapanthus*, in the Journal of the Royal Horticultural Society, 1913. The genus *Worsleya* (Amaryllidaceae) is also named in his honour.
PEDUNCLE: 60–75 cm.
FLOWER: "pale ageratum-blue."
NOTE: in van Tubergen's 1937 catalogue; it was double the price of the other two variegated plants and over six times as expensive as the other cultivars.

Agapanthus 'Azure' = *A*. RUBBISH

NOTE: offered seed is described variously. I have seen several plants under this name, both in England and in The Netherlands, but because of seed propagation the plants varied. Flower colour differed slightly; in one the leafbase was green, in the other purple—in the same batch of plants! The colouring of the leafbase in *Agapanthus* is critical; as I could not ignore this characteristic, I am unable to maintain this cultivar.

Agapanthus 'Baby Blue' = *A*. **'Blue Baby'**

Agapanthus **'Baby White'**

ORIGIN: known since 2001 from Australia.
LEAF: narrow.
PEDUNCLE: 40 cm.
FLOWER: pure white.
NOTE: details from the Internet [26].

Agapanthus **'Ballyrogan'** (Salver Group)

SYNONYM: *Agapanthus* 'Bally Rogan Blue'

ORIGIN: raised by Gary Dunlop, Ballyrogan Nurseries, UK, introduced in 1995, and still in cultivation.
LEAF: evergreen, up to 50 cm long and 3 cm wide, upright, pale to normal green, base green.
PEDUNCLE: up to 135 cm, green.
INFLORESCENCE: 12.5 cm across, 50 flowers, bud opens on 1 side.
PEDICEL: green with purple towards flower.
FLOWER: inside violet-blue (94C) with darker midrib (94AB), outside paler (97C) with darker midrib (97A), with more purple when out of flower, horizontal, 2 cm long, 3 cm across.

NOTE: details supplied by Gary Dunlop.
NOTE: nuclear DNA content = 23.3 pg.

Agapanthus 'Bally Rogan Blue' = *A.* **'Ballyrogan'**

Agapanthus **'Balmoral'**

ORIGIN: raised by The Crown Estate, Windsor, UK, introduced in 1975, and still in cultivation.
NAME: after the royal estate in Scotland.
LEAF: more or less deciduous.
PEDUNCLE: 70 cm.
FLOWER: dark violet-blue.

Agapanthus **'Bangor Blue'** (Funnel Group)

SYNONYM: *Agapanthus praecox* 'Bangor Blue'

ORIGIN: introduced in 1998 by Gary Dunlop, Ballyrogan Nurseries, UK, who obtained the plant from friends in Bangor, County Down.
LEAF: evergreen.
FLOWER: dark violet-blue.
NOTE: details supplied by Gary Dunlop.
NOTE: nuclear DNA content = 25.6 pg.

Agapanthus **'Basutoland'**

ORIGIN: known since 2003 when offered by the RHS Garden Wisley.

Agapanthus **'Beatrice'** (Trumpet Group)

ORIGIN: raised by Dick Fulcher, Pine Cottage Plants, UK, known since 2000.
NAME: in honour of the raiser's mother-in-law.
LEAF: evergreen, 50–60 cm long and 1.4–2.2 cm wide, arching, canaliculate, margin thick, normal green, base a bit caulescent and green.
PEDUNCLE: 120 cm.
INFLORESCENCE: 16 cm across, globular.
FLOWER: inside dark violet-blue (89C) with darker midrib (89A), horizontal to slightly nodding, 4.2 cm long (tube 1.8–2 cm long), stamens not exserted, anthers greyish.
NOTE: details supplied by Dick Fulcher.

Agapanthus **'Beauregard'**

ORIGIN: (**'Bressingham White'** × unknown) raised by J.-Y. Poiroux, Ets Horticole, France, known since 1998.
FLOWER: pale violet-blue.

Agapanthus **'Becky'** (Funnel Group)

ORIGIN: raised at NCCPG Bicton College, UK, selected by Dick Fulcher in 1993, and still in cultivation.

NAME: in honour of Dick Fulcher's eldest daughter.
LEAF: evergreen.
PEDUNCLE: 65 cm.
FLOWER: pale blue, up to 4.4 cm long (tube 1.4 cm long).
NOTE: details supplied by Dick Fulcher.

Agapanthus 'Beeches Dwarf'

ORIGIN: (chance seedling) discovered by Beeches Nursery, UK, in 1997, introduced in 2000, and still in cultivation.
LEAF: deciduous, 0.8–1 cm wide.
PEDUNCLE: 30–50 cm.
INFLORESCENCE: more or less drooping.
FLOWER: grey-blue with darker midrib.
NOTE: most details supplied by Beeches Nursery; some details from the Internet [12].

Agapanthus 'Ben Hope' (Salver Group)

ORIGIN: raised by The Crown Estate, Windsor, UK, introduced in 1972, and still in cultivation.
NAME: after the mountain in Scotland.
LEAF: deciduous, 15–40 cm long and up to 2 cm wide, upright to slightly arching, normal to dark green and glaucous, base purple.
PEDUNCLE: 40–50 cm, green, round.
INFLORESCENCE: 12 cm across, 40 flowers, globular.
PEDICEL: green with dull purple speckles towards flower.
FLOWERBUD: violet-blue, upright.
FLOWER: inside pale violet-blue (96CD), margin darker violet-blue (94C) with purple tint, midrib dark violet-blue (93C), outside violet-blue with base slightly darker, horizontal to slightly hanging downwards, 2.5–3 cm long (tube 0.8 cm long), 3–3.5 cm across, stamens not exserted, anthers violet.
NOTE: distinctly early flowering.
NOTE: details from plants grown at Wisley.
ILLUSTRATION: photograph, Phillips and Rix (1991).
AWARD: FCC in 1977.

Agapanthus Best New White Hybrids = A. RUBBISH

Agapanthus 'Beth Chatto' (Variegated Leaf Group)

SYNONYM: *Agapanthus campanulatus* subsp. *campanulatus* 'Albovittatus'
Agapanthus campanulatus var. *albo-vittatus* Philip & Lord
Agapanthus campanulatus var. *albovittatus* Philip & Lord
Agapanthus campanulatus 'Albovittatus'
Agapanthus campanulatus 'Variegatus'
Agapanthus campanulatus variegated

ORIGIN: known since 1865, UK. Still in cultivation, the main source being the plants sold at Beth Chatto Gardens, UK.

LEAF: deciduous, up to 15 cm long and 1 cm wide, upright to slightly arching, normal green with thin pale yellow stripes and usually a yellowish margin, the yellow colouring will become more greenish later in the season, base green-purple.

PEDUNCLE: 60–70 cm long, green and glaucous, round.

INFLORESCENCE: 9 cm across, 20 flowers, flat.

PEDICEL: green with violet.

FLOWERBUD: violet-blue and slightly paler in the middle, upright but quickly horizontal.

FLOWER: inside pale violet-blue with margin slightly darker, distinct white base, midrib violet-blue, outside violet-blue with darker base, when out of flower purple, irregular because of one reduced tepal, horizontal, up to 2.5 cm long (tube 1.2 cm long), 2–2.5 cm across, stamens not exserted, anthers violet-blue.

NOTE: this clone appeared in recent years under the provided name. Even though the name 'Variegatus' has precedence, I accept **'Beth Chatto'** to be rid of the name 'Variegatus', which is so confusing with regard to all variegated *Agapanthus* clones grown.

NOTE: nuclear DNA content = 22.2 pg.

ILLUSTRATION: photograph, Brickell (1996 as *A. campanulatus* 'Albovittatus').

Agapanthus 'Bethlehem Star'

ORIGIN: raised by Raveningham Gardens, UK, known since 1996, and still in cultivation.

LEAF: deciduous.

PEDUNCLE: 100 cm.

FLOWER: very pale violet-blue-white with "silvery transparent appearance."

Agapanthus 'Bianca Perla' (Funnel Group)

ERROR: 'Bianca-Perla'

ORIGIN: raised by C.H.A. van Eijk, Nootdorp, The Netherlands, who applied for European Plant Variety Right in 2002.

NAME: Italian, "white pearl," with reference to one of the raiser's daughters.

LEAF: evergreen, up to 60 cm long, 2–3 cm wide, arching, dark green, base green.

PEDUNCLE: 80–90 cm, green and glaucous, round.

INFLORESCENCE: 17–18 cm across, 80–100 flowers, globular, bud opens on 1 side, very long acuminate and caducous.

PEDICEL: pale green.

FLOWERBUD: cream-white with yellowish apex.

FLOWER: inside with cream midrib, outside white, horizontal, 4.7–5 cm long (tube 1 cm long), 6.5–7 cm across, stamens slightly exserted, anthers pale yellow with yellow pollen.

NOTE: details from plants grown by van Eijk. Selected as a year-round cut flower.

NOTE: European Plant Variety Right applied for, file no. 2002/1031, first published on the Internet [35] as 'Bianca-Perla' but now listed as **'Bianca Perla'**, which the raiser confirms.

Agapanthus 'Bianco' (Funnel Group)

ERROR: 'Bianca'

ORIGIN: introduced from Italy, known since 1997, originally offered as seed.
NAME: Italian, "white."
LEAF: evergreen.
PEDUNCLE: 85 cm.
INFLORESCENCE: 100 flowers, globular.
FLOWER: white, stamens exserted, anthers black.
NOTE: some details from the Internet [10].
NOTE: invalid name per the ICNCP-1995, art. 17.11.

Agapanthus bicolori Besant = *A.* 'Bicolori'

Besant (1903) Flora and Sylva, 1.

Agapanthus 'Bicolori'

SYNONYM: *Agapanthus bicolori* Besant

ORIGIN: known since 1903, UK.
FLOWER: "bearing flowers white and blue."

Agapanthus 'Bicton Bell' (Tubular Group)

SYNONYM: *Agapanthus* 'Bicton Bluebell'
Agapanthus 'Blue Bell'

ORIGIN: (probably hybrid with *A. inapertus*, possibly with some *A. caulescens*) raised at NCCPG Bicton College, UK, selected by Dick Fulcher in 1993, and still in cultivation.
LEAF: deciduous, up to 30 cm long and 3.5 cm wide, upright to 45° and twisted, normal but bright green and glaucous, base green.
PEDUNCLE: 95–120 cm, green and glaucous.
INFLORESCENCE: 15 cm across, 80 flowers, bud opens on 1 side.
PEDICEL: green.
FLOWER: inside pale violet-blue (92B) with dark violet-blue (93A) midrib, outside violet-blue (93D) flushing to dark violet-blue (93A) at the base, when out of flower purple with small violet-blue base, slightly hanging downwards but not vertically, 4 cm long, 2.5 cm across, stamens not exserted.
NOTE: details supplied by Gary Dunlop.
NOTE: nuclear DNA content = 25.3 pg.
ILLUSTRATION: *color plate.*

Agapanthus 'Bicton Bluebell' = *A.* 'Bicton Bell'

ERROR: 'Bicton Blue Bell', 'Bicton Blue Belle'

NOTE: invalid name per the ICNCP-1995, art. 17.13.

Agapanthus 'Bicton Bride' (Funnel Group)

ORIGIN: raised by Dick Fulcher, NCCPG Agapanthus National Collection, UK, introduced in 1998.
NAME: to mark the occasion of Rebecca Fulcher's wedding.
LEAF: evergreen.
PEDUNCLE: 80–90 cm.
FLOWER: white.
NOTE: details supplied by Dick Fulcher.

Agapanthus 'Big Blue' (Funnel Group)

SYNONYM: *Agapanthus africanus* 'Big Blue'
ORIGIN: known since 2000 when offered in the UK.
LEAF: evergreen, up to 3.5 cm wide.
PEDUNCLE: 150 cm.
INFLORESCENCE: "bold umbels."
FLOWER: "mid blue."
NOTE: details supplied by Beeches Nursery, UK.
NOTE: invalid name per the ICNCP-1995, art. 17.11.

Agapanthus 'Birkhall'

ORIGIN: raised by The Crown Estate, Windsor, UK, introduced in 1975, and still in cultivation at the NCCPG Agapanthus National Collection, UK.
NAME: after the royal estate in Scotland, near Balmoral.
LEAF: deciduous.
FLOWER: white.

Agapanthus 'Black Beauty' (Trumpet Group)

ORIGIN: raised by Kees Duivenvoorde, Beverwijk, The Netherlands, introduced in 1997, and still in cultivation.
LEAF: deciduous, up to 25 cm long and 2 cm wide, arching, dark green and slightly glaucous, base purple.
PEDUNCLE: 40(–60) cm, very dark violet with only the base green, flat.
INFLORESCENCE: 15–17 cm across, 40–50 flowers, globular.
PEDICEL: completely very dark violet-blue.
FLOWERBUD: dark violet-blue, upright but quickly horizontal.
FLOWER: inside pale violet-blue (93D) with margin darker (93C) with the 3 inner tepals almost white at lower half, midrib dark violet-blue (93A), outside violet-blue, midrib and base dark violet-blue, when out of flower dark purple, horizontal, 3.5 cm long (tube 1.2 cm long), 2.3 cm across, stamens not exserted, anthers black.
NOTE: details from plants grown by Duivenvoorde.
NOTE: similar to 'Intermedius', but darker in general appearance.
NOTE: registered in 2001.
NOTE: nuclear DNA content = 23 pg.
ILLUSTRATION: *color plate.*

Agapanthus 'Black Pantha' (Funnel Group)

SYNONYM: 'Black Panther'

ORIGIN: (chance seedling of *A. praecox* subsp. *orientalis*) raised by G. Morrison, Doncaster, Victoria, Australia, known since 1999.
LEAF: evergreen.
FLOWER: violet-blue.
NOTE: New Zealand Plant Variety Rights applied for, no. HOM092, on 7 July 1999, by Lyndale Nurseries Auckland Ltd, New Zealand.
NOTE: some details from the Internet [36].

Agapanthus 'Black Panther' = *A.* 'Black Pantha'

Agapanthus 'Blanc Méoni' (Funnel Group)

SYNONYM: *Agapanthus* 'Meoni'
Agapanthus praecox 'Blanc Méoni'
Agapanthus praecox 'Meoni'

ORIGIN: introduced in France, known since 2001.
LEAF: evergreen.
INFLORESCENCE: 80–100 flowers, globular, bract remains attached.
FLOWER: white, upright to horizontal, stamens not exserted, anthers yellow.
NOTE: details from Allemand and Pionnat (2001) and from the Internet [18].
ILLUSTRATION: photograph, Allemand and Pionnat (2001 as *A. praecox* var. 'Blanc Méoni').

Agapanthus 'Blauwe Valk' (Trumpet Group)

SYNONYM: *Agapanthus* 'Blue Bird' ex van der Zwet

ORIGIN: (selected from seedlings) introduced by van der Zwet, Roelofarendsveen, The Netherlands, around 1965, and still known in 1987. Probably no longer in cultivation.
LEAF: evergreen, horizontal arching.
PEDUNCLE: up to 65 cm.
INFLORESCENCE: "with less flowers compared with 'Josephine'."
FLOWER: violet-blue (95CD) with darker midrib (95A), tube shorter than 'Josephine' but opens more widely, 4 cm long (tube 1.5 cm long), 3 cm across.
NOTE: because this plant was different from the English 'Blue Bird', Gillissen (1980) changed the name to 'Blauwe Valk' in 1979, at the raiser's request.

Agapanthus 'Blauwe Wimpel' (Funnel Group)

TRANSLATION: BLUE RIBBON [in English]

ORIGIN: (chance seedling of *A. praecox* subsp. *orientalis*) known since 1961 when grown by J.A. van der Zwet & Zonen, Roelofarendsveen, The Netherlands, and still in cultivation. Saved from extinction by Reintjes, Veulen, The Netherlands, who donated a plant to the NPC in 2001.

LEAF: deciduous, up to 30 cm long and 2.5 cm wide, upright, dark glaucous green, base violet.

PEDUNCLE: 80–100 cm, dark green with a bit of purple towards inflorescence, flat.

INFLORESCENCE: 18 cm across, 100 flowers, globular.

PEDICEL: green with a bit of purple.

FLOWERBUD: greenish-white in the middle, apex violet-blue with a bit of green, base dark violet-blue, upright.

FLOWER: inside pale violet-blue (91B), midrib darker violet-blue (93C) and purple tint, outside pale violet-blue with midrib darker, base dark violet-blue, when out of flower purple, up to 4.7 cm long (tube 1.7 cm long), up to 4 cm across, upright to horizontal, stamens not exserted, anthers dark brown.

NOTE: details from plants grown by Reintjes.

NOTE: though the flower diameter is less than the length, I maintain this cultivar in the Funnel Group because of its flower shape and widely gappy tepal segments.

NOTE: nuclear DNA content = 24.9 pg.

ILLUSTRATION: *color plate.*

AWARD: GV in 1961.

Agapanthus 'Bleuet' (Salver Group)

ERROR: 'Bluet'

ORIGIN: raised by Griffioen, Wassenaar, The Netherlands, introduced in 1995, and still in cultivation.

LEAF: deciduous, 15 cm long and 0.8 cm wide, upright, normal green and slightly glaucous, base slightly dark purple.

PEDUNCLE: 40–50 cm, green and slightly flushed dull purple, round.

INFLORESCENCE: 9 cm across, 20–30 flowers, flat, bud opens on 1 side.

PEDICEL: greenish-violet.

FLOWERBUD: violet-blue, upright.

FLOWER: inside violet-blue (96BC) with purple tint, midrib darker, margin not distinctly darker, outside violet-blue with dark purple tint especially at midrib, when out of flower more purple, horizontal to slightly facing downwards, 2.2 cm long (tube 0.7 cm long), 2.8 cm across, stamens not exserted, anthers violet.

NOTE: details from plants grown by Griffioen.

NOTE: similar to '**Lilliput**' but the flower does not open so wide and is slightly paler in colour, and the leaves are somewhat wider.

NOTE: invalid name per the ICNCP-1995, art. 17.13.

Agapanthus '**Bleu Méoni**' (Funnel Group)

SYNONYM: *Agapanthus* 'Blue Méoni'
Agapanthus 'Hyères'
Agapanthus praecox 'Bleu Méoni'

ORIGIN: introduced by Enno Oudshoorn, France, known since 1998, and still in cultivation.

LEAF: evergreen.

INFLORESCENCE: 80–100 flowers, more or less globular, bract remains attached.
FLOWER: violet-blue with darker midrib, stamens not exserted, anthers violet.
NOTE: most details from Allemand and Pionnat (2001).
ILLUSTRATION: photograph, Allemand and Pionnat (2001 as *A. praecox* var. 'Bleu Méoni').

Agapanthus 'Bleu Triomphator' = *A.* **'Blue Triumphator'**

Agapanthus 'Blu' (Funnel Group)
ORIGIN: introduced from Italy, known since 1997, originally offered as seed.
NAME: Italian, "blue."
LEAF: evergreen.
PEDUNCLE: 85 cm.
INFLORESCENCE: 100 flowers, globular.
FLOWER: violet-blue, stamens not exserted, anthers violet.
NOTE: some details from the Internet [10].
NOTE: invalid name per the ICNCP-1995, art. 17.11.

Agapanthus blue = *A.* RUBBISH

'Blue' => *Agapanthus orientalis* 'Blue'

Agapanthus **'Blue Baby'** (Funnel Group)
SYNONYM: *Agapanthus africanus* 'Baby Blue'
Agapanthus 'Baby Blue'
Agapanthus praecox subsp. *orientalis* 'Baby Blue'
Agapanthus praecox 'Blue Baby'
ORIGIN: from New Zealand, known since 1987, and still in cultivation. Also offered as seed.
LEAF: evergreen, dark and narrow.
PEDUNCLE: 60 cm.
INFLORESCENCE: rather open.
FLOWER: pale violet-blue, "3.5 inches long."
NOTE: in my 1998 book I wrote that 'Baby Blue' was different from **'Blue Baby'**. But, having consulted more references, I am forced to admit the two names are used interchangeably for the same plant, and some nurseries sell plants under both names. Because of seed propagation, it is perhaps best to regard all offered plants as RUBBISH.

Agapanthus 'Blue Bell' = *A.* **'Bicton Bell'**

Agapanthus 'Blue Bird' ex van der Zwet = *A.* **'Blauwe Valk'**
NOTE: invalid name per the ICNCP-1995, art. 17.2.

Agapanthus '**Blue Bird**' ex Palmer (Trumpet Group)

  ERROR: 'Bluebird'

ORIGIN: raised and introduced by Lewis Palmer, known since 1974, and still in cultivation.

LEAF: deciduous, 30–50 cm long and up to 2 cm wide, upright, dark dull green, base purple.

PEDUNCLE: 60–75 cm, green with some purple and slightly glaucous, flat.

INFLORESCENCE: 15 cm across, more or less globular, bud opens on 1 side.

PEDICEL: green to dull purple towards flower.

FLOWERBUD: dark violet-blue, upright but quickly horizontal.

FLOWER: inside violet-blue (closest to 93D but with more blue), midrib slightly darker, margin violet-blue (93C), completely tinted with purple especially at margin, outside violet-blue with darker midrib, when out of flower more purple, horizontal, 2.8–3 cm long (tube 1 cm long), 2.5 cm across, stamens not exserted, anthers violet.

NOTE: details from plants grown at Wisley.

ILLUSTRATION: photograph, Bond (1978) and Warren (1995).

AWARD: HC in 1977.

Agapanthus '**Blue Bonnet**' (Funnel Group)

  SYNONYM: *Agapanthus praecox* 'Blue Bonnet'

ORIGIN: known since 1997, France.

LEAF: evergreen.

FLOWER: violet-blue.

Agapanthus '**Blue Boy**' ex Hackfalls Arboretum = *A.* '**Peter Pan**'

NOTE: Lady Anne Berry, Hackfalls Arboretum, Gisborne, New Zealand, informed me that the plant thought to bear the name 'Blue Boy' is actually '**Peter Pan**', because, when the plant was dug up for dividing, the original label was found.

Agapanthus '**Blue Boy**' ex Diacks Nurseries Ltd

ORIGIN: offered by Diacks, New Zealand, known since 1998.

LEAF: evergreen.

PEDUNCLE: 60 cm.

INFLORESCENCE: "huge."

FLOWER: "brilliant mid blue."

Agapanthus '**Blue Brush**' (Funnel Group)

  TRADE NAME: FRAGRANT BLUE

ORIGIN: raised by V.J. Hooper, Tauranga, New Zealand, in 2000; known in the UK since 2001 when offered by Fairhaven Nurseries.

LEAF: evergreen.

INFLORESCENCE: "large."

FLOWER: "strong blue."

NOTE: New Zealand Plant Variety Rights applied for, no. HOM121, on 4 August 2000, by Lifetech Laboratories Ltd, New Zealand.

NOTE: some details from the Internet [36].

Agapanthus 'Blue Cascade' (Funnel Group)

ORIGIN: introduced by Gary Dunlop, Ballyrogan Nurseries, UK, known since 1999.

LEAF: deciduous, 50 cm long and 2.5 cm wide, upright with arching apex, pale green, base green.

PEDUNCLE: 100 cm, green.

INFLORESCENCE: 18 cm across, 60–75 flowers, more or less globular, bud opens on 2 sides.

PEDICEL: bronze-green.

FLOWER: inside rather pale violet-blue (91B), margin violet-blue (90C), midrib slightly darker violet-blue (92A), outside violet-blue (91B) with darker margin (90C) and midrib (90B), nodding, up to 2.5 cm long, 4 cm across.

NOTE: details supplied by Gary Dunlop.

NOTE: nuclear DNA content = 22.7 pg.

Agapanthus 'Blue Companion' (Trumpet Group)

ORIGIN: introduced by Gary Dunlop, Ballyrogan Nurseries, UK, in 1998.

LEAF: deciduous, 6 per shoot, up to 50 cm long and 2.5 cm wide, slightly arching, normal green, leafbase green.

PEDUNCLE: 100–120 cm, green.

INFLORESCENCE: 15 cm across, 50–60 flowers, more or less flat, bud opens on 1 side, bract remains attached.

PEDICEL: green at the base to dark bronze towards the flower.

FLOWERBUD: rather dark violet-blue.

FLOWER: inside pale violet-blue (94D) with slightly darker midrib (94A), outside pale violet-blue (94D), midrib slightly darker (94A) and dark violet-blue base, when out of flower purple, upright to horizontal, 3 cm long, 3.5 cm across, stamens not exserted, anthers violet with yellow pollen.

NOTE: details supplied by Gary Dunlop.

NOTE: nuclear DNA content = 23.1 pg.

ILLUSTRATION: *color plate.*

Agapanthus 'Blue Danube' (Trumpet Group)

ORIGIN: raised by Don Duncan, Washington, USA, introduced by Wayside Gardens, South Carolina, USA, in 1995.

NAME: for the Danube River.

PEDUNCLE: up to 75 cm.

INFLORESCENCE: up to 11 cm across, 75–100 flowers, globular.

FLOWER: violet-blue.

NOTE: 'Blue Danube' is not a synonym of 'Donau', which see.

NOTE: details supplied by Wayside Gardens.

Agapanthus 'Blue Diamond'

ORIGIN: Japan, known since 2001 when offered by Komoriya Nursery Ltd.
PEDUNCLE: 85 cm.
FLOWER: dark purple-violet with darker midrib.
NOTE: details from the Internet [25].

Agapanthus 'Blue Diamond'

ORIGIN: known since 1998 when shown at Hampton Court Flower Show, UK, and since then offered through nurseries.
LEAF: deciduous.
PEDUNCLE: 60–80 cm.
INFLORESCENCE: "small."
FLOWER: pale violet-blue with darker midrib.
NOTE: selected because of early flowering.
NOTE: details supplied by Rosewood Daylilies, UK.
NOTE: I have not been able to determine which of the names—the UK or the Japanese—was published first.

Agapanthus 'Blue Dot'

ORIGIN: known since 1997, New Zealand, and still in cultivation.
LEAF: evergreen.
PEDUNCLE: 40 cm.
INFLORESCENCE: "small."
FLOWER: violet-blue.

Agapanthus 'Blue Dwarf' = *A*. RUBBISH

NOTE: invalid name per the ICNCP-1995, art. 17.11.

Agapanthus 'Blue Ensign'

SYNONYM: *Agapanthus pendulinus* 'Blue Ensign'
ORIGIN: known since 1954, as shown at the RHS show that August by Messrs M. Prichard & Son Ltd, Christchurch; no further records.

Agapanthus 'Blue Eyes' (Trumpet Group)

ORIGIN: raised by Haden Tebb, Mutare, Zimbabwe, known since 2001 when registered by Oudendijk Import B.V., De Kwakel, The Netherlands.
LEAF: evergreen.
PEDUNCLE: glossy green, flat.
INFLORESCENCE: 10.5 cm across, 30 flowers, more or less globular.
PEDICEL: green.
FLOWER: pale violet-blue (92C), margin and midrib slightly darker and with a bit of purple (92B), upright to horizontal, 3–4 cm long, 3–4 cm across.
NOTE: details from the Internet [18].

Agapanthus 'Blue Formality' (Funnel Group)

SYNONYM: *Agapanthus praecox* 'Blue Formality'

ORIGIN: raised and introduced by Gary Dunlop, Ballyrogan Nurseries, UK, known since 1999.

LEAF: evergreen, large.

PEDUNCLE: 120 cm.

INFLORESCENCE: 20 cm across.

FLOWER: violet-blue.

NOTE: details supplied by Gary Dunlop.

NOTE: nuclear DNA content = 25.2 pg.

Agapanthus 'Blue Fortune'

ORIGIN: known since 2000 when offered by Gerddi Fron Goch, UK.

Agapanthus 'Blue Giant' (Trumpet Group)

SYNONYM: *Agapanthus africanus* 'Blue Giant'
Agapanthus 'Dutch Blue Giant'
Agapanthus 'Dutch Giant'
Agapanthus orientalis 'Blue Giant'
Agapanthus umbellatus 'Blue Giant'

ORIGIN: (probably a selection of *A. praecox* subsp. *orientalis* with interbreeding of *A. africanus*) of Dutch origin but no further records. Known since 1951 when grown by J.K. Zandberg, Rijnsburg, The Netherlands, and still in cultivation.

LEAF: more or less evergreen, 25–60 cm long and 2.5–3.5 cm wide, upright to arching, pale to normal green and slightly glaucous, base green.

PEDUNCLE: 80–120(–150) cm, green with only some purple towards inflorescence, flat.

INFLORESCENCE: 17–23 cm across, (40–)90–130 flowers, globular, bud opens at 2 sides.

PEDICEL: greenish-purple.

FLOWERBUD: dark violet-blue with purple tint, upright.

FLOWER: pale violet-blue (92D) to almost white in the tube and purple tint towards apex, margin violet-blue (92B), midvein rather wide and darker than the margin (92A), outside pale violet-blue with darker margin, midvein darker with slightly purple tint towards apex, base darker with purple tint, when out of flower more white-purple, horizontal, 4–4.5 cm long (tube 1.8–2 cm), 2.5–3.5 cm across, stamens not exserted, anthers violet.

NOTE: details from plants grown at various nurseries.

NOTE: nuclear DNA content = 24.5 pg.

ILLUSTRATION: *color plate*; photograph, Brickell (1996), Snoeijer (1998, 1999), and van Dijk and Snoeijer (2001).

AWARD: GV in 1951; FCC in 1953.

Agapanthus 'Blue Globe' (Salver Group)

SYNONYM: *Agapanthus praecox* 'Blue Globe'
Agapanthus umbellatus 'Blue Globe'

ORIGIN: (selection from seedlings) introduced by Hoogervorst, Oegstgeest, The Netherlands, around 1964 and still in cultivation.

LEAF: more or less evergreen, 30–60 cm long and 2–3 cm wide, upright, normal to dark green and slightly glaucous, base green.

PEDUNCLE: 80–120 cm, green and glaucous, distinctly flat.

INFLORESCENCE: 15–22 cm across, 80–100 flowers, globular, bud opens on 2 sides.

PEDICEL: green to greenish-violet towards flower and with distinct violet-blue spot at the top.

FLOWERBUD: violet-blue with darker base and green apex, upright.

FLOWER: inside violet-blue (95B/97B but fading to 92B/91A) with purple tint at margin and base white, midrib slightly darker, outside violet-blue with distinct purple tint, base not darker, when out of flower whitish-purple, horizontal, 2.8 cm long (tube 0.7 cm long), 3.5 cm across, stamens not exserted, anthers yellow with a bit of violet and yellow pollen, becoming brown.

NOTE: the first flowers within an inflorescence tend to have 8 tepals.

NOTE: most details from plants grown by van der Valk.

NOTE: nuclear DNA content = 23.1 pg.

ILLUSTRATION: *color plate*; photograph, Gillissen (1980), Kostelijk (1986), and Snoeijer (1995, 1998, 2000).

Agapanthus 'Blue Gown' (Funnel Group)

ORIGIN: raised at NCCPG Bicton College, UK, selected by Dick Fulcher in 1993, and still in cultivation.

LEAF: evergreen.

PEDUNCLE: 95 cm.

INFLORESCENCE: "large," 60–70 flowers, more or less globular.

PEDICEL: green with a bit of violet tint.

FLOWERBUD: upright, starting pale violet with lower half cream, later more coloured but darker compared with open flowers.

FLOWER: inside very pale violet-white with margin slightly darker, midrib pale violet-blue, outside very pale violet-blue to almost white towards the base, midrib just slightly darker, when out of flower pale violet-white with purple apex, horizontal to slightly nodding, stamens exserted, anthers red-purple becoming dark brown.

NOTE: details supplied by Dick Fulcher.

ILLUSTRATION: photograph, Fulcher (2000).

Agapanthus 'Blue Haze'

ORIGIN: (seedling of 'Isis') raised by Rosewood Daylilies, UK, introduced in 2002.

LEAF: deciduous.

PEDUNCLE: 80 cm.

FLOWER: pale violet-blue.

NOTE: details supplied by Rosewood Daylilies.

Agapanthus 'Blue Heaven' (Funnel Group)

ORIGIN: raised by C.J. de Jong & A.Ph.M. Rijnbeek en Zoon B.V., Boskoop, The Netherlands, introduced in 1999.

LEAF: more or less deciduous, up to 40 cm long and up to 3 cm wide, arching, pale to normal green, base green.

PEDUNCLE: 70–80 cm, green, round.

INFLORESCENCE: 16 cm across, 30–50 flowers, more or less flat.

PEDICEL: green with just a little bit of purple towards the flower.

FLOWERBUD: violet-blue with seams just a bit darker.

FLOWER: inside pale violet-blue with a bit of a purple tint and to white near the base, margin slightly darker and purple tint, midrib dark violet-blue with purple tint, outside pale violet-blue with purple tint, midrib and base violet-blue with purple tint, when out of flower purple, horizontal, 4.2–4.4 cm long (tube 1.1 cm long), 5 cm across, stamens exserted, anthers dark violet-blue becoming black.

NOTE: European Plant Variety Right applied for and granted, file no. 1999/0782, grant no. 9477, expires 31 December 2027.

NOTE: details from plants grown by Rijnbeek.

ILLUSTRATION: *color plate.*

Agapanthus 'Blue Horizons'

ORIGIN: raised by Lyndale Nurseries Auckland Ltd, New Zealand, known since 2000.

NOTE: New Zealand Plant Variety Rights applied for, no. HOM104, on 17 January 2000, by Lyndale Nurseries Auckland Ltd.

NOTE: details from the Internet [36].

Agapanthus 'Blue Hybrid'

ORIGIN: offered by Ignace van Doorslaer, Belgium; known since 1997, Belgium, introduced from Northern Ireland. Still in cultivation.

LEAF: deciduous.

FLOWER: violet-blue.

NOTE: invalid name per the ICNCP-1995, art. 17.16.

Agapanthus 'Blue Ice' (Funnel Group)

ORIGIN: raised by Dick Fulcher, Pine Cottage Plants, UK, known since 2001.

PEDUNCLE: 100 cm.

INFLORESCENCE: 50 flowers, flat.

PEDICEL: green at the base to purplish towards the flower.

FLOWERBUD: upright, pale violet with a bit of cream towards base, base violet-blue.

FLOWER: very pale violet-blue with midrib hardly darker coloured, outside very pale violet-blue and distinct dark violet-blue base, horizontal, anthers brown.

NOTE: details supplied by Dick Fulcher.

Agapanthus 'Blue Imp' (Salver Group)

ORIGIN: introduced by Russell, known since 1971, and still in cultivation.

LEAF: deciduous, 30–50 cm long and up to 1.8 cm wide, upright, normal green and slightly glaucous, base with purple.

PEDUNCLE: (60–)80–100 cm, green and slightly glaucous, round.

INFLORESCENCE: up to 12 cm across, 40 flowers, globular, bud opens on 1 side.

PEDICEL: green to dull violet towards flower.

FLOWERBUD: upright, dark violet-blue with a bit of green in the middle and darker base.

FLOWER: inside violet-blue (96AB) with white base, margin slightly darker and with distinct purple tint, midrib dark violet-blue (94A), outside dark violet-blue with darker midrib and margin and base, horizontal to slightly facing downwards, 2.5–3 cm long (tube 1 cm long), 3 cm across, stamens slightly exserted, anthers violet-blue.

NOTE: most details from plants grown at Wisley.

ILLUSTRATION: photograph, Dunlop (2000).

Agapanthus 'Blue Lakes'

ERROR: 'Blue Lake'

ORIGIN: known since 1998 when grown by Ets Horticole, France.

FLOWER: violet-blue.

Agapanthus 'Blue Leap'

ORIGIN: (chance seedling) introduced by Heronswood Nursery, Washington, USA.

PEDUNCLE: 100 cm.

INFLORESCENCE: "large."

FLOWER: "medium blue with a white midrib."

Agapanthus 'Blue Méoni' = *A.* 'Bleu Méoni'

Agapanthus 'Blue Mercury' (Funnel Group)

SYNONYM: *Agapanthus praecox* 'Blue Mercury'

ORIGIN: raised by Gary Dunlop, Ballyrogan Nurseries, UK, named in 1998.

LEAF: evergreen, up to 35 cm long and 4 cm wide, upright to arching, normal green, base green.

PEDUNCLE: 70 cm, green.

INFLORESCENCE: 20 cm across, 50 flowers.

PEDICEL: green with brown-purple.

FLOWER: inside pale violet-blue (97C), midrib dark violet-blue (94B), outside pale violet-blue (97C) with darker base, horizontal, 4 cm long, 4.5 cm across, segments rather thick.

NOTE: details supplied by Gary Dunlop.

NOTE: invalid name per the ICNCP-1995, art. 17.13.

NOTE: nuclear DNA content = 23.8 pg.

Agapanthus 'Blue Meyb'

ORIGIN: known since 1995, France; no further records.

Agapanthus 'Blue Moon' (Trumpet Group)

SYNONYM: *Agapanthus praecox* subsp. *orientalis* 'Blue Moon'

ORIGIN: (selection of *A. praecox* subsp. *orientalis*) raised by Eric B. Smith, Buckshaw Gardens, UK. Known since 1987 but probably much older and still in cultivation.
LEAF: more or less evergreen, 30–50 cm long and up to 3.5 cm wide, upright, glossy green, base green.
PEDUNCLE: 70–90 cm, rather stout, green and glaucous, flat.
INFLORESCENCE: 12–14 cm across, 50 flowers, flat, bud opens on 1 side and bract remains attached.
PEDICEL: green with violet-blue towards flower.
FLOWERBUD: very pale violet-blue with cream apex and slightly darker base, upright.
FLOWER: inside pale violet-blue, margin and midrib slightly darker (92C) and with purple tint, outside pale violet-blue with purple tint and slightly darker base, horizontal but later slightly hanging downwards, 3 cm long (tube 1.1 cm long), 2.5–2.7 cm across, stamens not exserted, anthers dark violet.
NOTE: details from plants grown at Beth Chatto Gardens.
NOTE: very slow grower and rather late flowering.
NOTE: nuclear DNA content = 23.4 pg.
ILLUSTRATION: *color plate.*
AWARD: HC in 1977.

Agapanthus 'Blue Mountain'

ORIGIN: raised by D. Hughes, Blue Mountain Nurseries, Tapanui, New Zealand, known since 1996.
FLOWER: violet-blue.
NOTE: New Zealand Plant Variety Rights applied for and granted, no. HOM057, on 2 February 1996, by D. Hughes, Blue Mountain Nurseries, Tapanui, New Zealand, expires 30 July 2017.
NOTE: details from the Internet [36].

Agapanthus 'Blue Nile' (Funnel Group)

SYNONYM: *Agapanthus praecox* subsp. *orientalis* 'Blue Nile'
Agapanthus praecox 'Blue Nile'

ORIGIN: (selection of *A. praecox* subsp. *orientalis*) known since 1991, New Zealand, and still in cultivation.
NAME: for the Nile River.
LEAF: evergreen, glossy green, arching.
PEDUNCLE: 150–180 cm.
INFLORESCENCE: "rather large," 60 flowers.
FLOWER: inside pale violet-blue with darker midrib.
ILLUSTRATION: photograph, Redgrove (1991) and Fulcher (2002).

Agapanthus 'Blue Pale'

ORIGIN: known since 2001 when grown by Ets Horticole, France, and Ignace van Doorslaer, Belgium, obtained from Raveningham Gardens, UK.
LEAF: evergreen.
FLOWER: violet-blue.
NOTE: invalid name per ICNCP-1995, art. 17.11.

Agapanthus **'Blue Pearl'**

ORIGIN: known since 1967, UK.
FLOWER: very pale violet-blue.

Agapanthus **'Blue Penant'** (Trumpet Group)

SYNONYM: *Agapanthus africanus* 'Blue Penant'

ORIGIN: (selection from seedlings) introduced by van der Zwet, Roelofarendsveen, The Netherlands, around 1965 and still known in 1987. Probably no longer in cultivation.
LEAF: evergreen, horizontal bend.
PEDUNCLE: 80 cm, usually with a second peduncle but much shorter.
INFLORESCENCE: 16 cm across, globular.
FLOWER: violet-blue (98BC and 100A), up to 4.25 cm long, 2.5–2.9 cm across.
NOTE: very obvious that, during the development of the peduncle, the next season's leaves appear.
ILLUSTRATION: photograph, Gillissen (1980).

Agapanthus **'Blue Perfection'** (Funnel Group)

SYNONYM: *Agapanthus africanus* 'Blue Perfection'

ORIGIN: raised by Schoehuys, Uitgeest, The Netherlands, known since 1965 when grown by Fa J. de Jong & Zonen, Aalsmeer. Still grown by Kees Duivenvoorde, The Netherlands.
LEAF: more or less evergreen, 40–50 cm long and 3 cm wide, upright but the outer of the shoot spreading, pale green to normal green and slightly glaucous, base green.
PEDUNCLE: 80(–110) cm, rather stout, green and slightly glaucous, flat.
INFLORESCENCE: 15–20 cm across, 60 flowers, globular, bud opens on 2 sides and bracts remain attached.
PEDICEL: green flushed purple-violet.
FLOWERBUD: violet-blue with darker base and greenish apex, upright but later horizontal.
FLOWER: inside pale violet-blue (92BC) and a bit purple with margin slightly darker and distinct white base, midrib violet-blue (92A), outside pale violet-blue (92BC) with thin darker midrib (92A) and dark base (93A), when out of flower purple with small violet-blue base, upright to horizontal, 3.5–4 cm long (tube 1.5 cm), 3.7 cm across, stamens not exserted, anthers black with orange pollen.
NOTE: details from plants grown by Duivenvoorde.
NOTE: a robust plant.

NOTE: nuclear DNA content = 24.4 pg.

ILLUSTRATION: *color plate.*

AWARD: GV in 1965.

Agapanthus 'Blue Peter' (Salver Group)

ORIGIN: introduced by Palmer, known since 1974 but probably no longer in cultivation.

LEAF: deciduous, up to 45 cm long and 2.5 cm wide, upright, rather dark glossy green.

PEDUNCLE: 100–125 cm, pale green.

INFLORESCENCE: 12–15 cm across, globular.

PEDICEL: normal green and heavily dull purple towards flower.

FLOWER: inside violet-blue (91A) with white base, midrib violet-blue (93C), horizontal to slightly facing downwards, 2 cm long, 3.2 cm across.

Agapanthus 'Blue Queen' (Funnel Group)

SYNONYM: *Agapanthus orientalis* 'Blue Queen'
Agapanthus umbellatus 'Blue Queen'

ORIGIN: most likely Dutch but without any further information. Known since 1960 when grown by Fa J. de Jong & Zonen, Aalsmeer, The Netherlands. Probably no longer in cultivation.

LEAF: evergreen.

INFLORESCENCE: very large.

FLOWER: inside pale violet-blue with darker midrib (92B) and rather narrow, outside violet-blue (92B) with darker midrib (92A).

AWARD: GV in 1960.

Agapanthus 'Blue Riband' => *A.* 'Blue Ribbon'

Agapanthus 'Blue Ribband' => *A.* 'Blue Ribbon'

Agapanthus BLUE RIBBON => *A.* 'Blauwe Wimpel'

Agapanthus 'Blue Ribbon' (Funnel Group)

SYNONYM: *Agapanthus orientalis* 'Blue Ribbon'
Agapanthus umbellatus 'Blue Ribbon'

ERROR: 'Blue Riband', 'Blue Ribband'

ORIGIN: introduced by van Tubergen, The Netherlands, from import. Known since 1937 when offered by van Tubergen, which lasted on and off until the 1970s. The original clone may no longer be in cultivation, see further under note.

LEAF: evergreen.

PEDUNCLE: 150 cm.

INFLORESCENCE: 200 flowers.

FLOWER: violet-blue.

NOTE: van Tubergen's 1954 catalogue description reads thus: "150 cm, 200 flowers." Kees Duivenvoorde, Beverwijk, The Netherlands, who obtained his plant from a very reliable source, grows '**Blue Ribbon**', and he donated a plant to the NPC in 1999. It is most likely that this clone is grown only in these two collections and that this is the true plant, even though the inflorescence bears fewer flowers. A clone with this name is also grown in the Beth Chatto Gardens, UK. Both clones key out close to the same level, but the Duivenvoorde clone is remarkable in its very dark midrib colouring and wider tepals towards the apex compared with the Chatto clone. The length of the stamens too differs noticeably.

NOTE: seedlings are offered from the Beth Chatto Gardens plant. Seed offered in France as 'Blue Ribbon' is most likely from this English plant.

AWARD: GV in 1937.

Agapanthus '**Blue Ribbon**' ex Kees Duivenvoorde (Funnel Group)

LEAF: evergreen, 40–50 cm long and up to 3.5 cm wide, arching, dark glossy green but the older leaves starting with a yellowish apex, base green.

PEDUNCLE: 80–90 cm, green and slightly flushed purple towards inflorescence, round.

INFLORESCENCE: 19–22 cm across, 50–60 flowers, globular.

PEDICEL: dark purple with green base.

FLOWERBUD: violet-blue with base hardly darker, upright.

FLOWER: inside pale violet-blue, margin slightly with purple but hardly darker coloured, midrib obviously darker coloured, outside pale violet-blue with midrib a bit darker but at apex very dark violet-blue, base glossy dark violet-blue, when out of flower violet-blue with apex purple becoming completely purple, horizontal to slightly nodding, 4–4.2 cm long (tube 1.5 cm long), 4.5–5 cm across, stamens slightly exserted, anthers dark violet.

NOTE: nuclear DNA content = 24.8 pg.

ILLUSTRATION: *color plate.*

Agapanthus 'Blue Ribbon' ex Beth Chatto (Funnel Group)

LEAF: evergreen, up to 50 cm long and up to 4 cm wide, arching, normal green, base green.

PEDUNCLE: 80 cm, green and a bit violet-blue towards inflorescence, round.

INFLORESCENCE: 16 cm across, 50–70 flowers, globular.

PEDICEL: dark purple-violet.

FLOWERBUD: dark violet-blue, upright.

FLOWER: inside pale violet-blue with darker margin and purple tint, midrib dark violet-blue, outside violet-blue with base slightly darker, when out of flower more purple, horizontal, up to 5 cm long (tube 1.5 cm long), 5 cm across, stamens not exserted, anthers violet.

Agapanthus 'Blue Ribbon' ex France = *A.* '**Ruban Bleu**'

NOTE: invalid name per the ICNCP-1995, art. 17.12.

Agapanthus 'Blue Skies'

ORIGIN: probably from New Zealand. Known since 1991 and still in cultivation.
LEAF: evergreen.
PEDUNCLE: up to 60 cm.
FLOWER: pale violet-blue.

Agapanthus 'Blue Skies' (Trumpet Group)

ORIGIN: probably the UK; later known than the preceding cultivar.
LEAF: deciduous, 45 cm long and 2.5 cm wide, upright, normal green, base green.
PEDUNCLE: 95 cm, green.
INFLORESCENCE: 11 cm across, 40 flowers, bud opens on 1 side.
PEDICEL: green.
FLOWER: inside white flushed very pale violet-blue (92D), outside very pale violet-blue with midrib slightly darker (94D), base greenish, hanging downwards, 3.7 cm long, 2.5 cm across, stamens inserted.
NOTE: most details supplied by Gary Dunlop.
NOTE: invalid name per the ICNCP-1995, art. 17.12.

Agapanthus 'Blue Star' ex Raveningham Gardens

ORIGIN: raised by Raveningham Gardens, UK, known since 1989, and still in cultivation.
LEAF: evergreen.
PEDUNCLE: 100 cm.
FLOWER: violet-blue.
NOTE: invalid name per the ICNCP-1995, art. 17.13.
AWARD: PC in 1989.

Agapanthus 'Blue Star' ex Australia (Funnel Group)

SYNONYM: *Agapanthus praecox* 'Blue Star'

ORIGIN: introduced in Australia, known since 2003.
LEAF: evergreen.
PEDUNCLE: 30 cm.
INFLORESCENCE: 15–20 flowers, flat.
FLOWER: pale violet-blue with darker midrib.
NOTE: invalid name per the ICNCP-1995, art. 17.2 and 17.13.
NOTE: details from the Internet [37].

Agapanthus 'Blue Steel' (Tubular Group)

ORIGIN: (an *A. inapertus* hybrid) raised at NCCPG Bicton College, UK, selected by Dick Fulcher in 1993, and still in cultivation.
LEAF: deciduous, up to 85 cm long and 5 cm wide.
PEDUNCLE: 125 cm.
INFLORESCENCE: 13 cm across, globular.
FLOWER: violet-blue (93CD), "steel blue," 4.3–4.5 cm long.
NOTE: details supplied by Dick Fulcher; some details from the Internet [5].

Agapanthus 'Bluestorm' (Funnel Group)

SYNONYM: *Agapanthus* 'ATlblu'

TRADE NAME: BLUESTORM ex USA

ORIGIN: New Zealand. Known since 2002 when introduced by Anthony Tesselaar USA, California, USA.
LEAF: green to greenish-yellow.
PEDUNCLE: 75 cm.
INFLORESCENCE: 12 cm across, 100 flowers.
FLOWER: inside pale violet-blue with dark violet-blue midrib.
NOTE: some details from the Internet [30].
NOTE: U.S. Plant Patent applied for.

Agapanthus 'Blue Stripe' (Funnel Group)

ORIGIN: raised at NCCPG Bicton College, UK, selected by Dick Fulcher in 1993, and still in cultivation.
PEDUNCLE: 90 cm.
FLOWER: "pale blue with darker stripe."
NOTE: details supplied by Dick Fulcher; some details from the Internet [5].

Agapanthus 'Bluet' => *A.* 'Bleuet'

Agapanthus 'Blue Triumphator' (Salver Group)

SYNONYM: *Agapanthus africanus* 'Blue Triumphator'
Agapanthus 'Bleu Triomphator'
Agapanthus campanulatus 'Blue Triumphator'
Agapanthus orientalis 'Blue Triumphator'
Agapanthus umbellatus 'Blue Triumphator'

ORIGIN: (probably a selection of *A. caulescens*) most likely Dutch. Known since 1916 and still in cultivation.
LEAF: deciduous, (20–)30–50(–60) cm long and 1.5–2(–4) cm wide, upright, normal green and glaucous with apex slightly paler, base green.
PEDUNCLE: 70–120 cm, green and very glaucous, rather thin, round.
INFLORESCENCE: 12–15(–19) cm across, globular but loose, (30–)50–70 flowers, bud opens on 1 side.
PEDICEL: green with dull purple speckles.
FLOWERBUD: violet-blue with brownish apex and darker base, upright.
FLOWER: inside violet-blue (91AB), base almost white, margin and midrib darker with purple tint, outside violet-blue and purple tint and darker midrib, base distinctly darker, when out of flower bright purple, horizontal, 2.5–3 cm long (tube 1.1 cm long), (2.7–)3.5 cm across, stamens not exserted, anthers dark violet.
NOTE: most details from plants grown by van der Valk.
NOTE: nuclear DNA content = 22.4 pg.
NOTE: unfortunately, because of seed propagation, most plants offered under this name are not true. Because of this easy method of propagation, this plant is the

most widely grown of all cultivars, but with the result that is is better to regard this as a group of plants that look similar rather than a proper cultivar. The true cultivar, the details of which are given above, is still grown but rare. Seed-raised plants will still have the same flower colouring (which is called "grey") but are easily recognized by the flower shape, which will be typical of the Trumpet Group.

ILLUSTRATION: *color plate*; photograph, Gillissen (1980) and Snoeijer (1998, 1999).
AWARD: GI in 1961.

Agapanthus 'Bluety'

ORIGIN: known since 2002 when A.C. van Wijk, Rotterdam, The Netherlands, applied for European Plant Variety Right, file no. 2002/0671.

Agapanthus 'Blue Umbrella'

SYNONYM: *Agapanthus praecox* subsp. *orientalis* 'Blue Umbrella'

ORIGIN: known since 1996, Canada, and 1999, UK. Widely offered as seed or as plug seedlings.
LEAF: evergreen, arching, glossy green, base green.
PEDUNCLE: 100 cm.
FLOWER: violet-blue.

Agapanthus 'Blue Velvet' (Trumpet Group)

ORIGIN: raised at NCCPG Bicton College, UK, selected by Dick Fulcher in 1993, and still in cultivation.
LEAF: deciduous, 30–60 cm long and 2–2.7 cm wide, upright, dark glossy green, base green.
PEDUNCLE: 75–120 cm, dark green and glaucous and a bit flushed purple, flat.
INFLORESCENCE: 20 cm across, 50 flowers, globular.
PEDICEL: normal green with purple speckles.
FLOWER: inside pale violet-blue with distinct purple tint and margin slightly darker, midrib rather wide violet-purple, outside violet-blue with purple tint, midrib rather wide and dark violet-blue, base very dark violet-blue, horizontal to slightly nodding, 4.2 cm long (tube 1.5 cm long), 3.6 cm across, stamens not exserted, anthers dark violet.
NOTE: most details from plants grown by Coen Jansen.
ILLUSTRATION: photograph, Jansen (2002).

Agapanthus 'Blue Wave'

ORIGIN: offered as seed.
NOTE: name from the Internet [32].

Agapanthus 'Bressingham Blue' (Salver Group)

SYNONYM: *Agapanthus campanulatus* 'Bressingham Blue'
Agapanthus umbellatus 'Bressingham Blue'

ORIGIN: raised and introduced by Alan Bloom, Bressingham Gardens, UK. From a bed of over 2000 seedlings, nine were selected in 1967 and were planted out near

Bloom's house. After two years of cultivation these nine plants were still very similar, and it was decided to increase stock for introduction. Bloom (1991) wrote, "It
took nearly ten years to work up these nine plants to over 1,000 so as to make it a feature, pictured in colour in our catalogue as *Agapanthus* 'Bressingham Blue'."
Named in 1972 and still in cultivation.

LEAF: deciduous, 30–40 cm long and 2 cm wide, arching, normal green and glossy,
base green.

PEDUNCLE: (50–)80–90 cm, green and slightly glaucous, with purple towards inflorescence, round.

INFLORESCENCE: 12 cm across, 40 flowers, flat.

PEDICEL: green with purple-violet towards flower.

FLOWERBUD: dark violet-blue, upright but quickly nodding.

FLOWER: inside violet-blue with purple tint, margin dark violet-blue (94A) and midrib even darker, outside dark violet-blue (94A) with darker midrib and base, when
out of flower more purple, horizontal to slightly nodding, 2.8–3 cm long (tube 1 cm
long), 2.8–3 cm across, stamens not exserted, anthers violet-blue.

NOTE: details from plants grown at various nurseries and gardens.

NOTE: pale violet-blue flowering plants are also sold under this name.

NOTE: nuclear DNA content = 22.2 pg.

ILLUSTRATION: photograph, Bloom (1991), Phillips and Rix (1991), Warren (1995),
and Fulcher (2002).

Agapanthus 'Bressingham Bounty' (Trumpet Group)

SYNONYM: *Agapanthus campanulatus* 'Bressingham Bounty'

ORIGIN: raised and introduced by Bloom, Bressingham Gardens, UK. Selected from
seedbeds, including recent forms of Lewis Palmer Headbourne Hybrids. Raised in
1981, introduced in 1992, and still in cultivation.

LEAF: more or less evergreen, rather wide, arching, normal green.

PEDUNCLE: 80 cm, green, more or less round.

INFLORESCENCE: "rather large," 80–100 flowers, globular.

PEDICEL: green flushed purple.

FLOWERBUD: violet-blue with slightly darker base, upright but quickly horizontal.

FLOWER: inside pale violet-blue with margin slightly darker, midrib dark violet-
blue, outside pale violet-blue with midrib slightly darker and violet-blue base, when
out of flower purple, horizontal, stamens not exserted, anthers dark violet.

NOTE: details from plants grown by Bloom.

NOTE: two different clones are offered in the UK.

ILLUSTRATION: *color plate.*

Agapanthus 'Bressingham White' (Salver Group)

SYNONYM: *Agapanthus campanulatus* 'Bressingham White'

ORIGIN: raised and introduced by Bloom, Bressingham Gardens, UK. In the same
bed of over 2000 seedlings (from which **'Bressingham Blue'** was selected in 1967), a
few were flowering white. One was selected, named in 1972, and is still in cultivation.

LEAF: deciduous, 30 cm long and 1.8 cm wide, arching, normal green, base purple.
PEDUNCLE: 80–100 cm, green, flat, not so sturdy.
INFLORESCENCE: 15 cm across, 40–50 flowers, flat.
PEDICEL: green with purple towards flower.
FLOWER: inside white with transparent midrib, outside slightly violet at apex, when out of flower white with pale purple apex, horizontal, 3 cm long (tube 1 cm long), 2.5(–3) cm across, stamens not exserted, anthers black.
NOTE: most details from plants grown at Wisley; some details from Bloom.
NOTE: two different clones are offered in the UK.

Agapanthus 'Bright Blue' = *A.* RUBBISH
NOTE: invalid name per the ICNCP-1995, art. 17.11.

Agapanthus 'Bright Eyes' (Trumpet Group)
ORIGIN: raised by Gary Dunlop, Ballyrogan Nurseries, UK, named in 1998.
LEAF: deciduous, up to 30 cm long and 2 cm wide, upright, pale green, leafbase green.
PEDUNCLE: 30 cm, pale green.
INFLORESCENCE: 12 cm across, 30 flowers.
PEDICEL: bronze.
FLOWER: inside violet-blue with a white base, outside base violet-blue (93A), midrib fading (84B), flushed white, horizontal, 2.5 cm long, 2 cm across.
NOTE: details supplied by Gary Dunlop.

Agapanthus 'Bright White'
ORIGIN: known since 1997, Belgium, introduced from Northern Ireland.
LEAF: deciduous.
FLOWER: white.
NOTE: invalid name per the ICNCP-1995, art. 17.11.

Agapanthus 'Bristol' (Trumpet Group)
ORIGIN: ('Intermedius' × **'Donau'**) raised by Kees Duivenvoorde, Beverwijk, The Netherlands, introduced in 1999, and still in cultivation.
NAME: after the city in England.
LEAF: deciduous, up to 40 cm long and 2.5 cm wide, slightly arching, dark green, base dark violet-purple.
PEDUNCLE: 90 cm, green heavily speckled dark violet, flat.
INFLORESCENCE: 17 cm across, 70 flowers, globular.
PEDICEL: dark green and heavily speckled dark violet.
FLOWERBUD: very dark violet-blue with slightly darker base, upright.
FLOWER: inside violet-blue (93B), margin violet-blue with a bit of purple and inner tepals wavy, midrib very dark violet-blue (93A) and rather wide, outside dark violet-blue, midrib rather wide and dark violet-blue, base very dark violet-blue, when out of flower purple with midrib very dark violet-blue to almost black, horizontal,

2.2–2.8 cm long (tube 0.9 cm long), 1.8–2.2 cm across, stamens not exserted, anthers violet-blue with yellow pollen.

NOTE: details from plants grown by Duivenvoorde.

NOTE: registered in 1999.

NOTE: nuclear DNA content = 23.3 pg.

Agapanthus 'Buckingham Palace' (Salver Group)

ORIGIN: raised by The Crown Estate, Windsor, UK, introduced in 1975, and still in cultivation.

NAME: after the royal estate in London.

LEAF: deciduous, 20–30 cm long and up to 2.5 cm wide, arching, normal green, base purple.

PEDUNCLE: 100(–180) cm, usually bending over, green and glaucous, round.

INFLORESCENCE: 15–17 cm across, 40–50 flowers, more or less globular.

PEDICEL: dull purple-green.

FLOWERBUD: dark violet-blue, upright.

FLOWER: inside dark violet-blue (96A), margin with slightly purple tint, midrib darker (95A), outside dark violet-blue, base slightly darker, when out of flower more purple, horizontal, 3 cm long (tube 1.5 cm long), 3.5 cm across, stamens exserted, anthers dark violet.

NOTE: details from plants grown at Wisley.

NOTE: nuclear DNA content = 22.8 pg.

ILLUSTRATION: photograph, Phillips and Rix (1991).

Agapanthus 'Buckland' (Salver Group)

SYNONYM: *Agapanthus campanulatus* 'Buckland'

ORIGIN: (selection of *A. campanulatus*) introduced from The Garden House, Buckland Monachorum, near Yelverton, Devon, UK, known since 1995, and still in cultivation.

NAME: refers to location of The Garden House, begun by Lionel (d. 1981) and Katherine (d. 1983) Fortescue in 1945. The garden is now maintained by Keith and Ros Wiley and owned by The Fortescue Garden Trust.

LEAF: young leaves cream becoming green.

FLOWER: violet-blue.

NOTE: nuclear DNA content = 22.2 pg.

Agapanthus 'Buddy Blue'

ORIGIN: raised by Jim Holmes of Cape Seed & Bulb, South Africa. Known since 1999 when Plant Variety Right was applied for, commercially available since November 2003.

LEAF: evergreen.

PEDUNCLE: 60–80 cm.

INFLORESCENCE: 50–60 flowers, 15 cm across, globular.

PEDICEL: green flushed purple.

FLOWERBUD: obovate, seems not to open.

TEPALS: violet-blue (94B/96B) with purple apex and darker base.

NOTE: introduced as "long lasting cuflower (12–18 days)," the "tepals do not drop."

NOTE: details from sales leaflets and the Internet [38]; origin details supplied by Biofleur.

Agapanthus 'Caeruleus'

SYNONYM: *Agapanthus africanus* 'Caeruleus'
Agapanthus africanus 'Coerulea'

ORIGIN: offered by Ignace van Doorslaer, Belgium, known since 1997, introduced from France. Still in cultivation.

LEAF: evergreen.

FLOWER: violet-blue.

NOTE: invalid name per the ICNCP-1995, art. 17.9 and 17.11.

Agapanthus 'Caeruleus Selection'

SYNONYM: *Agapanthus africanus* 'Coerulea Selection'

ORIGIN: offered by Ignace van Doorslaer, Belgium, known since 1997, introduced from France.

LEAF: evergreen.

FLOWER: violet-blue.

NOTE: invalid name per the ICNCP-1995, art. 17.9, 17.11, and 17.16.

Agapanthus 'Cally Blue'

ORIGIN: (chance seedling of 'Lilliput') raised and introduced by Cally Gardens, Castle Douglas, UK, known since 2000.

PEDUNCLE: up to 45 cm.

FLOWER: violet-blue.

Agapanthus Cambourne Hybrids => see note under *A.* RUBBISH

ORIGIN: offered by Bridgemere Nurseries, UK, in 1999.

Agapanthus 'Cambridge' (Funnel Group)

ORIGIN: raised by Kees Duivenvoorde, Beverwijk, The Netherlands, introduced in 1999.

NAME: after the city in England.

LEAF: deciduous, up to 40 cm long and 2.7 cm wide, upright, pale green and slightly glaucous, base green.

PEDUNCLE: 80 cm, green with a bit of purple blush, flat.

INFLORESCENCE: 18 cm across, (40–)60–80 flowers, globular, bud opens on 2 sides and remains attached.

PEDICEL: dull purple to greenish at the base.

FLOWERBUD: cream-green and apex with a bit of dull pale purple, upright but later horizontal.

FLOWER: inside white with midrib transparent, outside white with outer tepals a bit purple at apex and base white to pale green, 3.5 cm long (tube 1 cm long), 4–4.5 cm across, stamens exserted, anthers opening purple with yellow pollen becoming brown.

NOTE: details from plants grown by Duivenvoorde.

NOTE: for a deciduous cultivar, this one has remarkably large and wide leaves, like those of an evergreen.

NOTE: nuclear DNA content = 23.9 pg.

ILLUSTRATION: *color plate.*

Agapanthus 'Cambridge Blue' (Tubular Group)

SYNONYM: *Agapanthus inapertus* subsp. *inapertus* 'Cambridge Blue'

ORIGIN: (selection of *A. inapertus*) introduced by RHS Garden Wisley, UK, and still in cultivation.

LEAF: deciduous.

FLOWER: pale violet-blue.

Agapanthus campanulatus F.M. Leight. (1965) J. South African Bot., Suppl.

DISTRIBUTION: central Natal, Basutoland and Orange Free State into the northeastern Cape Province, growing in grassy and rocky places, in moist soil. Known in cultivation since 1822, UK, and still widely cultivated.

LEAF: deciduous, from a short leek-like stem, 3–12 per shoot, 15–40(–50) cm long and 1–2.5 cm wide, green, shiny, purple at the base.

PEDUNCLE: 30–70(–100) cm.

INFLORESCENCE: few- to many-flowered, 10–30 flowers.

PEDICEL: 2–7 cm long, spreading.

FLOWER: pale to dark violet-blue or rarely white, 2–3.5 cm long (tube 0.5–1 cm long), segments spreading but not recurving, stamens shorter than the flower, exserted, pollen purple.

FLOWERING TIME: December into February.

NOTE: nuclear DNA content = 22.34 pg.

ILLUSTRATION: drawing, Synge (1986); photograph, Sheat and Schofield (1995), Brickell (1996), and Elsa Pooley (1998).

Agapanthus campanulatus subsp. *campanulatus*

DISTRIBUTION: northeastern Cape Province; Idutywa, Matatiele, Mount Currie, Tsolo, and Umtata. Natal; Helpmekaar, Lions River, Mpendle, Mtonjaneni, New Hanover, Nkandla, Nqutu, Pietermaritzburg, Port Shepstone, Richmond, Umvoti, Underberg, and Weenen. Not on high altitudes.

FLOWER: clear violet-blue, segments spreading to 45° (tube rather short).

NOTE: also offered as seed.

ILLUSTRATION: *color plate*; drawing, Leighton (1965), which is reproduced in Snoeijer (1998); photograph, Pienaar (1987) and Phillips and Rix (1991).

Agapanthus campanulatus subsp. *campanulatus* 'Albovittatus' = *A.* '**Beth Chatto**'
NOTE: invalid name per the ICNCP-1995, art. 17.9 and 17.11.

Agapanthus campanulatus subsp. *campanulatus* 'Albidus' => *A. campanulatus* 'Albidus'

Agapanthus campanulatus subsp. *campanulatus* 'Albus' = *A.* '**Franni**'
NOTE: invalid name per the ICNCP-1995, art. 17.2, 17.9, and 17.11.

Agapanthus campanulatus subsp. *campanulatus* 'Hardingsdale' = *A.* '**Hardingsdale**'

Agapanthus campanulatus subsp. *campanulatus* 'Intermedius' = *A.* 'Intermedius'

Agapanthus campanulatus subsp. *campanulatus* 'Iris' = *A.* 'Iris'

Agapanthus campanulatus subsp. *campanulatus* 'Isis' = *A.* '**Isis**'

Agapanthus campanulatus subsp. *campanulatus* 'Nanus' => *A. campanulatus* 'Nanus'

Agapanthus campanulatus subsp. *campanulatus* 'Slieve Donard' = *A.* '**Slieve Donard**'

Agapanthus campanulatus subsp. *campanulatus* 'Variegatus' = *A.* '**Beth Chatto**'

Agapanthus campanulatus subsp. *campanulatus* 'Wedgwood Blue' = *A.* '**Wedgwood Blue**'

Agapanthus campanulatus subsp. *campanulatus* 'Wendy' = *A.* '**Wendy**'

Agapanthus campanulatus subsp. **patens** F.M. Leight. (1965) J. South African Bot., Suppl.
SYNONYM: *Agapanthus patens* F.M. Leight.
Agapanthus 'Patens'

DISTRIBUTION: Orange Free State; Bethlehem, Clocolan, Ficksburg, Fouriesburg, and Harrismith. Natal; Bergville, Estcourt, Heidelberg in Transvaal, Mpendle, and Weenen. Basutoland. In mountainous rocky grassland, moist valley bottoms and slopes, damp places, and basalt cliffs, 1800–2400 m.
FLOWER: clear blue, tube rather short, segments spreading to 90°.
NOTE: widely grown; most plants grown as *A. campanulatus* belong here.
NOTE: probably the most frost-hardy *Agapanthus*.
NOTE: also offered as seed.
ILLUSTRATION: *color plate*; drawing, Turrill (1960 as *A. patens*), Leighton (1965), which is reproduced in Snoeijer (1998), and Dyer (1966a); photograph, Bloom (1969), Phillips and Rix (1991), and Fulcher (2000).

Agapanthus campanulatus subsp. *patens* 'Mooreanus' = *A.* '**Mooreanus**'

Agapanthus campanulatus subsp. *patens* 'Profusion' = *A.* '**Profusion**'

Agapanthus campanulatus subsp. *patens* 'Ultramarine' = *A.* '**Ultramarine**'

Agapanthus campanulatus var. *albidus* Philip & Lord = *A.* '**Franni**'
  Philip & Lord (1993) The Plant Finder. nom.nud.

Agapanthus campanulatus var. *albo-vittatus* Philip & Lord = *A.* '**Beth Chatto**'
  Philip & Lord (1989) The Plant Finder. nom.nud.

Agapanthus campanulatus var. *albovittatus* Philip & Lord = *A.* '**Beth Chatto**'
  Philip & Lord (1990) The Plant Finder. nom.nud.

Agapanthus campanulatus var. *albus* Philip & Lord = *A.* '**Franni**'
  Philip & Lord (1989) The Plant Finder. nom.nud.

Agapanthus campanulatus 'Alba' = *A. campanulatus* 'Albus'

Agapanthus campanulatus 'Albidus' ex today's plants = *A.* '**Franni**'

Agapanthus campanulatus '**Albidus**'
  ERROR: 'Alba'
  ORIGIN: known in cultivation since 1835, UK.
  NOTE: plants currently grown under this name have nothing to do with the species;
  see chapter 2.

Agapanthus campanulatus 'Albovittatus' = *A.* '**Beth Chatto**'
  NOTE: invalid name per the ICNCP-1995, art. 17.9 and 17.11.

Agapanthus campanulatus 'Albus' =
  = pro parte => *A. campanulatus* 'Albidus' = *A.* '**Franni**'
  = pro parte = *A. praecox* '**Albiflorus**'
  ERROR: 'Alba'
  NOTE: invalid name per the ICNCP-1995, art. 17.2, 17.9, and 17.11.

Agapanthus campanulatus 'Albus Nanus' = *A.* 'Albus Nanus'

Agapanthus campanulatus 'Blue Triumphator' = *A.* '**Blue Triumphator**'

Agapanthus campanulatus 'Bressingham Blue' = *A.* '**Bressingham Blue**'

Agapanthus campanulatus 'Bressingham Bounty' = *A.* '**Bressingham Bounty**'

Agapanthus campanulatus 'Bressingham White' = *A.* '**Bressingham White**'

Agapanthus campanulatus 'Bright Blue' = *A.* RUBBISH

Agapanthus campanulatus 'Buckland' = *A.* **'Buckland'**

Agapanthus campanulatus 'Chatto's Blue' = *A.* **'Cobalt Blue'**

Agapanthus campanulatus 'Cobalt Blue' = *A.* **'Cobalt Blue'**

Agapanthus campanulatus 'Dark Blue' = *A.* 'Dark Blue'

Agapanthus campanulatus 'Dwarf Bright Blue' = *A.* RUBBISH

Agapanthus campanulatus 'Gary Form' = *A.* 'Gary Form'

Agapanthus campanulatus 'Glockenturm' = *A.* **'Glockenturm'**

Agapanthus campanulatus 'Hardingsdale' = *A.* **'Hardingsdale'**

Agapanthus campanulatus 'Headbourne Hybrids' = *A.* RUBBISH

Agapanthus campanulatus 'Iris' = *A.* 'Iris'

Agapanthus campanulatus 'Isis' = *A.* **'Isis'**

Agapanthus campanulatus 'Kingston Blue' = *A.* **'Kingston Blue'**

Agapanthus campanulatus 'Kingston Blue Strain' = *A.* RUBBISH

Agapanthus campanulatus 'Kobold' = *A.* **'Kobold'**

Agapanthus campanulatus 'Meibont' = *A.* **'Meibont'**

Agapanthus campanulatus 'Midnight Blue' = *A.* **'Midnight Blue'**

Agapanthus campanulatus 'Nanus'

> NOTE: details of the origin of this cultivar were supplied by Gary Dunlop, Ballyrogan Nurseries, UK, who writes, "*Agapanthus nanus* was the name of a dwarf plant raised by the Slieve Donard Nursery from seed from South Africa, by that name. It is a dwarf form of *A. campanulatus*. Most were the typical agapanthus colour and the seedlings were sold. One of the seedlings was much darker than the rest and this was selected out and saved from being sold by Philip Wood, a director of the nursery, and named *A.* **'Midnight Blue'**. It was bulked up vegetatively and sold; it is slow to increase. The naming was I think prior to 1959 so the name nanus should be valid."
> NOTE: invalid name per the ICNCP-1995, art. 17.9 and 17.11 (unless pre-1959 published records are discovered).

Agapanthus campanulatus 'Navy Blue' = *A.* **'Navy Blue'**

Agapanthus campanulatus 'Oxbridge' = *A.* 'Oxbridge'

Agapanthus campanulatus 'Oxford Blue' = *A.* 'Oxford Blue'

Agapanthus campanulatus 'Pale Blue' = *A.* RUBBISH

Agapanthus campanulatus 'Pale Form' = *A.* RUBBISH

Agapanthus campanulatus 'Pinocchio' = *A.* 'Pinocchio'

Agapanthus campanulatus 'Premier' = *A.* 'Premier'

Agapanthus campanulatus 'Profusion' = *A.* 'Profusion'

Agapanthus campanulatus 'Rich Blue' = *A.* 'Rich Blue'

Agapanthus campanulatus 'Rosewarne' = *A.* 'Rosewarne'

Agapanthus campanulatus 'Royal Blue' = *A.* 'Royal Blue'

Agapanthus campanulatus 'Slieve Donard' = *A.* 'Slieve Donard'

Agapanthus campanulatus 'Slieve Donard Variety' = *A.* 'Slieve Donard'
     NOTE: invalid name per the ICNCP-1995, art. 17.15.

Agapanthus campanulatus 'Spokes' = *A.* 'Spokes'

Agapanthus campanulatus 'Ultramarine' = *A.* 'Ultramarine'

Agapanthus campanulatus 'Variegatus' = *A.* 'Beth Chatto'

Agapanthus campanulatus 'Wedgwood Blue' = *A.* 'Wedgwood Blue'

Agapanthus campanulatus 'Wendy' = *A.* 'Wendy'

Agapanthus campanulatus 'White Form' = *A.* RUBBISH

Agapanthus campanulatus 'White Hope' = *A.* 'White Hope'

Agapanthus campanulatus 'White Starlet' = *A.* 'White Starlet'

Agapanthus campanulatus 'White Triumphator' = *A.* 'White Triumphator'

Agapanthus campanulatus 'Wolkberg' = *A.* 'Wolkberg' (Salver Group)

Agapanthus campanulatus hybrids = *A.* RUBBISH

Agapanthus campanulatus variegated = *A.* 'Beth Chatto'

Agapanthus campanulatus white form = *A.* RUBBISH

Agapanthus candidus Besant = *A.* 'Candidus'

Besant (1903) Flora and Sylva, 1.

Agapanthus 'Candidus'

> SYNONYM: *Agapanthus candidus* Besant
> *Agapanthus umbellatus* var. *candidus* Baines
>
> ORIGIN: known since 1885, UK, and still referred to in 1903.
> FLOWER: "pure white form, with great substance."

Agapanthus 'Carlos Freile' (Funnel Group)

> ORIGIN: known since 2001 when shown by Flortec SA, Equador, at Horti Fair, the international flower trade show, in Amsterdam, The Netherlands.
> LEAF: evergreen.
> PEDUNCLE: 100 cm, green, round.
> INFLORESCENCE: 18 cm across, 80–100 flowers, globular.
> PEDICEL: green flushed purple.
> FLOWERBUD: dark violet-blue with a paler spot near the base.
> FLOWER: with a distinct purple tint, inside very pale violet-blue to white at the base, margin pale violet-blue and rather wide and slightly wavy, midrib pale violet-blue and rather wide, outside pale violet-blue with darker margin and midrib, base glossy dark violet-blue, when out of flower purple, upright to horizontal, 5–5.5 cm long (tube 2 cm long), 4.5–5.3 cm across, stamens exserted, anthers violet-blue with yellow pollen.
> NOTE: details from the 2001 Horti Fair.

Agapanthus 'Castle of Mey' (Salver Group)

> ORIGIN: raised by The Crown Estate, Windsor, UK, introduced in 1975, and still in cultivation.
> NAME: after the royal estate in England.
> LEAF: deciduous, 15–30 cm long and 1–1.5 cm wide, upright, normal green and slightly glaucous, base with purple.
> PEDUNCLE: 60–75 cm, green and with purple towards inflorescence, round.
> INFLORESCENCE: 12–14 cm across, 40–60 flowers, more or less flat, bud opens on 1 side.
> PEDICEL: green with dull purple towards flower.
> FLOWERBUD: violet-blue, upright.
> FLOWER: inside violet-blue (96BC), midrib slightly darker, margin with purple tint, outside pale violet-blue with purple tint, when out of flower more purple, horizontal to slightly nodding, 3.2 cm long (tube 1.2 cm long), 3–3.5 cm across, stamens exserted, anthers dark violet.
> NOTE: details from plants grown at various nurseries.

Agapanthus 'Catharina' (Trumpet Group)

> ERROR: 'Catherina'

ORIGIN: raised by Kees Duivenvoorde, Beverwijk, The Netherlands, introduced by him in 1995, and still in cultivation.

NAME: in honour of the raiser's wife, and also for their daughter of the same name.

LEAF: deciduous, up to 35 cm long and 3.5 cm wide, upright with apex bent, glaucous, base with purple.

PEDUNCLE: 90 cm, green with purple speckles, flat.

INFLORESCENCE: 20–23 cm across, 50–70 flowers, globular, bud opens on 2 sides.

PEDICEL: green with purple speckles to purple towards the flower.

FLOWERBUD: violet-blue, upright.

FLOWER: inside pale violet-blue (91BC) with darker midrib (93C) and margin with purple blush, outside pale violet-blue with darker base, when out of flower purple, horizontal, 3.5 cm long (tube 1.3 cm long), 3–3.5 cm across, stamens just slightly exserted, anthers dark violet.

NOTE: details from plants grown by Duivenvoorde.

NOTE: the first flowers within an inflorescence tend to have 6–8(–10) tepals; flowers tend towards the Salver Group when fully open.

NOTE: early flowering (early July in Holland).

NOTE: registered in 1995.

NOTE: nuclear DNA content = 24 pg.

ILLUSTRATION: *color plate.*

Agapanthus caulescens Sprenger ex Wittmack (1901) Gartenflora, 21.

SYNONYM: *Agapanthus africanus* subsp. *caulescens* (Sprenger) H.R. Wehrh.
Agapanthus nutans F.M. Leight.
Agapanthus umbellatus var. *caulescens* A. Worsley
Agapanthus umbellatus var. *maximum* Edwards ex Thomas

DISTRIBUTION: Natal, Swaziland and southeastern Transvaal. Growing in rocky areas, on grassy slopes, along mountain streams and cliffs.

LEAF: deciduous, from a leek-like stem that can be up to 25 cm long, 7–15 per shoot, basal leaves 5–15 cm long and the upper leaves 20–60 cm long, 1–4 cm wide, soft bright green to glaucous, shiny.

PEDUNCLE: 60–130(–180) cm.

INFLORESCENCE: few- to many-flowered.

PEDICEL: 3–7 cm long, spreading to slightly bending.

FLOWER: dark to clear violet-blue with base paler and midrib darker, 3–6 cm long (tube 1–2.7 cm long), segments slightly spreading to strongly bent or curved, horizontal to facing downwards, stamens and style shorter than the flower, pollen purple.

FLOWERING TIME: November into February.

NOTE: also offered as seed.

NOTE: in the year of its first mention (Sprenger 1901), a coloured plate was published by *Gartenflora*'s editor, and once again the main characteristic mentioned is the leaf-like stem "like **Musa**," which is clearly visible in the plate. Sprenger received seed at the end of the 1890s from a friend called Dietrich, collected in Transvaal. Sprenger raised the seed at his nursery in Naples, Italy. Because of this early introduction by Sprenger, who was Dutch, it is very likely that **'Blue Triumphator'** was a selection of this species, as suggested by Gillissen (1980).

NOTE: nuclear DNA content = 23.18 pg.

ILLUSTRATION: drawing, Leighton (1965, once as *A. nutans*) and both were reproduced in Snoeijer (1998); photograph, Palmer (1967), Phillips and Rix (1991, once as *A. nutans*), Scott (1997), Duncan (1998 as *A. nutans*), and Elsa Pooley (1998).

Agapanthus caulescens subsp. *angustifolius* F.M. Leight. (1965) J. South African Bot., Suppl.

SYNONYM: *Agapanthus angustifolius*

DISTRIBUTION: northeast Natal; Vryheid and Utrecht. Swaziland. Transvaal; Wakkerstroom.

LEAF: up to 3 cm wide, upright, apex acute-subacute.

PEDUNCLE: up to 100 cm.

FLOWER: very dark violet-blue, segments less recurved compared with subsp. *gracilis*.

ILLUSTRATION: photograph, Pienaar (1987) and Duncan (1998).

Agapanthus caulescens subsp. *angustifolius* 'Politique' = *A.* **'Politique'**

Agapanthus caulescens subsp. *caulescens*

DISTRIBUTION: Swaziland, shady sites on streambanks and in dolerite outcrops.

LEAF: 4 cm wide or more, apex obtuse, clear green.

PEDUNCLE: 25–60(–100) cm.

FLOWER: larger than those of the other two subspecies.

ILLUSTRATION: *color plate*; drawing, Wittmack (1901).

Agapanthus caulescens subsp. *gracilis* F.M. Leight. (1965) J. South African Bot., Suppl.

SYNONYM: *Agapanthus gracilis* F.M. Leight.

DISTRIBUTION: northern Natal; Ubombo. Known in cultivation since 1939 when introduced from open grassland, Lebombo Range, between Ubombo and Ingwavum.

LEAF: 7–9 per shoot, 30–60 cm long and 1.5–3 cm wide, weak.

PEDUNCLE: up to 60 cm, slender.

INFLORESCENCE: 20–40 flowers.

FLOWER: segments gracefully bent at the apex.

ILLUSTRATION: *color plate*; drawing, Leighton (1965), which is reproduced in Snoeijer (1998), and Hunt (1972).

Agapanthus caulescens 'Politique' = *A.* **'Politique'**

Agapanthus **'Cedric Morris'**

ORIGIN: from the garden of Cedric Morris, introduced by Raveningham Gardens. Known since 1994 and still in cultivation.

LEAF: deciduous.
PEDUNCLE: 50–90 cm.
FLOWER: white with pale purple.
NOTE: according to Gary Dunlop, similar to '**Ardernei**'.

Agapanthus 'Chandra'

ORIGIN: (probably a hybrid with *A. africanus* '**Albus**') raised by David Street, Devon, UK, introduced by Avon Bulbs. Known since 1995 and still in cultivation.
FLOWER: pure white, "thick textured."
NOTE: details supplied by Gary Dunlop.

Agapanthus 'Charlie Morrell'

ORIGIN: (selection from the same seedbatch as '**Woodcote Paleface**') raised by Brian Hiley, Wallington, Surrey, UK, introduced in 1997, and still in cultivation.
NAME: in honour of the raiser's late father-in-law.
LEAF: evergreen.
PEDUNCLE: 60–80 cm.
FLOWER: dark violet-blue.
NOTE: details supplied by Brian Hiley.

Agapanthus 'Charlotte'

ORIGIN: (seedling of '**Dawn Star**') raised by Ignace van Doorslaer, Belgium, named in 2001.
LEAF: deciduous.
FLOWER: pale violet-blue, slightly paler than '**Dawn Star**'.

'Chatto's Blue' => *Agapanthus campanulatus* 'Chatto's Blue'

Agapanthus 'Cherry Holley' (Funnel Group)

ORIGIN: raised in South Africa, introduced by Lewis Palmer. Known since 1955 and still in cultivation.
LEAF: deciduous, 25–45 cm long and 2–2.5 cm wide, arching, glossy green, base green.
PEDUNCLE: 60–75 cm, dark green but dark purple towards inflorescence, usually a second peduncle, flat.
INFLORESCENCE: 12–14 cm across, 30–50 flowers, more or less globular.
PEDICEL: dark green flushed purple-black.
FLOWERBUD: greyish-violet-blue with dark violet-blue base, upright but later more horizontal.
FLOWER: inside pale violet-blue, midrib violet-blue, margin violet-blue with purple, outside violet-blue with darker midrib, base dark violet-blue, when out of flower violet-blue with purple, horizontal, 3.8–4 cm long (tube 1.3 cm long), 4 cm across, stamens not exserted, anthers violet becoming black.
NOTE: details from plants grown at Wisley.
ILLUSTRATION: *color plate*.
AWARD: AM in 1955; FCC in 1977.

Agapanthus 'Christine' (Funnel Group)

ORIGIN: (selection of 'Goliath') probably raised by E.M.J. van der Valk, Zoeter-woude, The Netherlands, who registered the plant in 1979. Probably no longer in cultivation.

LEAF: evergreen.

FLOWER: violet-blue.

Agapanthus 'City of Lincoln' (Salver Group)

ORIGIN: raised by Kees Duivenvoorde, Beverwijk, The Netherlands, introduced in 1998.

NAME: after the city in England.

LEAF: deciduous.

PEDUNCLE: 75 cm.

INFLORESCENCE: 15 cm across.

FLOWER: inside violet-blue (93B) to white near the base, midrib violet-blue (93B), outside violet-blue (93A) with slightly paler margin, 2 cm long, 4 cm across.

NOTE: similar to 'Intermedius', differing in a longer peduncle and more flowers within an inflorescence.

NOTE: registered in 1998.

Agapanthus 'Clarence House'

ORIGIN: raised by The Crown Estate, Windsor, UK, introduced in 1975, and still in cultivation.

NAME: after the royal estate in England.

LEAF: deciduous.

PEDUNCLE: 75 cm.

FLOWER: dark violet-blue.

Agapanthus 'Cobalt Blue' (Salver Group)

SYNONYM: *Agapanthus campanulatus* 'Chatto's Blue'
Agapanthus campanulatus 'Cobalt Blue'

ORIGIN: (selection of *A. campanulatus*) raised by Beth Chatto, Elmstead Market, UK, introduced in 1988, and still in cultivation.

NAME: a reference to the flower colour.

LEAF: deciduous, 40–50 cm long, up to 2.5 cm wide, upright, normal green and slightly glaucous, base purple.

PEDUNCLE: 80–120 cm, green but purple tint towards inflorescence, round.

INFLORESCENCE: 11–13 cm across, 25–40 flowers, more or less globular, bud opens on 2 sides.

PEDICEL: dull violet-purple towards flower.

FLOWERBUD: violet-blue, upright but quickly nodded.

FLOWER: inside violet-blue (96B), midrib darker (96A), margin with purple tint, outside violet-blue with purple tint, base slightly darker, when out of flower purple with violet midrib, horizontal to slightly facing downwards, 3 cm long (tube 1.2 cm long), 3 cm across, stamens not exserted, anthers purple-violet becoming black.

NOTE: details from plants grown at Beth Chatto Gardens.

NOTE: formerly offered as 'Chatto's Blue', as the provided name was invalid under the ICNCP-1980; but per the ICNCP-1995, names of colours are allowed to be used as a cultivar name, making the name **'Cobalt Blue'** once again correct and valid.

NOTE: nuclear DNA content = 22.8 pg.

ILLUSTRATION: *color plate*; photograph, Snoeijer (1998).

Agapanthus coddii F.M. Leight. (1965) J. South African Bot., Suppl. Vol. IV. 36.

DISTRIBUTION: northwestern Transvaal; Waterberg, along streams and on mountainsides, 1400–1800 m. The plate in Letty (1962) was taken from material collected at Waterberg.

NAME: in honour of Dr Leslie Edward Wostall Codd, who collected, together with Dyer, the type specimen at Waterberg. Codd was director of the Botanical Research Institute (now part of the National Botanical Institute) from 1963 to 1973 and editor of *The Flowering Plants of Africa*, *Bothalia*, and *Flora of Southern Africa*.

LEAF: deciduous, distinctly from a leek-like stem, up to 10 per shoot, 15–45 cm long and 3–5 cm wide, more or less upright, clear green and slightly glaucous.

PEDUNCLE: rather stout, 100–150 cm.

PEDICEL: 3–6 cm long, upright to horizontal.

FLOWER: violet-blue, 3.5–4 cm long (tube 0.8–1.2 cm long), segments strongly spreading but not recurving, stamens and style shorter than the flower, pollen purple.

FLOWERING TIME: January.

NOTE: also offered as seed.

NOTE: nuclear DNA content = 24.03 pg.

ILLUSTRATION: drawing, Letty (1962 as *Agapanthus* sp.) and Leighton (1965); photograph, Duncan (1998).

Agapanthus coddii 'Lady Edith' = *A*. **'Lady Edith'**

Agapanthus 'Coerulea' => *A*. 'Caeruleus'

Agapanthus 'Coerulea Selection' => *A*. 'Caeruleus Selection'

Agapanthus 'Colossus' (Funnel Group)

ORIGIN: raised and introduced by Gary Dunlop, Ballyrogan Nurseries, UK, known since 2002.

LEAF: evergreen.

PEDUNCLE: 120 cm.

INFLORESCENCE: 30–40 cm across, globular.

FLOWER: violet-blue.

NOTE: details supplied by Gary Dunlop.

NOTE: nuclear DNA content = 25.2 pg.

Agapanthus 'Columba' (Trumpet Group)

ERROR: 'Colomba'

ORIGIN: raised by Kees Duivenvoorde, Beverwijk, The Netherlands, introduced by him in 1995, and still in cultivation.

NAME: in honour of the raiser's sister; it is also the family Christian name in Latin.

LEAF: deciduous, up to 40 cm long and 3 cm wide, upright, normal green and glaucous, base green.

PEDUNCLE: 70 cm, green flushed with dark purple, flat.

INFLORESCENCE: up to 18 cm across, 70 flowers, globular, bud opens on 1 side.

PEDICEL: almost completely dark purple with a green base.

FLOWERBUD: upright, dark violet-blue.

FLOWER: inside pale violet-blue (92A) with margin slightly darker, midrib violet-blue (93C), outside violet-blue with purple blush, base much darker, when out of flower purple with dark violet-blue base, horizontal, up to 4 cm long (tube 1.7 cm long), 3.5 cm across, stamens not exserted, anthers dark violet.

NOTE: details from plants grown by Duivenvoorde.

NOTE: early flowering (early July in Holland).

NOTE: flowers tend towards the Salver Group when fully open.

NOTE: registered in 1995.

NOTE: nuclear DNA content = 23.6 pg.

ILLUSTRATION: *color plate.*

Agapanthus comptonii F.M. Leight. = *A. praecox* subsp. *minimus* (Lindl.) F.M. Leight.

F.M. Leight. (1965) J. South African Bot., Suppl.

NAME: in honour of Compton, who collected the type specimen at Kaffir Drift, Bathurst.

Agapanthus comptoniii subsp. *longifolia* Hart => probably an error of subsp. *longitubus*

Hart (1995) Planten Vinder voor de lage landen. nom.nud.

Agapanthus comptonii subsp. *longitubus* F.M. Leight. = *A. praecox* subsp. *minimus* (Lindl.) F.M. Leight.

F.M. Leight. (1965) J. South African Bot., Suppl.

ERROR: *A. comptonii* subsp. *longifolia* Hart [?], *A. comptonii* 'Longifolia' [?]

Agapanthus comptonii 'Longifolia' => probably an error of subsp. *longitubus*

Agapanthus 'Cool Blue' (Funnel Group)

ORIGIN: raised by Dick Fulcher, Pine Cottage Plants, UK, known since 2000.

LEAF: deciduous, 40–70 cm long and 2–2.5 cm wide, wavy, canaliculate, normal green (138AB) with middle towards base slightly paler (144CD), base slightly caulescent and green.

PEDUNCLE: (70–)100 cm, rather stout.

INFLORESCENCE: 20 cm across, more or less flat.

PEDICEL: green with a purple tint.

FLOWERBUD: upright, violet-blue distinctly darker striped, base dark violet-blue.

FLOWER: inside violet-blue (89D) with dark violet-blue midrib (89A), outside violet-blue with darker midrib and base, horizontal to slightly nodding, up to 4.7 cm long (tube 2 cm long), stamens not exserted, anthers yellow-green (153D).

NOTE: details supplied by Dick Fulcher.

Agapanthus 'Cool Summer'

ORIGIN: known since 2001 when offered by Satoshi Komoriya, Komoriya Nursery Ltd, Japan.

NOTE: details supplied by Komoriya.

Agapanthus 'Corinne' (Trumpet Group)

ORIGIN: (mutant of **'Umbellatus Albus'**) raised by Karel Hooijman, Amstelveen, The Netherlands, in 1987 and still in cultivation.

NAME: in honour of the raiser's wife.

LEAF: deciduous, up to 50 cm long and 2.5 cm wide, arching, pale green, base dark purple.

PEDUNCLE: 70–100 cm, green and just slightly glaucous, round and a bit weak.

INFLORESCENCE: 15–16 cm across, 30–40 flowers, more or less flat, bud opens on 1 side.

PEDICEL: green with a bit of purple speckling.

FLOWERBUD: white with apex greenish and a bit dull purple, upright.

FLOWER: inside white, midrib transparent, outside white and the outer with a violet midrib towards apex, base cream-white, when out of flower purple, horizontal, 3.1 cm long (tube 1 cm long), 3–3.5 cm across, stamens not exserted, anthers dark purple-violet.

NOTE: most details from a living plant; some details supplied by Hooijman, some from Internet [18].

NOTE: grown by the raiser in Zimbabwe and Kenya to trade October through December as a cut flower.

ILLUSTRATION: *color plate*.

Agapanthus 'Crystal' (Trumpet Group)

ORIGIN: introduced by Lewis Palmer, known since 1974, and still in cultivation.

LEAF: deciduous, up to 50 cm long and 2 cm wide, upright, normal to dark green.

PEDUNCLE: 100–115 cm, normal green.

INFLORESCENCE: 13 cm across, flat.

FLOWER: white with margin violet-blue (94B) and midrib violet-blue (90B), upright to slightly facing downwards, 3.5 cm long, 3.5 cm across.

AWARD: HC in 1977.

Agapanthus 'Crystal Drop' (Tubular Group)

ORIGIN: New Zealand, known since 1996, and still in cultivation.
LEAF: deciduous, up to 50 cm long and 4 cm wide, upright with upper half arching, glossy green and rather canaliculate, base green.
PEDUNCLE: 60–140 cm, pale green and a bit glaucous, round.
INFLORESCENCE: 13 cm across, 30–40 flowers, drooping.
PEDICEL: pale green and a bit purple flushed towards the flower.
FLOWERBUD: upright but quickly nodding, cream base with upper half white with yellowish midrib.
FLOWER: inside white with margin very pale violet, midrib transparent pale purplish, outside white with margin slightly tinted very pale violet, base cream, when out of flower white with purple midrib at apex, drooping vertically, tepal segments slightly spreading, up to 4.2 cm long (tube 2 cm long), 2.4 cm across, stamens not or just 1–2 exserted, anthers purple becoming black.
NOTE: details from plants grown by Coen Jansen.
ILLUSTRATION: photograph, Fulcher (2002).

Agapanthus 'Cyan' (Tubular Group)

SYNONYM: *Agapanthus inapertus* subsp. *inapertus* 'Cyan'

ORIGIN: (selection of *A. inapertus* subsp. *intermedius*) raised and introduced by Gary Dunlop, Ballyrogan Nurseries, UK, known since 2002.
FLOWER: very dark violet-blue.
NOTE: details supplied by Gary Dunlop.
NOTE: nuclear DNA content = 24.9 pg.

Agapanthus DANUBE => *A.* 'Donau'

Agapanthus 'Dark'

ORIGIN: known since 1997 when grown by Ignace van Doorslaer, Belgium, obtained from Raveningham Gardens, UK. Still in cultivation.
LEAF: evergreen.
FLOWER: dark violet-blue.
NOTE: invalid name per the ICNCP-1995, art. 17.11.

Agapanthus 'Dark Blue'

SYNONYM: *Agapanthus campanulatus* 'Dark Blue'

ORIGIN: grown by Ignace van Doorslaer, Belgium, known since 1997, obtained from Northern Ireland. Still in cultivation.
LEAF: deciduous.
FLOWER: dark violet-blue.
NOTE: invalid name per the ICNCP-1995, art. 17.11.

Agapanthus dark hybrids = *A.* RUBBISH

Agapanthus 'Dark Navy Blue' = *A.* 'Navy Blue'

Agapanthus 'Dawn Star' (Funnel Group)

> ERROR: 'Dawnstar', 'Downstar'

ORIGIN: raised and introduced by Raveningham Gardens, UK. Known since 1989 and still in cultivation.
LEAF: deciduous.
PEDUNCLE: up to 50 cm.
INFLORESCENCE: 20–30 flowers, flat, bud opens on 1 side and remains attached during flowering.
FLOWER: inside pale violet-blue with dark midrib, outside pale violet-blue with darker midrib and a hint of purple.
ILLUSTRATION: photograph, Farger (1999).

Agapanthus 'Dayspring'

ORIGIN: known since 2000 when offered by Rowden Gardens, UK.

Agapanthus 'Debbie' (Trumpet Group)

ORIGIN: raised by Kees Duivenvoorde, Beverwijk, The Netherlands, introduced by him in 1997, and still in cultivation.
NAME: in honour of the raiser's granddaughter.
LEAF: deciduous, up to 20 cm long and 1.5 cm wide, more or less upright, in early stage distinctly yellow becoming normal green to dark green but some yellow colouring remains along the margin and apex, base green.
PEDUNCLE: 40(–60) cm, green speckled violet, round.
INFLORESCENCE: up to 15 cm across, 40–50 flowers, flat, bud opens on 1 side.
PEDICEL: purple.
FLOWERBUD: dark violet-blue, upright but quickly horizontal.
FLOWER: inside pale violet-blue (91AB) with margin slightly darker with purple blush, midrib dark violet-blue, outside violet-blue with purple blush at margin, base darker, when out of flower dark violet-blue with purple, horizontal, up to 3.5 cm long (tube 1.8 cm long), 2.5 cm across, stamens not exserted, anthers dark violet with yellow pollen.
NOTE: details from plants grown by Duivenvoorde.
NOTE: registered in 1997.
NOTE: nuclear DNA content = 23.8 pg.
ILLUSTRATION: *color plate*; photograph, Snoeijer (1998).

Agapanthus 'Defina's Blush' (Funnel Group)

> SYNONYM: *Agapanthus praecox* subsp. *orientalis* 'Defina's Blush'

ORIGIN: (seedling of *A. praecox* subsp. *orientalis*) introduced by San Marcos Growers, California, USA, in 2002.
FLOWER: white with violet-blue apex.
NOTE: details from the Internet [33].

Agapanthus 'Delft' (Funnel Group)

ORIGIN: introduced by Lewis Palmer, known since 1974, and still in cultivation.
NAME: after the city in The Netherlands, with reference to the flower colour.
LEAF: more or less evergreen, 50–60 cm long and up to 3.5 cm wide, arching, dark dull green, base purple.
PEDUNCLE: 120–150 cm, green, round.
INFLORESCENCE: 18 cm across, 80–100 flowers, globular.
PEDICEL: greenish with purple speckles.
FLOWERBUD: violet-blue, upright.
FLOWER: inside pale violet-blue (92B), margin and midrib slightly darker (92A), margin with purple tint, outside violet-blue and base slightly darker, when out of flower with purple, horizontal, 4 cm long (tube 1.1 cm long), 4–4.5 cm across, stamens not exserted, anthers dark violet with orange-brown pollen.
NOTE: details from plants grown at Wisley.
NOTE: nuclear DNA content = 23.6 pg.
ILLUSTRATION: photograph, Gough (1991), Phillips and Rix (1991), and Snoeijer (1998, 1999).
AWARD: FCC in 1977.

Agapanthus 'Dell Garden'

ORIGIN: known since 2003 when offered by the RHS Garden Wisley.

Agapanthus 'Density' (Trumpet Group)

ORIGIN: raised by Gary Dunlop, Ballyrogan Nurseries, UK, introduced in 1996, and still in cultivation.
LEAF: evergreen, up to 50 cm long and up to 2.5 cm wide, more or less upright at 45°, normal green and slightly glaucous, base green.
PEDUNCLE: up to 80 cm, green.
INFLORESCENCE: 17.5 cm across, over 100 flowers, bud opens on 2 sides.
PEDICEL: green.
FLOWER: pale violet-blue (97B), on both sides with darker midrib (96B), when out of flower more purple, 4 cm long, 3.5 cm across.
NOTE: details supplied by Gary Dunlop.

Agapanthus 'Devon Dawn' => see note under A. RUBBISH

ORIGIN: a seed strain, originating from an isolated planting of one clone in a Devon garden. Introduced by Dick Fulcher, Pine Cottage Plants, UK, known since 2001.

Agapanthus 'Diana' (Funnel Group)

ORIGIN: raised and introduced by Lewis Palmer. Known since 1974 and still in cultivation, but true plants are rare.
NAME: after an aristocratic lady.
LEAF: more or less evergreen, 40–50 cm long and up to 5 cm wide, arching, dark green.
PEDUNCLE: up to 100 cm long, dark green.

INFLORESCENCE: up to 25 cm across, globular.

PEDICEL: dark green heavily flushed very dark purple.

FLOWER: white with margin violet-blue (94B), midrib violet-blue (94A), horizontal to slightly facing downwards, up to 5 cm long, 4 cm across.

NOTE: most details from plants grown at Wisley. Different plants are grown under this name. Even though the diameter of the flower is less than the length, I keep this cultivar in the Funnel Group because of the leaves and the gappy tepal segments.

AWARD: AM in 1977.

Agapanthus 'Dnjepr' (Trumpet Group)

SYNONYM: *Agapanthus umbellatus* 'Dnjepr'

ORIGIN: (chance seedling) raised by W. Schoehuys, Uitgeest, The Netherlands, and introduced by Maas & van Stein, Hillegom, in 1981, and still in cultivation.

NAME: Dutch spelling of the Dnipro (Dnepr) River.

LEAF: deciduous, up to 30 cm long and 3 cm wide, upright, pale green, base green.

PEDUNCLE: 90 cm, green and slightly glaucous, flat.

INFLORESCENCE: 18 cm across, 70 flowers, globular, bud opens on 2 sides.

PEDICEL: green heavily flushed purple.

FLOWERBUD: upright, violet-blue.

FLOWER: inside pale violet-blue (91D) with margin slightly darker and purple blush, midrib violet-blue (93D), outside violet-blue with purple at apex, base dark violet-blue, when out of flower purple, horizontal, up to 3.8 cm long (tube 1.1 cm long), 3 cm across, stamens not exserted, anthers violet.

NOTE: details from plants grown by Maas & van Stein.

NOTE: the first flowers within the inflorescence tend to have extra tepals.

NOTE: registered in 1981.

NOTE: nuclear DNA content = 24.6 pg.

ILLUSTRATION: photograph, Snoeijer (1999).

AWARD: GV in 1981.

Agapanthus 'Doctor Brouwer' = *A.* 'Dr Brouwer'

Agapanthus 'Doktor Brouwer' = *A.* 'Dr Brouwer'

Agapanthus 'Donau' (Trumpet Group)

SYNONYM: *Agapanthus africanus* 'Donau'
Agapanthus umbellatus 'Donau'

TRANSLATION: DANUBE [in English]

ERROR: 'Donnau'

ORIGIN: (chance seedling) raised by W. Schoehuys, Uitgeest, The Netherlands, known since 1979. The plant was grown as "Blauw 912" by Gebroeders van Buggenum, who later named it 'Donau'. Still in cultivation.

NAME: Dutch translation of the Danube River.

LEAF: deciduous, 30 cm long and 2–2.5 cm wide, upright, dark green, base green.

PEDUNCLE: 60–80 cm, green and slightly glaucous, flat.

INFLORESCENCE: 15–20 cm across, (20–)40–60 flowers, bud opens on 2 sides.

PEDICEL: green with purple speckles and base purple.

FLOWERBUD: dark violet-blue, upright.

FLOWER: inside pale violet-blue (97B) with purple blush, midrib darker (96CD), outside darker especially at the base, when out of flower white-violet with purple, horizontal, 3.5 cm long (tube 1 cm long), 3(–3.5) cm across, stamens not exserted or just 1–2 slightly exserted, anthers dark violet.

NOTE: details from plants grown by Maas & van Stein.

NOTE: registered in 1979.

NOTE: nuclear DNA content = 24.7 pg.

ILLUSTRATION: *color plate*; photograph, Ganslmeier and Henseler (1985) and Snoeijer (1998).

AWARD: GV in 1979.

Agapanthus 'Doré'

ORIGIN: known since 2001 when grown by Ets Horticole, France.

FLOWER: violet-blue.

Agapanthus 'Dorothy Kate' (Funnel Group)

ORIGIN: raised by Dick Fulcher, Pine Cottage Plants, UK, known since 2000.

NAME: in honour of the raiser's mother.

LEAF: evergreen, rather unequal on one shoot, 20–86 cm long and 2–3.3 cm wide, upright, slightly channelled, normal green (137BC) and paler towards the base (141C), base long caulescent and pale green.

PEDUNCLE: 90(–130) cm, pale to normal green (143C), rather stout.

INFLORESCENCE: up to 21 cm across, globular.

FLOWER: inside violet-blue (94C) with darker midrib (94AB) and base with brown, outside similarly coloured, a bit upright but normally horizontal, 4–4.6 cm long (tube 1.2–1.4 cm long), stamens as long as the flower, anthers dark brown.

NOTE: details supplied by Dick Fulcher.

Agapanthus 'Dorothy Palmer' (Salver Group)

ERROR: 'Dorothy Parker'

ORIGIN: raised and introduced by Roland Jackman, Woking, UK. Known since 1970; still known in 1990.

NAME: in honour of Lewis Palmer's wife.

LEAF: deciduous, 40–45 cm long and up to 2.5 cm wide, upright, pale glossy green.

PEDUNCLE: up to 90 cm, pale green.

INFLORESCENCE: 13 cm across, 30–40 flowers, more or less flat.

PEDICEL: pale green flushed dark grey.

FLOWER: inside violet-blue (94B), margin and midrib darker violet-blue (94A), outside violet-blue with darker midrib and base, when out of flower purple-violet, horizontal or slightly facing downwards, 2.5 cm long, 2.5 cm across, stamens slightly exserted, anthers dark violet.

NOTE: details from plants grown at Wisley.

ILLUSTRATION: photograph, Paul and Ledward (1990 as 'Dorothy Parker').

AWARD: HC in 1977.

Agapanthus 'Double Diamond' (Funnel Group)

ORIGIN: raised by Jim Holmes of Cape Seed & Bulb, South Africa. Known since 2000 when Plant Variety Right was applied for, commercially available since November 2003.

LEAF: evergreen, 12–13 cm long.

PEDUNCLE: 20 cm.

INFLORESCENCE: 10–11 cm across, 18–20 flowers, flat.

FLOWERBUD: greenish-white, upright.

FLOWER: usually with 8 or 10 tepals, inside pure white with midrib slightly darker, outside white, horizontal, stamens slightly exserted, anthers yellow.

NOTE: a sterile cultivar, propagated by division and tissue culture.

NOTE: origin details were supplied by Biofleur; other details from sales leaflets, some from the Internet [38].

Agapanthus 'Downstar' => *A.* 'Dawn Star'

Agapanthus 'Dr Brouwer' (Trumpet Group)

SYNONYM: *Agapanthus africanus* 'Dr Brouwer'
Agapanthus 'Doctor Brouwer'
Agapanthus 'Doktor Brouwer'

ORIGIN: raised by Kees Duivenvoorde, Beverwijk, The Netherlands, introduced in 1987, and still in cultivation.

NAME: in honour of Dr T. Brouwer, specialist at the Heemskerk Hospital, The Netherlands.

LEAF: deciduous, 30–40 cm long and up to 2 cm wide, upright, normal green, base green.

PEDUNCLE: 80 cm, green to dark purple towards inflorescence, round.

INFLORESCENCE: 19 cm across, 50 flowers, globular, bud opens on 1 side.

PEDICEL: dark purple with green base.

FLOWERBUD: upright, dark violet-blue.

FLOWER: inside pale violet-blue (94D) with apex slightly purple and margin slightly darker, midrib darker violet-blue (94B), outside pale violet-blue with darker midrib, base dark violet-blue, when out of flower purple-violet, horizontal, 4–4.4 cm long (tube 1.6 cm), 3.5–4 cm across, stamens not exserted, anthers dark violet with orange-brown pollen becoming black.

NOTE: details from plants grown by Duivenvoorde.

NOTE: registered in 1987.

NOTE: selected for its early flowering.

NOTE: nuclear DNA content = 23.7 pg.

ILLUSTRATION: *color plate*; photograph, Snoeijer (1998) and van Dijk (2002).

Agapanthus 'Duivenbrugge Blue' (Trumpet Group)

ORIGIN: raised by Kees Duivenvoorde, Beverwijk, The Netherlands, introduced in 1998, and still in cultivation.

NAME: a compilation of the raiser's name and his wife's name, Verbrugge.

LEAF: deciduous, up to 35 cm long and 2.8 cm wide, upright, dull green and rather glaucous, base green.

PEDUNCLE: 100 cm, green and rather glaucous, slightly flat.

INFLORESCENCE: 18 cm across, 40 flowers, flat.

PEDICEL: green and slightly purple speckled.

FLOWERBUD: violet-blue, upright.

FLOWER: inside violet-blue (92B) with a purple tint towards the apex and slightly darker margin (94B), outside pale to normal violet-blue (94B) with margin darker (94A), midrib violet-blue (94A), when out of flower violet-blue with purple apex becoming completely purple, horizontal, up to 3.1 cm long (tube 1.2 cm long), 2.7 cm across, stamens not exserted, anthers violet becoming brown.

NOTE: details from plants grown by Duivenvoorde.

NOTE: flowers tend towards the Salver Group when fully open.

NOTE: registered in 2001.

NOTE: nuclear DNA content = 23 pg.

ILLUSTRATION: *color plate*; photograph, van der Wiel (1999).

Agapanthus 'Duivenbrugge White' (Salver Group)

ORIGIN: (white seedling × '**Prinses Marilène**') raised by Kees Duivenvoorde, Beverwijk, The Netherlands, introduced in 1998, and still in cultivation.

NAME: a compilation of the raiser's name and his wife's name, Verbrugge.

LEAF: deciduous.

PEDUNCLE: 90 cm, green, rather sturdy, more or less round.

INFLORESCENCE: 12 cm across, 50 flowers, globular.

PEDICEL: pale green.

FLOWERBUD: greenish-white with green apex, upright.

FLOWER: inside white with yellowish-transparent midrib, outside white with midrib very pale cream, when out of flower white with dull white base, upright to horizontal, 2.5–2.7 cm long (tube 0.9 cm long), 3.4 cm across, stamens exserted, anthers yellow.

NOTE: details from plants grown by Duivenvoorde.

NOTE: excellent cut flower with no bud loss.

NOTE: registered in 2001.

ILLUSTRATION: photograph, van der Wiel (2000).

Agapanthus 'Duná' (Trumpet Group)

ORIGIN: raised by Th. P.W. de Groot, Hillegom, The Netherlands, introduced by Maas & van Stein, also of Hillegom, introduced in 2001.

NAME: Hungarian for the Danube River.

LEAF: deciduous, up to 50 cm long and 3 cm wide, upright to arching, dark green, base dark purple.

PEDUNCLE: 120 cm, green and a bit purple speckled, slightly flat.
INFLORESCENCE: 20 cm across, 70 flowers, globular.
PEDICEL: green and a bit purple speckled.
FLOWERBUD: violet-blue with dull brownish apex and darker base, upright.
FLOWER: usually with 10–12 tepals, inside very pale violet-blue (92C) but slightly darker towards apex and with a purple tint, midrib violet-blue (92A), outside pale violet-blue (92B), midrib slightly darker (92A) but fading into the tepals, base violet-blue (93B), when out of flower purple-white, upright to horizontal, up to 3.1 cm long (tube 1.2 cm long), 3 cm across, 8–10 stamens not or just slightly exserted, anthers dark violet-brown.
NOTE: details from plants grown by Maas & van Stein.
ILLUSTRATION: *color plate.*

Agapanthus 'Dutch Blue Giant' = *A.* **'Blue Giant'**

Agapanthus 'Dutch Files' => *A.* **'Dutch Tiles'**

Agapanthus 'Dutch Giant' = *A.* **'Blue Giant'**

Agapanthus **'Dutch Tiles'** (Salver Group)

ERROR: 'Dutch Files'

ORIGIN: raised and introduced by Lewis Palmer. Known since 1955; still known in 1979.
LEAF: evergreen, up to 50 cm long, 3–4 cm wide, normal glossy green.
PEDUNCLE: twisted, 90–110 cm, pale green.
INFLORESCENCE: 16 cm across, up to 100 flowers, globular.
PEDICEL: green heavily flushed dark purple towards flowers.
FLOWER: pale violet-blue (92B), margin and midrib darker (92A), 2.5 cm long, 3 cm across.
ILLUSTRATION: photograph, Palmer (1967).
AWARD: PC in 1955.

Agapanthus 'Dwarf Alba'

ORIGIN: known since 2001 when offered by Magnolia Gardens Nursery, USA.
PEDUNCLE: 30–40 cm.
FLOWER: white.
NOTE: details from the Internet [23].
NOTE: invalid name per the ICNCP-1995, art. 17.9 and 17.11.

Agapanthus **'Dwarf Baby Blue'** (Funnel Group)

SYNONYM: *Agapanthus praecox* subsp. *orientalis* 'Dwarf Baby Blue'

ORIGIN: (selection of *A. praecox* subsp. *orientalis*) known since 1996, offered as seed.
LEAF: evergreen.
PEDUNCLE: 45 cm.
FLOWER: violet-blue.

Agapanthus 'Dwarf Blue' ex today's plants = *A*. RUBBISH

Agapanthus 'Dwarf Blue' ex Dobie (Funnel Group)

SYNONYM: *Agapanthus praecox* 'Dwarf Blue'

ORIGIN: introduced by Messrs Samuel Dobie & Son Ltd, Llangollen, Clwyd, known since 1974. Because of seed propagation, the true plant is probably no longer in cultivation.

LEAF: more or less evergreen, 20–40 cm long and 2 cm wide, arching, dark glossy green and slightly glaucous.

PEDUNCLE: 70 cm, normal green.

INFLORESCENCE: 18 cm across, globular.

FLOWER: white flushed pale violet-blue, margin and midrib violet-blue (94B), horizontal, 5 cm long, 5 cm across.

NOTE: invalid name per the ICNCP-1995, art. 17.11.

AWARD: AM in 1977.

Agapanthus 'Dwarf Bright Blue' = *A*. RUBBISH

NOTE: invalid name per the ICNCP-1995, art. 17.11.

Agapanthus 'Dwarf White' ex today's plants = *A*. RUBBISH

Agapanthus 'Dwarf White' ex Giridlian

SYNONYM: *Agapanthus orientalis* 'Dwarf White'

ORIGIN: raised and introduced by J.N. Giridlian's Oakhurst Gardens, California, USA, known since 1962. Because of seed propagation, the true plant is probably no longer in cultivation.

LEAF: evergreen.

INFLORESCENCE: "large and many flowered."

PEDUNCLE: "eighteen inches."

FLOWER: white.

NOTE: invalid name per the ICNCP-1995, art. 17.11.

Agapanthus dyeri F.M. Leight. = *A. inapertus* subsp. *intermedius* F.M. Leight.

F.M. Leight. (1965) J. South African Bot., Suppl. Vol. IV. 46.

NAME: in honour of Dr Robert Allen Dyer, who collected, together with Codd, the type specimen at the Mohlakeng Plateau, Blouberg. Dyer was a taxonomist and director of the Botanical Research Institute (now part of the National Botanical Institute) from 1944 until 1963.

Agapanthus 'Early Variegated' (Variegated Leaf Group)

ORIGIN: most likely introduced in the UK, known since 1997.

LEAF: deciduous, variegated.

NOTE: invalid name per the ICNCP-1995, art. 17.11.

Agapanthus 'Ed Carman' (Variegated Leaf Group)

ORIGIN: known since 2003 when offered by Cotswold Garden Flowers, UK.
LEAF: yellow variegated.
PEDUNCLE: 65 cm.
INFLORESCENCE: 60–70 flowers, globular.
FLOWER: white.
NOTE: details from the Internet [39].

Agapanthus 'Edinburgh' (Trumpet Group)

ORIGIN: (selected seedling × 'Sunfield') raised by Kees Duivenvoorde, introduced in 2002.
NAME: after the capital of Scotland.
LEAF: deciduous.
PEDUNCLE: 80 cm.
INFLORESCENCE: 20 cm across, 60 flowers.
FLOWER: violet-blue.
NOTE: selected for its late flowering and remarkably large flowers.
NOTE: details supplied by Duivenvoorde.

Agapanthus 'Elaine' (Trumpet Group)

SYNONYM: *Agapanthus africanus* 'Elaine'

ORIGIN: raised by Los Angeles State and County Arboretum, California, USA, introduced in 1990, and still in cultivation.
LEAF: evergreen, rather large, arching.
PEDUNCLE: 100(–150) cm.
INFLORESCENCE: 16 cm across, globular.
FLOWER: dark violet-blue, slightly facing downwards.
NOTE: most details from the Internet [22] and [31].
NOTE: from the images on the Internet, this cultivar is similar to 'Purple Cloud' in inflorescence shape.
NOTE: U.S. Plant Patent no. 7303.

Agapanthus 'Elegans' (Funnel Group)

SYNONYM: *Agapanthus praecox* 'Elegans'

ORIGIN: (selection of *A. praecox*) known since 1994, Kirstenbosch National Botanical Garden, South Africa. Also offered as seed.
LEAF: evergreen.
PEDUNCLE: 50 cm.
FLOWER: violet-blue.
NOTE: invalid name per the ICNCP-1995, art. 17.9 and 17.11.

Agapanthus 'Elisabeth' (Trumpet Group)

ORIGIN: raised by Kees Duivenvoorde, Beverwijk, The Netherlands, introduced in 1996, and still in cultivation.

NAME: in honour of the raiser's daughter.

LEAF: deciduous, 30–40 cm long and 2.5 cm wide, slightly arching, dark green, base green.

PEDUNCLE: 90 cm, green and flushed purple, flat.

INFLORESCENCE: up to 17 cm across, 60 flowers, globular, bud opens on 1 side.

PEDICEL: green flushed purple to purple towards flower.

FLOWERBUD: upright, dark violet-blue.

FLOWER: inside pale violet-blue with purple blush at apex and margin slightly darker, midrib slightly darker violet-blue, outside violet-blue with purple towards apex and darker coloured midrib, base dark violet-blue, when out of flower purple-violet, horizontal, up to 3.4 cm long (tube 1.5 cm long), 2.5–3 cm across, stamens not exserted, anthers violet becoming black.

NOTE: details from plants grown by Duivenvoorde.

NOTE: registered in 1995.

NOTE: nuclear DNA content = 23.9 pg.

ILLUSTRATION: *color plate*; photograph, van der Wiel (1996).

Agapanthus 'Elizabeth Salisbury' (Salver Group)

ORIGIN: raised by Lewis Palmer, known since 1974, and still in cultivation.

LEAF: deciduous, 40–50 cm long and 1.5–2 cm wide, arching, normal green, base with purple.

PEDUNCLE: 60–80 cm, green, round.

INFLORESCENCE: 10–14 cm across, globular, bud opens on 1 side.

PEDICEL: green with dull purple speckles.

FLOWERBUD: violet-blue, upright.

FLOWER: inside pale violet-blue (97A) to white, midrib slightly darker (94B), margin darker with purple tint, outside violet-blue with darker midrib, when out of flower more purple, horizontal, 2.5–3 cm long (tube 0.8 cm long), 3 cm across.

NOTE: most details from plants grown at Wisley.

Agapanthus 'Elize'

ORIGIN: ('**Corinne**' × '**Wolga**') raised by Koert Scheepers, Zimbabwe, in 2001, introduced by Karel Hooijman, Amstelveen, The Netherlands, in 2003.

PEDUNCLE: 50–55 cm.

FLOWER: pure white, 3–4.5 cm across, anthers yellow.

NOTE: details supplied by Hooijman.

Agapanthus 'Ellamae' (Funnel Group)

SYNONYM: *Agapanthus africanus* 'Ellamae'

ERROR: 'Ella Mae'

ORIGIN: raised by the Los Angeles State and County Arboretum, California, USA, introduced in 1990, and still in cultivation.

LEAF: more or less deciduous, "broad."

PEDUNCLE: up to 130 cm.

INFLORESCENCE: 100 flowers, globular.
FLOWER: inside pale violet-blue with white base, margin violet-blue, midrib dark violet-blue, horizontal, stamens just slightly exserted.
NOTE: most details from the Internet [22], [30], [31], and [33].
NOTE: U.S. Plant Patent no. 7297.

Agapanthus 'Emba' (Funnel Group)

ORIGIN: raised by Th. P.W. de Groot, Hillegom, The Netherlands, introduced by Maas & van Stein, also of Hillegom, introduced in 2001.
NAME: for the Emba River, in Kazakhstan.
LEAF: deciduous, up to 45 cm long and 3 cm wide, upright to spreading, dark green, base violet.
PEDUNCLE: 110 cm, dark green, slightly purple speckled, round.
INFLORESCENCE: 16 cm across, 80 flowers, globular, bud opens on 1 side.
PEDICEL: green and heavily flushed purple.
FLOWERBUD: violet-blue with slightly darker midrib and base, upright but quickly horizontal.
FLOWER: inside pale violet-blue (93D) and slightly darker towards apex with purple tint, midrib violet-blue (93C), outside pale violet-blue (93D) with purple tint, midrib and base violet-blue (93C), when out of flower purple, horizontal, up to 3.4 cm long (tube 1.4 cm long), 3.8 cm across, stamens exserted, anthers purplish with yellow pollen.
NOTE: details from plants grown by Maas & van Stein.
NOTE: flowers tend towards the Salver Group when fully open.
ILLUSTRATION: *color plate.*

Agapanthus 'Enchanting'

ORIGIN: introduced by Mrs D. Palmer, known since 1974; no further records.

Agapanthus ensifolius Willd. = *Polyxena pygmaea* Kunth (Hyacinthaceae)

Willd. (1799) Sp. Plant. II.

Agapanthus 'Ethel's Joy'

ORIGIN: known since 2003 when offered by Pennard Plants, UK.

Agapanthus 'Eve' (Trumpet Group)

ORIGIN: raised by Lewis Palmer, known since 1972, and still in cultivation.
NAME: after an aristocratic lady.
LEAF: more or less evergreen, 40–50 cm long, 3 cm wide, upright, pale glossy green, base with purple.
PEDUNCLE: 70 cm, yellowish-green.
INFLORESCENCE: 11 cm across, globular.
PEDICEL: yellowish to dark green towards flower.
FLOWER: very pale violet-blue, margin violet-blue (94B), midrib greyish-blue, horizontal, 2.5 cm long, 3 cm across.
AWARD: HC in 1977.

Agapanthus 'Evening Star'

ORIGIN: raised and introduced by Raveningham Gardens, UK, known since 1995, and still in cultivation.
LEAF: deciduous.
PEDUNCLE: 60–75 cm, purple.
FLOWER: violet-blue with darker midrib.
NOTE: invalid name per the ICNCP-1995, art. 17.13.

Agapanthus ex

NOTE: in Holland, some nurseries offers both the clone and seed-raised plants of that clone. The clone is offered under its cultivar name (e.g., **'Midnight Star'**), while the seed-raised plants of this cultivar are offered as "ex **Midnight Star.**"

Agapanthus excelsus Besant = *A.* 'Excelsus'

Besant (1903) Flora and Sylva, 1.

Agapanthus 'Excelsus'

SYNONYM: *Agapanthus excelsus* Besant
Agapanthus umbellatus var. *excelsa* Lemoine
Agapanthus umbellatus var. *excelsus* Leichtlin

ORIGIN: known since 1878 when offered by Lemoine, France. Also offered by Mater, Leiden, The Netherlands, for 100 cents—one of the more expensive listed. Still offered by van Tubergen, The Netherlands, in 1926, but probably no longer in cultivation.
PEDUNCLE: 150–180 cm.
INFLORESCENCE: "immense."
FLOWER: violet-blue.
NOTE: late flowering.

Agapanthus 'Fafner' (Funnel Group)

ORIGIN: introduced by Gary Dunlop, Ballyrogan Nurseries, UK, known since 1999.
NAME: one of the giants in Wagner's *Das Rheingold*.
LEAF: evergreen, up to 42.5 cm long and 3 cm wide, a bit arching with apex bent, normal green, base green.
PEDUNCLE: 90 cm, green.
INFLORESCENCE: 25 cm across, over 100 flowers, globular, bud opens on 2 sides.
PEDICEL: green to bronze near the flower.
FLOWERBUD: pale violet-blue.
FLOWER: inside pale violet-blue (92C) with slightly darker margin (94C), midrib dark violet-blue (94A), outside violet-blue (94C), midrib dark violet-blue (94A), when out of flower purple, slightly upright to horizontal, up to 4 cm long, up to 4.25 cm across, stamens slightly exserted, anthers violet with yellow pollen.
NOTE: details supplied by Gary Dunlop.

NOTE: nuclear DNA content = 25.1 pg.
ILLUSTRATION: *color plate.*

Agapanthus 'Far Horizon' (Funnel Group)

ORIGIN: raised at NCCPG Bicton College, UK, selected by Dick Fulcher in 1993, and still in cultivation.
LEAF: evergreen.
PEDUNCLE: 70 cm.
INFLORESCENCE: 50–60 flowers, globular.
PEDICEL: green.
FLOWERBUD: upright, pale violet with cream towards the base and base slightly darker.
FLOWER: on both sides pale violet with midrib slightly darker, horizontal, 3.7 cm long (tube 1.2 cm long), stamens exserted, anthers brown.
NOTE: the flower colour gives a "pale blue grey" impression.
NOTE: details supplied by Dick Fulcher; some details from the Internet [5].

Agapanthus 'Fasolt' (Funnel Group)

ORIGIN: introduced by Gary Dunlop, Ballyrogan Nurseries, UK, known since 1999.
NAME: one of the giants in Wagner's *Das Rheingold.*
LEAF: evergreen, up to 35 cm long and 3 cm wide, upright, yellow-green, base green.
PEDUNCLE: 100 cm, green.
INFLORESCENCE: 22.5 cm across, over 120 flowers, globular, bud opens on 2 sides.
PEDICEL: green to violet near the flower.
FLOWERBUD: pale violet-blue.
FLOWER: inside pale violet-blue (95D), midrib dark violet-blue (95B), outside pale violet-blue (94D), midrib dark violet-blue (95B), when out of flower purple, slightly upright to horizontal, up to 5 cm long, up to 4.5 cm across, a couple or so stamens exserted, anthers violet with yellow pollen.
NOTE: details supplied by Gary Dunlop.
NOTE: nuclear DNA content = 25.6 pg.

Agapanthus 'Fin'

NOTE: name from the Internet [33].

Agapanthus 'Findlay's Blue' (Salver Group)

ORIGIN: known since 1972, UK, and still in cultivation.
LEAF: deciduous, 30–40 cm long and 1.5–2 cm wide, upright, dark green and slightly glaucous, base purple.
PEDUNCLE: 80–90 cm, green, round, rather weak.
INFLORESCENCE: 12 cm across, 30(–50) flowers, flat, bud opens on 1 side.
PEDICEL: green with some dull purple speckles.
FLOWERBUD: dark violet-blue, upright.
FLOWER: inside violet-blue (96DC) to dark violet-blue (96A), midrib darker (93A), margin slightly darker with purple tint, outside dark violet-blue with darker base,

when out of flower hardly any purple and only near the base, horizontal, 2.5 cm long (tube 1 cm long), 3 cm across, stamens exserted, anthers violet.
NOTE: most details from plants grown at Wisley.

Agapanthus 'Finnline'
ORIGIN: raised by Parva Plants, New Zealand, known since 2003.
NOTE: New Zealand Plant Variety Rights applied for, no. HOM161, on 26 March 2003, by Parva Plants.
NOTE: details from the Internet [36].

Agapanthus 'First Blue'
ORIGIN: known from The Netherlands in 1999; no further records.
NOTE: name from Allemand and Pionnat (2001).
NOTE: invalid name per the ICNCP-1995, art. 17.11.

Agapanthus flore pleno Besant = *A.* 'Flore Pleno'
Besant (1903) Flora and Sylva, 1.

Agapanthus 'Flore Pleno'
SYNONYM: *Agapanthus africanus* subsp. *umbellatus* var. *plenus* H.R. Wehrh.
Agapanthus africanus 'Flore Pleno'
Agapanthus flore pleno Besant
Agapanthus globosus 'Flora Plena'
Agapanthus orientalis var. *flore pleno* Synge
Agapanthus orientalis 'Flore Pleno'
Agapanthus praecox subsp. *orientalis* 'Flore Pleno'
Agapanthus praecox subsp. *praecox* 'Flore Pleno'
Agapanthus praecox subsp. *praecox* 'Plenus'
Agapanthus praecox 'Flore Pleno'
Agapanthus praecox 'Plenus'
Agapanthus umbellatus var. *flore pleno* Lemoine
Agapanthus umbellatus var. *plenus* Bonstedt

ERROR: 'Flora Plena', 'Flora Pleno', 'Flore Plena'

ORIGIN: known since 1878 in France, 1885 in England, and 1888 in The Netherlands. Most likely discovered in France, as E.-A. Carrière (1880) wrote concerning a plant grown by M. Godefroy-Lebeuf, Argenteuil, France, and accompanied his next mention of the same plant, in 1882, with a line drawing (shown here). The plant was listed by nearly all fin de siècle nurseries that offered *Agapanthus*, for a rather cheap price compared with other cultivars offered. Still in cultivation, especially in collections, and readily available commercially, at least not rare.
LEAF: evergreen, up to 25 cm long and 2 cm wide, arching, normal green, base green.
PEDUNCLE: 80 cm, green with pale purple speckles, round.
INFLORESCENCE: 18 cm across, 30 flowers.
PEDICEL: green with dull violet towards flower.

FLOWERBUD: violet-blue, upright.

FLOWER: on both sides pale violet-blue with purple tint, midrib darker, when out of flower more purple, horizontal, 4–4.5 cm long (tube 1–1.5 cm long), 4 cm across, stamens and pistil changed into segment-like staminodes.

NOTE: details from plants grown by Coen Jansen.

NOTE: nuclear DNA content = 25.4 pg.

ILLUSTRATION: *color plate*; drawing, Carrière (1882); photograph, Snoeijer (1998, 1999).

Figure 34 from Carrière (1882)

Agapanthus 'Floribundus' (Funnel Group)

SYNONYM: *Agapanthus praecox* subsp. *floribundus* Erhardt
Agapanthus praecox subsp. *orientalis* 'Floribundus'
Agapanthus praecox subsp. *praecox* 'Floribundus'
Agapanthus praecox var. *floribundus* Platt

ERROR: 'Floribunda'

ORIGIN: (selection of *A. praecox* subsp. *orientalis*) introduced from South Africa. Known since 1990, UK, and still in cultivation. Also offered as seed.

LEAF: evergreen, 30–40 cm long and 2.5 cm wide, upright, pale green, base green.

PEDUNCLE: 90–100 cm, green, round.

INFLORESCENCE: 22 cm across, 50 flowers, more or less globular.

PEDICEL: green with dull purple towards flower.

FLOWERBUD: violet-blue with purple tint, upright but quickly horizontal.

FLOWER: inside pale violet-blue (92BC) with purple tint, midrib violet-blue (92A), outside pale violet-blue with purple tint, midrib and base slightly darker, when out of flower more purple, horizontal, 4.5 cm long (tube 1.8 cm long), 4 cm across, stamens slightly exserted, anthers dark violet becoming brown.

NOTE: most details from plants grown by Coen Jansen. Because of seed propagation, better to regard this as a group of plants that look similar rather than a proper cultivar.

NOTE: invalid name per the ICNCP-1995, art. 17.9 and 17.11.

ILLUSTRATION: photograph, Snoeijer (1998).

Agapanthus 'Florist Select Blue'

SYNONYM: *Agapanthus orientalis* 'Florist Select Blue'

ORIGIN: (selection of *A. praecox* subsp. *orientalis*) known since 1990 when offered as seed.

FLOWER: violet-blue.

Agapanthus 'Florist Select White'

SYNONYM: *Agapanthus orientalis* 'Florist Select White'

ORIGIN: (selection of *A. praecox* subsp. *orientalis*) known since 1990 when offered as seed.

FLOWER: white.

Agapanthus 'Foremost's Variegated Nana' (Variegated Leaf Group)

ORIGIN: known since 2001, South Africa.

LEAF: variegated.

PEDUNCLE: 30 cm.

FLOWER: violet-blue.

NOTE: not so free-flowering.

NOTE: propagated by tissue culture.

NOTE: invalid name per the ICNCP-1995, art. 17.9.

Agapanthus 'Formality' (Funnel Group)

SYNONYM: *Agapanthus praecox* 'Formality'

ORIGIN: (selection of *A. praecox*) raised by Gary Dunlop, Ballyrogan Nurseries, UK, known since 1998.

LEAF: evergreen, 10–12 per shoot, up to 45 cm long and 4.5 cm wide, arching, normal green, leafbase slightly bronze.

PEDUNCLE: up to 110 cm, green.

INFLORESCENCE: 20 cm across, 70 flowers, more or less globular, bud opens on 1 side.

PEDICEL: green flushed purple.

FLOWERBUD: violet-blue with darker midrib and dark dull violet-blue base, upright but quickly horizontal.

FLOWER: inside pale violet-blue (97B) with margin slightly darker, midrib violet-blue (97A), outside pale violet-blue with midrib and base slightly darker, when out of flower with purple, horizontal, 4.5 cm long, 5.5 cm across, stamens not exserted, anthers dark purple-violet.

NOTE: details supplied by Gary Dunlop.

ILLUSTRATION: *color plate.*

Agapanthus 'Formosus'

SYNONYM: *Agapanthus umbellatus* var. *formosus* Mater

ORIGIN: known since 1892 when offered by J. Mater & Fils, Leiden, The Netherlands. The plant was offered for 90 cents—one of the more expensive cultivars listed. No description known.

Agapanthus FRAGRANT BLUE = *A.* 'Blue Brush'

Agapanthus FRAGRANT GLEN = *A.* 'Glen Avon'

Agapanthus FRAGRANT SNOW = *A.* 'Snow Cloud'

Agapanthus 'Franni' (Salver Group)

SYNONYM: *Agapanthus africanus* 'Albidus' pro parte
Agapanthus campanulatus subsp. *campanulatus* 'Albus'
Agapanthus campanulatus var. *albidus* Philip & Lord
Agapanthus campanulatus var. *albus* Philip & Lord
Agapanthus campanulatus 'Albidus' ex today's plants
Agapanthus campanulatus 'Albus' pro parte

ORIGIN: known for several decades in the UK under its synonyms. While this manuscript was being edited, I decided to give this plant a valid cultivar name because it has nothing to do with *A. campanulatus*; see chapter 2.

NAME: in honour of Franni, editor for Timber Press.

LEAF: deciduous, 30(–40) cm long and up to 2 cm wide, upright, pale green, base purple.

PEDUNCLE: 50–100 cm, green with a white bloom, round.

INFLORESCENCE: 6–11 cm across, 30–50 flowers, bud opens on 2 sides.

PEDICEL: green with purple tint.

FLOWERBUD: dull white with dull but pale purple apex, upright.

FLOWER: inside white, midrib transparent, outside white with apex yellowish-purple and greenish base, when out of flower white and rarely with pale purple apex, horizontal, 2–2.5 cm long (tube 0.8–1 cm long), 2 cm across, stamens slightly exserted, anthers black.

NOTE: details from plants grown at Beth Chatto Gardens as *A. campanulatus* 'Albidus'.

NOTE: also offered as seed, which are all kinds of different white-flowering hybrids (= RUBBISH).

NOTE: nuclear DNA content = 23.8 pg.

ILLUSTRATION: *color plate*; photograph, Phillips and Rix (1991 as *A. campanulatus* 'Albus') and Snoeijer (1998, 1999 as *A. campanulatus* 'Albidus').

AWARD: AM in 1960 as *A. campanulatus albus*.

Agapanthus 'Frederick Street Park'

SYNONYM: *Agapanthus* 'Frederick Street Pink'

ORIGIN: (seedling of '**Peter Pan**') introduced by Monterey Bay Nursery, California, USA, in 2000.

LEAF: evergreen, dark green.

PEDUNCLE: 25–30 cm.

FLOWER: "darker blue flowers than usually seen on plants sold as '**Peter Pan**'."

NOTE: most details from the Internet [20].

Agapanthus 'Frederick Street Pink' = *A.* '**Frederick Street Park**'

Agapanthus 'Fukuro-yae-murasaki'

ORIGIN: Japan, known since 2001 when offered by Kokkaen.

INFLORESCENCE: more or less globular.

FLOWER: violet-blue, usually more than 6 tepals.

NOTE: details supplied by Y. Aihara.

Agapanthus 'Fulsome' (Salver Group)

ORIGIN: raised by Gary Dunlop, Ballyrogan Nurseries, UK, named in 1998.

LEAF: deciduous.

PEDUNCLE: 100 cm.

INFLORESCENCE: 15 cm across, 200 flowers, globular.

FLOWER: dark violet-blue.

NOTE: details supplied by Gary Dunlop.

Agapanthus 'F.W. Moore'

ORIGIN: known since 1903, UK. Probably no longer in cultivation.

NAME: see '**Mooreanus**'.

FLOWER: "large blue."

Agapanthus 'Garden Blue' (Funnel Group)

ORIGIN: Japan, known since 2001 when offered by Sakata.

INFLORESCENCE: more or less globular.

FLOWER: pale violet-blue with dark violet-blue midrib.

NOTE: details supplied by Y. Aihara.

Agapanthus 'Garden King' (Funnel Group)

ORIGIN: Japan, known since 1998 when offered by Sakata, still in cultivation.

PEDUNCLE: 60 cm.

INFLORESCENCE: flat, of all the base bostryces one pedicel is elongated, which gives the impression of an extra row of smaller inflorescence nicely arranged around the main inflorescence; this elongated pedicel is as long as or slightly longer than the main inflorescence.

FLOWER: violet-blue.

NOTE: details supplied by Y. Aihara.

Agapanthus 'Garden Queen'

ORIGIN: Japan, known since 2001 when offered by Komoriya Nursery Ltd.

LEAF: evergreen.

PEDUNCLE: 70 cm.

FLOWER: very pale purple.

NOTE: details from the Internet [25].

Agapanthus 'Garden White' (Funnel Group)

ORIGIN: Japan, known since 2001 when offered by Sakata.

INFLORESCENCE: flat.

FLOWER: pure white, stamens exserted, anthers yellow.

NOTE: details supplied by Y. Aihara.

Agapanthus 'Gary Form'

SYNONYM: *Agapanthus campanulatus* 'Gary Form'

ORIGIN: known since 1997, Belgium, obtained from Gary Dunlop, Ballyrogan Nurseries, UK, and still in cultivation.

LEAF: deciduous.

NOTE: invalid name per the ICNCP-1995, art. 17.15.

Agapanthus 'Gayle's Lilac' (Funnel Group)

ORIGIN: introduced in New Zealand, known since 1997, and still in cultivation.

LEAF: evergreen, narrow.

PEDUNCLE: 40–50 cm.

INFLORESCENCE: 30–40 flowers.

FLOWER: inside very pale violet to white, margin pale violet, midrib violet, horizontal, stamens exserted, anthers purple with yellow pollen.

NOTE: invalid name per the ICNCP-1995, art. 17.13.

Agapanthus 'Geagold' (Variegated Leaf Group)

ORIGIN: raised by I.R. Gear, Heritage Horticulture, New Zealand, known since 1995, and still in cultivation.

LEAF: evergreen, green with a yellow margin, arching.

PEDUNCLE: 70 cm.

INFLORESCENCE: 25 flowers.

FLOWER: violet-blue.

NOTE: New Zealand Plant Variety Rights applied for, no. HOM054, on 5 October 1995, by I.R. Gear, Heritage Horticulture, New Zealand.

NOTE: some details from the Internet [36].

Agapanthus 'Gem'

> ORIGIN: raised at NCCPG Bicton College, UK, selected by Dick Fulcher in 1993, and still in cultivation.
> LEAF: evergreen.
> PEDUNCLE: 100 cm.
> FLOWER: "mid to dark blue," 3.8 cm long (tube 0.8 cm long).
> NOTE: details supplied by Dick Fulcher.

Agapanthus **'Getty White'** (Funnel Group)

> SYNONYM: *Agapanthus africanus* 'Getty White'
> *Agapanthus praecox* subsp. *praecox* 'Getty White'
> *Agapanthus praecox* 'Getty White'
>
> ORIGIN: introduced in the USA, known since 1990 in the UK when offered as seed. Still in cultivation.
> LEAF: evergreen, arching, dark green.
> PEDUNCLE: (25–)50 cm.
> INFLORESCENCE: "large," 50–80 flowers, globular.
> FLOWER: white.
> NOTE: some details from the Internet [21] and [31].

Agapanthus 'Giant Blue'

> SYNONYM: *Agapanthus praecox* 'Giant Blue'
>
> ORIGIN: known since 1995, Kirstenbosch National Botanical Garden, South Africa.
> NOTE: invalid name per the ICNCP-1995, art. 17.11.
> NOTE: plants offered in the UK under this name are best regarded as seed-raised RUBBISH.

Agapanthus 'Giant Hybrids' = *A.* RUBBISH

> NOTE: invalid name per the ICNCP-1995, art. 17.16.

Agapanthus Giant Hybrids = *A.* RUBBISH

Agapanthus gigantea Erhardt (1995) PPP Index. nom.nud.

Agapanthus gigantea 'Albus' = *A.* 'Giganteus Albus'

Agapanthus giganteus = **A.** **'Giganteus'**

> Kolb & Weiss (1882) Dr. Neubert's Deutsches Garten-Magazin.
> Leichtlin (1884) catalogue.
> Besant (1903) Flora and Sylva, 1.

Agapanthus **'Giganteus'** (Funnel Group)

> SYNONYM: *Agapanthus africanus* subsp. *umbellatus* var. *giganteus* H.R. Wehrh.
> *Agapanthus giganteus* Kolb & Weiss
> *Agapanthus orientalis* var. *giganteus* Synge

Agapanthus praecox subsp. *praecox* 'Giganteus'
Agapanthus praecox 'Giganteus'
Agapanthus umbellatus var. *giganteus* Lemoine

ORIGIN: (probably a selection of *A. praecox*) introduced by Frœbel, Zurich, Switzerland, known since 1880. The name is still referred to, but it is most unlikely the true plant is still in cultivation.
LEAF: evergreen, 60–65 cm long and up to 5.5 cm wide.
PEDUNCLE: 110–125 cm.
INFLORESCENCE: "huge," 150–200 flowers.
FLOWERBUD: dark violet-blue.
FLOWER: violet-blue, "Gentian-blue."

Agapanthus 'Giganteus Albus' (Funnel Group)

SYNONYM: *Agapanthus gigantea* 'Albus'

ORIGIN: known since 1995; no further records.
PEDUNCLE: 130 cm, green.
INFLORESCENCE: 100 flowers, globular.
PEDICEL: green.
FLOWERBUD: upright, white with cream base.
FLOWER: on both sides white, when out of flower white, margin on outer segments short wavy, horizontal, stamens exserted, anthers yellow.
NOTE: most details supplied by Dick Fulcher.
NOTE: invalid name per the ICNCP-1995, art. 17.9 and 17.11.

Agapanthus 'Glacier Stream' (Trumpet Group)

ORIGIN: introduced by Maas & van Stein, Hillegom, The Netherlands. Grown for many years as "WitC," named **'Glacier Stream'** in 1995. Still in cultivation.
LEAF: more or less deciduous, 40–50 cm long and 2 cm wide, upright, normal green and slightly glaucous, apex paler, base purple.
PEDUNCLE: 100 cm, green with purple towards inflorescence, flat.
INFLORESCENCE: 15 cm across, 50–60 flowers, more or less globular, bud opens on 1 side.
PEDICEL: dull greenish-purple.
FLOWERBUD: white with dull purple apex, upright.
FLOWER: inside white, transparent midrib on which the violet colour of the outside is visible, outside white with some violet at apex and base, when out of flower brownish-white with purple apex, horizontal, 3 cm long (tube 1 cm long), 3 cm across, stamens not exserted, anthers black with orange-brown pollen.
NOTE: details from plants grown by Maas & van Stein.
NOTE: nuclear DNA content = 23.9 pg.
ILLUSTRATION: *color plate.*

Agapanthus 'Glamis Castle'

ORIGIN: raised by The Crown Estate, Windsor, UK, introduced in 1975, and still in cultivation.

NAME: after the royal estate in Scotland.
LEAF: deciduous.
FLOWER: white.

Agapanthus 'Glen Avon' (Funnel Group)

ERROR: 'Glenavon'

TRADE NAME: FRAGRANT GLEN

ORIGIN: raised by A.D. Gray, Glen Avon, New Plymouth, New Zealand, known since 1997, and still in cultivation.
LEAF: evergreen, rather wide and glaucous.
PEDUNCLE: 100 cm.
INFLORESCENCE: 20 cm across, "up to 350 flowers," globular.
FLOWER: usually with 10 tepals, inside violet-blue with darker midrib, stamens not exserted.
NOTE: New Zealand Plant Variety Rights applied for and granted, no. HOM066, on 24 January 1997, by Lifetech Laboratories Ltd, New Zealand, expires 8 March 2020.
NOTE: introduced, for its fragrance, as 'Fragrant Glen', a name that was altered when the cultivar proved not to be so fragrant. It remains unclear which name was published first; with the PVR office in New Zealand, I use the name 'Glen Avon'.
NOTE: according to a sales leaflet sent together with the June 2003 issue of *The Garden*, the cultivar has Plant Variety Right as 'Glenavon', but this is not yet recorded on the Internet [35]. The plant is, however, widely sold in the UK as 'Glenavon'.
NOTE: some details from the Internet [19], [35], and [36].

Agapanthus globosus Bull ex Boom = *A.* 'Globosus'

Lemoine (1909) catalogue. nom.nud.
van Tubergen (1936, 1950) Catalogue. nom.nud.
Bull ex Boom (1950) Flora der gekweekte kruidachtige gewassen.

Agapanthus globosus 'Flora Plena' = *A.* 'Flore Pleno'

J.N. Giridlian's Oakhurst Gardens (1962) catalogue.

Agapanthus 'Globosus' (Salver Group)

SYNONYM: *Agapanthus africanus* subsp. *minor* var. *globosus* H.R. Wehrh.
Agapanthus africanus var. *globosus* (Bull) Bail. ex Boom
Agapanthus globosus Bull ex Boom
Agapanthus minor var. *globosus* Bonstedt
Agapanthus umbellatus var. *globosus* Lemoine

ORIGIN: (probably a selection of *A. campanulatus*) known since 1905, when shown by Messrs William Bull & Sons, Chelsea, UK. The plant was sent to Bull by a correspondent in the Orange River Colony. Offered by Lemoine in 1909 and as late as 1952 by van Tubergen. Sometimes referred to but probably no longer in cultivation.
LEAF: deciduous.
PEDUNCLE: very long.

INFLORESCENCE: many-flowered, globular.

PEDICEL: very short.

FLOWER: violet-blue with white base, 2.5 cm across.

NOTE: very free-flowering.

ILLUSTRATION: drawing, Gardeners' Chronicle Editor (1905 as *A. umbellatus globosus*).

Agapanthus 'Glockenturm'

SYNONYM: *Agapanthus campanulatus* 'Glockenturm'

ORIGIN: Germany.

NAME: German, "bell-tower."

FLOWER: violet-blue.

NOTE: registered in 1983.

Agapanthus 'Golden Rule' (Variegated Leaf Group)

ORIGIN: raised by J.C. Archibald, introduced by Buckshaw Gardens, UK. Known since 1988 and still in cultivation.

LEAF: deciduous, 15 cm long and up to 0.8 cm wide, upright, pale green with thin cream-yellow stripes especially along the margin, base green.

PEDUNCLE: 40–70 cm, green with purple towards inflorescence, round.

INFLORESCENCE: 8 cm across, 30 flowers.

PEDICEL: violet-purple.

FLOWERBUD: violet-blue, upright.

FLOWER: violet-blue on both sides, when out of flower with purple, horizontal to slightly nodding, 2.5 cm long (tube 1 cm long), 2 cm across.

NOTE: details from plants grown by Coen Jansen.

Agapanthus 'Goldfinger' (Variegated Leaf Group)

ERROR: 'Gold Finger'

ORIGIN: raised by Kees Duivenvoorde, The Netherlands, in 1990. Offered since 2001 by Ignace van Doorslaer, Belgium.

LEAF: more or less evergreen, up to 20 cm long and 0.9 cm wide, arching to almost flat on the soil, canaliculate, pale green with yellow stripes and usually with a rather wide yellow margin, base violet.

NOTE: details from plants grown by Duivenvoorde.

NOTE: the plant has never flowered.

NOTE: nuclear DNA content = 23.4 pg.

ILLUSTRATION: *color plate*.

Agapanthus 'Goliath' (Funnel Group)

ORIGIN: (selection of **A. praecox** subsp. **orientalis**) origin unknown but most likely Dutch. Known since 1960, when grown by Simon de Goede NV, Elst, The Netherlands, and still in cultivation.

LEAF: evergreen, 30–60 cm long, up to 3.8 cm wide, arching, dark glossy green, base green.

PEDUNCLE: 60–80 cm, green and slightly glaucous, round.

INFLORESCENCE: up to 20 cm across, 70–100 flowers, globular, bud opens on 1 side.

PEDICEL: green and heavily flushed purple towards flower.

FLOWERBUD: violet-blue, upright.

FLOWER: inside pale violet-blue (98D), margin just slightly darker and purple blush, midrib distinctly dark violet-blue (95B), outside violet-blue with purple blush and midrib and base slightly darker, when out of flower purple, upright and horizontal, 5 cm long (tube 1.5 cm long), 5.5 cm across, stamens slightly exserted, anthers dark violet.

NOTE: most details from CNB show garden, Heemstede.

NOTE: seed-propagated and so better to regard this as a group of plants that look similar rather than a proper cultivar.

ILLUSTRATION: drawing, Gillissen (1982); photograph, Snoeijer (1998).

ILLUSTRATION: *color plate.*

AWARD: GV in 1960.

Agapanthus gracilis F.M. Leight. = *A. caulescens* subsp. *gracilis* F.M. Leight.

F.M. Leight. (1945) Journal of South African Botany.

Agapanthus 'Graskop' (Tubular Group)

SYNONYM: *Agapanthus inapertus* subsp. *pendulus* 'Graskop'
Agapanthus inapertus 'Graskop'

ERROR: 'Grasskop'

ORIGIN: (selection of *A. inapertus* subsp. *pendulus*) from Graskop, northeast Transvaal. Introduced by Kirstenbosch National Botanical Garden, South Africa. Known since 1987 and still in cultivation.

LEAF: deciduous, up to 40 cm long and 3.8 cm wide, upright with upper half arching, greenish-blue and glaucous, base green.

PEDUNCLE: 80–150 cm, green and strongly glaucous, round.

INFLORESCENCE: up to 12 cm across, 30–40 flowers, drooping.

PEDICEL: pale green flushed purple.

FLOWERBUD: upright but quickly nodding, very dark violet-blue with green at the base.

FLOWER: inside pale violet-blue with dark margin, midrib violet-blue, outside dark violet-blue (89B) with purple tint, midrib slightly darker with distinctly purple tint and base a bit green, drooping vertically, up to 4.7 cm long (tube 2.6 cm), 1.5 cm across, stamens as long as the flower or just visible, anthers black.

NOTE: most details from a plant grown by Coen Jansen.

NOTE: sometimes offered as seed, and so differences in flower colour, especially paler-coloured forms, appear (see 'Graskopje'). Also propagated by tissue culture (the true clone, it is hoped).

ILLUSTRATION: *color plate*; drawing, du Plessis and Duncan (1989); photograph, Duncan (1985 as *A. inapertus* subsp. *pendulus* 'Graskop', 1998 as *A. inapertus* subsp. *pendulus* 'Graskop').

Agapanthus 'Graskopje' (Tubular Group)

> SYNONYM: *Agapanthus inapertus* 'Graskopje'

ORIGIN: introduced by Hans Kramer, De Hessenhof nursery, The Netherlands, in 2002 as a seedling of '**Graskop**'.
FLOWER: violet-blue but slightly variable.

Agapanthus 'Grey' = *A.* '**Windsor Grey**'

Agapanthus 'Grey Blue'

ORIGIN: known since 2002 in the collection of Ignace van Doorslaer, Belgium, but no description yet published.
NOTE: invalid name per the ICNCP-1995, art. 17.11.

Agapanthus '**Grey Pearl**'

> SYNONYM: *Agapanthus praecox* 'Grey Pearl'

ORIGIN: known since 1996, UK, offered as seed; no further records.

Agapanthus '**Guilfoyle**' (Funnel Group)

> SYNONYM: *Agapanthus praecox* 'Guilfoyle'

ORIGIN: known since 2001 when offered by Lambley, Australia.
LEAF: evergreen, more or less upright, dark green.
PEDUNCLE: usually with a secondary peduncle.
FLOWER: violet-blue.
NOTE: details from the Internet [24].

Agapanthus '**Hadspen**'

ORIGIN: known since 1998, UK (Pope 1999).
FLOWER: pale violet-blue, slightly nodding.

Agapanthus '**Hardingsdale**' (Salver Group)

> SYNONYM: *Agapanthus campanulatus* subsp. *campanulatus* 'Hardinsdale'
> *Agapanthus campanulatus* 'Hardinsdale'

ORIGIN: (selection of *A. campanulatus*) from the Hardingsdale farm near Pietermaritzburg, Natal, introduced by Kirstenbosch National Botanical Garden, South Africa. Known since 1989.
LEAF: deciduous, pale green, upright.
PEDUNCLE: 100–140 cm, green.
FLOWER: violet-blue with darker midrib (93C), stamens not exserted.
ILLUSTRATION: photograph, Duncan (1998 as *A. campanulatus* subsp. *campanulatus* 'Hardingsdale').

Agapanthus Hardy Hybrid = *A.* RUBBISH

ORIGIN: known since 1987 when offered by Great Dixter Nurseries, UK.

Agapanthus 'Harvest Blue'

ORIGIN: raised by Dick Fulcher, Pine Cottage Plants, UK, named in 1998, and still in cultivation.
LEAF: evergreen.
PEDUNCLE: 80–90 cm.
INFLORESCENCE: 18 cm across, flat.
PEDICEL: green with dark violet speckles.
FLOWER: violet-blue, base darker.
NOTE: very late flowering, into October in the UK.
NOTE: details supplied by Dick Fulcher.

Agapanthus 'Hazy Days'

ORIGIN: known since 1997 when offered by Diacks, New Zealand, and still in cultivation.
PEDUNCLE: up to 150 cm.
FLOWER: "soft lavender blue."

Agapanthus 'H.C. Hart'

ORIGIN: known since 1903, UK.
NAME: in honour of Irish naturalist Henry Chichester Hart (1847–1908), who collected plants on the British Polar Expedition 1875–76 and in Palestine 1883–84.
FLOWER: violet-blue.
NOTE: the plant was described by Besant (1903) as "similar but dwarfer habit," compared with 'F.W. Moore'.

Agapanthus 'Headbourne A' = *A.* RUBBISH

Agapanthus 'Headbourne Blue' = *A.* RUBBISH

Agapanthus 'Headbourne White' = *A.* RUBBISH

Agapanthus Headbourne Hybrids ex today's plants = *A.* RUBBISH

Agapanthus Headbourne Hybrids ex Lewis Palmer

SYNONYM: *Agapanthus* Headbourne Worthy Hybrids
ORIGIN: a group of plants raised by Lewis Palmer, Winchester, Hantshire, UK, who requested seed after a visit to the Kirstenbosch National Botanical Garden, South Africa. He found that all 300 of the seedlings that resulted appeared to be hybrids. Palmer selected and named many plants during the 1950s and 1960s. The parents could not be recovered but seem to be at least *A. campanulatus*, and probably *A. inapertus* and *A. praecox*. Palmer also himself collected seeds in South Africa in 1963 (see *A. africanus* subsp. *walshii*).
NAME: after Lewis Palmer's garden.
NOTE: according to Hanneke van Dijk (1996), Palmer's original plants, introduced by him as Headbourne Hybrids, are still growing in the gardens of Howick Hall,

Alnwick, Northumberland, UK. The Hall is now owned by the Howick Trustees Ltd and managed by Lord Howick, son of Lady Mary Howick; Lewis Palmer was the brother of Lady Grey, Lady Mary Howick's mother.

NOTE: many different selections are offered in the trade, both as plants and as seed—which last suggests that plants are not necessarily derived from Palmer's introductions, either directly or indirectly. With no selection whatsoever, every manner of seed-propagated RUBBISH is sold as Headbourne Hybrids, simply because the name is well known and so sells.

Agapanthus Headbourne Worthy Hybrids = *A.* Headbourne Hybrids

Agapanthus 'Hekiun' (Salver Group)

ORIGIN: raised and introduced in Japan, known since 1999, and still in cultivation.
INFLORESCENCE: flat.
FLOWER: pale violet-blue with midrib dark violet-blue.
NOTE: some details from the Internet [25].

Agapanthus 'Helen' (Salver Group)

ORIGIN: raised by Gary Dunlop, Ballyrogan Nurseries, UK, introduced in 2001.
LEAF: deciduous, 45 cm long and 3 cm wide, arching, yellowish-green, base green.
PEDUNCLE: 100 cm, green.
INFLORESCENCE: 16 cm across, 70 flowers, bud opens on 2 sides.
PEDICEL: green.
FLOWER: inside pale violet-blue (97B) to white at the base, outside pale violet-blue (97B flushed 97A), horizontal, up to 2.5 cm long, 3.5 cm across, anthers yellow.
NOTE: details supplied by Gary Dunlop.
NOTE: nuclear DNA content = 22.5 pg.

Agapanthus 'Helsinki' (Trumpet Group)

ORIGIN: ('**Blue Triumphator**' × '**Dr Brouwer**') raised by Kees Duivenvoorde, introduced in 2002.
NAME: after the capital of Finland.
LEAF: deciduous, up to 50 cm long and 2 cm wide, upright, normal green and glaucous, base green.
PEDUNCLE: 100–125 cm, green and glaucous, rather sturdy, more or less round.
INFLORESCENCE: 15–20 cm across, 30–60 flowers, more or less flat, bud opens on 2 sides.
PEDICEL: green.
FLOWERBUD: violet-blue with paler stripes, upright.
FLOWER: inside pale violet-blue with margin slightly darker and with purple tint, midrib dark violet-blue, outside pale violet-blue, midrib dark violet-blue and base violet-blue, when out of flower purple with violet-blue base, horizontal, 3.5–3.8 cm long (tube 1.7 cm long), 3 cm across, stamens exserted, anthers violet-blue with yellow pollen.
NOTE: details from plants grown by Duivenvoorde.

Agapanthus 'Henderson's White'

ORIGIN: known since 2001 when offered by San Marcos Growers, California, USA.
LEAF: evergreen.
FLOWER: white.
NOTE: details from the Internet [32].

Agapanthus Heronswood Hybrids => see note under *A.* RUBBISH

ORIGIN: seedling mixture introduced and offered by Heronswood Nursery, Washington, USA.

Agapanthus 'Hinag' (Variegated Leaf Group)

SYNONYM: *Agapanthus africanus* 'Hinag'

TRADE NAME: SUMMER GOLD

ORIGIN: (seedling of **'Peter Pan'** pollinated by unknown parent, probably a variegated plant) raised by Ramon Alaniz Mendoza, California, USA, in 1986. Introduced by Hines Horticulture, also of California, and still in cultivation.
LEAF: evergreen, up to 42 cm long and 2 cm wide, upright but later arching, green with yellow (11AB) stripes and yellow (11BC) margin.
PEDUNCLE: 45–60 cm, green with yellow.
INFLORESCENCE: 10.5 cm across, up to 50 flowers.
PEDICEL: yellow.
FLOWER: inside violet-blue (92B) with darker midrib (92A), 3 cm long, 3.5 cm across, stamens not exserted, anthers yellow.
NOTE: details from the Internet [17] and some from [36].
NOTE: rather free-flowering for a variegated cultivar.
NOTE: Internet [17] suggests a relation to *A. africanus*, but I see no link to this species.
NOTE: New Zealand Plant Variety Rights applied for, no. HOM138, on 23 November 2001, by A.J. Park, Wellington, New Zealand.

Agapanthus 'Holbeach' (Funnel Group)

ORIGIN: raised by Kees Duivenvoorde, Beverwijk, The Netherlands, introduced in 1997.
NAME: after the city in England.
LEAF: deciduous.
PEDUNCLE: 40 cm, green and just a bit violet speckled, rather sturdy, flat.
INFLORESCENCE: 14 cm across, 50 flowers, flat, bud opens on 2 sides and remains attached.
PEDICEL: green and heavily speckled violet-blue.
FLOWERBUD: violet-blue, paler base with a bit of green, later violet-blue with darker midrib, upright.
FLOWER: inside very pale violet-blue (97BC) with purple tint towards apex, midrib dark violet-blue (93C) and rather wide, outside pale violet-blue (92C), midrib and base dark violet-blue (93A), margin slightly wavy, when out of flower dark purple

with violet-blue base, horizontal, 3.2 cm long (tube 0.9 cm long), 4 cm across, stamens not exserted, anthers violet-blue with yellow pollen.
NOTE: details from plants grown by Duivenvoorde.
NOTE: the first flowers tend to have (7–)8 tepals.
NOTE: nuclear DNA content = 23.8 pg.
ILLUSTRATION: *color plate.*

Agapanthus 'Holbrook'

ORIGIN: raised by Sampford Shrubs, UK. Introduced in 1993, and still in cultivation.
NAME: after the hill in Devon where the nursery is located.
LEAF: deciduous, slightly glaucous.
PEDUNCLE: 75–80 cm.
FLOWER: dark violet-blue.

Agapanthus hollandii F.M. Leight. = *A. inapertus* subsp. *hollandii* F.M. Leight.

F.M. Leight. (1934) South African Gardening, Vol. XXIV, 82.

Agapanthus 'Huntington Blue' (Funnel Group)

ORIGIN: introduced in the USA, known since 1998.
PEDUNCLE: 75–90 cm.
FLOWER: violet-blue.
NOTE: details from the Internet [6].

Agapanthus hybrid = *A*. RUBBISH

Agapanthus hybrida Scheubel ex A. Worsley (1913) J. Roy. Hort. Soc.

NOTE: Worsley (1913) "A fertile hybrid between *Agapanthus umbellatus* and *Agapanthus* 'Mooreanus', and fairly equipoised between them. It is deciduous, and is heavily coloured blue or purple on the short stem."

Agapanthus hybrid miniature = *A*. RUBBISH

Agapanthus hybrids = *A*. RUBBISH

Agapanthus hybrids new = *A*. RUBBISH

Agapanthus hybrids white = *A*. RUBBISH

Agapanthus 'Hydon Mist' (Salver Group)

ORIGIN: introduced by Hydon Nurseries, UK. Known since 1990 and still in cultivation.
LEAF: deciduous, up to 40 cm long and 1.8 cm wide, upright, normal green, base with purple.
PEDUNCLE: 80–100 cm, green and slightly glaucous, round.
INFLORESCENCE: 15 cm across, 40–50 flowers, bud opens on 1 side.
PEDICEL: green with dull purple speckles.

FLOWERBUD: dark violet-blue, upright.

FLOWER: inside violet-blue, midrib darker (93B), margin violet-blue (93C) with purple tint, outside violet-blue with base slightly darker, when out of flower extremely purple coloured, horizontal, 3 cm long (tube 1 cm long), 3.5 cm across.

NOTE: details from plants grown at Hydon Nurseries.

Agapanthus 'Hyères' = *A.* '**Bleu Méoni**'

Agapanthus 'Ice Blue Star'

ORIGIN: raised and introduced by Raveningham Gardens, UK, known since 1999.
LEAF: deciduous.
PEDUNCLE: 100 cm.
FLOWER: pale violet-blue.
NOTE: invalid name per the ICNCP-1995, art. 17.13.

Agapanthus '**Ice Crystal**'

ORIGIN: Australia, known since 2001; no further records.

Agapanthus '**Ice Lolly**' (Funnel Group)

ORIGIN: introduced by Maas & van Stein, Hillegom, The Netherlands. Grown for many years as no. 57a, named '**Ice Lolly**' in 1995, and still in cultivation.
LEAF: deciduous, 30–40 cm long and 2.5 cm wide, upright, pale green and slightly glaucous, base green.
PEDUNCLE: 80–100 cm, green and slightly glaucous, round.
INFLORESCENCE: 18 cm across, 80 flowers, more or less globular, bud opens on 1 side.
PEDICEL: green.
FLOWERBUD: white with yellow apex, upright.
FLOWER: inside white, midrib transparent to yellowish, outside white, midrib near apex pale yellow, when out of flower white, horizontal, 3(–3.5) cm long (tube 1.2 cm long), 3.5–4 cm across, stamens not exserted, anthers yellow.
NOTE: details from plants grown by Maas & van Stein.
NOTE: nuclear DNA content = 24.5 pg.
ILLUSTRATION: *color plate.*

Agapanthus '**Ice Maiden**'

ORIGIN: collected as an unnamed plant from New Zealand and introduced by Max Schleipfer, Kakteen- und Staudengärtnerei, Germany, in 1992. Still in cultivation.
FLOWER: white with pale violet-blue tint.

Agapanthus '**Ice Queen**' (Trumpet Group)

ORIGIN: offered by Mill House Nursery, Akaroa, New Zealand, who obtained the plant from Bay Bloom Nurseries, Tauranga, New Zealand, in November 1994.
PEDUNCLE: 80–150 cm.
INFLORESCENCE: flat.

PEDICEL: purple.

FLOWER: inside white, outside white, midrib near the apex violet, when out of flower purple, anthers yellow.

NOTE: details supplied by Lucie Wenmakers, Mill House Nursery.

Agapanthus 'Imaru' = *A.* 'Timaru'

Agapanthus 'Ile d'Yeu'

ORIGIN: (selection of **'Blue Baby'**) selected by J.-Y. Poiroux, Ets Horticole, France, known since 1998.

NAME: after the island off the coast of Vendée, France.

LEAF: evergreen.

FLOWER: violet-blue.

Agapanthus inapertus Beauv. ex F.M. Leight. (1965) J. South African Bot., Suppl.

SYNONYM: *Agapanthus africanus* subsp. *insignis* (Bull) H.R. Wehrh.

DISTRIBUTION: southeastern Transvaal and northwestern Swaziland to north of Transvaal; eastern Drakensberg, Zoutpansberg, Lydenburg, and Piet Retief. In open grassland and forest clearings and along streams, in high rainfall areas.

LEAF: deciduous, from a short leek-like stem, 6–8 per shoot, 30–50(–70) cm long and 2–3(–6) cm wide, more or less upright, pale green and glaucous, base green or purple, apex acute.

PEDUNCLE: (30–)60–200 cm, usually green.

INFLORESCENCE: 20–40(–80) flowers, 6–12.5 cm across, drooping.

PEDICEL: 2–5.5 cm long, first upright later more bent to drooping, green or green flushed purple.

FLOWER: pale violet-blue to dark violet-blue or rarely white (in cultivation => *A. inapertus* 'Albus' and 'White'), 2.5–5 cm long, 1–1.5 cm across, hanging downwards, stamens as long as the flower, pollen yellow, style slightly longer than the flowers.

FLOWERING TIME: December into March.

NOTE: according to Onderstall (1984), *A. inapertus* is a protected species.

NOTE: nuclear DNA content = 25.16 pg.

ILLUSTRATION: drawing, Beauverd (1910), Letty (1962), Duncan (1985), and Gillissen (1982); photograph, Onderstall (1984), Redgrove (1991), Sheat and Schofield (1995), Brickell (1996), Elsa Pooley (1998), Wray (1998a), Snoeijer (1999, 2000), Dunlop (2000), Fulcher (2000), van Wyk (2000), and Jansen (2002).

Agapanthus inapertus subsp. *hollandii* F.M. Leight. (1965) J. South African Bot., Suppl.

SYNONYM: *Agapanthus hollandii* F.M. Leight.

DISTRIBUTION: east Transvaal; Lydenburg, in grassland and among rocks.

NAME: in honour of Holland, who collected the type specimen at Alkmaar, Lydenburg.

FLOWER: "magenta-blue," segments shorter that the tube, more spreading compared with subsp. *inapertus* and subsp. *pendulus.*
NOTE: also offered as seed.
ILLUSTRATION: drawing, Leighton (1965); photograph, Pienaar (1987), Phillips and Rix (1991), and Fulcher (2000).

Agapanthus inapertus subsp. *hollandii* 'Lydenburg' = *A.* 'Lydenburg'

Agapanthus inapertus subsp. *hollandii* 'Sky' =

= pro parte = *A.* 'Sky'
= pro parte = *A.* 'Sky Blue'

Agapanthus inapertus subsp. *hollandii* 'Sky Blue' = *A.* 'Sky Blue'

Agapanthus inapertus subsp. **inapertus** Beauv. (1910) Bull. Soc. Bot. Geneve.

DISTRIBUTION: Transvaal; Letaba, Lydenburg, and Pietersburg.
PEDICEL: 4–5 cm long.
FLOWER: violet-blue or rarely white (in cultivation => 'Albus' and 'White'), 4–5 cm long, segments shorter than the tube, segments not or slightly spreading, stamens as long as the flowers.
NOTE: the drawing in Dyer (1966b) by Cythna Letty was produced from specimens collected by Dr I.B. Pole Evans at Pietersburg in 1931.
ILLUSTRATION: *color plate*; drawing, Leighton (1965), which is reproduced in Snoeijer (1998) and Dyer (1966b).

Agapanthus inapertus subsp. *inapertus* 'Albus' = *A. inapertus* 'Albus'

Agapanthus inapertus subsp. *inapertus* 'Cambridge Blue' = *A.* **'Cambridge Blue'**

Agapanthus inapertus subsp. *inapertus* 'Cyan' = *A.* 'Cyan'

Agapanthus inapertus subsp. *inapertus* 'White' = *A.* 'White'

Agapanthus inapertus subsp. *inapertus* white = *A.* 'White'

Agapanthus inapertus subsp. **intermedius** F.M. Leight. (1965) J. South African Bot., Suppl.

SYNONYM: *Agapanthus dyeri* F.M. Leight.

DISTRIBUTION: Transvaal; in Namaachas on the border between Transvaal and southern Mozambique, Blouberg, Carolina, Ermelo, Standerton, Volksrust, and Wakkerstroom. Swaziland; Mbabane. Growing throughout the complete distribution of the species, in grassy and rocky mountainsides and along streams.
FLOWER: violet-blue, 2.5–4.5 cm long, tube 1.3 cm long to as long as segments, segments not or hardly spreading.
NOTE: the plate in Duncan (1993 as *A. dyeri*) by Gillian Condy was from material collected at the Blouberg (see under *A. dyeri*).
NOTE: rather variable in leaf shape and amount of flowers in the inflorescence.

ILLUSTRATION: drawing, Leighton (1965 also as *A. dyeri*) and Duncan (1993 as *A. dyeri*, 1998 as *A. dyeri*); photograph, Leighton (1965 as *A. dyeri*), which is reproduced in Snoeijer (1998), Phillips and Rix (1991 also as *A. dyeri*), and Duncan (1993 as *A. dyeri*).

Agapanthus inapertus subsp. *intermedius* 'Wolkberg' =

   = pro parte = *A.* '**Wolkberg**' (Tubular Group)
   = pro parte = *A.* 'Wolkberg' (Salver Group)

Agapanthus inapertus subsp. *parviflorus* F.M. Leight. (1965) J. South African Bot., Suppl.

DISTRIBUTION: Transvaal; Lydenburg, in grassland, between boulders.
FLOWER: blue or purple, 2.3–3.5 cm long, segments not or hardly spreading and rather small.
NOTE: in the late 1980s, the Hortus Botanicus Amsterdam gave me a shoot of a plant labelled *A. inapertus*. The original plant came from France. A couple of years ago I sent a shoot to Gary Dunlop, who identified it as subsp. *parviflorus*. The description is as follows.
LEAF: deciduous, 8 per shoot, up to 60 cm long and 2.5 cm wide, upright, normal green and slightly glaucous, base green.
PEDUNCLE: 100 cm, green flushed bronze towards the inflorescence, slightly glaucous.
INFLORESCENCE: 7 cm across, 30–60 flowers, bud opens on 1 side.
PEDICEL: green.
FLOWER: inside very pale violet-blue (92C) with margin and midrib dark violet-blue (93A), outside pale violet-blue (93D/92B), drooping, up to 2.5 cm long, 1.25 cm across.

Agapanthus inapertus subsp. *pendulus* (L. Bol.) F.M. Leight. (1965) J. South African Bot., Suppl.

   SYNONYM: *Agapanthus inapertus* Beauv. ex Sealy pro parte
   Agapanthus inapertus 'Pendula'
   Agapanthus 'Pendulinus'
   Agapanthus pendulus L. Bol.

DISTRIBUTION: Transvaal; Belfast, Dullstroom, and Lydenburg, in grassland and rocky slopes, up to 2000 m.
LEAF: upright, pale yellow-green, purple base.
PEDUNCLE: up to 160 cm, green flushed bronze towards the inflorescence.
INFLORESCENCE: 10 cm across, 40 flowers, drooping.
PEDICEL: bronze.
FLOWER: dark blue to violet-blue to very pale violet-blue or rarely white, 2.5–4 cm long, 1.5 cm across with segments hardly spreading, anthers black.
NOTE: also offered as seed.
ILLUSTRATION: *color plate*; drawing, Sealy (1940–42 as *A. inapertus* pro parte), Leighton (1965), which is reproduced in Snoeijer (1998), and Dyer (1966c); pho-

tograph, Pienaar (1987), Phillips and Rix (1991), and Allemand and Pionnat (2001 as *A. inapertus* subsp. *pendulus* var. 'Graskop', a white-flowering form).

Agapanthus inapertus subsp. *pendulus* 'Graskop' = **A. 'Graskop'**

Agapanthus inapertus var. *albus* Synge = *A. inapertus* 'Albus'
 Synge (1986) Dictionary of Gardening.

Agapanthus inapertus 'Albus'
    synonym: *Agapanthus inapertus* subsp. *inapertus* 'Albus'
    Agapanthus inapertus var. *albus* Synge
 origin: known since 1976, UK, as Thomas (1976) included in his book a photo-graph taken at the RHS Garden Wisley.
 flower: cream-white.
 note: several different clones are grown under this name.
 note: invalid name per the ICNCP-1995, art. 17.2, 17.9, and 17.11.
 illustration: photograph, Thomas (1976).

Agapanthus inapertus 'Graskop' = **A. 'Graskop'**

Agapanthus inapertus 'Graskopje' = **A. 'Graskopje'**

Agapanthus inapertus 'Inky Tears' = **A. 'Inky Tears'**

Agapanthus inapertus 'Ivory Bells' = **A. 'Ivory Bells'**

Agapanthus inapertus 'Lady Moore' = **A. 'Lady Moore'**

Agapanthus inapertus 'Mood Indigo' = *A.* **'Mood Indigo'**

Agapanthus inapertus 'Pendula' = **A. inapertus** subsp. **pendulus**

Agapanthus inapertus 'Purple Cloud' = **A. 'Purple Cloud'**

Agapanthus inapertus 'White' = *A.* 'White'

Agapanthus inapertus Beauv. ex Sealy =
    = pro parte = **A. inapertus** subsp. **pendulus** (L. Bol.) F.M. Leight.
    = pro parte = **A. 'Weillighii'**
 Sealy (1940–42) Curtis's Botanical Magazine, t.9621.

Agapanthus 'Indigo'
    synonym: *Agapanthus praecox* subsp. *orientalis* 'Indigo'
 origin: (selection of *A. praecox* subsp. *orientalis*) known since 1990 and still in cul-tivation. Also offered as seed.
 flower: violet-blue.
 note: invalid name per the ICNCP-1995, art. 17.13.

Agapanthus 'Inky Tears' (Tubular Group)

> SYNONYM: *Agapanthus inapertus* 'Inky Tears'

ORIGIN: known since 1996, Australia, and still in cultivation.
LEAF: deciduous.
PEDUNCLE: 50 cm.
FLOWER: dark violet-blue.
NOTE: some details from the Internet [24].

Agapanthus 'Innocence' (Trumpet Group)

ORIGIN: known since 2001 when offered by Gary Dunlop, Ballyrogan Nurseries, UK.
LEAF: deciduous.
PEDUNCLE: 100 cm.
INFLORESCENCE: 15 cm across.
FLOWER: white.
NOTE: details supplied by Gary Dunlop.

Agapanthus insignis RHS = *A.* 'Insignis'

RHS (1903) The Garden.
Besant (1903) Flora and Sylva, 1.
Ch. Penninck (1906) Revue de l'Horticulture Belge.

Agapanthus 'Insignis' (Funnel Group)

> SYNONYM: *Agapanthus insignis* RHS
> *Agapanthus umbellatus* var. *insignis* Thomas

ORIGIN: known since 1903, UK, and 1906, Belgium. Introduced from South Africa. Referred to by Thomas (1990) but probably no longer in cultivation.
LEAF: deciduous, with white base.
INFLORESCENCE: many-flowered, globular.
FLOWER: "peculiar pale shade of lilac-blue," slightly facing downwards.
NOTE: a description was published by Penninck (1906).
ILLUSTRATION: photograph, Penninck (1906 as *A. insignis*).

Agapanthus 'Intermedia' => *A.* 'Intermedius'

Agapanthus 'Intermediate White'

ORIGIN: introduced by Monterey Bay Nursery, California, USA, known since 1998.
PEDUNCLE: "taller than most types."
INFLORESCENCE: many-flowered, globular.
FLOWER: white.
NOTE: invalid name per the ICNCP-1995, art. 17.11.

Agapanthus intermedius Leichtlin = *A.* 'Intermedius'

Leichtlin (1889) Pflanzen-Liste.
Besant (1903) Flora and Sylva, 1.

Agapanthus intermedius van Tubergen = *A.* 'Intermedius'
van Tubergen (1946) catalogue.

Agapanthus intermedius 'Albus'
PEDUNCLE: 50 cm.
FLOWER: white.
NOTE: invalid name per the ICNCP-1995, art. 17.2, 17.9, and 17.11.

Agapanthus 'Intermedius'

SYNONYM: *Agapanthus intermedius* Leichtlin
Agapanthus umbellatus var. *intermedius* van Tubergen (1920)

ORIGIN: known since 1887 when offered by Leichtlin, Germany, who described the plant in his 1889 catalogue. The plant was also offered by van Tubergen, The Netherlands, in their 1920 catalogue only, and is probably no longer in cultivation.
PEDUNCLE: up to 120 cm.
INFLORESCENCE: up to 150 flowers.
FLOWER: "deep bright violet-blue."

Agapanthus 'Intermedius' (Trumpet Group)

SYNONYM: *Agapanthus africanus* 'Intermedius'
Agapanthus campanulatus subsp. *campanulatus* 'Intermedius'
Agapanthus intermedius van Tubergen (1946)

ERROR: 'Intermedia'

ORIGIN: known since 1946 when offered by van Tubergen, The Netherlands, and still in cultivation.
LEAF: deciduous, 20–30 cm long and up to 1.8 cm wide, arching, pale green but darker towards base and distinctly glaucous, base with purple.
PEDUNCLE: 70 cm, base green and glaucous but towards inflorescence violet, round.
INFLORESCENCE: 14 cm across, 50 flowers, more or less flat, bud opens on 2 sides.
PEDICEL: dark violet-purple.
FLOWERBUD: very dark violet-blue with paler apex, upright.
FLOWER: inside violet-blue, midrib slightly darker (93B), margin slightly darker, outside dark violet-blue (92A) with darker midrib (90A) and darker base, when out of flower purple-violet, horizontal, 2.5–3 cm long (tube 1 cm long), 2–3 cm across, stamens not exserted, anthers dark violet.
NOTE: details from plants grown by Maas & van Stein.
NOTE: registered in 1979.
NOTE: nuclear DNA content = 22.9 pg.
NOTE: the 1946 description by van Tubergen differs distinctly from the description by Leichtlin. Because van Tubergen did not offer a plant under this name for 25 years, without question the cultivar now grown with this name is the 1946 van Tubergen clone.
NOTE: invalid name per the ICNCP-1995, art. 17.2 and 17.9. It would be nice if this clone had a correct cultivar name; on the other hand, it is still widely grown and

traded, mainly as 'Intermedia', and so it is perhaps better to conserve the name.
ILLUSTRATION: *color plates*; photograph, Snoeijer (1998, 1999).

Agapanthus 'Iris' (Salver Group)

SYNONYM: *Agapanthus campanulatus* subsp. *campanulatus* 'Iris'
Agapanthus campanulatus 'Iris'

ORIGIN: known since 1991, and still in cultivation.
LEAF: deciduous.
INFLORESCENCE: many-flowered.
FLOWER: dark violet-blue.
NOTE: invalid name per the ICNCP-1995, art. 17.13.

Agapanthus 'Irving Cantor'

ORIGIN: known since 1997, Australia, when referred to by Cheers (1997).
FLOWER: violet-blue.
ILLUSTRATION: photograph, Cheers (1997, but not very good).

Agapanthus 'Isis' (Salver Group)

SYNONYM: *Agapanthus campanulatus* subsp. *campanulatus* 'Isis'
Agapanthus campanulatus 'Isis'
Agapanthus umbellatus 'Isis'

ORIGIN: (probably a selection of *A. campanulatus*) raised and introduced by Bloom, Bressingham Gardens, UK. Known since 1968 and still in cultivation. Also offered as seed.
LEAF: deciduous, up to 40 cm long and 1.5(–2) cm wide, upright, normal green and slightly glaucous, base with purple.
PEDUNCLE: 75–100 cm, green, round.
INFLORESCENCE: 12 cm across, 40–50 flowers, flat, bud opens on 2 sides.
PEDICEL: greenish-purple.
FLOWERBUD: dark violet-blue, upright.
FLOWER: inside violet-blue (94AB) to white at the base, midrib darker, margin slightly darker with purple tint, outside violet-blue with purple tint at apex and midrib, base darker, when out of flower more purple especially at midrib, horizontal to slightly facing downwards, 2.5 cm long (tube 1 cm long), 2.5 cm across, stamens not exserted, anthers purplish-yellow.
NOTE: details from plants grown by Coen Jansen.
NOTE: two different clones are grown under this name, especially in the UK, so it is possible that the description just given is of the wrong clone.
NOTE: Bloom (1991) "One [plant] had been acquired under the name *weillighii*, but a visiting taxonomist told me that it was an info name and was in fact a hybrid which needed to have a cultivar name. Being a fairly deep blue I called it 'Isis', and so it has remained."
NOTE: nuclear DNA content = 22.7 pg.
ILLUSTRATION: *color plate*; photograph, Hay and Beckett (1979) and Scott (1997).

Agapanthus 'Albatross'

Agapanthus 'Amethyst'

Agapanthus 'Argenteus Vittatus'

Agapanthus 'Atlantic Ocean'

Agapanthus 'Aureovittatus'

Agapanthus 'Bicton Bell"

Agapanthus 'Black Beauty'

Agapanthus 'Blauwe Wimpel'

Agapanthus 'Blue Companion'

Agapanthus 'Blue Giant'

Agapanthus 'Blue Globe'

Agapanthus 'Blue Heaven'

Agapanthus 'Blue Moon'

Agapanthus 'Blue Perfection'

Agapanthus 'Blue Ribbon'

Agapanthus 'Blue
Triumphator'

Agapanthus 'Bressingham Bounty'

Agapanthus
'Cambridge'

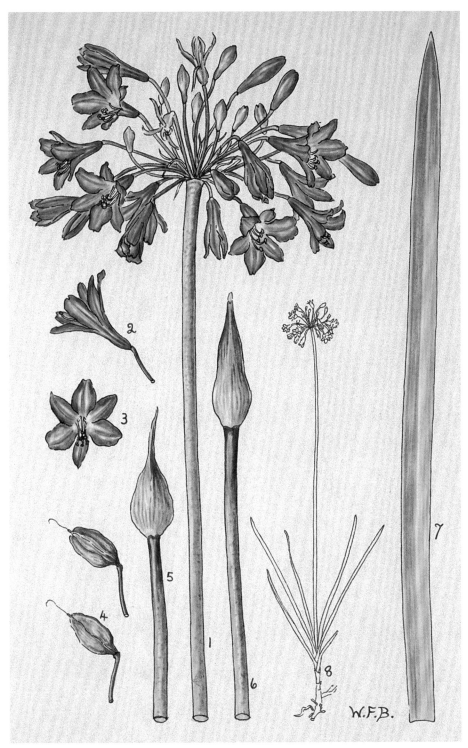

Agapanthus campanulatus subsp. *campanulatus*. Plate 7, Leighton (1965)

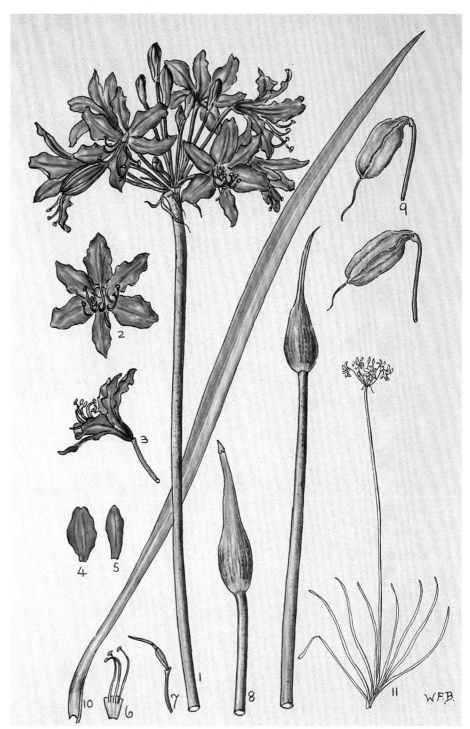

Agapanthus campanulatus subsp. *patens*. Plate 8, Leighton (1965)

Agapanthus 'Catharina'

Agapanthus caulescens. Plate 1487, Wittmack (1901)

Agapanthus caulescens subsp. *gracilis*. Plate 9, Leighton (1965)

Agapanthus 'Cherry Holley'

Agapanthus 'Cobalt Blue'

Agapanthus 'Columba'

Agapanthus 'Corinne'

Agapanthus 'Debbie'

Agapanthus 'Donau'

Agapanthus 'Dr Brouwer'

Agapanthus 'Duivenbrugge Blue'

Agapanthus 'Duná'

Agapanthus 'Elisabeth'

Agapanthus 'Emba'

Agapanthus 'Fafner'

Agapanthus
'Flore Pleno'

Agapanthus
'Formality'

Agapanthus
'Franni'

Agapanthus
'Glacier Stream'

Agapanthus
'Goldfinger'

Agapanthus
'Goliath'

Agapanthus 'Graskop'

Agapanthus
'Holbeach'

Agapanthus 'Ice
Lolly'

Agapanthus inapertus subsp. *inapertus*. Plate 11, Leighton (1965)

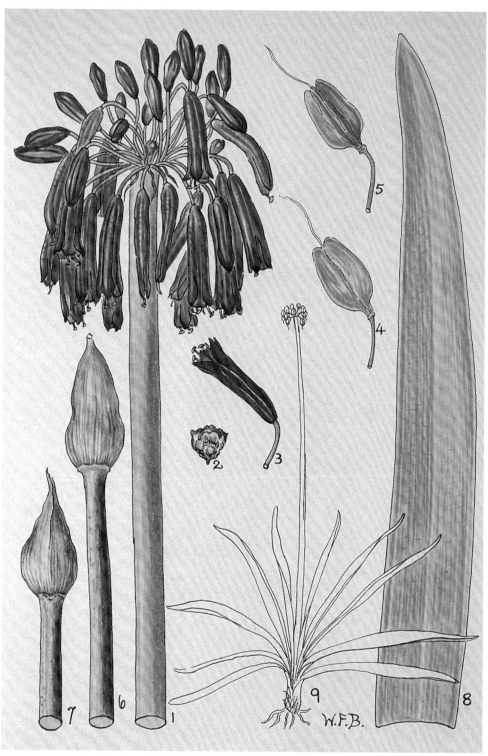

Agapanthus inapertus subsp. *pendulus*. Plate 12, Leighton (1965)

Agapanthus 'Intermedius'

Agapanthus 'Intermedius', fruit

Agapanthus 'Isis'

Agapanthus
'Johanna'

Agapanthus
'Jolanda'

Agapanthus 'Josephine'

Agapanthus 'Joyful Blue'

Agapanthus 'Kama'

Agapanthus 'Lady Moore'

Agapanthus 'Lady Wimborne'

Agapanthus 'Lena'

Agapanthus 'Lilliput'

Agapanthus 'Loch Hope'

Agapanthus 'Marianne'

Agapanthus 'Mariètte'

Agapanthus 'Maximus'

Agapanthus 'Midnight Blue'

Agapanthus 'Monmid'

Agapanthus 'Notfred'

Agapanthus 'Nottingham'

Agapanthus 'Oslo'

Agapanthus
'Parijs'

Agapanthus
'Pinchbeck'

Agapanthus 'Pinocchio'

Agapanthus 'Polar Ice'

Agapanthus praecox subsp. *minimus.* Plate 5, Leighton (1965)

Agapanthus praecox subsp. *orientalis.* Plate 4, Leighton (1965)

Agapanthus praecox 'Albiflorus'

Agapanthus praecox 'Albiflorus' on Madeira

Agapanthus 'Prinses Marilène'

Agapanthus 'Profusion'

Agapanthus 'Purple Cloud'

Agapanthus 'Queen Anne'

Agapanthus 'Queen Mother'

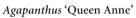

Agapanthus 'Rhone'

Agapanthus 'Rosemary'

Agapanthus 'Rotterdam'

Agapanthus 'Royal Blue' ex UK

Agapanthus 'San Gabriel'

Agapanthus 'San Gabriel', leaves

Agapanthus 'Septemberhemel'

Agapanthus 'Sky Rocket'

Agapanthus 'Stéphanie Charm'

Agapanthus 'Sunfield'

Agapanthus 'Suzan'

Agapanthus 'Sylvine'

Agapanthus 'Tall Boy'

Agapanthus 'Tinkerbell'

Agapanthus 'Umbellatus Albus'

Agapanthus 'Umbellatus Albus',
Dutch field

Agapanthus 'Violetta'

Agapanthus 'Virginia'

Agapanthus 'Waga'

Agapanthus 'Weaver'

Agapanthus 'Weillighii' [?] at Wisley

Agapanthus 'Weillighii' (on left). Plate 9621, Sealy (1940–42)

Agapanthus
'White'

Agapanthus
'White Beauty'

Agapanthus
'White Heaven'

Agapanthus 'White Smile'

Agapanthus 'Whitney'

Agapanthus
'Windsor Castle'

Agapanthus
'Windsor Grey'

Agapanthus
'Wolga'

Agapanthus 'Isleworth Blue' (Funnel Group)

SYNONYM: *Agapanthus orientalis* 'Isleworth Blue'
Agapanthus umbellatus 'Isleworth Blue'

ORIGIN: known since 1937 when offered by van Tubergen, The Netherlands. The plant was imported, with no accompanying records.
INFLORESCENCE: very large.
FLOWER: soft lavender-blue with darker midrib.
AWARD: GV in 1937.

Agapanthus 'Itsa Twista'

ORIGIN: introduced by Monterey Bay Nursery, California, USA, in 2000.
INFLORESCENCE: "dense."
FLOWER: usually more than 6 tepals, "pure white."
NOTE: details from the Internet [20].

Agapanthus 'Ivory'

ORIGIN: known since 2003 when offered by Lodge Lane Nursery, UK, which had obtained the micropropagated plants from Cotswold Garden Flowers, also of the UK; no further records.

Agapanthus 'Ivory Bells' (Funnel Group)

SYNONYM: *Agapanthus inapertus* 'Ivory Bells'

ORIGIN: known since 2001 when offered by Lambley, Australia.
PEDUNCLE: 150 cm.
FLOWER: pure white, "open, campanulate."

Agapanthus 'Jack's Blue' (Funnel Group)

ORIGIN: New Zealand, known since 2001 when offered widely in the UK.
NAME: in honour of Jack Blyth, a New Zealand nurseryman.
LEAF: evergreen, dark green.
PEDUNCLE: 120–150 cm.
INFLORESCENCE: 25 cm across.
FLOWERBUD: dark violet-blue (89B), upright but quickly horizontal to slightly nodding.
FLOWER: violet-blue (89D), horizontal to slightly nodding, 6 cm long (tube 2 cm long), 5 cm across, anthers green.
NOTE: details supplied by Dick Fulcher, who continued thus: "Very fine hybrid similar in shape and stature to **'Purple Cloud'** but with larger individual flowers, the dark violet-blue flowerbuds opening much paler, producing a distinct contrast in colour."

Agapanthus 'Jahan' (Variegated Leaf Group)

ORIGIN: known since 1996, Australia.
LEAF: variegated.

Agapanthus 'Jeanette Dean'

SYNONYM: *Agapanthus orientalis* 'Jeanette Dean'

ORIGIN: introduced by J.N. Giridlian's Oakhurst Gardens, California, USA, in 1962, and listed as "the first to flower and the brightest blue. Medium height, profuse bloomer." Probably no longer in cultivation.

Agapanthus 'Jersey Giant'

ORIGIN: known since 2001, UK.
PEDUNCLE: 60 cm, rather sturdy.
INFLORESCENCE: "very large."
FLOWER: violet-blue.
NOTE: some details from the Internet [12].

Agapanthus 'Jodie' (Funnel Group)

ORIGIN: raised by Dick Fulcher, Pine Cottage Plants, UK, known since 2000.
NAME: in honour of the raiser's youngest granddaughter.
LEAF: evergreen.
PEDUNCLE: 140–150 cm.
FLOWER: inside violet-blue with dark violet-blue midrib, horizontal, stamens not exserted, anthers violet.
NOTE: details supplied by Dick Fulcher.
ILLUSTRATION: photograph, Fulcher (2000).

Agapanthus 'Johanna' (Trumpet Group)

ORIGIN: raised by Kees Duivenvoorde, Beverwijk, The Netherlands, introduced in 1996, and still in cultivation.
NAME: in honour of the raiser's daughter.
LEAF: deciduous, up to 30 cm long and 2.3 cm wide, upright, pale green, base green.
PEDUNCLE: 90 cm, green and flushed purple, round.
INFLORESCENCE: up to 17 cm across, 50 flowers, globular, bud opens on 1 side.
PEDICEL: heavily flushed purple.
FLOWERBUD: upright, dark violet-blue.
FLOWER: inside very pale violet-blue but darker towards apex and with margin slightly darker, midrib violet-blue, outside violet-blue with very wide darker coloured midrib, base darker, when out of flower purple, horizontal, up to 3.5 cm long (tube 1.2 cm), 3 cm across, stamens as long as the flower or just slightly exserted, anthers dark violet.
NOTE: details from plants grown by Duivenvoorde.
NOTE: the first flowers within the inflorescence tend to have 8 tepals.
NOTE: registered in 1995.
NOTE: nuclear DNA content = 24 pg.
ILLUSTRATION: *color plate.*

Agapanthus 'Johanna Gärtner' (Funnel Group)

SYNONYM: *Agapanthus umbellatus* 'Johanna Gärtner'

ORIGIN: raised and introduced by Heinz Klose Staudengärtnerei, Germany, known since 1991, and still in cultivation.

NAME: in honour of the raiser's former employer.

PEDUNCLE: 120 cm.

FLOWER: dark violet-blue.

Agapanthus Johannesburg Hybrids => see note under *A*. RUBBISH

ORIGIN: (selected from seedlings grown from wild-collected seed) raised and introduced by Beth Chatto Gardens, UK, in 1999.

Agapanthus 'Jolanda' (Trumpet Group)

ORIGIN: raised by Kees Duivenvoorde, Beverwijk, The Netherlands, introduced in 1996, and still in cultivation.

NAME: in honour of the raiser's granddaughter.

LEAF: deciduous, up to 40 cm long and 3 cm wide, upright to slightly arching, green and strongly glaucous, base green.

PEDUNCLE: 100 cm, green and slightly flushed purple, flat.

INFLORESCENCE: up to 18 cm across, 50 flowers, globular, bud opens on 1 side.

PEDICEL: green with paler base and flushed purple towards flower.

FLOWERBUD: dark violet-blue, upright.

FLOWER: inside violet-blue with purple blush at apex and margin slightly darker, midrib dark violet-blue, outside violet-blue with darker coloured midrib, base darker, when out of flower purple-violet, horizontal, 3.4 cm long (tube 1.4 cm long), 3 cm across, stamens not exserted, anthers dark violet-blue.

NOTE: details from plants grown by Duivenvoorde.

NOTE: selected for its late flowering.

NOTE: registered in 1995.

NOTE: nuclear DNA content = 23.8 pg.

ILLUSTRATION: *color plate.*

Agapanthus 'Josephine' ex Holland (Trumpet Group)

ORIGIN: (selection from seedlings) introduced by van der Zwet, Roelofarendsveen, The Netherlands, around 1965, and still in cultivation.

LEAF: more or less evergreen, up to 40 cm long and 3.5 cm wide, arching to horizontal bend, slightly caniculate, dark green, base green.

PEDUNCLE: (70–)90–120 cm, green, distinctly flat.

INFLORESCENCE: 20 cm across, globular, 100–130 flowers.

PEDICEL: green to pale green with some purple speckles towards the flower.

FLOWERBUD: violet blue with darker base, in the early stage with a pale green band, upright.

FLOWER: inside violet-blue (95C), margin darker, midrib dark violet-blue (95AB), base white, outside violet-blue with a purple tint and slightly darker coloured midrib and margin, base green-violet-blue, upright, 4.3 cm long (tube 1.7 cm long), 2.5–3 cm across, stamens not exserted, anthers dull violet with yellow pollen.

NOTE: most details from plants grown by Reintjes.

NOTE: with their gappy tepal segments, flowers tend towards the Funnel Group when fully open but because of the diameter are maintained in the Trumpet Group.

NOTE: nuclear DNA content = 24.6 pg.

ILLUSTRATION: *color plate.*

Agapanthus 'Josephine' ex Germany (Salver Group)

ORIGIN: introduced in Germany, known since 1970, and still in cultivation.

NOTE: very similar to **'Blue Globe'** and probably the same; see chapter 2.

NOTE: invalid name per the ICNCP-1995, art. 17.2.

Agapanthus 'Joyce' (Funnel Group)

ORIGIN: raised by Lewis Palmer. Known since 1972; still known in 1979.

LEAF: evergreen, 25–30 cm long and 3–4 cm wide, upright, dark green and glaucous.

PEDUNCLE: up to 70 cm high, dark green.

INFLORESCENCE: 18 cm across, flat.

PEDICEL: green to dark green.

FLOWER: white flushed with pale violet-blue, margin violet-blue (93D), midrib violet-blue (94B), upright, 3.5 cm long, 5 cm across, filaments pale violet-blue, anthers black.

AWARD: AM in 1977.

Agapanthus 'Joyful Blue' (Salver Group)

ORIGIN: selected by Joy Creek Nursery, Oregon, USA, known since 1998, and still in cultivation.

LEAF: deciduous, up to 30 cm long and 2 cm wide, upright, normal green.

PEDUNCLE: up to 100 cm, green flushed purple towards inflorescence.

INFLORESCENCE: 13 cm across, 20–30 flowers, flat, bud opens on 2 sides.

PEDICEL: purple.

FLOWERBUD: pale violet-blue with midrib and base slightly darker, upright but quickly horizontal.

FLOWER: inside pale violet-blue, midrib slightly darker and with purple tint, outside pale violet-blue with midrib and base slightly darker, stamens not exserted, anthers dark violet.

NOTE: details from plants grown at Joy Creek Nursery.

ILLUSTRATION: *color plate.*

Agapanthus 'June' (Trumpet Group)

ERROR: 'Juno'

ORIGIN: raised by Lewis Palmer, introduced by Mrs D. Palmer. Known since 1974.

LEAF: deciduous, up to 50 cm long and 3 cm wide, upright, pale green and slightly glaucous.

PEDUNCLE: up to 70 cm, normal green.

INFLORESCENCE: 17 cm across, globular.

PEDICEL: pale green flushed dark purple.

FLOWER: very pale violet-blue, margin darker violet-blue (94CD), midrib violet-blue (93C), horizontal, 4 cm long, 3–3.5 cm across.

AWARD: HC in 1977.

Agapanthus 'June Bond'

SYNONYM: *Agapanthus praecox* 'June Bond'

ORIGIN: (chance seedling) selected by Randy Baldwin in June Bond's Santa Barbara, California, garden, USA, known since 2001.

LEAF: evergreen, up to 30 cm long.

PEDUNCLE: 50 cm.

INFLORESCENCE: "full heads."

FLOWER: "bright blue."

NOTE: details from the Internet [21].

Agapanthus 'June Bride' = *A.* 'Komos June Bride'

Agapanthus 'Juno' => *A.* 'June'

Agapanthus 'Kalmthout' = *A.* 'Kalmthout Blue'

Agapanthus 'Kalmthout Blue'

SYNONYM: *Agapanthus* 'Kalmthout'

ORIGIN: introduced by Kalmthout Arboretum, Belgium. The plants were grown for many years but commercially known since 1996, UK.

LEAF: deciduous.

PEDUNCLE: 80–100 cm.

FLOWER: violet-blue.

Agapanthus 'Kalmthout White'

ORIGIN: introduced by Kalmthout Arboretum, Belgium. The plants were grown for many years but commercially known since 1998, UK.

LEAF: deciduous.

PEDUNCLE: 80–100 cm.

FLOWER: white.

Agapanthus 'Kama' (Trumpet Group)

ORIGIN: raised by Th. P.W. de Groot, Hillegom, The Netherlands, introduced by Maas & van Stein, also of Hillegom, introduced in 2001.

NAME: for the Kama River, in Russia.

LEAF: deciduous, up to 30 cm long and 3 cm wide, spreading, normal green and glaucous, base green.

PEDUNCLE: 80 cm, dark green and dark violet speckled, usually with a secondary shorter peduncle.

INFLORESCENCE: 19 cm across, 50 flowers, globular.

PEDICEL: dark green and heavily dark purple speckled.

FLOWERBUD: violet-blue with darker base, upright but quickly horizontal.

FLOWER: inside pale violet-blue (92BC) and slightly darker margin and purple tint, midrib violet-blue (93B) in sometimes 3 stripes, outside pale violet-blue (93D), midrib violet-blue (93B), base violet-blue (93A), when out of flower purple with violet-blue base, horizontal, 4 cm long (tube 1.5 cm long), 3–3.5 cm across, stamens not exserted, anthers purple becoming yellowish-white.

NOTE: details from plants grown by Maas & van Stein.

ILLUSTRATION: *color plate*.

Agapanthus 'Kew White'

ORIGIN: from RBG Kew, known since 1996, UK, when offered by Great Dixter, and still in cultivation.

FLOWER: white.

NOTE: nuclear DNA content = 23.4 pg.

Agapanthus 'Kingston Blue' (Salver Group)

SYNONYM: *Agapanthus campanulatus* 'Kingston Blue'

ORIGIN: (selection of **A. campanulatus** subsp. **patens**) introduced by Miss Raphael, Kingston Bagpuize, UK. Known since 1990 and still in cultivation. Also offered as seed.

LEAF: deciduous, 10–20 cm long and 0.6–0.8 cm wide, arching, dark green, base purple.

PEDUNCLE: 50–60 cm, green, round.

INFLORESCENCE: 11–13 cm across, 20–30 flowers, flat.

PEDICEL: dull greenish-violet.

FLOWERBUD: dark violet-blue, upright.

FLOWER: inside violet-blue (94A/95C), midrib dark violet-blue with purple tint, margin slightly darker with distinct purple tint, outside dark violet-blue, base slightly darker, when out of flower more purple, horizontal, 2.7 cm long (tube 0.8 cm long), 3.5 cm across, stamens exserted, anther violet with yellow pollen.

NOTE: details from plants grown at different gardens and nurseries.

NOTE: very good grower and free-flowering.

NOTE: sometimes called similar to '**Lilliput**', but besides having a different origin, this plant has slightly wider leaves and a taller peduncle than '**Lilliput**'.

NOTE: nuclear DNA content = 22.3 pg.

Agapanthus Kingston Blue Strain = A. RUBBISH

Agapanthus 'Kirstenbosch' (Trumpet Group)

ORIGIN: introduced by Lewis Palmer. Known since 1974; still known in 1977.

LEAF: 50 cm long, 3 cm wide, arching, pale dull green.

PEDUNCLE: 80 cm, pale green with dull purple tint.

INFLORESCENCE: 16 cm across, flat.

FLOWER: very pale violet-blue, margin violet-blue (93C), midrib violet-blue (94B), upright to slightly facing downwards, 3 cm long, 3 cm across.
AWARD: C in 1977.

Agapanthus 'Kirsty' (Funnel Group)

ORIGIN: raised by Dick Fulcher, introduced in 1999.
PEDUNCLE: 100 cm.
INFLORESCENCE: 70 flowers, more or less globular.
FLOWER: pale violet-blue with darker midrib, horizontal, stamens not exserted, anthers violet.
ILLUSTRATION: photograph, Fulcher (2000).

Agapanthus 'Kobold' (Salver Group)

SYNONYM: *Agapanthus campanulatus* 'Kobold'

ERROR: 'Kobolt'

ORIGIN: most likely Dutch, known since 1979, and still in cultivation.
LEAF: deciduous, 25–40 cm long and 1.5–2 cm wide, upright but later more arching, pale green, base purple.
PEDUNCLE: 30–50(–70) cm, green, round.
INFLORESCENCE: 10–14 cm across, (30–)40(–60) flowers, flat, bud opens on 1 side, bract usually remains attached.
PEDICEL: green with violet.
FLOWERBUD: violet-blue, upright.
FLOWER: inside pale violet-blue, midrib darker, margin with purple tint, outside violet-blue but with more violet at base, when out of flower more purple, horizontal, 2.6–2.8 cm long (tube 1 cm long), 2.5–3 cm across, stamens not exserted, anthers dark violet.
NOTE: most details from plants grown at Buitenhof, Lisse, The Netherlands.
NOTE: nuclear DNA content = 23 pg.
ILLUSTRATION: drawing, Gillissen (1982).

Agapanthus 'Komos Blue Cloud'

ERROR: 'Komos Blue Claud'

ORIGIN: raised and introduced by Satoshi Komoriya, Komoriya Nursery Ltd, Japan, known since 1999, and still in cultivation.
NAME: a reference to raiser's surname.
PEDUNCLE: 125 cm.
FLOWER: pale purple-violet.
NOTE: name from Allemand and Pionnat (2001); some details from the Internet [25 as 'Komos Blue Claud'], origin details supplied by Komoriya.

Agapanthus 'Komos Blue Sky'

ORIGIN: raised and introduced by Satoshi Komoriya, Komoriya Nursery Ltd, Japan, known since 2001.
NOTE: details supplied by Komoriya.

Agapanthus 'Komos Cherry Blossom'

ERROR: 'Komos Cherry Blossum'

ORIGIN: raised and introduced by Satoshi Komoriya, Komoriya Nursery Ltd, Japan, known since 2001.

NOTE: details supplied by Komoriya.

Agapanthus 'Komos June Bride' (Funnel Group)

SYNONYM: *Agapanthus* 'June Bride'

ORIGIN: raised and introduced by Satoshi Komoriya, Komoriya Nursery Ltd, Japan, known since 1998, and still in cultivation.

NAME: a reference to the raiser's surname.

PEDUNCLE: 50 cm.

INFLORESCENCE: flat.

FLOWER: pure white, anthers yellow.

NOTE: name from Allemand and Pionnat (2001); details from the Internet [25], origin details supplied by Komoriya.

Agapanthus 'Komos Lake Eye'

ORIGIN: raised and introduced by Satoshi Komoriya, Komoriya Nursery Ltd, Japan, known since 2001.

NOTE: details supplied by Komoriya.

Agapanthus 'Komos Ryoufuu'

ORIGIN: raised and introduced by Satoshi Komoriya, Komoriya Nursery Ltd, Japan, known since 2000, and still in cultivation.

NAME: a reference to the raiser's surname.

PEDUNCLE: 100 cm.

FLOWER: pale violet-blue.

NOTE: details from the Internet [25] and the origin details supplied by Komoriya.

Agapanthus 'Komos Violette'

ORIGIN: raised and introduced by Satoshi Komoriya, Komoriya Nursery Ltd, Japan, known since 2001, and still in cultivation.

NAME: a reference to the raiser's surname.

PEDUNCLE: 100 cm.

FLOWER: pale purple-violet.

NOTE: details from the Internet [25] and origin details supplied by Komoriya.

Agapanthus 'Kopenhagen' (Trumpet Group)

ORIGIN: (selected seedling 93 × 'Wolga') raised by Kees Duivenvoorde, introduced in 2002.

NAME: Dutch spelling of the capital of Denmark.

LEAF: deciduous.

PEDUNCLE: 100 cm.

INFLORESCENCE: 15 cm across, 50 flowers.
FLOWER: an even violet-blue.
NOTE: selected for its late flowering.
NOTE: details supplied by Duivenvoorde.

Agapanthus 'Kosui-no-hitomi' (Salver Group)

ORIGIN: raised and introduced in Japan, known since 1998 when offered by Takii. Still in cultivation.
PEDUNCLE: 100 cm.
INFLORESCENCE: more or less globular.
FLOWER: dark purple-violet, stamens exserted.
NOTE: some details supplied by Y. Aihara and some from the Internet [25].

Agapanthus 'Kosui-no-kaze'

ORIGIN: Japan, known since 2001 when offered by Komoriya Nursery Ltd.
PEDUNCLE: 85 cm.
FLOWER: dark purple-violet.
NOTE: details from the Internet [25].

Agapanthus 'Krelagei'

SYNONYM: *Agapanthus maximus* 'Krelagei'
Agapanthus umbellatus var. *maximus* 'Krelagei'
Agapanthus umbellatus 'Krelagei'

ORIGIN: known since 1880 when offered by Leichtlin, who described the plant in 1895. Leichtlin still offered the plant in 1901. Probably no longer in cultivation.
INFLORESCENCE: very large.
FLOWER: deep violet-blue.
NOTE: late flowering, October and November.

Agapanthus 'K. Wiley'

ORIGIN: known since 2002 when offered by Prime Perennials, UK.
FLOWER: violet-blue.

Agapanthus 'Lady Edith' (Funnel Group)

SYNONYM: *Agapanthus coddii* 'Lady Edith'

ORIGIN: introduced by Mount Stewart, the famous garden in Northern Ireland.
LEAF: deciduous, very caulescent.
NOTE: details supplied by Gary Dunlop.
NOTE: nuclear DNA content = 24.2 pg.

Agapanthus 'Lady Grey' (Salver Group)

SYNONYM: *Agapanthus* 'Mabel Grey'

ORIGIN: raised and introduced by Lewis Palmer, known since 1951, and still in cultivation.
NAME: in honour of Palmer's sister.

LEAF: deciduous, 40–50 cm long and 1.5 cm wide, upright and arching, normal green and a bit glaucous, base green.

PEDUNCLE: 50–85 cm, green and slightly glaucous, round.

INFLORESCENCE: 10–13 cm, 40 flowers.

PEDICEL: purple-violet.

FLOWERBUD: dark violet-blue with purplish apex, upright.

FLOWER: inside violet-blue (95C) with white base, midrib darker, margin slightly darker and with purple tint, the outer tepals with distinct white tip, outside violet-blue, midrib and base darker, when out of flower purple, horizontal, 2.3 cm long (tube 0.8 cm long), 2.3 cm across, stamens not exserted, anthers violet.

NOTE: most details from plants grown at Wisley.

NOTE: Palmer showed the plant as *A. patens*, which was changed to '**Lady Grey**'. It seems, according to the Wisley trial, that the name later changed once again, to 'Mabel Grey'.

AWARD: AM in 1951 as '**Lady Grey**'; HC in 1977 as 'Mabel Grey'.

Agapanthus '**Lady Moore**' (Salver Group)

SYNONYM: *Agapanthus inapertus* 'Lady Moore'

ERROR: 'Lady Moor'

ORIGIN: from the garden of Miss Raphael, Kingston Bagpuize, and introduced by Elizabeth Parker Jervis in the early 1960s. Still in cultivation.

NAME: in honour of Lady Phyllis Moore, wife of Sir Frederick Moore (see 'Mooreanus') and a very good gardener and plantswoman.

LEAF: deciduous, up to 40 cm long and 1.5 cm wide, upright to arching, dark green and slightly glaucous, base with purple.

PEDUNCLE: 40–70 cm, green and slightly glaucous, round.

INFLORESCENCE: 12 cm across, 10–40 flowers, flat, bud opens on 1 side.

PEDICEL: green with purple speckles and purple at the top.

FLOWERBUD: greenish-white with dark dull purple apex, upright.

FLOWER: white with transparent midrib, outside white and the three outer segments with violet apex, base greenish, when out of flower white becoming pale brown, horizontal to slightly facing downwards, up to 2.5 cm long (tube 0.8 cm long), 2.5 cm across, stamens not exserted, anthers dark purple-violet.

NOTE: details from plants grown in different gardens.

NOTE: very slow grower.

NOTE: some plants sold as 'White Dwarf' are actually '**Lady Moore**'.

ILLUSTRATION: *color plate.*

Agapanthus '**Lady Wimborne**' (Salver Group)

ERROR: 'Lady Wimbourne'

ORIGIN: raised and introduced by Lewis Palmer, known since 1972, and still in cultivation.

LEAF: deciduous, 40 cm long and 2.5–3 cm wide, upright, normal to dark green and glaucous.

PEDUNCLE: 100 cm, pale green.

INFLORESCENCE: 14 cm across, 30–40 flowers, flat.

PEDICEL: green and slightly flushed purple.

FLOWERBUD: greyish with midrib at apex green-violet and small violet-blue base, becoming more coloured, upright but quickly horizontal.

FLOWER: almost white with margin and midrib violet-blue (91A), outside pale violet-blue with rather wide darker midrib and violet-blue base, horizontal to slightly facing downwards, 2.5 cm long, 3.5 cm across, stamens not exserted, anthers very dark violet.

NOTE: details from plants grown at Wisley.

ILLUSTRATION: *color plate.*

AWARD: HC in 1977.

Agapanthus 'Large Blue'

ORIGIN: known since 2001 from Australia.

FLOWER: violet-blue.

NOTE: details from the Internet [26].

NOTE: invalid name per the ICNCP-1995, art. 17.11.

Agapanthus 'Large White'

ORIGIN: known since 2001 from Australia.

FLOWER: white.

NOTE: details from the Internet [26].

NOTE: invalid name per the ICNCP-1995, art. 17.11.

Agapanthus 'L'Armandèche'

SYNONYM: *Agapanthus praecox* subsp. *orientalis* 'L'Armandèche'

ORIGIN: known since 2001 when grown by Ets Horticole, France.

FLOWER: white with violet-blue midrib.

Agapanthus 'Latent Blue' (Funnel Group)

ORIGIN: raised by Gary Dunlop, Ballyrogan Nurseries, UK, named in 1998.

LEAF: up to 40 cm long and 2.5 cm wide, normal green with paler apex, base green.

PEDUNCLE: 100 cm, green.

INFLORESCENCE: 15 cm across, 50 flowers.

PEDICEL: purple.

FLOWER: inside violet-blue (94A) with darker midrib and base (95A), outside violet-blue (94A) with darker midrib (95A), horizontal, 3 cm long, 4 cm across.

NOTE: details supplied by Gary Dunlop.

NOTE: invalid name per the ICNCP-1995, art. 17.11 and 17.12.

Agapanthus 'Latifolius'

SYNONYM: *Agapanthus africanus* subsp. *umbellatus* var. *latifolius* H.R. Wehrh.

Agapanthus umbellatus var. *latifolius* Voss ex Bonstedt

ORIGIN: known since 1931, Germany. Probably no longer in cultivation.
LEAF: very wide, glossy green.
PEDUNCLE: up to 120 cm.
INFLORESCENCE: up to 200 flowers.
NOTE: not so free-flowering.

Agapanthus 'Lavender Girl' (Trumpet Group)

ORIGIN: raised by Dick Fulcher, Pine Cottage Plants, UK, known since 2000.
LEAF: deciduous, 48–70 cm long and 2–2.5 cm wide, spreading, normal green (143A), base green.
PEDUNCLE: 120 cm, rather stout.
INFLORESCENCE: 12 cm across.
PEDICEL: normal green with purple-violet speckles towards the flower.
FLOWER: inside violet-blue (93C) with a darker tint (93B), horizontal to slightly nodding, up to 3.5 cm long (tube 1.1 cm long), 3.2 cm across, anthers black.
NOTE: rather late flowering, in the UK in September, and "noticeably fragrant."
NOTE: details supplied by Dick Fulcher.

Agapanthus 'Lavender Haze'

ORIGIN: raised by R.J. and D.M.L. Wood, New Plymouth, New Zealand, known since 2001.
NOTE: New Zealand Plant Variety Rights applied for, no. HOM133, on 5 June 2001, by Lifetech Laboratories Ltd, New Zealand.
NOTE: details from the Internet [36].

Agapanthus 'Leicester' (Funnel Group)

ORIGIN: raised by Kees Duivenvoorde, Beverwijk, The Netherlands, introduced in 1999.
NAME: after the city in England.
LEAF: deciduous, up to 35 cm long and 2.3 cm wide, upright, normal green, base green.
PEDUNCLE: 60–70 cm, green flushed purple, a bit flat.
INFLORESCENCE: 15–17 cm across, 40–70 flowers, flat, bract caducous.
PEDICEL: green with dull purple and a violet blush.
FLOWERBUD: cream-white with a bit of pale purple at apex, upright but later horizontal.
FLOWER: inside white, midrib thin transparent, outside white with base very pale green, when out of flower white with a bit of pale purple at the base and a pale purple tint at apex, upright to horizontal, 4 cm long (tube 1.2 cm long), 4.7 cm across, stamens exserted, anthers purple becoming black with yellow pollen.
NOTE: details from plants grown by Duivenvoorde.
NOTE: similar to 'Spalding' but 'Leicester' has a shorter peduncle.
NOTE: flowers tend towards the Salver Group when fully open.
NOTE: nuclear DNA content = 24.9 pg.

Agapanthus leichtlinii Baker = *A.* 'Leichtlinii'

Baker (1878) Gardeners Chronicle.

Agapanthus 'Leichtlinii' (Trumpet Group)

SYNONYM: *Agapanthus africanus* subsp. *minor* var. *leichtlinii* H.R. Wehrh.
Agapanthus africanus var. *leichtlinii* (Baker) Beauverd
Agapanthus africanus 'Leichtlinii'
Agapanthus leichtlinii Baker
Agapanthus minor var. *leichtlinii* Bonstedt
Agapanthus minor 'Leichtlinii'
Agapanthus orientalis var. *leichtlinii* Synge
Agapanthus praecox subsp. *orientalis* 'Leichtlinii'
Agapanthus umbellatus var. *leichtlinii* Baker

ERROR: 'Leitchlinii'

ORIGIN: (selection of *A. africanus*) introduced from the Cape, known since 1878, when offered by Leichtlin. Still referred to in 1986 but probably no longer in cultivation.
NAME: in honour of Max Leichtlin, famous nurseryman in Baden-Baden, Germany.
LEAF: evergreen, similar to *A. africanus* but shorter and wider.
PEDUNCLE: up to 45 cm long.
INFLORESCENCE: compact.
FLOWER: dark violet-blue, up to 3 cm long.
NOTE: Leichtlin refers to the plant as flowering semi-double; no other reference mentions this detail.

Agapanthus 'Leighton Blue'

ORIGIN: offered by Bridgemere Nurseries, UK, in 1999.

Agapanthus 'Leitchlinii' => *A.* 'Leichtlinii'

Agapanthus 'Lena' (Funnel Group)

ORIGIN: raised by Th. P.W. de Groot, Hillegom, The Netherlands, introduced by Maas & van Stein, also of Hillegom, introduced in 2001.
NAME: for the Lena River, in Russia.
LEAF: deciduous, up to 35 cm long and 2.8 cm wide, upright to slightly spreading, normal to apple-green and glaucous, base green.
PEDUNCLE: 80 cm, green and slightly purple speckled, round.
INFLORESCENCE: 19 cm across, 80 flowers, globular, bud opens on 2 sides.
PEDICEL: green and slightly purple speckled.
FLOWERBUD: violet-blue with darker base, upright.
FLOWER: inside pale violet-blue (93D) and margin with distinct purple tint, midrib violet-blue (93A), outside pale violet-blue (93CD), midrib violet-blue (93B) and base slightly darker (93A), when out of flower purple with small violet-blue base, horizontal, 3.6 cm long (tube 1.7 cm long), 3.7 cm across, stamens slightly exserted, anthers brownish.

NOTE: details from plants grown by Maas & van Stein.
ILLUSTRATION: *color plate.*

Agapanthus 'Les Barges'

ORIGIN: raised by J.-Y. Poiroux, Ets Horticole, France, in 2000.
FLOWER: pale violet-blue with darker midrib.

Agapanthus 'Lewis Palmer' (Trumpet Group)

ORIGIN: raised and introduced by the RHS Garden Wisley, known since 1954.
NAME: in honour of Lewis Palmer (d. 1971), The Grange, Headbourne Worthy, Winchester, Hantshire, UK.
LEAF: "long and wide."
PEDUNCLE: up to 130 cm.
INFLORESCENCE: 25 cm across, globular.
PEDICEL: up to 5 cm long.
FLOWER: blue-green (113B), up to 4.5 cm long and 2.5 cm across.
AWARD: AM in 1954.

Agapanthus Lewis Palmer hybrid = *A.* RUBBISH

Agapanthus 'Liam's Lilac' (Funnel Group)

ORIGIN: (an *A. caulescens* hybrid) raised by Dick Fulcher, Pine Cottage Plants, UK, selected in 1997, and still in cultivation.
NAME: in honour of the raiser's oldest grandson.
LEAF: deciduous.
PEDUNCLE: 80–100 cm.
FLOWER: purple-violet with darker base, "flared."
NOTE: invalid name per the ICNCP-1995, art. 17.13, but as the name refers to the colour and not to a plant, it is accepted here.

Agapanthus 'Light Star'

ORIGIN: raised by Raveningham Gardens, UK, known since 1989.

Agapanthus 'Lilac Bells'

ORIGIN: (an *A. inapertus* hybrid) raised at NCCPG Bicton College, UK, selected by Dick Fulcher in 1993, and still in cultivation.
LEAF: more or less deciduous, 30–60 cm long and 2.5–3.3 cm wide.
PEDUNCLE: 80–100 cm, rather stout.
INFLORESCENCE: 16 cm across, globular.
FLOWER: violet-blue (94C) with a "hint of lilac," 3.5 cm long, stamens longer than the flower.
NOTE: details supplied by Dick Fulcher and some from the Internet [5].

Agapanthus 'Lilacinus'

SYNONYM: *Agapanthus umbellatus* var. *lilacinus* Krelage
ORIGIN: known since 1888 when offered by Krelage; no further records.

Agapanthus 'Lilac Time' (Funnel Group)

ORIGIN: raised at NCCPG Bicton College, UK, selected by Dick Fulcher in 1993, and still in cultivation.
LEAF: evergreen, 30–66 cm long and 3–3.8 cm wide, base purple.
PEDUNCLE: stout, 90–125 cm.
INFLORESCENCE: 19 cm across, 60–70 flowers, globular.
PEDICEL: green with purple towards flower.
FLOWERBUD: upright, pale violet-blue with a bit of cream towards base, base slightly darker.
FLOWER: inside pale violet-blue (91BC) with slightly darker midrib (90A), outside pale violet-blue with slightly darker midrib and base, when out of flower purple, horizontal to slightly facing downwards, 3.2–3.5 cm long (tube 1 cm long), segments recurving when fully open, stamens not exserted, anthers blue becoming brown.
NOTE: details supplied by Dick Fulcher.
NOTE: tends towards the Salver Group when the flower is fully open.
NOTE: nuclear DNA content = 23.3 pg.
ILLUSTRATION: photograph, Fulcher (2000, 2002).

Agapanthus 'Lilliput' (Salver Group)

ORIGIN: raised by Roland Jackman, Woking, UK, 1950s and still widely cultivated. Also offered as seed.
LEAF: deciduous, 10–20 cm long and 0.3–1.2 cm wide, upright to arching, dark green, base dark purple.
PEDUNCLE: 20–60 cm, green with violet towards inflorescence, round.
INFLORESCENCE: 10 cm across, 20–25 flowers, flat, bud opens on 1 side.
PEDICEL: violet.
FLOWERBUD: dark violet-blue, upright.
FLOWER: inside dark violet-blue (95C), midrib darker (94A), margin with very pale purple tint, outside dark violet-blue with slightly darker base, segments recurving when fully open, when out of flower purple-violet, horizontal to slightly facing downwards, 2.5 cm long (tube 0.8 cm long), 3–3.5 cm across, stamens exserted, anthers violet with yellowish pollen.
NOTE: details from plants grown at different gardens and nurseries.
NOTE: sometimes regarded as being similar to **Kingston Blue**.
ILLUSTRATION: *color plate*; photograph, Vermeulen (1996), Snoeijer (1998, 2000), Wray (1998a), and Jansen (2002).
AWARD: AM in 1977.

Agapanthus 'Little Diamond'

ORIGIN: known since 2003 when offered by Beeches Nursery, UK.

Agapanthus 'Little White' (Funnel Group)

SYNONYM: *Agapanthus africanus* 'Little White'
Agapanthus 'Nana White'

ORIGIN: known since 2001, South Africa, and 2002, USA.

LEAF: evergreen.

PEDUNCLE: 30–60 cm, green.

INFLORESCENCE: "large," 100 flowers, globular.

PEDICEL: green.

FLOWERBUD: white with greenish base, upright.

FLOWER: inside white, outside white, when out of flower dull white, horizontal, stamens slightly exserted, anthers yellow.

NOTE: propagated by tissue culture.

NOTE: though traded as a selection of *A. africanus*, it is clear that this clone is a selection of *A. praecox* 'Albiflorus'.

NOTE: invalid name per the ICNCP-1995, art. 17.11.

Agapanthus 'Loch Hope' (Funnel Group)

ORIGIN: (a form of *A. dyeri* [*A. inapertus* subsp. *intermedius*] per Gillissen 1980) raised by The Crown Estate, Windsor, UK, introduced in 1974, and still in cultivation.

NAME: after the lake in Scotland.

LEAF: deciduous, 30–50 cm long and up to 3 cm wide, upright, dark green, base green.

PEDUNCLE: 60–100(–150) cm, green with dull purple, slightly weak, round.

INFLORESCENCE: 12–16 cm across, 50–70 flowers, flat, bud opens on 1 side.

PEDICEL: dark violet-purple.

FLOWERBUD: dark violet-blue, upright.

FLOWER: inside violet-blue (94AB), midrib darker, margin slightly darker with purple tint, outside violet-blue with purple tint, base and midrib darker, when out of flower purple, horizontal to facing downwards, 3.8 cm long (tube 1.1–1.3 cm long), 3.5–4 cm across, stamens not exserted, anthers dark violet.

NOTE: most details from plants grown at different gardens and nurseries.

NOTE: probably the most popular of the taller *Agapanthus* cultivars, but because of the slightly weak peduncle best grown without any higher plants nearby.

NOTE: seed-raised plants are offered under this name, so be sure you buy the clone.

NOTE: nuclear DNA content = 23.6 pg.

ILLUSTRATION: *color plate*; photograph, Phillips and Rix (1991), Cheers (1997), Kramer (1998), Snoeijer (1998, 1999, 2000), and Fulcher (2000, 2002).

AWARD: AM in 1977; AGM.

Agapanthus 'Loch Hope Variegated' (Variegated Leaf Group)

ORIGIN: (seedling of 'Loch Hope') raised by Dick Fulcher, UK, introduced in 2002.

LEAF: evergreen, green with cream-yellow variegation.

Agapanthus 'Loch Inch'

ORIGIN: known since 1991, UK; no further records.

NAME: after the lake in Scotland.

'Longifolia' => *Agapanthus comptonii* 'Longifolia'

Agapanthus longispathus F.M. Leight. = *A. praecox* subsp. *minimus* (Lindl.)
F.M. Leight.

F.M. Leight. (1934) South African Gardening, Vol. XXIV, 82.

Agapanthus 'Lorna' (Salver Group)

ORIGIN: (an *A. campanulatus* hybrid) raised by Dick Fulcher, Pine Cottage Plants,
UK, named in 1998.
NAME: in honour of the raiser's wife.
PEDUNCLE: 130 cm.
INFLORESCENCE: 18 cm across.
FLOWER: "a rich very dark blue."
NOTE: details supplied by Dick Fulcher.

Agapanthus 'Lost Horizon' (Funnel Group)

ORIGIN: raised at NCCPG Bicton College, UK, selected by Dick Fulcher in 1993,
and still in cultivation.
LEAF: more or less deciduous.
PEDUNCLE: 60 cm, green, round.
INFLORESCENCE: 70 flowers, globular.
PEDICEL: green with purple towards the flower.
FLOWERBUD: upright, pale violet-blue with cream towards base, base violet-blue,
later more coloured.
FLOWER: inside very pale violet-blue with midrib slightly darker, outside very pale
violet-blue with midrib and base slightly darker, when out of flower purple, hori-
zontal, stamens exserted, anthers purple with yellowish pollen, becoming dark
brown.
NOTE: details supplied by Dick Fulcher and some from the Internet [5].

Agapanthus 'Luly' (Funnel Group)

ORIGIN: raised by Lewis Palmer, known since 1972, and still in cultivation.
NAME: after Lewis Palmer's pet.
LEAF: more or less evergreen, 50–60 cm long and 3–4 cm wide, fairly upright to
arching, dark green and glaucous, large dark glossy purple base.
PEDUNCLE: up to 90 cm.
INFLORESCENCE: 17 cm across, 50–80 flowers, globular.
PEDICEL: normal green.
FLOWER: pale violet-blue, margin darker (92B), midrib dark violet-blue (92A), hor-
izontal, 3.5 cm long, 3 cm across, stamens not exserted, anthers violet.
ILLUSTRATION: photograph, Phillips and Rix (1991), Warren (1995) and Fulcher
(2000).
AWARD: FCC in 1977.

Agapanthus 'Lydenburg' (Tubular Group)

SYNONYM: *Agapanthus inapertus* subsp. *hollandii* 'Lydenburg'

ORIGIN: (selection of *A. inapertus* subsp. *hollandii*) from Lydenburg, eastern Transvaal. Introduced by Kirstenbosch National Botanical Garden, known since 1983, and still in cultivation. Also offered as seed.

LEAF: deciduous.

PEDUNCLE: 80–120 cm, green and glaucous, round.

INFLORESCENCE: 25–40 flowers, drooping.

PEDICEL: green flush slightly with purple.

FLOWERBUD: very dark violet-blue, upright but quickly hanging downwards before opening.

FLOWER: outside dark violet-blue (93B) with base slightly darker, hanging downwards but not vertically, stamens not exserted.

NOTE: nuclear DNA content = 23.8 pg.

ILLUSTRATION: drawing, du Plessis and Duncan (1989); photograph, Duncan (1985 as *A. inapertus* subsp. *hollandii* 'Lydenburg', 1998 as *A. inapertus* subsp. *hollandii* 'Lydenburg'), Allemand and Pionnat (2001 as *A. inapertus* subsp. *hollandii* var. 'Lydenburg'), and Fulcher (2002).

Agapanthus 'Mabel Grey' = *A.* 'Lady Grey'

Agapanthus 'Macho' (Funnel Group)

ORIGIN: raised by Jo Dame, Kenya, in 2002, introduced by Karel Hooijman, Amstelveen, The Netherlands.

LEAF: evergreen.

PEDUNCLE: 140 cm.

FLOWER: violet-blue, 6–6.5 cm across.

NOTE: details supplied by Hooijman.

Agapanthus 'Magnifico' (Funnel Group)

SYNONYM: *Agapanthus praecox* 'Magnifico'

ORIGIN: (selection of *A. praecox*) introduced by Gary Dunlop, Ballyrogan Nurseries, UK, in 1998, who received the plant from a friend.

LEAF: evergreen, 10 per shoot, up to 50 cm long and 4 cm wide, upright to slightly arching, normal green, leafbase green.

PEDUNCLE: 120 cm, green.

INFLORESCENCE: 25 cm across, 100 flowers.

PEDICEL: slightly bronze.

FLOWER: inside dark violet-blue (93A), midrib violet-blue (94A), outside violet-blue (94A) flushed purple, horizontal, 4.5 cm long, 4 cm across.

NOTE: details supplied by Gary Dunlop.

NOTE: nuclear DNA content = 25.1 pg.

Agapanthus MAIBONT = *A.* 'Meibont'

Agapanthus 'Majestic'

SYNONYM: *Agapanthus umbellatus* 'Majestic'

ORIGIN: known since 1964, France, when referred to by Schauenberg.

FLOWER: violet-blue with dark midrib.

Agapanthus 'Major'

SYNONYM: *Agapanthus umbellatus* var. *major* Leichtlin

ORIGIN: known since 1873 when offered by Leichtlin, Germany, and still referred to in 1920.

PEDUNCLE: 90 cm.

FLOWER: "unicoloured."

Agapanthus 'Malvern'

SYNONYM: *Agapanthus* 'Malvern Hills'

ORIGIN: raised by John Tooby, Bransford, UK, "on a nursery based on the outskirts of Malvern." Known since 2000 when offered by Webbs of Wychbold, UK.

PEDUNCLE: 75–90 cm.

FLOWER: dark violet-blue.

Agapanthus 'Malvern Hills' = *A.* 'Malvern'

Agapanthus 'Marcus' (Trumpet Group)

ORIGIN: raised by Kees Duivenvoorde, Beverwijk, The Netherlands, introduced in 1995, and still in cultivation.

NAME: in honour of the raiser's grandson.

LEAF: deciduous, 30–40 cm long and 2.5 cm wide, upright, dark green and slightly glaucous, base green.

PEDUNCLE: 70 cm, green and slightly glaucous, flat.

INFLORESCENCE: 16 cm across, 50 flowers, globular, bud opens on 2 sides.

PEDICEL: purple with green base.

FLOWERBUD: violet-blue, upright.

FLOWER: inside pale violet-blue with purple at apex, margin slightly darker, midrib violet-blue, outside pale violet-blue with darker midrib and base, when out of flower purple, 3.5 cm long (tube 1 cm long), 3.5 cm across, stamens not exserted, anthers purple-brown with yellowish pollen.

NOTE: details from plants grown by Duivenvoorde.

NOTE: first flowers tend to have 8 tepals.

NOTE: registered in 1995.

ILLUSTRATION: photograph, Snoeijer (1998).

Agapanthus 'Margaret Wakehurst' (Funnel Group)

ORIGIN: raised and introduced by Lewis Palmer, known since 1973, and still in cultivation.

NAME: after an aristocratic lady.

LEAF: probably evergreen, 50–60 cm long and 2.5–4 cm wide, upright to slightly arching, dark glossy green, base green.

PEDUNCLE: 80–100 cm, green with violet blush towards inflorescence, round.

INFLORESCENCE: 16 cm across, 50–70 flowers, globular, bud opens on 1 side.

PEDICEL: dark violet-blue to almost black towards the flower.

FLOWERBUD: dark violet-blue, upright.

FLOWER: pale violet-blue (93CD) with a white base, margin slightly darker, midrib dark violet-blue (93AB), outside dark violet-blue with purple tint, base slightly darker, when out of flower more purple, horizontal, 4 cm long (tube 1.5 cm long), 4.5 cm across, stamens not exserted, anthers violet.

NOTE: details from plants grown at Wisley.

AWARD: AM in 1977.

Agapanthus 'Marianne' (Trumpet Group)

ORIGIN: raised by Kees Duivenvoorde, Beverwijk, The Netherlands, introduced in 1987, and still in cultivation.

NAME: in honour of Marianne Hendriks, a friend of the raiser.

LEAF: deciduous, up to 20 cm long and 2.5 cm wide, upright, normal to pale green, base green.

PEDUNCLE: 50 cm, normal green and slightly glaucous towards the base, round.

INFLORESCENCE: 17 cm across, 60–90 flowers, globular.

PEDICEL: green and purple speckled, base slightly dark purple.

FLOWERBUD: violet-blue, upright.

FLOWER: pale violet-blue (92AB), midrib violet-blue (93C), margin with purple blush, outside pale violet-blue with darker midrib and base, when out of flower purple, horizontal, 4.5 cm long (tube 1.8 cm long), 4(–4.5) cm across, stamens not exserted, anthers violet.

NOTE: details from plants grown by Duivenvoorde.

NOTE: registered in 1987.

NOTE: nuclear DNA content = 24 pg.

ILLUSTRATION: *color plate*; photograph, Snoeijer (1998, 2000), van Dijk and Snoeijer (2001), and van Dijk (2002).

Agapanthus 'Mariètte' (Trumpet Group)

ERROR: 'Marietta', 'Marriette'

ORIGIN: ('Intermedius' × unknown) raised by Kees Duivenvoorde, Beverwijk, The Netherlands, introduced in 1998, and still in cultivation.

LEAF: deciduous, 25–30 cm long and up to 1.8 cm wide, upright, dark green, base green.

PEDUNCLE: 40(–60) cm, green, rather sturdy, flat.

INFLORESCENCE: 14 cm across, 80 flowers, globular.

PEDICEL: green and slightly violet speckled.

FLOWERBUD: pale green with violet-blue apex, later pale violet-blue with dark apex, upright.

FLOWER: inside very pale violet-blue, midrib violet-blue (97C), margin pale violet-blue with a hint of purple (97D), outside pale violet-blue and purple tint but darker towards apex (97B), midrib violet-blue, base not particularly darker, when out of flower purple, upright to horizontal, 3–3.5 cm long (tube 0.8–1 cm long), 2.9 cm across, stamens not exserted, anthers black.
NOTE: details from plants grown by Duivenvoorde.
NOTE: selected for its late flowering.
NOTE: registered in 1999.
NOTE: nuclear DNA content = 24.5 pg.
ILLUSTRATION: *color plate.*

Agapanthus 'Marike'

ORIGIN: (**'Corinne'** × **'Ice Lolly'**) raised by Wayne Hundertmark, Zimbabwe, in 1999, introduced by Karel Hooijman, Amstelveen, The Netherlands, in 2002.
PEDUNCLE: 40 cm.
FLOWER: pure white, 3–3.5 cm across, anthers yellow.
NOTE: details supplied by Hooijman.

Agapanthus 'Marjorie'

ORIGIN: from Bert Hopwood, introduced by Buckshaw Gardens, UK. Known since 1989 and still in cultivation.
NAME: in honour of Hopwood's wife.
PEDUNCLE: 50–60 cm.
INFLORESCENCE: "large."
FLOWER: pale violet-blue.

Agapanthus 'Martine' (Trumpet Group)

ORIGIN: raised by Kees Duivenvoorde, Beverwijk, The Netherlands, introduced in 1996, and still in cultivation.
NAME: in honour of the raiser's granddaughter.
LEAF: deciduous, up to 40 cm long and 2 cm wide, upright, pale green, base green.
PEDUNCLE: 80 cm, green and flushed purple, round.
INFLORESCENCE: up to 16 cm across, 70 flowers, globular, bud opens on 1 side.
PEDICEL: almost completely dark purple with a green base.
FLOWERBUD: upright, dark violet-blue but when very young distinctly with a white base.
FLOWER: inside pale violet-blue with margin slightly darker, midrib violet-blue, outside violet-blue with midrib darker and purple apex, base very dark, when out of flower purple-violet, horizontal, up to 4 cm long (tube 1.3 cm), 3.5 cm across, stamens not exserted, anthers very dark violet.
NOTE: details from plants grown by Duivenvoorde.
NOTE: within an inflorescence usually some flowers will have 8 tepals.
NOTE: registered in 1995.
NOTE: nuclear DNA content = 23.6 pg.
ILLUSTRATION: photograph, Snoeijer (1998).

Agapanthus 'Martyr Worthy'

ORIGIN: raised by Mrs Nelson, Winchester, UK, known since 1974; no further records.

Agapanthus maximus Besant = *A*. 'Maximus'

Besant (1903) Flora and Sylva, 1.
Erhardt (1995) PPP Index.

Agapanthus maximus albidus Numa Schneider (1911) Revue Horticole. nom.nud.

Agapanthus maximus 'Albus' = *A*. 'Maximus Albus'

NOTE: invalid name per the ICNCP-1995, art. 17.2, 17.9, and 17.11.

Agapanthus maximus 'Krelagei' = *A*. 'Krelagei'

Agapanthus 'Maximus' (Funnel Group)

SYNONYM: *Agapanthus africanus* var. *maximus* (Lindl.) Durand & Schinz
Agapanthus maximus Besant
Agapanthus praecox subsp. *maximus* Erhardt
Agapanthus praecox subsp. *orientalis* 'Maximus'
Agapanthus praecox subsp. *praecox* 'Maximus'
Agapanthus umbellatus var. *maximus* Lindl.
Agapanthus umbellatus 'Maximus'

ORIGIN: (selection of *A. praecox*) obtained by J.H. Krelage, Haarlem, The Netherlands, from Mr Ring, Frankfurt am Main, Germany, in about 1843; Max Leichtlin of Baden-Baden, Germany, bought a plant from Krelage. The plant was a very slow grower and was not readily available commercially until the 1890s. Krelage showed the plant in October 1892 as *A. umbellatus maximus*.
LEAF: evergreen, "broad and massive."
PEDUNCLE: 120 cm or more.
INFLORESCENCE: "huge," "immense," 300 flowers.
FLOWER: "levendige fraai blauwe kleur," violet-blue, up to 6.25 cm across.
NOTE: according to Beauverd (1910), 'Maximus' is a synonym of 'Multiflorus'.
NOTE: nuclear DNA content = 24.9 pg.
NOTE: Koen van Poucke, Sint Niklaas, Belgium, still offers a clone from a plant known from before World War II, but this is not positively the true 'Maximus'; its description is as follows:
LEAF: evergreen, 30–50 cm long and up to 5 cm wide, arching, normal green, base green.
PEDUNCLE: 100 cm, green, round.
INFLORESCENCE: 18–20 cm across, over 100 flowers, globular, bud opens on 1 side.
PEDICEL: pale to normal green.
FLOWERBUD: violet-blue with paler base, upright.
FLOWER: inside very pale violet-blue to almost white at the base, margin and midrib

slightly darker (94BC), purple tint, outside pale violet-blue but darker towards apex, base very pale violet-blue, when out of flower dark violet-blue with purple, horizontal, 5.5–6 cm long (tube 2 cm long), 6–6.5 cm across, stamens exserted, anthers violet-brown.

ILLUSTRATION: *color plate.*

Agapanthus 'Maximus Albus' ex Snoeijer (1998) = *A.* 'Umbellatus Albus'

NOTE: the description published in my 1998 book is excluded here as I had to accept the plant used for the description as a synonym of 'Umbellatus Albus'.

Agapanthus 'Maximus Albus' (Funnel Group)

SYNONYM: *Agapanthus maximus* 'Albus'
Agapanthus orientalis var. *maximus albus* Synge
Agapanthus praecox subsp. *maximus* 'Albus'
Agapanthus praecox subsp. *praecox* 'Maximus Albus'
Agapanthus praecox 'Maximus Albus'
Agapanthus umbellatus var. *maximus albus* Lemoine

ORIGIN: (selection of **A. praecox**) most likely Dutch, known since 1888, The Netherlands. Plants are still offered but may not be true.
LEAF: evergreen.
INFLORESCENCE: "large," over 100 flowers.
FLOWER: white.

Agapanthus 'Mediterranee' (Funnel Group)

ORIGIN: known since 2002 when listed on the Internet.
FLOWER: violet-blue (92C).
NOTE: details from the Internet [18].

Agapanthus 'Medium White' (Funnel Group)

SYNONYM: *Agapanthus* praecox 'Medium White'

ORIGIN: (selection of **A. praecox**) known since 1993, Kirstenbosch National Botanical Garden, South Africa. Also offered as seed.
LEAF: evergreen.
PEDUNCLE: 50–80 cm.
FLOWER: white.
NOTE: invalid name per the ICNCP-1995, art. 17.11.

Agapanthus medius Roem. & Schult. (1830) Systema vegetabilium. nom.nud.

NOTE: Roemer and Schultes refer to this name but with a question mark and no description.

Agapanthus 'Meibont' (Salver Group)

SYNONYM: *Agapanthus campanulatus* 'Meibont'
TRANSLATION: MAIBONT [in German]

ORIGIN: ('**Lilliput**' × '**Midnight Star**') raised by Hans Kramer, De Hessenhof nursery, The Netherlands. Selected from approximately 2000 seedlings and introduced in 1998. Still in cultivation.

NAME: Dutch, "variegated in May," a reference to the leaf colouring.

LEAF: more or less deciduous, up to 40 cm long and 2.3 cm wide, green with upper half cream-yellow in spring, in summer green with a yellow tip or green, base dark purple.

PEDUNCLE: 80 cm.

INFLORESCENCE: 15 cm across, 50–60 flowers, more or less globular.

PEDICEL: green at the base to dark purple-violet towards the flower.

FLOWERBUD: violet-blue with dark violet-blue base, upright but quickly horizontal.

FLOWER: inside violet-blue with darker midrib, purple tint, outside violet-blue with darker midrib and base, horizontal to slightly facing downwards, stamens not exserted, anthers violet.

NOTE: details from plants grown at De Hessenhof.

NOTE: '**Septemberhemel**' is from the same batch.

NOTE: nuclear DNA content = 22.7 pg.

Agapanthus 'Meoni' = *A.* '**Blanc Méoni**'

Agapanthus 'Mercury' (Trumpet Group)

ORIGIN: raised at NCCPG Bicton College, UK, selected by Dick Fulcher in 1993, and still in cultivation.

LEAF: more or less evergreen.

PEDUNCLE: 90–95 cm.

INFLORESCENCE: 70 flowers, globular.

FLOWER: very pale violet-blue ("an unusual silver, mercury shade—off white with grey stripe"), when out of flower a bit purple, horizontal, 3.7 cm long (tube 1.5 cm), stamens not exserted, anthers yellow.

NOTE: details supplied by Dick Fulcher.

NOTE: invalid name per the ICNCP-1995, art. 17.13.

ILLUSTRATION: photograph, Fulcher (2002).

Agapanthus '**Meryden White**'

ORIGIN: known since 2001 when offered by Fir Tree Farm.

NOTE: name from the Internet [19].

Agapanthus 'Mid Blue'

ORIGIN: known since 1997, New Zealand, and still in cultivation.

FLOWER: violet-blue with darker midrib.

NOTE: invalid name per the ICNCP-1995, art. 17.11.

Agapanthus 'Mid Blue Dark'

ORIGIN: known since 1997 when grown by Ignace van Doorslaer, Belgium, obtained from Raveningham Gardens, UK. Still in cultivation.

LEAF: evergreen.
FLOWER: violet-blue with darker midrib.
NOTE: invalid name per the ICNCP-1995, art. 17.11.

Agapanthus MIDKNIGHT BLUE = *A.* 'Monmid'

Agapanthus 'Midnight'

ORIGIN: known since 1999 when offered by RHS Garden Wisley, but this plant is probably either 'Midnight Blue' or 'Midnight Star'.

Agapanthus 'Midnight Blue' ex South Africa

ORIGIN: tissue-cultured plants are offered in South Africa, but the description clearly differs from the original Philip Wood cultivar.
INFLORESCENCE: 50–70 flowers.
FLOWER: violet-blue.
NOTE: invalid name per the ICNCP-1995, art. 17.2.

Agapanthus 'Midnight Blue' ex Philip Wood (Salver Group)

SYNONYM: *Agapanthus campanulatus* 'Midnight Blue'

ORIGIN: (seedling of *A. campanulatus*, raised from seed received from South Africa, see further at *A. campanulatus* 'Nanus') raised by Philip Wood, introduced by Slieve Donard Nursery, UK. Known since 1976 and still in cultivation. Also offered as seed.
LEAF: deciduous, upright, normal green.
PEDUNCLE: 30 cm, green to violet near the inflorescence.
INFLORESCENCE: 20 flowers.
PEDICEL: purple-violet.
FLOWER: inside dark violet-blue with white base, outside dark violet-blue, when out of flower purple-violet, 1.5 cm across.
NOTE: details supplied by Gary Dunlop; those from my 1998 book are excluded.
NOTE: nuclear DNA content = 22.6 pg.
NOTE: most plants grown under this name have nothing to do with Wood's plant and should be regarded as RUBBISH.
ILLUSTRATION: *color plate.*

Agapanthus 'Midnight Star' (Trumpet Group)

ORIGIN: raised by Raveningham Gardens, UK, known since 1989, and still in cultivation.
LEAF: deciduous, up to 40 cm long and 2.6 cm wide, arching, dark green, base dark purple.
PEDUNCLE: 50–90 cm, green with dark purple below the inflorescence, round.
INFLORESCENCE: 13–15 cm across, 40–50(–80) flowers, flat.
PEDICEL: dark purple to green at the base.
FLOWERBUD: dark violet-blue with darker base, rather glossy, upright.
FLOWER: inside pale violet-blue (92B) with a purple tint, midrib dark violet-blue

(93A), outside pale violet-blue (92A) with distinct purple tint, midrib violet-blue (93B) and base glossy violet-blue (93A), when out of flower purple-violet, horizontal to just a bit nodding, up to 3.5 cm long (tube 1.2 cm long), 2.8 cm across, stamens not exserted, anthers dark violet.

NOTE: details from plants grown by van Doorslaer; those from my 1998 book are excluded.

NOTE: widely propagated by seed and so better to regard this as a group of plants that look similar rather than a proper cultivar.

NOTE: nuclear DNA content = 23.2 pg.

ILLUSTRATION: photograph, Kramer (1998).

AWARD: PC in 1989.

Agapanthus 'Milky Blue'

ORIGIN: known since 1997, New Zealand. Also offered as seed.

Agapanthus 'Miniature Blue'

SYNONYM: *Agapanthus praecox* 'Miniature Blue'

ORIGIN: known since 1998, UK.

NOTE: invalid name per the ICNCP-1995, art. 17.11.

Agapanthus 'Miniature White'

SYNONYM: *Agapanthus praecox* 'Miniature White'

ORIGIN: known since 1992, Kirstenbosch National Botanical Garden, and 1997, France, imported from South Africa.

NOTE: invalid name per the ICNCP-1995, art. 17.11.

Agapanthus 'Mini Blue'

ORIGIN: known since 1997, New Zealand.

NOTE: invalid name per the ICNCP-1995, art. 17.11.

Agapanthus 'Mini Twista'

ORIGIN: introduced by Monterey Bay Nursery, California, USA, introduced in 2000.

LEAF: "rather broad foliage for a dwarf form."

PEDUNCLE: "thick, chunky, sturdy stalks."

INFLORESCENCE: "dense, round clusters."

FLOWER: "pure white."

NOTE: details from the Internet [20].

Agapanthus minor Lodd. = *A. africanus* (L.) Hoffmanns. subsp. *africanus*

Lodd. (1817) Bot. Cab. I, 42.

Agapanthus minor var. globusus Bonstedt = *A.* 'Globosus'

Bonstedt (1931) Pareys Blumengärtnerei.

Agapanthus minor var. *leichtlinii* Bonstedt = *A.* 'Leichtlinii'
Bonstedt (1931) Pareys Blumengärtnerei.

Agapanthus minor var. *mooreanus* Bonstedt = *A.* 'Mooreanus'
Bonstedt (1931) Pareys Blumengärtnerei.

Agapanthus minor var. *saintpaulii* Bonstedt = *A.* 'Saintpaulii'
Bonstedt (1931) Pareys Blumengärtnerei.

Agapanthus minor alba => *A. africanus* 'Albus'
ORIGIN: offered as seed.

Agapanthus minor 'Leichtlinii' = *A.* 'Leichtlinii'

Agapanthus minor 'Mooreanus' = *A.* 'Mooreanus'

Agapanthus minor 'Morei' = *A.* 'Mooreanus'
NOTE: offered by Lemoine, France, in 1877 and still offered by him in 1911; Lemoine's 1877 description reads, "Rustique espèce produisant des ombelles de 20 fleurs, en clochettes et d'un bleu intense." The plant probably refers to 'Mooreanus'; however, this contradicts stories concerning that cultivar's year of introduction.

Agapanthus minor 'Saintpaulii' = *A.* 'Saintpaulii'

'Minor' => *Agapanthus africanus* 'Minor'

Agapanthus 'Minor Alba' => *A. africanus* 'Albus'
NOTE: invalid name per the ICNCP-1995, art. 17.9 and 17.11.

Agapanthus Mixed Giant Hybrids = *A.* RUBBISH

Agapanthus 'Mixed White' = *A.* RUBBISH

Agapanthus mixed whites = *A.* RUBBISH

Agapanthus 'Miss Latimer'
ORIGIN: known since 1995, UK; no further records.

Agapanthus 'Moira' (Trumpet Group)
ORIGIN: (selection from seedlings) introduced by van der Zwet, Roelofarendsveen, The Netherlands, around 1965 and still known in 1987. Probably no longer in cultivation.
LEAF: evergreen, horizontal.
PEDUNCLE: up to 50 cm.
INFLORESCENCE: up to 15 cm, with 60–70 flowers.

FLOWERBUD: distinctly dark coloured and small.
FLOWER: violet-blue (98BC and 100AC), 4 cm long (tube 1.7 cm), 2.5 cm across.
NOTE: very often with a second short peduncle next to the main peduncle.
NOTE: seed brown.

Agapanthus 'Molly Fenwick' (Funnel Group)

ORIGIN: known since 1991, from Savill Gardens, Windsor, UK.
PEDUNCLE: up to 75 cm.
FLOWER: violet-blue.
ILLUSTRATION: photograph, Phillips and Rix (1991).

Agapanthus 'Molly Howick' (Trumpet Group)

ERROR: 'Molly Hawick'

ORIGIN: raised by Lewis Palmer, known since 1972, and still in cultivation.
LEAF: up to 40 cm long and 2.5 cm wide, upright, pale green, base purple.
PEDUNCLE: 60–70 cm, pale green, round.
INFLORESCENCE: 15 cm across, 60 flowers, globular.
PEDICEL: green flushed with dark violet.
FLOWERBUD: dark violet-blue, upright but quickly horizontal.
FLOWER: inside violet-blue (94AB) with margin slightly darker, midrib dark violet-blue, outside dark violet-blue, midrib with darker apex and slightly purple, when out of flower more purple, horizontal, 2.8 cm long (tube 1 cm long), 2–2.5 cm across, stamens not exserted, anthers dark violet.
NOTE: most details from plants grown by Coen Jansen.
AWARD: AM in 1977.

Agapanthus 'Momid, T.M.' = *A.* 'Monmid'

NOTE: name from the Internet [8].

Agapanthus 'Mondrian'

ORIGIN: introduced by Lambley Nursery, Australia, before 2000.
PEDUNCLE: 80 cm.
INFLORESCENCE: globular.
FLOWER: white.

Agapanthus 'Monmid' (Salver Group)

ERROR: 'Momid'

TRADE NAME: MIDKNIGHT BLUE ex USA

ORIGIN: introduced by Monrovia, USA, in 1995 and still in cultivation.
NAME: a compilation of Monrovia and MIDKNIGHT.
LEAF: deciduous, up to 35 cm long, normal green.
PEDUNCLE: 75–100 cm.
INFLORESCENCE: 12–14 cm across, 40–70 flowers, more or less globular.
PEDICEL: green flushed purple towards the flower.

FLOWERBUD: violet-blue apex to greyish towards the base and base green, quickly more coloured, upright.

FLOWER: inside pale violet-blue, midrib darker violet-blue and tend to be in two stripes, outside pale violet-blue with darker midrib and base, horizontal to slightly facing downwards, stamens slightly exserted, anthers violet.

NOTE: details from plants offered at a garden center in Portland, Oregon, USA, some details from the Internet [30], and some sent by Wendy Proud of Monrovia. This cultivar is propagated by Monrovia via tissue culture.

NOTE: offered with a trademark in the USA.

ILLUSTRATION: *color plate.*

Agapanthus 'Monstrosus'

SYNONYM: *Agapanthus orientalis* var. *monstrosus* Synge
Agapanthus praecox subsp. *praecox* 'Monstrosus'
Agapanthus umbellatus var. *fl. monst.* Mater
Agapanthus umbellatus var. *monstrosus* A. Worsley

ORIGIN: (chance seedling from a flower with 12 tepals) known since 1892 when offered by Mater, Leiden, The Netherlands, for 25 cents, one of the cheapest of the 10 cultivars listed. Probably no longer in cultivation.

LEAF: evergreen, 5–7.5 cm wide, green and glaucous.

INFLORESCENCE: several hundred flowers.

FLOWER: with more than 6 tepals, violet-blue.

Agapanthus 'Mood Indigo' (Trumpet Group)

SYNONYM: *Agapanthus inapertus* 'Mood Indigo'

ORIGIN: (selection of *A. inapertus*) introduced from the Los Angeles State and County Arboretum, California, USA. Known since 1991 and still in cultivation.

LEAF: deciduous, up to 30 cm long and 2 cm wide, arching, pale green, base violet.

PEDUNCLE: 60–80 cm long, pale green slightly flushed purple, round.

INFLORESCENCE: 15 cm across, 30–50 flowers, globular.

PEDICEL: pale green flushed purple towards the flower.

FLOWERBUD: upright, violet-blue and darker ribbed.

FLOWER: inside pale purple-violet with margin darker and paler base, midrib purple-violet, outside violet-blue with purple tint, midrib and base dark violet-blue, when out of flower purple, horizontal to slightly nodding, up to 2.4 cm long (tube 0.7 cm long), 2.4 cm across, stamens not exserted, anthers green-violet becoming brown.

NOTE: details from plants grown by Coen Jansen.

NOTE: invalid name per the ICNCP-1995, art. 17.13, but as the name refers to the colour, not to a plant, it is accepted here.

Agapanthus 'Moonstar'

ERROR: 'Moon Star'

ORIGIN: raised and introduced by Raveningham Gardens, UK, known since 1993, and still in cultivation.

LEAF: deciduous.

PEDUNCLE: 50 cm.

FLOWER: "pale violet-blue."

NOTE: said to be mixed up with 'Sky Star'.

Agapanthus 'Mooreanus' (Salver Group)

SYNONYM: *Agapanthus africanus* subsp. *minor* var. *mooreanus* H.R. Wehrh.
Agapanthus africanus var. *mooreanus* Nich. ex Boom
Agapanthus campanulatus subsp. *patens* 'Mooreanus'
Agapanthus minor var. *mooreanus* Bonstedt
Agapanthus minor 'Mooreanus'
Agapanthus minor 'Morei'
Agapanthus orientalis Mooreanus'
Agapanthus praecox Mooreanus'
Agapanthus umbellatus var. *mooreanus* G. Nicholson
Agapanthus umbellatus 'Mooreanus'

ORIGIN: (selection of *A. campanulatus* subsp. *patens*) still in cultivation.

NAME: in honour of the Moore family, as both David Moore and Frederick Moore were directors of the Glasnevin Botanic Garden. Horticulturist David Moore (1807–1879) was born Muir but changed his name when he moved from Scotland to Ireland; he was director from 1838 until his death in 1879. His son, Frederick William Moore (1857–1950), succeeded him in that year and continued as director until 1922; he was knighted in 1911.

LEAF: deciduous, up to 28 cm long and 1.3 cm wide, upright, strongly ribbed beneath.

PEDUNCLE: 45–70 cm.

INFLORESCENCE: 20–25 flowers.

FLOWER: inside violet-blue (92A), segments sometimes recurved, 2.9 cm long (tube 1 cm), 3.8 cm across.

NOTE: the usual story of its introduction is that, around 1890, a German student, working at the Glasnevin Botanic Garden, Dublin, Ireland, went to South Africa and sent a plant to Sir Frederick Moore, the garden's director. The student labelled the plant *mooreanus*. It is also said that the plant was introduced by Julius Wilhelm Keit, curator of the Natal Botanical Gardens from 1872, who sent it to the Glasnevin Botanic Garden in the late 1870s. Lemoine listed an *A. minor* 'Morei' in 1877, as did Krelage, The Netherlands, in 1888 (the plant was referred to as "new"). Van Tubergen showed the plant in August 1891 in Artis Zoo, Amsterdam. In 1954, Lady Moore told Lewis Palmer she was almost certain the plant received at Glasnevin originated in Orange Free State, in which case it is surely a selection of *A. campanulatus* subsp. *patens*.

NOTE: mainly seed-propagated since its introduction and so better to regard this as a group of plants that look similar rather than a proper cultivar.

AWARD: AGM in 1928 as *A. africanus mooreanus*.

Agapanthus 'Mooreanus Minor' = *A.* RUBBISH

Agapanthus Mooreanus Minor Hybrids = *A*. RUBBISH

Agapanthus 'Mori-no-fuji'

ORIGIN: Japan, known since 2001 when offered by Komoriya Nursery Ltd.
PEDUNCLE: 100 cm.
FLOWER: purple-violet.
NOTE: details from the Internet [25].

Agapanthus 'Mori-no-hirugao'

ERROR: 'Morino-hirugao'

ORIGIN: Japan, known since 2001 when offered by Komoriya Nursery Ltd.
PEDUNCLE: 80 cm.
FLOWER: pale violet-blue.
NOTE: details from the Internet [25].

Agapanthus 'Mori-no-izumi' (Salver Group)

ORIGIN: raised and introduced in Japan, known since 1999, and still in cultivation.
NAME: Japanese, "soft breeze in the forest."
PEDUNCLE: 80 cm.
INFLORESCENCE: flat.
FLOWER: pale violet-blue, midrib and margin dark violet-blue.
NOTE: details supplied by Y. Aihara and some from the Internet [25].

Agapanthus 'Mori-no-rindou' (Salver Group)

ERROR: 'Mori-no-rinndou'

ORIGIN: raised and introduced in Japan, known since 1999, and still in cultivation.
PEDUNCLE: 60 cm.
INFLORESCENCE: flat.
FLOWER: pale purple-violet with darker midrib.
NOTE: details supplied by Y. Aihara and some from the Internet [25].

Agapanthus 'Mori-no-ryoufuu'

ORIGIN: Japan, known since 2001 when offered by Komoriya Nursery Ltd.
NAME: Japanese, "purple cloud."
PEDUNCLE: 120 cm.
FLOWER: pale purple-violet.
NOTE: details from the Internet [25].

Agapanthus 'Mori-no-ryozu' (Salver Group)

ORIGIN: raised and introduced in Japan, known since 1999.
NAME: Japanese, "soft breeze in the forest."
FLOWER: dark violet-blue.
NOTE: details supplied by Y. Aihara.

Agapanthus 'Morning Star'

ORIGIN: raised by Raveningham Gardens, UK, known since 1996, and still in cultivation.
LEAF: deciduous.
PEDUNCLE: 80 cm.
FLOWER: violet-blue.

Agapanthus Mosswood Hybrids => see note under *A.* RUBBISH

ORIGIN: seedlings selected by Ron Pal, Victoria, British Columbia, Canada, known since 1996, and still offered.
NOTE: details from the Internet [4].

Agapanthus 'Mount Stewart' (Funnel Group)

SYNONYM: *Agapanthus africanus* 'Mount Stewart'
Agapanthus 'Mount Stewart Form'
Agapanthus praecox 'Mount Stewart'
Agapanthus praecox 'Mount Stewart Form'

ORIGIN: introduced by Gary Dunlop, Ballyrogan Nurseries, UK, known since 1996, and still in cultivation.
NAME: after the famous garden in Northern Ireland.
LEAF: evergreen, up to 45 cm long and 2 cm wide, arching, normal green and glaucous, base green.
PEDUNCLE: up to 115 cm, green.
INFLORESCENCE: 20 cm across, 85 flowers, distinctly globular, bud opens at 2 sides.
PEDICEL: green-bronze.
FLOWER: violet-blue.
NOTE: regarded as a selection of *A. africanus* but because of the peduncle length, the size of the inflorescence, and the amount of flowers, it seems more a selection of *A. praecox* subsp. *orientalis*.
NOTE: nuclear DNA content = 25 pg.

Agapanthus 'Mount Stewart Form' = *A.* 'Mount Stewart'

NOTE: invalid name per the ICNCP-1995, art. 17.15.

Agapanthus 'Mount Thomas', *A.* 'Mt Thomas' (Funnel Group)

SYNONYM: *Agapanthus praecox* subsp. *orientalis* 'Mount Thomas'

ORIGIN: (selection of *A. praecox* subsp. *orientalis*) from Mount Thomas, eastern Cape. Introduced by Kirstenbosch National Botanical Garden, South Africa. Known since 1976 and still in cultivation. Also offered as seed.
LEAF: evergreen, green and glaucous.
PEDUNCLE: 80–120 cm.
INFLORESCENCE: rather small but many-flowered, 60–80 flowers, globular.
FLOWER: inside pale violet-blue (96D) with midrib just slightly darker, outside similar but slightly darker, when out of flower purple, horizontal, stamens not exserted, anthers yellow becoming black.

NOTE: seed-propagated and so better to regard this as a group of plants that look similar rather than a proper cultivar.
ILLUSTRATION: drawing, du Plessis and Duncan (1989); photograph, Duncan (1985 as *A. praecox* subsp. *orientalis* 'Mt. Thomas').
NOTE: Kirstenbosch offered this cultivar as seed in 1997 described as "very dark blue."

Agapanthus 'Mt Thomas' => *A.* 'Mount Thomas'

Agapanthus multiflorus Willd. = *A.* 'Multiflorus'

Willd. (1809) Enum. Plant. 353. nom.nud.
Roem. & Schult. (1830) Systema vegetabilium.

Agapanthus 'Multiflorus'

SYNONYM: *Agapanthus africanus* subsp. *umbellatus* var. *multifloris* Voss ex H.R. Wehrh.
Agapanthus multiflorus Willd.
Agapanthus umbellatus var. *multiflorus* Baker
ORIGIN: known since 1809 and still referred to in 1931.
LEAF: up to 2.5 cm wide.
INFLORESCENCE: 60–80 flowers.
FLOWER: dark violet-blue, 4.5–6 cm long.
NOTE: according to Beauverd (1910), 'Multiflorus' is a synonym of 'Maximus'.

Agapanthus 'Murasaki Shikibu' (Salver Group)

ORIGIN: Japan, known since 2001 when offered by Takii.
FLOWER: violet-blue with darker midrib, stamens exserted.
NOTE: details supplied by Y. Aihara.

Agapanthus 'My Joy'

ORIGIN: raised by J.N. Giridlian's Oakhurst Gardens, Arcadia, California, introduced in 1943; they offered the plant for several years, but demand was so high they stopped sales to build up stock, offering it again in 1962. Probably no longer in cultivation.
LEAF: "grassy."
PEDUNCLE: 40 cm.
FLOWER: "bright blue."

Agapanthus 'Mystery' (Trumpet Group)

ORIGIN: raised by Lewis Palmer, known since 1972, and still in cultivation.
LEAF: deciduous, 35 cm long and 3 cm wide, slightly arching, normal to dark dull green.
PEDUNCLE: 70–80 cm, normal green.
INFLORESCENCE: 16 cm across, globular.

FLOWER: white with margin violet-blue (94B) and midrib violet-blue (94A), upright to horizontal, 3.8 cm long, 3.8 cm across.
AWARD: HC in 1977.

Agapanthus 'Nana Blue'

ORIGIN: known since 2001, South Africa.
PEDUNCLE: 30 cm.
FLOWER: violet-blue.
NOTE: propagated by tissue culture.
NOTE: invalid name per the ICNCP-1995, art. 17.9 and 17.11.

Agapanthus 'Nana White' = A. 'Little White'

NOTE: invalid name per the ICNCP-1995, art. 17.9 and 17.11.

Agapanthus nanus L.H. Bailey = A. 'Nanus'

L.H. Bailey (1977) Hortus Third.

'Nanus' => Agapanthus campanulatus subsp. campanulatus 'Nanus'

Agapanthus 'Nanus' (Funnel Group)

SYNONYM: Agapanthus nanus L.H. Bailey
Agapanthus orientalis 'Nanus'

ORIGIN: known since 1977, USA, when referred to by Bailey, and again by Pienaar in 1987, South Africa, but it is doubtful that both are one and the same plant.
FLOWER: violet-blue with darker midrib.
NOTE: usually referred to as being "dwarf and compact."
NOTE: invalid name per the ICNCP-1995, art. 17.9 and 17.11.
ILLUSTRATION: photograph, Pienaar (1987 as A. orientalis 'Nanus').

Agapanthus 'Naomi'

ORIGIN: known since 2001 when it was to be offered by Asterby & Chalkcroft Nurseries, UK, according to the RHS Plant Finder. But the nursery informs me they never received stock from the wholesale nursery, which has since gone out of business, so the existence of plants seems uncertain.

Agapanthus natalensis Gaddum = A. 'Natalensis'

Gaddum (1997) New Zealand Plant Finder. nom.nud.

Agapanthus 'Natalensis'

SYNONYM: Agapanthus natalensis Gaddum

ORIGIN: known since 1997, New Zealand, and still in cultivation.
FLOWER: "deep electric blue."
NOTE: according to Bulbes d'Opale, probably a form of A. campanulatus.
NOTE: invalid name per the ICNCP-1995, art. 17.9.

Agapanthus 'Navy Blue'

SYNONYM: *Agapanthus campanulatus* 'Navy Blue'
Agapanthus 'Dark Navy Blue'

ORIGIN: known since 1995, UK, and still in cultivation.
LEAF: deciduous.
FLOWER: dark violet-blue.

Agapanthus 'Neuseeland'

ORIGIN: collected as an unnamed plant from New Zealand and introduced by Heinrich Hagemann Staudenkulturen, Germany. Known since 1995 and still in cultivation.
FLOWER: pale violet-blue.

Agapanthus 'Newa' (Trumpet Group)

ORIGIN: raised by Th. P.W. de Groot, Hillegom, The Netherlands, introduced by Maas & van Stein, also of Hillegom, introduced in 2001.
NAME: Dutch spelling of the Neva River.
LEAF: deciduous, up to 35 cm long and 1.9 cm wide, slightly arching, pale green, base green.
PEDUNCLE: 70 cm, pale to normal green and a bit purple speckled, flat.
INFLORESCENCE: 20 cm across, 40 flowers, flat.
PEDICEL: green with purple speckles.
FLOWERBUD: pale violet-blue with darker base, upright but quickly horizontal.
FLOWER: inside very pale violet-blue (92CD) with slight purple tint at the margin, midrib violet-blue (92A) with purple tint, outside pale violet-blue (92C) with midrib slightly darker (92B), base violet-blue (92AB), when out of flower purple with violet-blue base becoming white, horizontal, up to 4 cm long (tube 1.5 cm long), 3.5 cm across, only 1–2 stamens exserted, anthers violet with yellow pollen.
NOTE: details from plants grown by Maas & van Stein.

Agapanthus 'New Blue' = A. RUBBISH

NOTE: various countries offer different seed-propagated plants, and it is therefore best to regard this as RUBBISH. A clone grown under this name in the UK by a few nurseries has been propagated by tissue culture; the description of this clone is as follows:
LEAF: evergreen.
PEDUNCLE: 50–70 cm.
INFLORESCENCE: "elegant loose," 15–20 flowers, flat.
FLOWER: inside pale violet-blue to almost white near the base, margin violet-blue, midrib dark violet-blue, horizontal, stamens exserted, anthers violet.
NOTE: details send by Dick Fulcher.
ILLUSTRATION: photograph, Fulcher (2002 as *A.* 'New Blue').

Agapanthus 'New Giant' = A. RUBBISH

Agapanthus 'New Giant Blue' = *A.* RUBBISH

Agapanthus 'New Giant Blue Pale' = *A.* RUBBISH

Agapanthus New Giant Hybrids = *A.* RUBBISH

> NOTE: plants offered are seed-raised and therefore variable. Selections in violet-blue or white are offered as 'New Giant Blue', 'New Giant White', etc., but since seedlings that have not yet flowered are also sold, it is possible that plants sold as flowering violet-blue might actually flower white and vice versa, hence: RUBBISH.

Agapanthus 'New Giant Pale' = *A.* RUBBISH

Agapanthus 'New Giant Pale Blue' = *A.* RUBBISH

Agapanthus 'New Giant White' = *A.* RUBBISH

Agapanthus New Hybrids Mixed = *A.* RUBBISH

Agapanthus 'Newstead Blue'

> ORIGIN: known since 1998 when offered by Diacks, New Zealand, and still in cultivation.
> PEDUNCLE: 80–100 cm.
> FLOWER: violet-blue.

Agapanthus 'Nicky' = *A.* **'Nikki'**

Agapanthus 'Nikki' (Salver Group)

> SYNONYM: *Agapanthus* 'Nicky'

> ORIGIN: (an *A. campanulatus* hybrid) raised by Dick Fulcher, Pine Cottage Plants, UK, named in 1998, and still in cultivation.
> NAME: in honour of the raiser's second daughter.
> LEAF: deciduous, up to 46 cm long and 2.2 cm wide, arching, dark green and a bit glaucous, base slightly purple.
> PEDUNCLE: 60–80 cm, green and slightly purple speckled, round.
> INFLORESCENCE: 15–16 cm across, 30–50 flowers, flat.
> PEDICEL: green to dark violet towards flower.
> FLOWERBUD: upright, very dark violet-blue with a white spot in the middle when young.
> FLOWER: inside violet-blue with a purple tint and a white base, midrib dark violet-blue, outside violet-blue with midrib and base slightly darker, sometimes with a white spot at the end of the tube, when out of flower dark violet-blue with purple, horizontal to slightly nodding, 3.5–3.7 cm long (tube 1 cm long), 4–4.2 cm across, stamens not exserted, anthers violet.
> NOTE: most details supplied by Dick Fulcher.
> ILLUSTRATION: photograph, Fulcher (2000 as *A.* 'Nicky').

Agapanthus 'Norman Hadden' (Salver Group)

ORIGIN: (probably a selection of *A. campanulatus* subsp. *patens*) obtained by Gary Dunlop from David Fax, a specialist in the Liliaceae sensu lato, of Bullwood Nurseries, UK (no longer trading). Known since 1989, UK, and still in cultivation.
NAME: in honour of the late Norman Hadden, who owned the nursery Underway in Porlock, UK.
LEAF: deciduous.
FLOWER: "deep blue."
NOTE: details supplied by Gary Dunlop.

Agapanthus 'Notfred' (Variegated Leaf Group)

TRADE NAME: SILVER MOON

ORIGIN: (mutant found in "seedlings of Headbourne Hybrids") discovered by Fred Nichols, staff member of Notcutts Nurseries, UK, introduced by Notcutts in 2001.
NAME: a compilation of Notcutts and Fred Nichols.
LEAF: evergreen, up to 40 cm long and 1.7 cm wide, arching, green with cream stripes especially along the margin (young leaves more yellowish coloured), base purple.
PEDUNCLE: 70 cm, pale green and slightly cream striped, round.
INFLORESCENCE: up to 19 cm across, 40 flowers, flat.
PEDICEL: green with a bit of purple speckles.
FLOWERBUD: violet-blue, upright.
FLOWER: inside pale violet-blue with distinct purple tint, midrib slightly darker, outside pale violet-blue with a distinct purple tint, midrib slightly darker, base violet-blue, when out of flower strongly purple coloured, horizontal, 3.2 cm long (tube 1.2 cm long), 3.5 cm across, stamens not exserted, anthers black.
NOTE: European Plant Variety Right applied for, file no. 2000/1679.
NOTE: plant details from plants shown at Plantarium 2001, details on its origin supplied by David Clark of Notcutts.
NOTE: nuclear DNA content = 21.9 pg.
ILLUSTRATION: *color plate.*
AWARD: Best New Plant Award at the trade show GLEE 2000, Birmingham, UK; silver medal at Plantarium, Boskoop, The Netherlands, in 2001.

Agapanthus 'Nottingham' (Salver Group)

ORIGIN: (unnamed seedling × 'Prinses Marilène') raised by Kees Duivenvoorde, Beverwijk, The Netherlands, introduced in 1999.
NAME: after the city in England.
LEAF: deciduous, up to 40 cm long and 2.3 cm wide, upright to slightly arching, pale to normal green and a bit glaucous in the middle, base green.
PEDUNCLE: 90 cm, green and distinctly glaucous, round.
INFLORESCENCE: 15–18 cm across, 30 flowers, flat.
PEDICEL: pale green but slightly darker at the base.
FLOWERBUD: white with pale yellow apex and base, upright but quickly horizontal.

FLOWER: inside pure white with midrib transparent, outside white with pale green-white base, when out of flower dull white, horizontal, 3.4 cm long (tube 1.3 cm long), 4–4.5 cm across, stamens slightly exserted, anthers yellow becoming dark yellow, connective tissue pale purple, slightly fragrant.
NOTE: details from plants grown by Duivenvoorde.
NOTE: registered in 1999.
NOTE: nuclear DNA content = 22.3 pg.
ILLUSTRATION: *color plate.*

Agapanthus nutans F.M. Leight. = ***A. caulescens*** Sprenger ex Wittmack

F.M. Leight (1965) J. South African Bot., Suppl. Vol. IV. 38.

Agapanthus nutans 'Albus'

ORIGIN: known since 1991, UK, and still in cultivation.
FLOWER: white.
NOTE: invalid name per the ICNCP-1995, art. 17.2, 17.9, and 17.11.
ILLUSTRATION: photograph, Phillips and Rix (1991)

Agapanthus nutans 'Polar Ice' = *A.* **'Polar Ice'**

Agapanthus **'Nyx'** (Salver Group)

ORIGIN: introduced by Gary Dunlop, Ballyrogan Nurseries, UK, known since 1999.
LEAF: deciduous, up to 30 cm long and 1.5 cm wide, arching, dark green, base purple.
PEDUNCLE: 60 cm, bronze.
INFLORESCENCE: 12.5 cm across, 30–60 flowers, bud opens on 2 sides.
PEDICEL: purple-bronze.
FLOWER: inside pale violet-blue (93D) with apex slightly darker (93C), margin violet-blue (93B), midrib dark violet-blue (93A), outside violet-blue (93B) with midrib and base dark violet-blue (93A), when fully open a white spot on the inner tepals along the margin, horizontal to nodding, up to 2.5 cm long, 3 cm across.
NOTE: details supplied by Gary Dunlop.
NOTE: nuclear DNA content = 23.1 pg.

Agapanthus **'Ocean Blue'** (Trumpet Group)

ORIGIN: Japan, known since 2001 when offered by Kokkaen.
INFLORESCENCE: flat.
FLOWER: pale violet-blue.
NOTE: details supplied by Y. Aihara.

Agapanthus **'October Blue'**

ORIGIN: known since 1965, when shown at the RHS show in October, exhibited by The Crown Estate, Windsor, UK; no further records.

Agapanthus **'Olinda'**

ORIGIN: known since 1996, Australia; no further records.

Agapanthus orientalis F.M. Leight. = *A. praecox* subsp. *orientalis* F.M. Leight.
   F.M. Leight. (1939) J. South African Bot., Vol. 5. 57.

Agapanthus orientalis var. *albiflorus* (Hend.) Boom = *A. praecox* 'Albiflorus'
   Boom (1950) Flora der gekweekte, kruidachtige gewassen.

Agapanthus orientalis var. *albus* Synge = *A. praecox* 'Albiflorus'
   Synge (1986) Dictionary of Gardening.

Agapanthus orientalis var. *aurivittatus* Synge = *A.* 'Aureovittatus'
   Synge (1986) Dictionary of Gardening.

Agapanthus orientalis var. *flore pleno* Synge = *A.* 'Flore Pleno'
   Synge (1986) Dictionary of Gardening.

Agapanthus orientalis var. *foliis argenteis vittatis* van Tubergen = *A.* 'Argenteus
   Vittatus'
   van Tubergen (1968) catalogue.

Agapanthus orientalis var. *giganteus* Synge = *A.* 'Giganteus'
   Synge (1986) Dictionary of Gardening. nom.nud.

Agapanthus orientalis var. *leichtlinii* Synge = *A.* 'Leichtlinii'
   Synge (1986) Dictionary of Gardening. nom.nud.

Agapanthus orientalis var. *maximus albus* Synge = *A.* 'Maximus Albus'
   Synge (1986) Dictionary of Gardening. nom.nud.

Agapanthus orientalis var. *monstrosus* Synge = *A.* 'Monstrosus'
   Synge (1986) Dictionary of Gardening. nom.nud.

Agapanthus orientalis var. *pallidus* Synge = *A.* 'Pallidus'
   Synge (1986) Dictionary of Gardening. nom.nud.

Agapanthus orientalis var. *variegatus* Synge = *A.* 'Argenteus Vittatus'
   Synge (1986) Dictionary of Gardening. nom.nud.

Agapanthus orientalis var. *variegatus falcatus* Synge = *A.* 'Variegatus Falcatus'
   Synge (1986) Dictionary of Gardening. nom.nud.

Agapanthus orientalis 'Albidus' = *A. praecox* 'Albiflorus'
   NOTE: invalid name per the ICNCP-1995, art. 17.2, 17.9, and 17.11.

Agapanthus orientalis 'Albus Select' = *A.* 'Albus Select'

Agapanthus orientalis 'Argenteis Variegatus' = *A*. **'Argenteus Vittatus'**

Agapanthus orientalis 'Blue'
> ORIGIN: known since 1997, New Zealand. Also offered as seed.
> NOTE: invalid name per the ICNCP-1995, art. 17.11.

Agapanthus orientalis 'Blue Giant' = *A*. **'Blue Giant'**

Agapanthus orientalis 'Blue Queen' = *A*. **'Blue Queen'**

Agapanthus orientalis 'Blue Ribbon' = *A*. **'Blue Ribbon'**

Agapanthus orientalis 'Blue Triumphator' = *A*. **'Blue Triumphator'**

Agapanthus orientalis 'Dwarf White' = *A*. **'Dwarf White'**

Agapanthus orientalis 'Flore Pleno' = *A*. **'Flore Pleno'**

Agapanthus orientalis 'Florist Select Blue' = *A*. **'Florist Select Blue'**

Agapanthus orientalis 'Florist Select White' = *A*. **'Florist Select White'**

Agapanthus orientalis 'Isleworth Blue' = *A*. **'Isleworth Blue'**

Agapanthus orientalis 'Jeanette Dean' = *A*. **'Jeanette Dean'**

Agapanthus orientalis 'Mooreanus' = *A*. **'Mooreanus'**

Agapanthus orientalis 'Nanus' = *A*. **'Nanus'**

Agapanthus orientalis 'Snow Queen' = *A*. **'Snow Queen'**

Agapanthus orientalis 'Trudy' = *A*. **'Trudy'**

Agapanthus orientalis 'Variegatus' = *A*. **'ArgenteusVittatus'**
> NOTE: invalid name per the ICNCP-1995, art. 17.2, 17.9, and 17.11.

Agapanthus orientalis 'White Ice' = *A*. **'White Ice'**

Agapanthus orientalis hybrids = *A*. RUBBISH

Agapanthus orientalis white
> ORIGIN: known since 1997, New Zealand. Also offered as seed.

Agapanthus 'Oslo' (Trumpet Group)
> ORIGIN: (**'Blue Triumphator'** × **'Dr Brouwer'**) raised by Kees Duivenvoorde, Beverwijk, The Netherlands, introduced in 2001.
> NAME: after the capital of Norway.
> LEAF: deciduous, up to 40 cm long and 2.5 cm wide, upright, normal to dark green, base green.

PEDUNCLE: 100 cm, green and just a bit violet speckled, rather sturdy, more or less round.

INFLORESCENCE: 12 cm across, 40 flowers, globular.

PEDICEL: dark green-violet.

FLOWERBUD: greenish-violet with violet apex, upright.

FLOWER: inside pale violet-blue (92CD) with a bit of a purple tint, midrib violet-blue (92A), outside pale violet-blue (92AC), thin midrib violet-blue (92A), base greenish-violet, when out of flower purple with small violet-blue base, horizontal, up to 3.2 cm long (tube 1 cm long), 3.4 cm across, stamens exserted, anthers violet-blue with yellow pollen.

NOTE: details from plants grown by Duivenvoorde.

NOTE: registered in 2001.

NOTE: nuclear DNA content = 23.6 pg.

ILLUSTRATION: *color plate.*

Agapanthus 'Ossato Snow Queen'

ORIGIN: raised by Nico van Os Veredeling B.V., Bergschenhoek, The Netherlands, introduced in 1994.

NAME: a reference to the raiser's surname.

LEAF: evergreen, 40–60 cm long, 3–3.5 cm wide, upright, normal green, base green.

PEDUNCLE: 80 cm, just a bit flat, green and glaucous.

INFLORESCENCE: 18 cm across, 150 flowers, globular, bud opens on 1 side, bract caducous.

PEDICEL: green.

FLOWERBUD: cream with yellowish apex.

FLOWER: inside with transparent midrib, outside white, horizontal, up to 4.5 cm long (tube 1 cm long), 5–6 cm across, stamens inserted, anthers cream with yellow pollen.

NOTE: details from plants grown by van Os.

NOTE: Kwekersrecht (plant variety right) applied for and granted, The Netherlands only, no. AGP2.

Agapanthus 'Oxbridge' (Salver Group)

SYNONYM: *Agapanthus campanulatus* 'Oxbridge'

ORIGIN: raised by Gary Dunlop, Ballyrogan Nurseries, UK, introduced in 1996, and still in cultivation.

NAME: alludes to the two tints of violet-blue in the flower.

LEAF: arching, normal green.

PEDUNCLE: 70 cm, green.

INFLORESCENCE: 20–30 flowers.

PEDICEL: purple.

FLOWERBUD: dark violet-blue.

FLOWER: inside violet-blue with white base.

NOTE: details supplied by Gary Dunlop.

Agapanthus 'Oxford Blue' (Salver Group)

> synonym: *Agapanthus campanulatus* 'Oxford Blue'

origin: (selection of *A. campanulatus*) raised by Gary Dunlop, Ballyrogan Nurseries, UK, introduced in 1995, and still in cultivation.
leaf: deciduous, up to 22.5 cm long and 1.5 cm wide, upright, normal green and glaucous, base green.
peduncle: 75 cm, green.
inflorescence: 10 cm across, 30 flowers, bud opens on 2 sides.
pedicel: purple.
flower: violet-blue (97B) with darker coloured midrib (95A) on both sides, up to 1.5 cm long, 1.25 cm across.
note: details supplied by Gary Dunlop.
note: nuclear DNA content = 22.5 pg.

Agapanthus 'Pacific Ocean' (Funnel Group)

origin: raised by C.H.A. van Eijk, Nootdorp, The Netherlands. Known since 2003 when the breeder applied for European Plant Variety Right.
leaf: evergreen, 40–50 cm long, 3(–4) cm wide, more or less upright, dark green, base green.
peduncle: 100 cm, green and glaucous, round.
inflorescence: 20 cm across, 100(–150) flowers, globular, bud opens on 1 side, bract rather long acuminate and caducous.
pedicel: green with purple speckles towards the flower.
flowerbud: dark violet-blue with paler seams.
flower: inside very pale violet-blue with purple tint and to white at the base, margin violet-blue with purple tint (93C), midrib very dark violet-blue (93A), outside violet-blue with purple tint and darker midrib, base violet-blue, horizontal, 4–4.3 cm long (tube 1 cm long), 5.5 cm across, stamens slightly exserted, anthers dark purple with dark yellow pollen.
note: the first flowers within an inflorescence tend to have 8 tepals. Selected as a year-round cut flower.
note: details from plants grown by van Eijk.
note: European Plant Variety Right applied for, file no. 2003/0048.

Agapanthus 'Pale' = *A.* RUBBISH

Agapanthus 'Pale Blue' = *A.* RUBBISH

Agapanthus 'Pale Form' = *A.* RUBBISH

Agapanthus pallidus Besant = *A.* 'Pallidus'

> Besant (1903) Flora and Sylva, 1.

Agapanthus 'Pallidus'

> synonym: *Agapanthus africanus* subsp. *umbellatus* var. *pallidus* H.R. Wehrh.
> *Agapanthus orientalis* var. *pallidus* Synge

Agapanthus pallidus Besant
Agapanthus praecox subsp. *praecox* 'Pallidus'
Agapanthus praecox 'Pallidus'
Agapanthus umbellatus var. *pallidus* Krelage

ERROR: 'Pallida'

ORIGIN: known since 1888 when offered by Krelage, The Netherlands, and, incredibly, still offered by Lambley Nursery in Australia in 2001. Most likely Dutch growers who left Holland after World War II carried plants with them; this is known to have happened with *Tulipa* and other bulbs and corms that are no longer in cultivation in Holland but are still surviving in New Zealand, Australia, or Canada. Lambley's description of it as "an old cultivar," coupled with a reference to its "china blue flowers," suggests this might be the true cultivar.

NOTE: according to the description in Krelage's catalogues, leaves are "rigid" and flowers are "pale china-blue." In early 2002 Lambley Nursery offered the Dutch Plant Collection a plant, which flowered in late autumn of that year; a brief description follows:

LEAF: more or less upright, normal green and glaucous, base green.

PEDUNCLE: green and glaucous, round.

INFLORESCENCE: 15–16 flowers, flat.

PEDICEL: green and a bit purple speckled.

FLOWERBUD: pale to normal violet-blue but distinctly paler towards the apex with darker ribs, apex greenish, upright but quickly horizontal.

FLOWER: inside very pale violet-blue with margin just slightly darker and purple tinted, midrib violet-blue, outside pale violet-blue with slightly darker margin, midrib and base violet-blue, when out of flower purple, horizontal, 4.5 cm long (tube 1.5 cm long), 3.5 cm across, stamens not exserted or just 1–2 slightly exserted, anthers brown.

Agapanthus Palmer's Hybrids = *A.* RUBBISH

Agapanthus 'Parijs' (Funnel Group)

SYNONYM: *Agapanthus* 'Paris'

ORIGIN: raised by Kees Duivenvoorde, Beverwijk, The Netherlands, introduced in 2001. After registration and before this publication, Duivenvoorde changed the name to 'Parijs', which is valid per the ICNCP-1995.

NAME: Dutch spelling of the capital of France.

LEAF: deciduous, upright, normal green.

PEDUNCLE: 80 cm, very dark purple-violet but paler towards base.

INFLORESCENCE: 20 cm across, 40–50 flowers, flat.

PEDICEL: dark purple.

FLOWERBUD: starting pale violet-blue with apex dull pale purple becoming more coloured later violet-blue with dark base, upright but quickly horizontal.

FLOWER: inside rather equally pale violet-blue, midrib violet-blue, outside pale violet-blue with dark glossy violet-blue base, on both sides with distinct purple tint,

when out of flower purple with dark violet-blue base, horizontal, stamens not
exserted, anthers violet-black.
NOTE: details from plants grown by Duivenvoorde.
NOTE: registered in 2001 (as 'Paris').
ILLUSTRATION: *color plate.*

Agapanthus 'Paris' = *A.* **'Parijs'**
NOTE: invalid name per the ICNCP-1995, art. 17.13.

Agapanthus patens F.M. Leight. = *A.* **campanulatus** subsp. **patens** F.M. Leight.
F.M. Leight. (1945) J. South African Bot., Vol. XI. 99.

Agapanthus patens 'Profusion' = *A.* **'Profusion'**

Agapanthus 'Patens' = *A.* **campanulatus** subsp. **patens** F.M. Leight.
NOTE: invalid name per the ICNCP-1995, art. 17.9.

Agapanthus 'Patent Blue' (Salver Group)
ORIGIN: raised by Gary Dunlop, Ballyrogan Nurseries, UK, named in 1998.
LEAF: deciduous, up to 40 cm long and 2 cm wide, upright, normal green, leafbase
green.
PEDUNCLE: 90 cm, green.
INFLORESCENCE: 15 cm across, 60 flowers.
PEDICEL: bronze-purple.
FLOWERBUD: very dark violet-blue, upright.
FLOWER: inside violet-blue (94A) with midrib very dark violet (95A), outside violet-
blue (94A) with base and midrib violet (85A), slightly facing downwards, 2.5 cm
long, 2.5 cm across, anthers shorter than the flower.
NOTE: details supplied by Gary Dunlop.
NOTE: invalid name per the ICNCP-1995, art. 17.11 and 17.12.
NOTE: nuclear DNA content = 22.5 pg.
ILLUSTRATION: photograph, Snoeijer (1998).

Agapanthus pendulinus 'Blue Ensign' = *A.* **'Blue Ensign'**

Agapanthus 'Pendulinus' = *A.* **inapertus** subsp. **pendulus** (L. Bol.) F.M. Leight.
NOTE: invalid name per the ICNCP-1995, art. 17.9.

Agapanthus pendulus L. Bol. = *A.* **inapertus** subsp. **pendulus** (L. Bol.) F.M.
Leight.
L. Bol. (1923) Ann. Bol. Herb. III, 80.

Agapanthus **'Penelope Palmer'** (Funnel Group)
ORIGIN: raised by Lewis Palmer, known since 1964, and still in cultivation.
LEAF: probably more or less evergreen, up to 50 cm long and 2.5 cm wide, arching,
normal glossy green, base green.

PEDUNCLE: 120 cm, green and slightly glaucous, round.

INFLORESCENCE: 15 cm across, 50 flowers, flat.

PEDICEL: green with violet-purple towards flower.

FLOWERBUD: dark violet-blue with white spots in middle, upright.

FLOWER: inside pale to normal violet-blue (96D) with a white base, margin slightly darker with purple tint, midrib dark violet-blue (94A), outside violet-blue with darker base and midrib, when out of flower more purple and segments curling distinctly, horizontal, 4 cm long (tube 1–1.2 cm long), 5 cm across, stamens slightly exserted, anthers violet with yellow pollen.

NOTE: most details from plants grown at Wisley.

NOTE: nuclear DNA content = 23.9 pg.

ILLUSTRATION: photograph, Snoeijer (1998).

AWARD: PC in 1964.

Agapanthus 'Penny Slade'

ORIGIN: introduced by Apple Court, UK, in 1997, and still in cultivation.

NAME: in honour of Penny Slade, the nursery customer who brought them the plant.

LEAF: evergreen.

PEDUNCLE: 35 cm.

FLOWER: "mid blue."

Agapanthus 'Penn's White' (Funnel Group)

SYNONYM: *Agapanthus praecox* subsp. *orientalis* 'Penn's White'

ORIGIN: (seedling of *A. praecox* subsp. *orientalis*) introduced by San Marcos Growers, California, USA, in 2002.

LEAF: evergreen.

PEDUNCLE: 80–100 cm.

PEDICEL: "dark."

FLOWER: white.

NOTE: details from the Internet [33].

Agapanthus 'Peter Pan' (Funnel Group)

SYNONYM: *Agapanthus africanus* 'Peter Pan'
Agapanthus 'Blue Boy' ex Hackfalls Arboretum
Agapanthus praecox subsp. *minimus* 'Peter Pan'
Agapanthus praecox subsp. *orientalis* 'Peter Pan'

ORIGIN: (selection of *A. praecox* subsp. *minimus*) raised by J.N. Giridlian's Oakhurst Gardens, California, USA, in 1949. Still widely cultivated but mainly propagated by seed, which is offered throughout the world.

NAME: hero of J.M. Barrie's play (1904) of the same name.

LEAF: evergreen, 15–25 cm long and 1 cm wide, arching, pale green, base green.

PEDUNCLE: 30–50 cm, green, round.

INFLORESCENCE: 10–12 cm across, 10–15 flowers, flat.

PEDICEL: green.

FLOWERBUD: violet-blue, upright.

FLOWER: pale violet-blue with purple tint and midrib slightly darker, when out of flower more purple, upright to horizontal, 3.8 cm long (tube 1–1.2 cm long), 4 cm across, stamens not exserted, anthers violet with yellow pollen becoming brown-black.

NOTE: details from plants grown by Coen Jansen and at Wisley, but, with the plant's being seed-propagated, it is doubtful the preceding details are correct. Dick Fulcher claims to grow the original stock, but most plants offered probably have nothing to do with Giridlian's introduction.

NOTE: despite its being among the most widely grown seed-propagated plants, some nurseries state that the plant is sterile.

NOTE: although the plant is now sometimes propagated by tissue culture, it unfortunately had been (and still is) seed-propagated worldwide since its introduction. It is therefore best to regard today's plants as RUBBISH.

Agapanthus 'Peter Pan Albus' = *A.* '**Rancho Dwarf**'

NOTE: invalid name per the ICNCP-1995, art. 17.2.

Agapanthus 'Peter Pan American'

SYNONYM: *Agapanthus* 'Peter Pan US form'

ORIGIN: introduced by Washfield Nursery, UK, an import from the USA. Known since 1996 and still in cultivation.
LEAF: evergreen.
PEDUNCLE: 25–30.
FLOWER: pale violet-blue.

Agapanthus 'Peter Pan Selection'

ORIGIN: (a uniform selection of '**Peter Pan**') known since 2001 when offered by San Marcos Growers, California, USA.
PEDUNCLE: 30–50 cm.
FLOWER: violet-blue.
NOTE: details from the Internet [33].
NOTE: invalid name per the ICNCP-1995, art. 17.16.

Agapanthus 'Peter Pan US Form' = *A.* '**Peter Pan American**'

NOTE: invalid name per the ICNCP-1995, art. 17.16.

Agapanthus 'Peter Pan Variegated' => *A.* '**Tinkerbell**' [?]

Agapanthus 'Petite Blue'

ORIGIN: known since 2001 when grown by Ets Horticole, France, and offered in the same year by Monterey Bay Nursery, California, USA.
LEAF: deciduous, upright.
INFLORESCENCE: "compact rounded clusters."
FLOWER: "deep, rich blue."
NOTE: invalid name per the ICNCP-1995, art. 17.11.

Agapanthus 'Phantom' (Funnel Group)

ORIGIN: seedling from the Coleton Fishacre garden, Devon, UK, around 1990, and still in cultivation.
LEAF: evergreen, up to 25 cm long and 4.5 cm wide, low arching, normal green and slightly glaucous, base green.
PEDUNCLE: 90–110 cm, green.
INFLORESCENCE: 20 cm across, 75 flowers, more or less flat, bud opens at 2 sides.
PEDICEL: pale yellow-green.
FLOWERBUD: cream-white with violet-blue apex, upright.
FLOWER: on both sides white flushed with pale violet-blue (97A) at apex, horizontal, up to 4.5 cm long, 4 cm across, stamens not or just 1–2 exserted, anthers pale violet with yellow pollen.
NOTE: details supplied by Gary Dunlop.
NOTE: nuclear DNA content = 25 pg.
ILLUSTRATION: photograph, Royal Horticultural Society (1998, 1999), Snoeijer (1998), and Fulcher (2000, 2002).

Agapanthus 'Pinchbeck' (Funnel Group)

ERROR: 'Pinck Deck'

ORIGIN: ('Intermedius' × **'Columba'**) raised by Kees Duivenvoorde, Beverwijk, The Netherlands, introduced in 1999, and still in cultivation.
NAME: after the city in England.
LEAF: deciduous, up to 25 cm long and 1.6 cm wide, upright, normal green, base green.
PEDUNCLE: 50 cm, green and purple speckled, round.
INFLORESCENCE: 16 cm across, 40–50 flowers, globular.
PEDICEL: green and heavily flushed purple.
FLOWERBUD: dark violet-blue with darker base, upright but quickly horizontal.
FLOWER: inside pale violet-blue with margin slightly darker, midrib violet-blue and rather wide, outside violet-blue with darker midrib, when out of flower purple, horizontal, up to 3.5 cm long (tube 1 cm long), 4 cm across, stamens not or just slightly exserted, anthers brown, slightly fragrant.
NOTE: details from plants grown by Duivenvoorde.
NOTE: registered in 2001.
NOTE: nuclear DNA content = 23.7 pg.
ILLUSTRATION: *color plate.*

Agapanthus Pine Cottage seedlings = *A.* RUBBISH

NOTE: mixed seedlings in mixed colours, raised by Dick Fulcher from seed collected at the NCCPG at Pine Cottage Plants, UK.

Agapanthus 'Pinocchio' (Salver Group)

SYNONYM: *Agapanthus campanulatus* 'Pinocchio'
ERROR: 'Pinnocchio'

ORIGIN: introduced by Maas & van Stein, Hillegom, The Netherlands, in 1996 and still in cultivation.

LEAF: deciduous, 30–40 cm long and up to 1.5 cm wide, upright, pale green and slightly glaucous, base with dark violet.

PEDUNCLE: 60 cm, green with purple towards inflorescence, round.

INFLORESCENCE: 10–13 cm across, (20–)30(–40) flowers, flat, bud opens on 2 sides.

PEDICEL: purple with green base.

FLOWERBUD: violet-blue with a paler coloured ring above the darker base, upright.

FLOWER: inside pale violet-blue (97AB) with a purple blush and margin slightly darker with more purple, midrib violet-blue, outside violet-blue with darker midrib, base dark violet-blue, when out of flower slightly purple, horizontal, 2.5 cm long (tube 1–1.2 cm long), 2.5 cm across, stamens not exserted, anthers violet with brownish pollen.

NOTE: details from plants grown by Maas & van Stein.

NOTE: registered in 1996.

NOTE: nuclear DNA content = 22.8 pg.

ILLUSTRATION: *color plate*; photograph, Snoeijer (1998).

Agapanthus 'Plas Merdyn Blue' (Trumpet Group)

ERROR: 'Plasmerdyn Blue'

ORIGIN: received from Plas Merdyn, introduced by Gary Dunlop, Ballyrogan Nurseries, UK, introduced in 1995, and still in cultivation.

NAME: refers to Plas Merdyn, the garden of the late Bill and Gretta Lennon, Holywood, County Down, Northern Ireland. These friends of the introducer had grown *Agapanthus* for many years, having originally obtained their plants from a neighbour who had grown them from before World War II, predating the Lewis Palmer introductions.

LEAF: up to 25 cm long and 2 cm wide, upright, normal green, base green.

PEDUNCLE: up to 55 cm, green.

INFLORESCENCE: 15 cm across, 40–50 flowers, globular, bud opens at 2 sides.

PEDICEL: purple.

FLOWER: inside pale violet-blue (97B) with much darker midrib (96A) which is rather wide, outside pale violet with darker midrib and base, on both sides with distinct purple tint, when out of flower purple becoming grey-white, horizontal to slightly facing downwards, 3 cm long, 3 cm across, stamens not exserted, anthers violet.

NOTE: details supplied by Gary Dunlop.

NOTE: nuclear DNA content = 24.2 pg.

Agapanthus 'Plas Merdyn White' (Funnel Group)

ORIGIN: received from Plas Merdyn, introduced by Gary Dunlop, Ballyrogan Nurseries, UK, introduced in 1995, and still in cultivation.

NAME: see 'Plas Merdyn Blue'.

LEAF: up to 25 cm long and 1.5 cm wide, upright, normal green and glaucous, base green.

PEDUNCLE: up to 60 cm, green.

INFLORESCENCE: 13 cm across, 40–50 flowers, bud opens on 2 sides.

PEDICEL: green.

FLOWER: white, more pale purple when out of flower, upright, 4 cm long, 4 cm across.

NOTE: details supplied by Gary Dunlop.

NOTE: nuclear DNA content = 25.3 pg.

Agapanthus 'Platinum Pearl' (Funnel Group)

ORIGIN: (chance seedling of **'Snow Cloud'**) raised by Parva Plants, New Zealand, known since 1998.

PEDUNCLE: up to 90 cm, usually with a second peduncle.

INFLORESCENCE: up to 170 flowers, globular.

FLOWER: inside very pale violet-blue with slightly darker midrib, stamens as long as the flower, anthers violet.

NOTE: details from the Internet [2].

Agapanthus 'Platinum Pink' (Funnel Group)

ORIGIN: (chance seedling of **'Snow Cloud'**) raised by Parva Plants, New Zealand, known since 1998.

PEDUNCLE: 70–90 cm, usually with a second peduncle.

INFLORESCENCE: 90–120 flowers, globular.

FLOWER: inside pale violet-blue with darker midrib, stamens not exserted, anthers violet.

NOTE: details from the Internet [2].

NOTE: invalid name per the ICNCP-1995, art. 17.13, but as the name refers to the colour, not to a plant, it is accepted here.

Agapanthus 'Plenitude' (Trumpet Group)

ORIGIN: raised by Gary Dunlop, Ballyrogan Nurseries, UK, named in 1998.

LEAF: evergreen, up to 40 cm long and 4 cm wide, leafbase green.

PEDUNCLE: 90 cm, green.

INFLORESCENCE: 14 cm across, 120 flowers.

PEDICEL: green.

FLOWER: on both sides pale violet-blue, outside with darker base (92A), horizontal, 3 cm long, 3 cm across.

NOTE: details supplied by Gary Dunlop.

NOTE: invalid name per the ICNCP-1995, art. 17.9.

'Plenus' => *Agapanthus praecox* 'Plenus'

Agapanthus 'Pluto Veil' (Trumpet Group)

ORIGIN: offered by Miyoshi Flowers, Japan, as new in 1999.

FLOWER: violet-blue.

Agapanthus 'Podge Mill' (Trumpet Group)

ORIGIN: introduced in Ireland, known since 1994, and still in cultivation.

LEAF: deciduous, 30–40 cm long and 2.5 cm wide, upright, normal to dark green, base purple.

PEDUNCLE: 50–80 cm, green with dull purple towards inflorescence, round.

INFLORESCENCE: 17.5 cm across, 50–70 flowers.

PEDICEL: violet-purple.

FLOWERBUD: violet-blue, upright.

FLOWER: inside violet-blue (94C), midrib darker (94A), outside violet-blue, when out of flower more purple, horizontal, 4 cm long (tube 1.2 cm), 3.5 cm across, stamens not exserted, anthers dark violet.

NOTE: details from plants grown by Coen Jansen.

NOTE: the flower tends towards the Salver Group when fully open.

Agapanthus 'Polar Ice' (Trumpet Group)

SYNONYM: *Agapanthus nutans* 'Polar Ice'
Agapanthus umbellatus 'Polar Ice'

ERROR: 'Pola Ice'

TRANSLATION: POOLIJS [in Dutch]

ORIGIN: (chance seedling) raised by Maas & van Stein, Hillegom, The Netherlands, introduced in 1981, and still in cultivation.

LEAF: deciduous, 20–30 cm long and up to 2.5 cm wide, upright to spreading, pale green, base green.

PEDUNCLE: 60–80 cm, green, round.

INFLORESCENCE: 12–15 cm across, 60–80 flowers, flat, often with pagoda fasciation, bud opens on 1 side.

PEDICEL: green.

FLOWERBUD: white with yellowish apex, upright.

FLOWER: inside white with transparent midrib, outside white with apex very pale yellow, when out of flower white to pale brown, 3.2 cm long (tube 1 cm long), 3 cm across, stamens not exserted, anthers yellow.

NOTE: details from plants grown by Maas & van Stein.

NOTE: registered in 1981.

NOTE: nuclear DNA content = 24.5 pg.

ILLUSTRATION: *color plate*; photograph, Snoeijer (1998), Fulcher (2002), and Jansen (2002).

AWARD: GV in 1981.

Agapanthus 'Politique' (Funnel Group)

SYNONYM: *Agapanthus caulescens* subsp. *angustifolius* 'Politique'
Agapanthus caulescens 'Politique'

ORIGIN: (selection of *A. caulescens* subsp. *angustifolius*) from the Politique farm, near Pietermaritzburg, Natal. Introduced by Kirstenbosch National Botanical Garden, South Africa, known since 1989, and still in cultivation.

LEAF: deciduous, upright, glaucous.

PEDUNCLE: 100–150 cm.

INFLORESCENCE: 50 flowers, more or less globular, bract remains more or less attached.

PEDICEL: green with purple towards flower.

FLOWER: very pale violet-blue with darker midrib, outside pale violet-blue with darker midrib and base, horizontal to slightly nodding, stamens not exserted, anthers violet.

NOTE: slow grower.

NOTE: flower colour in the references ranges from normal blue to very dark blue.

ILLUSTRATION: photograph, Duncan (1985 as *A. caulescens* subsp. *angustifolius* 'Politique').

Agapanthus POOLIJS => *A.* 'Polar Ice'

Agapanthus 'Porcelain'

ORIGIN: known since 2003 when offered by Gary Dunlop, Ballyrogan Nurseries, UK.

Agapanthus 'Porlock' (Funnel Group)

ORIGIN: introduced by Norman Hadden. Known since 1991 and still in cultivation.

NAME: after the town in the UK where the late Norman Hadden had his nursery, Underway.

LEAF: evergreen, up to 30 cm long and 4 cm wide, arching, normal green, base green.

FLOWER: pale violet-blue with darker margin, midrib dark violet-blue, rather large.

NOTE: some details from plants grown by Coen Jansen.

ILLUSTRATION: photograph, Jansen (2002).

Agapanthus praecox Willd. ex F.M. Leight. (1965) J. South African Bot., Suppl.

SYNONYM: *Agapanthus africanus* subsp. *praecox* (Willd.) H.R. Wehrh.
Agapanthus umbellatus var. *angustifolius* Redouté ex Roem. & Schult.
Tulbaghia africana var. *praecox* (Willd.) Kuntze

DISTRIBUTION: eastern Cape Province; from Port Elizabeth to Natal. Growing in grassland, on rocky places and along forest margins, in high rainfall areas.

LEAF: evergreen, 7–20 per shoot, 20–70 cm long and 1.5–5.5 cm wide, leathery, upright but usually arching, apex obtuse to acute.

PEDUNCLE: slender to stout, 40–150 cm.

INFLORESCENCE: few- to many-flowered.

PEDICEL: 4–12 cm long.

FLOWER: violet-blue or sometimes white (in cultivation => *A. praecox* 'Albiflorus'), rather thin in texture, 3–7 cm long (tube 0.7–2.6 cm long), segments spreading, stamens and style usually as long as the flower but sometimes shorter, exserted, pollen yellow.

FLOWERING TIME: December into April.

NOTE: very variable shape and habitus. All variations appear throughout its distribution and grow next to each other; therefore better, perhaps, to disregard the sub-species and maintain only the species.

NOTE: widely cultivated in all parts of the world, from the tropics to Mediterranean climates, where it can become an invasive weed, threatening the local flora.

NOTE: nuclear DNA content = 25.46 pg.

ILLUSTRATION: drawing, Nieuman and Smit (1987); photograph, Kostelijk (1986), Nieuman and Smit (1987), Pienaar (1987), Kramer (1998), Elsa Pooley (1998), Wray (1998a), Snoeijer (1999), Dunlop (2000), Fulcher (2000, 2002), and van Wyk (2000).

Agapanthus praecox subsp. *floribundus* Erhardt = *A.* 'Floribundus'

Erhardt (1997) PPP Index. nom.nud.
Philip & Lord (1998) The RHS Plant Finder. nom.nud.

Agapanthus praecox subsp. *floribundus* 'Saint Ivel' = *A.* 'Saint Ivel'

Agapanthus praecox subsp. *maximus* Erhardt = *A.* 'Maximus'

Erhardt (1995) PPP Index. nom.nud.
Philip & Lord (1998) The RHS Plant Finder. nom.nud.

Agapanthus praecox subsp. *maximus* 'Albus' = *A.* 'Maximus Albus'

NOTE: invalid name per the ICNCP-1995, art. 17.2.

***Agapanthus praecox* subsp. *minimus* (Lindl.) F.M. Leight. (1965) J. South African Bot., Suppl.**

SYNONYM: *Agapanthus africanus* var. *minimus* (Lindl.) Beauverd
Agapanthus comptonii F.M. Leight.
Agapanthus comptonii subsp. *longitubus* F.M. Leight.
Agapanthus longispathus F.M. Leight.
Agapanthus umbellatus var. *minimus* Lindl.
Agapanthus umbellatus var. *praecox* Baker

DISTRIBUTION: eastern Cape Province; Adelaide, Albany, Alexandria, Bathurst, Chalumna, Humansdorp, Kingwilliamstown, Knysna, Komgha, Peddie, and Port Elizabeth, growing in large clusters on rocky slopes.

LEAF: 6–10 per shoot, 20–60 cm long and 1–2.5 cm wide, leathery, usually horizontal spreading.

PEDUNCLE: slender, 40–100 cm.

INFLORESCENCE: few- to many-flowered but not so dense as in subsp. *orientalis*.

FLOWER: pale violet-blue to normal violet-blue, 3–6.5 cm long, segments spreading and with recurved apex, stamens shorter than the flowers.

ILLUSTRATION: *color plate*; drawing, Leighton (1965 and also as *A. comptonii, A. c.* subsp. *longitubus*, and *A. c.* subsp. *comptonii*, which last is reproduced in Snoeijer 1998), Batten and Bokelmann (1966 as *A. c.* subsp. *longitubus*), and Courtenay-Latimer and Smith (1967); photograph, Palmer (1967 as *A. comptonii*), Doutt (1994

as *A. comptonii*), Phillips and Rix (1991 as *A. c.* subsp. *longitubus*), Wray (1995 as *A. comptonii*), and Duncan (1998 as *A. c.* subsp. *longitubus*).

Agapanthus praecox subsp. *minimus* 'Adelaide' = *A.* **'Adelaide'**

Agapanthus praecox subsp. *minimus* 'Forma' = *A.* RUBBISH

Agapanthus praecox subsp. *minimus* 'Peter Pan' = *A.* **'Peter Pan'**

Agapanthus praecox subsp. *minimus* 'Storms River' = *A.* **'Storms River'**

Agapanthus praecox subsp. *minimus* 'Supreme' = *A.* 'Supreme'

Agapanthus praecox subsp. *minimus* 'Tinkerbell' = *A.* **'Tinkerbell'**

Agapanthus praecox subsp. *minimus* 'Variegatus' = *A.* **'Argenteus Vittatus'**
NOTE: invalid name per the ICNCP-1995, art. 17.2, 17.9, and 17.11.

Agapanthus praecox subsp. ***orientalis*** F.M. Leight. (1965) J. South African Bot., Suppl.

SYNONYM: *Agapanthus africanus* subsp. *umbellatus* (Hoffmanns.) H.R. Wehrh. pro parte
Agapanthus orientalis F.M. Leight.
Agapanthus umbellatus L'Hér. pro parte
Agapanthus umbellatus Redouté pro parte

ORIGIN: eastern Cape Province; Albany, Cathcart, Cradock, Kentani, Kingwilliams-town, Lusikisiki, Tsolo, Uitenhage, Umtata, and Victoria East. Natal; Port Shep-stone. Known in cultivation since 1813, France, and still widely grown. Also offered as seed.
LEAF: 16–20 per shoot, up to 70 cm long and 5.5 cm wide, arching, green.
PEDUNCLE: 60–140 cm, rather stout.
INFLORESCENCE: up to 100 or more flowers.
PEDICEL: 9–12 cm long.
FLOWER: pale to normal violet-blue or rarely white (in cultivation => *A. praecox* 'Albiflorus'), segments spreading and wavy, 4–5.5 cm long (tube 1.4–2 cm long), 4 cm across, stamens as long as or slightly longer than the flower.
NOTE: the drawing in Pole Evans (1921) by artist K.A. Landsell was the first colour plate in the first volume of *The Flowering Plants of South Africa*—a good choice to start with (this magazine is still produced, as *The Flowering Plants of Africa*, by the National Botanical Institute).
ILLUSTRATION: *color plate*; drawing, Pole Evans (1921 as *A. umbellatus*), Doutt (1994), Leighton (1965), which is reproduced in Snoeijer (1998), Dyer (1966), Mallary, Waltermire, and Levin (1986 as *A. umbellatus*); photograph, Hay and Beckett (1979 as *A. orientalis*), Brickell (1996), Vermeulen (1996), Cheers (1997), Duncan (1998), and Allemand and Pionnat (2001).

Agapanthus praecox subsp. *orientalis* var. *albiflorus* Philip & Lord = *A. praecox* 'Albiflorus'

Philip & Lord (1993) The Plant Finder. nom.nud.

Agapanthus praecox subsp. *orientalis* 'Albatross' = *A.* 'Albatross'

Agapanthus praecox subsp. *orientalis* 'Albidus' = *A. praecox* 'Albiflorus'
    NOTE: invalid name per the ICNCP-1995, art. 17.2, 17.9, and 17.11.

Agapanthus praecox subsp. *orientalis* 'Albiflorus' = *A. praecox* 'Albiflorus'

Agapanthus praecox subsp. *orientalis* 'Albus' = *A. praecox* 'Albiflorus'
    NOTE: invalid name per the ICNCP-1995, art. 17.2, 17.9, and 17.11.

Agapanthus praecox subsp. *orientalis* 'Albo Roseus' = *A.* 'Albus Roseus'

Agapanthus praecox subsp. *orientalis* 'Albus Roseus' = *A.* 'Albus Roseus'

Agapanthus praecox subsp. *orientalis* 'Argenteus Vittatus' = *A.* 'Argenteus Vittatus'

Agapanthus praecox subsp. *orientalis* 'Aureovittatus' = *A.* 'Aureovittatus'

Agapanthus praecox subsp. *orientalis* 'Azure' = *A.* RUBBISH

Agapanthus praecox subsp. *orientalis* 'Baby Blue' = *A.* 'Blue Baby'

Agapanthus praecox subsp. *orientalis* 'Blue Moon' = *A.* 'Blue Moon'

Agapanthus praecox subsp. *orientalis* 'Blue Nile' = *A.* 'Blue Nile'

Agapanthus praecox subsp. *orientalis* 'Blue Umbrella' = *A.* 'Blue Umbrella'

Agapanthus praecox subsp. *orientalis* 'Defina's Blush' = *A.* 'Defina's Blush'

Agapanthus praecox subsp. *orientalis* 'Dwarf Baby Blue' = *A.* 'Dwarf Baby Blue'

Agapanthus praecox subsp. *orientalis* 'Dwarf White' = *A.* RUBBISH

Agapanthus praecox subsp. *orientalis* 'Flore Pleno' = *A.* 'Flore Pleno'

Agapanthus praecox subsp. *orientalis* 'Floribundus' = *A.* 'Floribundus'

Agapanthus praecox subsp. *orientalis* 'Indigo' = *A.* 'Indigo'

Agapanthus praecox subsp. *orientalis* 'L'Armandèche' = *A.* 'L'Armandèche'

Agapanthus praecox subsp. *orientalis* 'Leichtlinii' = *A.* 'Leichtlinii'

Agapanthus praecox subsp. *orientalis* 'Maximus' = *A.* '**Maximus**'

Agapanthus praecox subsp. *orientalis* 'Mount Thomas' = *A.* '**Mount Thomas**'

Agapanthus praecox subsp. *orientalis* 'Penn's White' = *A.* '**Penn's White**'

Agapanthus praecox subsp. *orientalis* 'Peter Pan' = *A.* '**Peter Pan**'

Agapanthus praecox subsp. *orientalis* 'Rancho Dwarf' = *A.* '**Rancho Dwarf**'

Agapanthus praecox subsp. *orientalis* 'Silver Streak' = *A.* '**Silver Streak**'

Agapanthus praecox subsp. *orientalis* 'Snowball' = *A.* '**Snowball**'

Agapanthus praecox subsp. *orientalis* 'Snowstorm' = *A.* '**Snowstorm**'

Agapanthus praecox subsp. *orientalis* 'Streamline' = *A.* '**Streamline**'

Agapanthus praecox subsp. *orientalis* 'Tigerleaf' = *A.* '**Tigerleaf**'

Agapanthus praecox subsp. *orientalis* 'Variegatus' = *A.* '**Argenteus Vittatus**'
NOTE: invalid name per the ICNCP-1995, art. 17.2, 17.9, and 17.11.

Agapanthus praecox subsp. *orientalis* 'Weaver' = *A.* '**Weaver**'

Agapanthus praecox subsp. *orientalis* 'Weaver Lineata' = *A.* 'Weaver Lineata'

Agapanthus praecox subsp. *orientalis* blue
NOTE: offered as seed.

Agapanthus praecox subsp. *orientalis* large blue selection
NOTE: offered as seed.

Agapanthus praecox subsp. *orientalis* white
NOTE: offered as seed.

**Agapanthus praecox* subsp. *praecox* Willd. (1809) Enum Hort. Berol. 353.
ORIGIN: eastern Cape Province; Cathcart, Humansdorp, and Uitenhage.
LEAF: 10–11 per shoot, 60–70 cm long and 4 cm wide, leathery, more or less upright.
PEDUNCLE: rather stout, 80–100 cm.
INFLORESCENCE: many-flowered.
PEDICEL: 10–12 cm long, spreading.
FLOWER: violet-blue, 5–7 cm long (tube 0.2–2.6 cm long), segments spreading, stamens and pistil sometimes longer than the flower.
NOTE: also offered as seed.
ILLUSTRATION: drawing, Leighton (1965) and Batten and Bokelmann (1966); photograph, Duncan (1998).

Agapanthus praecox subsp. *praecox* 'Albatross' = *A.* **'Albatross'**

Agapanthus praecox subsp. *praecox* 'Albus' = *A. praecox* **'Albiflorus'**
  NOTE: invalid name per the ICNCP-1995, art. 17.2, 17.9, and 17.11.

Agapanthus praecox subsp. *praecox* 'Argenteus Vittatus' = *A.* **'Argenteus Vittatus'**

Agapanthus praecox subsp. *praecox* 'Aureovariegatus' = *A.* **'Aureovittatus'**
  NOTE: invalid name per the ICNCP-1995, art. 17.9 and 17.11.

Agapanthus praecox subsp. *praecox* 'Aureovittatus' = *A.* **'Aureovittatus'**

Agapanthus praecox subsp. *praecox* 'Azure' = *A.* RUBBISH

Agapanthus praecox subsp. *praecox* 'Dwarf White' = *A.* RUBBISH

Agapanthus praecox subsp. *praecox* 'Flore Pleno' = *A.* **'Flore Pleno'**

Agapanthus praecox subsp. *praecox* 'Floribunda' = *A.* 'Floribundus'

Agapanthus praecox subsp. *praecox* 'Floribundus' = *A.* 'Floribundus'

Agapanthus praecox subsp. *praecox* 'Getty White' = *A.* **'Getty White'**

Agapanthus praecox subsp. *praecox* 'Giganteus' = *A.* **'Giganteus'**

Agapanthus praecox subsp. *praecox* 'Maximus' = *A.* **'Maximus'**

Agapanthus praecox subsp. *praecox* 'Maximus Albus' = *A.* **'Maximus Albus'**

Agapanthus praecox subsp. *praecox* 'Monstrosus' = *A.* **'Monstrosus'**

Agapanthus praecox subsp. *praecox* 'Pallidus' = *A.* **'Pallidus'**

Agapanthus praecox subsp. *praecox* 'Plenus' = *A.* **'Flore Pleno'**
  NOTE: invalid name per the ICNCP-1995, art. 17.9 and 17.11.

Agapanthus praecox subsp. *praecox* 'Robusta' = *A.* 'Robusta'

Agapanthus praecox subsp. *praecox* 'Silver Sceptre' = *A.* **'Silver Sceptre'**

Agapanthus praecox subsp. *praecox* 'Variegatus' = *A.* **'Argenteus Vittatus'**
  NOTE: invalid name per the ICNCP-1995, art. 17.2, 17.9, and 17.11.

Agapanthus praecox subsp. *praecox* 'Vittatus' = *A.* **'Aureovittatus'**
  NOTE: invalid name per the ICNCP-1995, art. 17.2, 17.9, and 17.11.

Agapanthus praecox subsp. *praecox* white
  NOTE: offered as seed.

Agapanthus praecox var. *albiflora* Dunlop = *A. praecox* 'Albiflorus'
  Gary Dunlop (2000) Gardens Illustrated. nom.nud.

Agapanthus praecox var. *albiflorus* Erhardt = *A. praecox* 'Albiflorus'
  Erhardt (1995) PPP Index. nom.nud.

Agapanthus praecox var. *floribundus* Platt = *A.* 'Floribundus'
  Platt (1997) Seed Search. Second Edition. nom.nud.

Agapanthus praecox var. *vittatus* Philip & Lord = *A.* 'Aureovittatus'
  Philip & Lord (1993) The Plant Finder. nom.nud.

Agapanthus praecox 'Albidus' = *A. praecox* 'Albiflorus'
  NOTE: invalid name per the ICNCP-1995, art. 17.2, 17.9, and 17.11.

Agapanthus praecox 'Albiflorus'

  SYNONYM: *Agapanthus albidus* L.H. Bailey
  Agapanthus albiflorus Erhardt
  Agapanthus campanulatus 'Albus' pro parte
  Agapanthus orientalis var. *albiflorus* (Hend.) Boom
  Agapanthus orientalis var. *albus* Synge
  Agapanthus orientalis 'Albidus'
  Agapanthus praecox subsp. *orientalis* var. *albiflorus* Philip & Lord
  Agapanthus praecox subsp. *orientalis* 'Albidus'
  Agapanthus praecox subsp. *orientalis* 'Albiflorus'
  Agapanthus praecox subsp. *orientalis* 'Albus'
  Agapanthus praecox subsp. *praecox* 'Albus'
  Agapanthus praecox var. *albiflora* Dunlop
  Agapanthus praecox var. *albiflorus* Erhardt
  Agapanthus praecox 'Albidus'
  Agapanthus praecox 'Albus'
  Agapanthus umbellatus var. *albidus* L.H. Bailey
  Agapanthus umbellatus var. *albidus* Numa Schneider
  Agapanthus umbellatus var. *albiflorus* Hend. ex Boom
  Agapanthus umbellatus var. *albus* hort. pro parte
  Agapanthus umbellatus var. *fl. albis* Mater
  ORIGIN: known in cultivation since 1864, England, and still widely grown.
  LEAF: evergreen, 40–70 cm long and 4–5 cm wide, upright but later arching, normal green, base green.
  PEDUNCLE: (75–)100(–125) cm, green, round.
  INFLORESCENCE: 20–25 cm, over 100 flowers, globular.

PEDICEL: green but sometimes with some purple towards flower.

FLOWERBUD: white, upright.

FLOWER: white on both sides, midrib transparent, when out of flower more white to pale brown, horizontal, up to 5 cm long (tube 1.5 cm long), up to 4.5 cm across, anthers yellow or black.

NOTE: details from plants grown at various nurseries and gardens.

NOTE: as the plant was and still is seed-propagated, it is better to regard this as a group of plants that look similar rather than a proper cultivar.

NOTE: nuclear DNA content = 25.3 pg (material taken from plants cultivated on Madeira).

ILLUSTRATION: *color plates*; photograph, Pienaar (1987 as *A. orientalis* 'Albidus'), Snoeijer (1998, 2000), Dunlop (2000 as *A. praecox* var. *albiflora*), and Fulcher (2002).

AWARD: the plant that received an FCC in 1879 as *A. umbellatus albus* probably refers to ***A. praecox* 'Albiflorus'**.

Agapanthus praecox 'Albus' = ***A. praecox* 'Albiflorus'**

NOTE: invalid name per the ICNCP-1995, art. 17.2, 17.9, and 17.11.

Agapanthus praecox 'Argenteus Vittatus' = *A.* **'Argenteus Vittatus'**

Agapanthus praecox 'Atlas' = *A.* **'Atlas'**

Agapanthus praecox 'Aureovittatus' = *A.* **'Aureovittatus'**

Agapanthus praecox 'Bangor Blue' = *A.* **'Bangor Blue'**

Agapanthus praecox 'Blanc Méoni' = *A.* **'Blanc Méoni'**

Agapanthus praecox 'Bleu Méoni' = *A.* **'Bleu Méoni'**

Agapanthus praecox 'Blue Baby' = *A.* **'Blue Baby'**

Agapanthus praecox 'Blue Bonnet' = *A.* **'Blue Bonnet'**

Agapanthus praecox 'Blue Formality' = *A.* **'Blue Formality'**

Agapanthus praecox 'Blue Globe' = *A.* **'Blue Globe'**

Agapanthus praecox 'Blue Mercury' = *A.* 'Blue Mercury'

Agapanthus praecox 'Blue Nile' = *A.* **'Blue Nile'**

Agapanthus praecox 'Blue Star' = *A.* 'Blue Star' ex Australia

Agapanthus praecox 'Dwarf Blue' = *A.* 'Dwarf Blue'

Agapanthus praecox 'Dwarf White' = *A.* RUBBISH

Agapanthus praecox 'Elegans' = *A.* 'Elegans'

Agapanthus praecox 'Flore Plena' = *A.* **'Flore Pleno'**

Agapanthus praecox 'Flore Pleno' = *A.* **'Flore Pleno'**

Agapanthus praecox 'Formality' = *A.* **'Formality'**

Agapanthus praecox 'Getty White' = *A.* **'Getty White'**

Agapanthus praecox 'Giant Blue' = *A.* 'Giant Blue'

Agapanthus praecox 'Giganteus' = *A.* **'Giganteus'**

Agapanthus praecox 'Grey Pearl' = *A.* **'Grey Pearl'**

Agapanthus praecox 'Guilfoyle' = *A.* **'Guilfoyle'**

Agapanthus praecox 'Headbourne' = *A.* RUBBISH

Agapanthus praecox 'June Bond' = *A.* **'June Bond'**

Agapanthus praecox 'Magnifico' = *A.* **'Magnifico'**

Agapanthus praecox 'Maximus Albus' = *A.* **'Maximus Albus'**

Agapanthus praecox 'Medium White' = *A.* 'Medium White'

Agapanthus praecox 'Meoni' = *A.* **'Blanc Méoni'**

Agapanthus praecox 'Miniature Blue' = *A.* 'Miniature Blue'

Agapanthus praecox 'Miniature White' = *A.* 'Miniature White'

Agapanthus praecox 'Mooreanus' = *A.* **'Mooreanus'**

Agapanthus praecox 'Mount Stewart' = *A.* **'Mount Stewart'**

Agapanthus praecox 'Mount Stewart Form' = *A.* **'Mount Stewart'**

Agapanthus praecox 'Pallida' = *A.* **'Pallidus'**

Agapanthus praecox 'Pallidus' = *A.* **'Pallidus'**

Agapanthus praecox 'Plenus' = *A.* **'Flore Pleno'**
    NOTE: invalid name per the ICNCP-1995, art. 17.9 and 17.11.

Agapanthus praecox 'Saint Ivel' = *A.* **'Saint Ivel'**

Agapanthus praecox 'San Gabriel' = *A.* **'San Gabriel'**

Agapanthus praecox 'Select' = *A*. 'Select'

Agapanthus praecox 'Selma Bock' = *A*. **'Selma Bock'**

Agapanthus praecox 'Silver Streak' = *A*. **'Silver Streak'**

Agapanthus praecox 'Slieve Donard Form' = *A*. 'Slieve Donard Form'

Agapanthus praecox 'Small White' = *A*. 'Small White'

Agapanthus praecox 'Snowstorm' = *A*. **'Snowstorm'**

Agapanthus praecox 'Storms River' = *A*. **'Storms River'**

Agapanthus praecox 'Tall Double' = *A*. 'Tall Double'

Agapanthus praecox 'Tall White' = *A*. 'Tall White'

Agapanthus praecox 'Tinkerbell' = *A*. **'Tinkerbell'**

Agapanthus praecox 'Titan' = *A*. **'Titan'**

Agapanthus praecox 'Umbellatus Albus' = *A*. **'Umbellatus Albus'**

Agapanthus praecox 'Variegatus' = *A*. **'Argenteus Vittatus'**
    NOTE: invalid name per the ICNCP-1995, art. 17.2, 17.9, and 17.11.

Agapanthus praecox 'Vittatus' = *A*. **'Aureovittatus'**
    NOTE: invalid name per the ICNCP-1995, art. 17.9 and 17.11.

Agapanthus praecox 'White Smile' = *A*. **'White Smile'**

Agapanthus praecox Adelaide Seedlings = *A*. RUBBISH

Agapanthus **'Premier'** (Salver Group)
    SYNONYM: *Agapanthus campanulatus* 'Premier'
    ORIGIN: raised by Gary Dunlop, Ballyrogan Nurseries, UK, known since 1997, and still in cultivation.
    PEDUNCLE: 100 cm, stout.
    FLOWER: violet-blue.
    NOTE: details supplied by Gary Dunlop.
    NOTE: nuclear DNA content = 21.9 pg.

Agapanthus **'Pride of Bicton'**
    ORIGIN: (an *A. praecox* hybrid) raised at NCCPG Bicton College, UK, selected by Dick Fulcher in 1993, and still in cultivation.
    LEAF: deciduous.
    PEDUNCLE: 100 cm.

FLOWER: "deep blue."
NOTE: details supplied by Dick Fulcher.

Agapanthus 'Primley Double'

ORIGIN: introduced by Treseder, UK. Known since 1974 and still in cultivation.
LEAF: 30–45 cm long and 2.5–3 cm wide, arching, dark glossy green.
PEDUNCLE: up to 45 cm high, normal green with yellowish flush.
INFLORESCENCE: 19 cm across, globular.
PEDICEL: normal green heavily flushed black-purple.
FLOWER: inside white flushed violet-blue (92B), outside violet-blue (94B), upright to slightly hanging downwards, 5 cm long, 3 cm across.
NOTE: flowers have more than the usual 6 tepals.

Agapanthus 'Princess Margaret'

ORIGIN: raised by The Crown Estate, Windsor, UK, introduced in 1975, and still in cultivation.
NAME: in honour of HRH Princess Margaret (1930–2002), sister of HM Queen Elizabeth II.
LEAF: deciduous.
PEDUNCLE: 50 cm.
FLOWER: violet-blue.

Agapanthus 'Prinses Marilène' (Salver Group)

ORIGIN: raised by Kees Duivenvoorde, Beverwijk, The Netherlands, introduced in 1998.
NAME: in honour of Marilène van den Broek (b. 1970), who married Maurits, prince of Oranje-Nassau (b. 1968), in June 1998, The Netherlands.
LEAF: deciduous, up to 30 cm long and 2 cm wide, arching, pale green, base pale green.
PEDUNCLE: 70–100 cm, pale green and slightly glaucous, round.
INFLORESCENCE: 15–18 cm across, 15–50 flowers, more or less flat.
PEDICEL: pale green.
FLOWERBUD: white with yellow apex.
FLOWER: white with transparent midrib, when out of flower white, horizontal, 3 cm long (tube 1 cm long), 3.5 cm across, stamens exserted, anthers cream.
NOTE: details from plants grown by Duivenvoorde.
NOTE: registered in 1998.
NOTE: nuclear DNA content = 22.2 pg.
ILLUSTRATION: *color plate*; photograph, Snoeijer (1998, 1999).

Agapanthus 'Profusion' (Salver Group)

SYNONYM: *Agapanthus campanulatus* subsp. *patens* 'Profusion'
Agapanthus campanulatus 'Profusion'
Agapanthus patens 'Profusion'
Agapanthus umbellatus 'Profusion'

ORIGIN: (selection of *A. campanulatus* subsp. *patens*) known since 1978 and still in cultivation. Also offered as seed.

LEAF: deciduous, 30–40 cm long and 1.2 cm wide, upright to arching, normal green and glaucous, base purple.

PEDUNCLE: (60–)80–100 cm, green with pale purple speckles, round.

INFLORESCENCE: 11–12 cm across, 40 flowers, bud opens on 1 side, bract usually not caducous.

PEDICEL: dull purple.

FLOWERBUD: violet-blue at upper half, lower half greenish with violet-blue at the base, upright.

FLOWER: inside rather equally violet-blue (96D), midrib darker (96B), margin with purple tint, outside violet-blue with dark margin, base distinctly very dark violet-blue, when out of flower more purple, horizontal, 2–2.5 cm long (tube 0.9 cm long), 2.7 cm across, stamens not or just slightly exserted, anthers dark violet.

NOTE: details from plants grown at Beth Chatto Gardens.

NOTE: nuclear DNA content = 22.2 pg.

ILLUSTRATION: *color plate*; photograph, Fulcher (2000).

Agapanthus 'Prolific Blue' (Salver Group)

ORIGIN: from Don Duncan, Washington, USA. Introduced by Wayside Gardens, South Carolina, USA, in 1993 and still in cultivation.

PEDUNCLE: 50–75 cm.

INFLORESCENCE: 100(–160) flowers, globular.

FLOWER: pale violet-blue to almost white near the base, midrib dark violet-blue.

NOTE: invalid name per the ICNCP-1995, art. 17.11.

Agapanthus 'Prolific White' (Trumpet Group)

ORIGIN: raised by Don Duncan, Washington, USA, introduced by Wayside Gardens, South Carolina, USA, in 1995.

PEDUNCLE: 50–65 cm.

INFLORESCENCE: flat.

FLOWER: clear white.

NOTE: invalid name per the ICNCP-1995, art. 17.11.

Agapanthus 'Proteas'

ORIGIN: known since 1998, UK.

LEAF: deciduous.

PEDUNCLE: 75 cm.

FLOWER: dark violet-blue.

Agapanthus 'Pure White'

ORIGIN: known since 1989, UK.

NOTE: invalid name per the ICNCP-1995, art. 17.11.

Agapanthus 'Purple Cloud' (Trumpet Group)

SYNONYM: *Agapanthus inapertus* 'Purple Cloud'
Agapanthus 'Storm Cloud' ex Reads Nursery

ERROR: 'Purple Choud'

ORIGIN: (probably a hybrid between *A. praecox* subsp. *orientalis* and *A. inapertus*) introduced in New Zealand, known since 1991, and still in cultivation. Also offered as seed.

LEAF: evergreen, up to 50 cm long and 4 cm wide, upright with upper half arching, distinctly glaucous, base purple.

PEDUNCLE: 150–200 cm, green and slightly glaucous, more or less round, sometimes with a secondary but shorter peduncle.

INFLORESCENCE: 20–25 cm across, 50–70 flowers, globular, bud opens on 1 side.

PEDICEL: green but heavily violet-purple speckled.

FLOWERBUD: dark violet-blue, upright.

FLOWER: inside pale to normal violet-blue with paler base, midrib and margin dark violet-blue with purple tint, outside dark violet-blue, base with purple, when out of flower more purple, the first flowers hang downwards but otherwise more or less horizontal, 4.5(–5) cm long (tube 1.6–2 cm long), 3–3.5 cm across, stamens just slightly exserted, anthers violet, good fruits by open pollination, elliptic, on the sunside violet at the base and along the inner rib towards apex, otherwise glossy green.

NOTE: details from plants grown at various nurseries.

NOTE: some prefer to regard this cultivar as an *A. inapertus* hybrid, because of commercial interest; however, its flower diameter, together with its being evergreen, places it within the Trumpet Group.

NOTE: very impressive cultivar, both in and out of flower, as a plant. Very slow to propagate as the plant will hardly make any side shoots.

NOTE: initially seed-propagated but now widely propagated by tissue culture. Obviously, seed-raised plants are variable, less impressive plants, mainly recognized by having a shorter peduncle.

NOTE: the plant that was offered by Reads Nursery, UK, as 'Storm Cloud' is the same as **'Purple Cloud'**.

NOTE: nuclear DNA content = 24.9 pg.

ILLUSTRATION: *color plate*; photograph, Snoeijer (1998, 1999), van Dijk (2002), and Fulcher (2002).

Agapanthus 'Purple Splendour'

ORIGIN: known since 1991, New Zealand.

INFLORESCENCE: globular.

FLOWER: violet-blue.

NOTE: very similar to **'Purple Cloud'** but said to have a more globular inflorescence.

Agapanthus 'Purple Star'

ORIGIN: known since 2000 when offered by The Village Nurseries, UK. The nursery suspects it might be the same as **'Purple Cloud'**.

Agapanthus 'Queen Anne' (Funnel Group)

SYNONYM: *Agapanthus africanus* 'Queen Anne'

ERROR: 'Queen Ann'

ORIGIN: introduced in New Zealand. Known since 1990 and still in cultivation. Also offered as seed.

LEAF: evergreen, arching, normal to dark green.

PEDUNCLE: up to 60 cm.

INFLORESCENCE: 50–70 flowers, more or less globular.

PEDICEL: green and slightly flushed purple towards the flower.

FLOWERBUD: starting cream with dull pale violet flush, later more coloured, upright.

FLOWER: inside very pale violet-blue-white with margin slightly more coloured, midrib pale violet-blue, outside very pale violet-blue with midrib and base just slightly darker, when out of flower pale purple-violet, horizontal to just slightly facing downwards, stamens exserted, anthers purple becoming black and pollen orange-brown.

NOTE: most details from plants offered at a garden centre in Portland, Oregon, USA. Unfortunately, this cultivar is widely propagated by seed, and it will not be long before it is best to regard this name as a synonym of RUBBISH.

ILLUSTRATION: *color plate.*

Agapanthus 'Queen Elizabeth the Queen Mother' = *A.* 'Queen Mother'

NOTE: invalid name per the ICNCP-1995, art. 17.10.

Agapanthus 'Queen Mother' (Salver Group)

SYNONYM: *Agapanthus* 'Queen Elizabeth the Queen Mother'

ORIGIN: raised by The Crown Estate, Windsor, UK, introduced in 1995, still in cultivation.

NAME: in honour of Lady Elizabeth Bowes-Lyon (1900–2002), HM Queen Elizabeth, mother of HM Queen Elizabeth II.

LEAF: deciduous, up to 50 cm long and 2.5 cm wide, upright, dark glossy green, base with a bit of purple.

PEDUNCLE: 60–85 cm, green and glaucous, round.

INFLORESCENCE: 12–15 cm across, 30–40(–80) flowers, more or less flat.

PEDICEL: green and a bit purple towards flower.

FLOWERBUD: dark violet-blue with very dark violet-blue base, upright but later horizontal.

FLOWER: inside violet-blue with base very pale violet-blue, midrib dark violet-blue, margin violet-blue with purple, outside violet-blue with slightly darker midrib and base, when out of flower violet-blue with purple, horizontal to a bit nodding, 2.7–3 cm long (tube 1.1 cm long), 2.5–3 cm across, stamens not exserted, anthers violet-blue.

NOTE: details from plants grown at Wisley and by Hans Kramer.

ILLUSTRATION: *color plate.*

Agapanthus 'Rancho Dwarf'

> SYNONYM: *Agapanthus africanus* 'Rancho Dwarf'
> *Agapanthus* 'Peter Pan Albus'
> *Agapanthus praecox* subsp. *orientalis* 'Rancho Dwarf'
> *Agapanthus* 'Rancho White'

ORIGIN: introduced by Brown Bulb Ranch, USA. Known since 1974. The true plant is probably no longer in cultivation.
FLOWER: white.
NOTE: seed-propagated and so best to regard plants under this name as RUBBISH.

Agapanthus 'Rancho White' = *A.* **'Rancho Dwarf'**

Agapanthus **'Raveningham Hall'** (Funnel Group)

ORIGIN: obtained by Coen Jansen, Dalfsen, The Netherlands, as an unnamed seedling from Raveningham Gardens in 1990. Named by him and still in cultivation.
NAME: after Raveningham Hall, Norfolk, UK, which is famous for its walled garden and its *Agapanthus* selections, all of which contain the word "star." The garden was the particular domain of Lady Priscilla Bacon, mother of Sir Nichols Bacon, the current owner.
LEAF: deciduous, up to 40 cm long and 3 cm wide, arching, normal green and slightly glaucous, base green.
PEDUNCLE: 80 cm, green, flat.
INFLORESCENCE: 18 cm across, 60 flowers, globular.
PEDICEL: green with violet-purple towards flower.
FLOWERBUD: violet-blue, upright.
FLOWER: inside pale violet-blue with margin slightly darker and purple tint, midrib dark violet-blue (94A) and rather wide, outside violet-blue, midrib and base dark violet-blue, when out of flower more purple, horizontal, 4 cm long (tube 1 cm long), 4 cm across, stamens slightly exserted, anthers dark violet with yellow pollen.
NOTE: details from plants grown by Coen Jansen.
NOTE: nuclear DNA content = 24.4 pg.

Agapanthus **'Regal Beauty'**

ORIGIN: raised by R.J. and D.M.L. Wood, New Plymouth, New Zealand.
NOTE: New Zealand Plant Variety Rights applied for, no. HOM124, on 6 October 2000, by Lifetech Laboratories Ltd, New Zealand.
NOTE: details from the Internet [36].

Agapanthus **'Repens'**

> SYNONYM: *Agapanthus umbellatus* var. *repens* A. Worsley

NOTE: Worsley (1913) "A small-growing form with creeping rootstock, narrow and short leaves and flowers like *Agapanthus* **'Mooreanus'**."

Agapanthus 'Rhone' (Trumpet Group)

ORIGIN: introduced by Maas & van Stein, Hillegom, The Netherlands, known since 1989, and still in cultivation.

NAME: Dutch spelling of the Rhône River.

LEAF: deciduous, 20–30 cm long and 2 cm wide, upright but later almost flat on the ground, dark green and slightly glaucous, base green.

PEDUNCLE: 80 cm, green at lower half, upper half with violet, flat.

INFLORESCENCE: 11–13 cm across, 30–40 flowers, flat, bud opens on 2 sides.

PEDICEL: dark dull purple.

FLOWERBUD: dark violet-blue, upright.

FLOWER: inside with a rather wide violet-blue (92A) midrib, margin pale violet-blue (97AB) with purple tint, outside violet-blue with slightly darker base, when out of flower more purple, horizontal, 2.5 cm long (tube 0.8 cm long), 2.5 cm across, stamens not exserted, anthers violet with yellow pollen.

NOTE: details from plants grown by Maas & van Stein.

NOTE: easily recognized by its peduncle, which is almost bicoloured in full sun.

NOTE: nuclear DNA content = 24 pg.

ILLUSTRATION: *color plate.*

Agapanthus 'Rich Blue'

SYNONYM: *Agapanthus campanulatus* 'Rich Blue'

ORIGIN: known since 1987, UK, and still in cultivation.

LEAF: deciduous.

FLOWER: violet-blue.

NOTE: invalid name per the ICNCP-1995, art. 17.11.

Agapanthus 'Robusta'

SYNONYM: *Agapanthus praecox* subsp. *praecox* 'Robusta'

ORIGIN: known since 1995, Kirstenbosch National Botanical Garden; no further records.

NOTE: invalid name per the ICNCP-1995, art. 17.9 and 17.11.

Agapanthus 'Rohline'

ORIGIN: Australia, known since 1994; no further records.

NOTE: Kwekersrecht (plant variety right) applied for, The Netherlands only, not granted, no. AGP1.

NOTE: name from Allemand and Pionnat (2001) and the Internet [28].

Agapanthus 'Rosemary' (Trumpet Group)

ERROR: 'Rose Mary'

ORIGIN: raised by Lewis Palmer, known since 1974, and still in cultivation.

LEAF: deciduous, up to 50(–70) cm long and 3.5 cm wide, upright, normal glossy green.

PEDUNCLE: 100–140 cm, normal green and distinctly glaucous, rather sturdy, round.

INFLORESCENCE: 15–19 cm across, 50–70 flowers, more or less flat.

PEDICEL: dark green.

FLOWERBUD: greenish-white but before opening a bit violet, upright.

FLOWER: inside dull white to very pale purple-grey especially along the margin, midrib transparent with a purple tint, outside white to very pale greyish-violet at the margin and greenish base, midrib transparent, when out of flower almost completely pale purple, horizontal to slightly facing downwards, 3.7–4 cm long (tube 1.9 cm long), 2.5 cm across, stamens not exserted, anthers black.

NOTE: most details from plants grown by van Doorslaer.

NOTE: very similar to '**Windsor Grey**' but in general 'Rosemary' has a smaller inflorescence with fewer, slightly paler flowers.

NOTE: invalid name per the ICNCP-1995, art. 17.13.

NOTE: nuclear DNA content = 23.9 pg.

ILLUSTRATION: *color plate*; photograph, Phillips and Rix (1991) and Snoeijer (1998).

AWARD: AM in 1977.

Agapanthus 'Rosewarne' (Trumpet Group)

SYNONYM: *Agapanthus campanulatus* 'Rosewarne'

ERROR: 'Rose Warne', 'Rosewarn'

ORIGIN: (selection of *A. campanulatus*) grown at a college in Rosewarne, UK, introduced by Burncoose & South Down Nurseries, Redruth, Cornwall, in 1995, and still in cultivation.

LEAF: evergreen, 12 per shoot, up to 45 cm long and 4 cm wide, upright to arching, normal green, base green.

PEDUNCLE: 75–100 cm, green.

INFLORESCENCE: 22.5 cm across, 100 flowers.

PEDICEL: bronze.

FLOWER: inside pale violet-blue (91C), broad and darker midrib (91A), outside pale violet-blue (91C), base and midrib darker (91A), horizontal, 4 cm long, 3 cm across.

NOTE: most details supplied by Gary Dunlop.

NOTE: nuclear DNA content = 25.2 pg.

Agapanthus 'Rotterdam' (Funnel Group)

ORIGIN: ('**Blue Perfection**' × seedling) raised by Kees Duivenvoorde, Beverwijk, The Netherlands, introduced in 1999, and still in cultivation.

NAME: after the city in The Netherlands.

LEAF: deciduous, up to 40 cm long and 2.2 cm wide, upright, dark green, base green.

PEDUNCLE: 70 cm, green, rather sturdy, flat.

INFLORESCENCE: 13 cm across, 80–100 flowers, globular.

PEDICEL: green to violet to the flower.

FLOWERBUD: pale violet-blue with a bit of green in the middle, upright.

FLOWER: inside very pale violet-blue (92D) with a bit of a purple tint, midrib violet-blue (97A), outside pale violet-blue (97B) with purple tint, midrib violet-blue, base glossy violet-blue (96A), when out of flower purple with violet-blue base, up to 3 cm

long (tube 1 cm long), 3.3 cm across, stamens exserted, anthers dark violet becom-
ing black, pollen orange-brown.
NOTE: details from plants grown by Duivenvoorde.
NOTE: flowers tend towards the Salver Group when fully open.
NOTE: registered in 1999.
NOTE: nuclear DNA content = 23.9 pg.
ILLUSTRATION: *color plate*; photograph, Arie in't Veld (2001).

Agapanthus 'Rotunda' (Funnel Group)

ORIGIN: raised and introduced by Gary Dunlop, Ballyrogan Nurseries, UK.
LEAF: deciduous, 75 cm long and 3 cm wide, upright, normal green, base slightly
purple.
PEDUNCLE: 120 cm, green.
INFLORESCENCE: 17.5 cm across, 100 flowers, bud opens on 2 sides.
PEDICEL: green.
FLOWER: inside rather pale violet-blue (92C) with midrib slightly darker (92B), out-
side pale violet-blue (92B) with darker midrib (93A), horizontal, 3 cm long, 5 cm
across.
NOTE: details supplied by Gary Dunlop.

Agapanthus 'Roy' (Salver Group)

ORIGIN: introduced by Lewis Palmer, known since 1973.
LEAF: deciduous, up to 40 cm long and 2 cm wide, upright, dull green and glaucous.
PEDUNCLE: 90–100 cm, pale green-yellow.
INFLORESCENCE: 11 cm across, globular.
PEDICEL: green with almost black spots towards flower.
FLOWER: inside white with violet-blue margin and midrib (94B), slightly facing
downwards, 2 cm long, 3 cm across.

Agapanthus ROYAL AMA = a series that includes the cultivars 'Elaine' and 'Ellamae'

Agapanthus 'Royal Blue' ex The Netherlands

ORIGIN: known since 1966 when grown by Fa J. de Jong & Zonen, Aalsmeer, The
Netherlands. Probably no longer in cultivation.
FLOWER: inside violet-blue, outside dark violet-blue with darker midrib.
AWARD: GV in 1966.

Agapanthus 'Royal Blue' ex UK (Salver Group)

SYNONYM: *Agapanthus campanulatus* 'Royal Blue'

ORIGIN: (probably a selection of *A. campanulatus*) raised by The Crown Estate,
Windsor, UK, introduced in 1974, and still in cultivation.
LEAF: deciduous, 30–40 cm long and 2–2.5 cm wide, arching, normal green, base
purple.
PEDUNCLE: 40–75 cm, pale green, round.

INFLORESCENCE: 12 cm across, (10–)30 flowers, flat.

PEDICEL: green with dull purple towards flower.

FLOWERBUD: dark violet-blue, upright.

FLOWER: inside dark violet-blue (94AB) but paler towards base, midrib darker, margin with purple tint, outside violet-blue with midrib and base dark violet-blue, segments recurved, horizontal to facing downwards, 3 cm long (tube 0.8 cm long), 3.5 cm across, stamens exserted, anthers dark violet.

NOTE: details from plants grown at Wisley.

ILLUSTRATION: photograph, Snoeijer (1998) and Wray (1998a).

NOTE: invalid name per the ICNCP-1995, art. 17.2.

ILLUSTRATION: *color plate.*

AWARD: AM in 1977.

Agapanthus 'Royale' (Funnel Group)

ORIGIN: raised by Gary Dunlop, Ballyrogan Nurseries, UK, named in 1995.

LEAF: evergreen, up to 42.5 cm long and 3.5 cm wide, upright to 60°, normal green, base green.

PEDUNCLE: up to 90 cm, green.

INFLORESCENCE: up to 22.5 cm across, 50 flowers, bud usually opens on 1 side.

PEDICEL: green-bronze.

FLOWER: inside white with margin and midrib dark violet-blue (95A), outside pale violet-blue (94D) with wide darker coloured midrib (95A), horizontal but mostly facing towards the sun, up to 4 cm long, 4.5 cm across.

NOTE: details supplied by Gary Dunlop.

Agapanthus 'Royal Lodge'

ORIGIN: raised by The Crown Estate, Windsor, UK, introduced in 1975, and still in cultivation.

NAME: after the royal estate.

LEAF: deciduous.

PEDUNCLE: 110 cm.

FLOWER: violet-blue.

Agapanthus 'Royal Purple'

ORIGIN: known since 1995, UK; no further records.

Agapanthus 'Ruban Bleu' (Funnel Group)

SYNONYM: *Agapanthus* 'Blue Ribbon'

ORIGIN: known since 2001 when offered as seed in France.

NAME: French, "blue ribbon."

FLOWER: violet-blue with a very dark midrib, stamens exserted.

NOTE: because I am not certain we are dealing with the same cultivar, I separate the one grown and introduced in Holland from the one grown and introduced in England. The Dutch plant, however, is rather rare (known in only two collections) and not propagated from seed, as far as I know; it is most likely, therefore, any 'Ruban Bleu' seed offered is from the English plant.

NOTE: details from the Internet [11].

Agapanthus 'Ruban Blanc'

SYNONYM: *Agapanthus* 'White Ribbon'

ORIGIN: known since 2001 when offered as seed in France.
NAME: French, "white ribbon."
FLOWER: white.
NOTE: details from the Internet [11].

Agapanthus RUBBISH

SYNONYM: *Agapanthus* Adelaide Seedlings
Agapanthus africanus 'New Blue'
Agapanthus africanus Headbourne Hybrids
Agapanthus 'Azure'
Agapanthus Best New White Hybrids
Agapanthus blue
Agapanthus 'Blue Dwarf'
Agapanthus 'Bright Blue'
Agapanthus campanulatus 'Bright Blue'
Agapanthus campanulatus 'Dwarf Bright Blue'
Agapanthus campanulatus 'Headbourne Hybrids'
Agapanthus campanulatus 'Kingston Blue Strain'
Agapanthus campanulatus 'Pale Blue'
Agapanthus campanulatus 'Pale Form'
Agapanthus campanulatus 'White Form'
Agapanthus campanulatus hybrids
Agapanthus campanulatus white form
Agapanthus dark hybrids
Agapanthus 'Devon Dawn'
Agapanthus 'Dwarf Blue' ex today's plants
Agapanthus 'Dwarf Bright Blue'
Agapanthus 'Dwarf White'
Agapanthus 'Giant Hybrids'
Agapanthus Giant Hybrids
Agapanthus Hardy Hybrid
Agapanthus 'Headbourne A'
Agapanthus 'Headbourne Blue'
Agapanthus 'Headbourne White'
Agapanthus Headbourne Hybrids ex today's plants
Agapanthus hybrid
Agapanthus hybrid miniature
Agapanthus hybrids
Agapanthus hybrids new

Agapanthus hybrids white
Agapanthus Kingston Blue Strain
Agapanthus Lewis Palmer hybrid
Agapanthus Mixed Giant Hybrids
Agapanthus 'Mixed White'
Agapanthus mixed whites
Agapanthus 'Mooreanus Minor'
Agapanthus Mooreanus Minor Hybrids
Agapanthus 'New Blue'
Agapanthus 'New Giant'
Agapanthus 'New Giant Blue'
Agapanthus 'New Giant Blue Pale'
Agapanthus New Giant Hybrids
Agapanthus 'New Giant Pale'
Agapanthus 'New Giant Pale Blue'
Agapanthus 'New Giant White'
Agapanthus New Hybrids Mixed
Agapanthus orientalis hybrids
Agapanthus 'Pale'
Agapanthus 'Pale Blue'
Agapanthus 'Pale Form'
Agapanthus Palmer's Hybrids
Agapanthus Pine Cottage seedlings
Agapanthus praecox subsp. *minimus* 'Forma'
Agapanthus praecox subsp. *orientalis* 'Azure'
Agapanthus praecox subsp. *orientalis* 'Dwarf White'
Agapanthus praecox subsp. *praecox* 'Azure'
Agapanthus praecox subsp. *praecox* 'Dwarf White'
Agapanthus praecox 'Dwarf White'
Agapanthus praecox 'Headbourne'
Agapanthus praecox Adelaide Seedlings
Agapanthus 'Stormcloud' ex today's plants
Agapanthus Trudy Seedlings
Agapanthus umbellatus 'Headbourne'
Agapanthus umbellatus 'Headbourne Hybrids'
Agapanthus umbellatus 'Underway'
Agapanthus 'Underway'
Agapanthus white
Agapanthus 'White Dwarf'
Agapanthus White Dwarf Hybrids
Agapanthus 'White Form'

NOTE: the term dates from the mid 19th century, when it was widely used in the bulbs/corms and bare-rooted perennials trade, including **Agapanthus**. Small parcels of leftover bulbs/plants (i.e., cloned and named cultivars) were mixed and sold as "rubbish" (*rommel* in Dutch), in the sense of "mixture of leftovers." The term is hardly used anymore because the trade is no longer interested in unnamed mixtures.

I maintain the term here because so many *Agapanthus* cultivars are propagated by seed and hence are not true to type; they are offered without any notice of how they were propagated and sometimes even before they have flowered, under a variety of terms, such as "seedlings," "hybrids," and especially "Headbourne Hybrids." The term RUBBISH in this book, therefore, should be read as "mixture of seedlings." I have included all seedlings and hybrids under RUBBISH (even those I have not seen myself, based on reference descriptions).

Several cultivars I came across, listed here as synonyms of RUBBISH, are actually cloned cultivars; they are listed thus simply because I found the names were applied to other plants in other countries. Such cloned cultivars should get a correct cultivar name, rather than a RUBBISH name like 'New Blue' or 'White Dwarf'.

Many seed-propagated cultivars are still accepted in this book, either as a cultivar or as a group of plants that look similar to each other. But in time, even these correctly named and originally cloned cultivars (**'Blue Baby'**, **'Peter Pan'**, **'Queen Anne'**, **'Rancho White'**, and **'Streamline'**, to name but a few) will become mere RUBBISH, which is unfortunate. Worse yet, some cultivars are now propagated by tissue culture even though it is known the cultivar was propagated by seed in the first place. Consumers are increasingly aware of these unacceptable seed-raising practices. It's time that growers stop propagating by seed, that nurseries and garden centres stop selling seed-raised plants, and, of course, that all consumers stop buying this RUBBISH.

Of course, the ICNCP-1995 accepts seed-raised cultivars, maintaining them as seed strains. In fact, most of our crops, vegetables, and ornamental annuals are raised and maintained as seed. But in *Agapanthus*, plants raised from seed are so variable, even when collected from an isolated plant, that a seed-propagated cultivar is unacceptable.

Agapanthus 'Saint Ivel'

SYNONYM: *Agapanthus praecox* subsp. *floribundus* 'Saint Ivel'
Agapanthus praecox 'Saint Ivel'

ORIGIN: known since 1997, UK.
LEAF: evergreen.
PEDUNCLE: 80 cm.
FLOWER: violet-blue.

Agapanthus 'Saint Michael'

ORIGIN: raised and introduced by Lewis Palmer, known since 1974; no further records.

Agapanthus 'Saintpaulii'

SYNONYM: *Agapanthus africanus* subsp. *minor* var. *saintpaulii* H.R. Wehrh.
Agapanthus minor var. *saintpaulii* Bonstedt
Agapanthus minor 'Saintpaulii'

ORIGIN: known since 1903 when offered by Leichtlin. Still referred to in 1931 but probably no longer in cultivation.

PEDUNCLE: 60 cm.

INFLORESCENCE: 50–120 flowers.

FLOWER: "snow" white, rather small.

NOTE: habitus "dwarf and compact."

Agapanthus 'Sandringham' (Salver Group)

ORIGIN: raised by The Crown Estate, Windsor, UK, introduced in 1995, and still in cultivation.

NAME: after the royal estate in Norfolk, England.

LEAF: deciduous, 20–30 cm long and 1.3 cm wide, upright to arching, normal green, base purple.

PEDUNCLE: 50–80 cm, green with just a bit of purple towards the inflorescence, round.

INFLORESCENCE: 12 cm across, (10–)40 flowers, flat.

PEDICEL: green with some dull violet speckles.

FLOWERBUD: dark violet-blue, upright.

FLOWER: inside dark violet-blue (95C), midrib darker (93AB), margin darker and with purple tint, outside dark violet-blue with slightly darker base, horizontal, 3 cm long (tube 1.1 cm long), 3 cm across, stamens not exserted, anthers violet.

NOTE: details from plants grown at Wisley.

ILLUSTRATION: photograph, Snoeijer (1998).

Agapanthus 'San Gabriel' (Variegated Leaf Group)

SYNONYM: *Agapanthus praecox* 'San Gabriel'

ORIGIN: (chance seedling) discovered at Monrovia's Azusa, California, site, in a large batch of seedlings, in 1986. Joe Sharman sent some offsets of the plant to friends in the UK. Still in cultivation.

NAME: named by Joe Sharman, Monksilver Nursery, UK, after the hills above the nursery in California.

LEAF: evergreen, up to 30 cm long and 2.2 cm wide, arching, on one plant leaves should be a mixture of a few dark glossy green leaves and a few variably striped with pale to dark yellow to even rather wide bands (some leaves might be even completely yellow), base green.

PEDUNCLE: 60–75 cm, normal green with cream stripes, round.

INFLORESCENCE: up to 15 cm across, 40 flowers, flat, bud green and variably striped rich cream to pale green, opens on 1 side.

PEDICEL: bright green with violet towards the flowers.

FLOWERBUD: upright, violet-blue but when very young with a paler coloured base.

FLOWER: inside very pale violet-blue (92D) to almost white, margin pale violet-blue (92C) with purple tint, midrib pale violet-blue (92B), outside violet-blue with darker coloured midrib and base slightly darker, when out of flower slightly purple, horizontal, 4 cm long (tube 1.5 cm long), 4 cm across, stamens exserted, anthers dark violet with orange-brown pollen, fruit yellow, green or variably striped in one inflorescence.

NOTE: details from plants grown by Monksilver Nursery, UK.

NOTE: registered in 1986.

NOTE: variegated seedlings of 'San Gabriel' are offered under this name, but they are no longer true.

NOTE: nuclear DNA content = 24.7 pg.

ILLUSTRATION: *color plates*; photograph, Hirose and Yokoi (1998), Snoeijer (1998), Fulcher (2002), Jansen (2002), and van Dijk (2002).

Agapanthus 'Sapphire'

> SYNONYM: *Agapanthus africanus* 'Sapphire'

ORIGIN: known since 1987, UK, and still in cultivation.

LEAF: evergreen.

PEDUNCLE: 60 cm.

FLOWER: dark violet-blue.

NOTE: nuclear DNA content = 21.9 pg.

Agapanthus 'Sarah' (Funnel Group)

ORIGIN: raised by M.F. Geenty, Hamilton, New Zealand, known since 2000, and still in cultivation.

LEAF: deciduous, up to 25 cm long and 1 cm wide, rather spreading, pale green, base green-cream.

PEDUNCLE: 60 cm, green, round.

INFLORESCENCE: 8–10 cm across, 15–25 flowers, upright.

PEDICEL: green.

FLOWERBUD: violet-blue with apex dark green, base green with white spot to the violet-blue.

FLOWER: inside pale violet-blue-white and purple tint, margin slightly darker and purple tint, slightly wavy, midrib pale violet-blue, outside pale violet-blue, apex and base greenish, when out of flower strongly purple, upright, up to 3.8 cm long (tube 1 cm long), 4 cm across, stamens slightly exserted, anthers yellow becoming brown.

NOTE: some flowers within an inflorescence tend to have 8 tepals.

NOTE: details from plants shown at the 2001 Horti Fair, in Amsterdam, The Netherlands; some details from the Internet [36].

NOTE: European Plant Variety Right applied for and granted, file no. 2001/0188, grant no. 10661, expires 31 December 2028.

NOTE: New Zealand Plant Variety Rights applied for, no. HOM105, on 17 January 2000, by Lyndale Nurseries Auckland Ltd, New Zealand.

Agapanthus 'Saundersonianus'

> SYNONYM: *Agapanthus africanus* subsp. *umbellatus* var. *saundersonianus* H.R. Wehrh.
>
> *Agapanthus umbellatus* var. *saundersonianus* Bonstedt

ORIGIN: known since 1903, UK, and 1905, The Netherlands. Still referred to in 1931 but probably no longer in cultivation.

FLOWER: dark violet-blue.

Agapanthus 'Sea Coral'

ERROR: 'Seacoral'

ORIGIN: introduced in New Zealand, known since 2000 when offered in the UK, and still in cultivation.
LEAF: evergreen, "narrow."
PEDUNCLE: 60–80 cm.
INFLORESCENCE: flat.
FLOWER: white with purple apex.

Agapanthus 'Sea Foam'

ERROR: 'Sea Form'

ORIGIN: raised by the curator of the Botanical Garden Auckland, New Zealand, introduced in 1998, and still in cultivation.
LEAF: evergreen, "strong and broad."
PEDUNCLE: 120 cm.
FLOWER: "pure white," anthers yellow.
NOTE: some details from the Internet [12].

Agapanthus 'Sea Mist' (Funnel Group)

ORIGIN: raised by the curator of the Botanical Garden Auckland, New Zealand, introduced in 1998. Still in cultivation.
LEAF: evergreen, "strong and broad."
PEDUNCLE: 75 cm.
INFLORESCENCE: 60 flowers, flat.
FLOWER: violet-blue with darker midrib.
NOTE: New Zealand Plant Variety Rights applied for and granted, no. HOM079, by Auckland Regional Council, Manurewa, Auckland, New Zealand, expires 12 July 2019.
NOTE: some details from the Internet [36].

Agapanthus 'Sea Spray' (Funnel Group)

ERROR: 'Seaspray'

ORIGIN: raised by the curator of the Botanical Garden Auckland, New Zealand, introduced in 1998, and still in cultivation.
LEAF: evergreen.
PEDUNCLE: 120 cm.
INFLORESCENCE: 60 flowers, flat.
FLOWER: white, anthers yellow.

Agapanthus 'Select'

SYNONYM: *Agapanthus praecox* 'Select'
ORIGIN: offered as seed.
NOTE: name from the Internet [32].
NOTE: invalid name per the ICNCP-1995, art. 17.16.

Agapanthus 'Selected White'

ORIGIN: offered as seed.
NOTE: name from the Internet [32].
NOTE: invalid name per the ICNCP-1995, art. 17.11.

Agapanthus 'Selma Bock'

SYNONYM: *Agapanthus praecox* 'Selma Bock'

ORIGIN: known since 1995, Kirstenbosch National Botanical Garden; no further records.

Agapanthus 'Septemberhemel' (Funnel Group)

ERROR: 'September Hemel'

ORIGIN: ('**Lilliput**' × '**Midnight Star**') raised by Hans Kramer, De Hessenhof nursery, The Netherlands. Selected from a bed of approximately 2000 seedlings and introduced in 2000. Still in cultivation.
NAME: Dutch, "September sky," with reference to the late flowering.
LEAF: deciduous, up to 35 cm long and 2.3 cm wide, arching, normal green, base purple-violet.
PEDUNCLE: 70 cm, green and glaucous and a bit purple speckled towards the inflorescence, rather sturdy, round.
INFLORESCENCE: 14 cm across, 60–70 flowers, flat, bud opens on 1 side, bract not caducous.
PEDICEL: dark purple.
FLOWERBUD: dark violet-blue with darker base, upright.
FLOWER: inside pale violet-blue (94B) with a slight purple tint at apex and margin dark violet-blue (95B), midrib violet-blue (94A), outside violet-blue (94B) with purple tint, midrib slightly darker (94A), base dark violet-blue (95A), when out of flower purple-violet, horizontal to slightly nodding, up to 3.6 cm long (tube 1.1 cm long), 3.4 cm across, stamens not exserted, anthers violet becoming black, just a bit fragrant.
NOTE: details from plants grown by Kramer.
NOTE: '**Meibont**' is from the same batch.
NOTE: similar to '**Loch Hope**', but the peduncle of '**Septemberhemel**' is sturdier and straighter.
NOTE: nuclear DNA content = 23.1 pg.
ILLUSTRATION: *color plate*; photograph, van Dijk (2002).

Agapanthus 'Shidarefuji'

ORIGIN: Japan, known since 2001 when offered by Komoriya Nursery Ltd.
NAME: Japanese, "weeping wisteria."
PEDUNCLE: 70 cm.
FLOWER: pale purple-violet.
NOTE: details from the Internet [25].

Agapanthus 'Shinkai' (Salver Group)

ORIGIN: Japan, known since 1999 when offered by Sakata, and still in cultivation.
NAME: Japanese, "deep sea," "deep ocean."
PEDUNCLE: 100 cm.
INFLORESCENCE: flat.
FLOWER: dark violet-blue.
NOTE: most details supplied by Y. Aihara and some from the Internet [25].

Agapanthus 'Shinryoku'

ORIGIN: Japan, known since 1999.
NOTE: name from Allemand and Pionnat (2001).

Agapanthus 'Shisei'

ORIGIN: Japan, known since 2001 when offered by Komoriya Nursery Ltd.
NAME: Japanese, "purple star."
PEDUNCLE: 95 cm.
FLOWER: very dark purple-violet.
NOTE: details from the Internet [25].

Agapanthus 'Silver Baby'

ORIGIN: known since 2001, New Zealand.
FLOWER: "steely silver."
NOTE: habitus dwarf.

Agapanthus 'Silver Jubilee' (Funnel Group)

ORIGIN: raised by The Crown Estate, Windsor, UK, introduced in 1975, and still in cultivation.
NAME: refers to the celebration marking 25 years of HM Queen Elizabeth II's reign.
LEAF: probably evergreen, 30–40 cm long and up to 3 cm wide, arching, normal green and slightly glaucous, base green.
PEDUNCLE: 60–70 cm, green, round.
INFLORESCENCE: 16 cm across, 50 flowers, globular.
PEDICEL: green with purple tint towards flower.
FLOWERBUD: white, upright.
FLOWER: inside white with thick transparent midrib, outside white with sometimes yellowish apex, horizontal, 4 cm long (tube 1.2 cm long), 4 cm across, stamens not exserted, anthers becoming purple.
NOTE: details from plants grown at Wisley.
AWARD: HC in 1977.

Agapanthus 'Silver Mist' (Funnel Group)

ORIGIN: raised at NCCPG Bicton College, UK, selected by Dick Fulcher in 1993, and still in cultivation.
LEAF: evergreen, 20–65 cm long and up to 4 cm wide, upright to arching, dark green, base green.

PEDUNCLE: stout, 75–95 cm, dark green, flat.

INFLORESCENCE: 20 cm across, up to 70 flowers, globular.

PEDICEL: glossy green flushed with purple.

FLOWERBUD: upright but quickly horizontal, pale violet-blue with purple tint and greenish-purple apex.

FLOWER: inside very pale violet-blue (91D) with margin slightly purple tinted, midrib violet-blue (91A), outside very pale violet-blue (91D) with purple tint and midrib slightly darker (91B), when out of flower pale purple, horizontal, 3–3.4 cm long (tube 0.9 cm long), 3.7 cm across, stamens not or just slightly exserted, anthers dark purple.

NOTE: details from plants grown by Coen Jansen; some details supplied by Gary Dunlop.

Agapanthus SILVER MOON = *A.* 'Notfred'

Agapanthus 'Silver Sceptre' (Funnel Group)

SYNONYM: *Agapanthus praecox* subsp. *praecox* 'Silver Sceptre'

ORIGIN: introduced by Gary Dunlop, Ballyrogan Nurseries, UK, known since 1999.

LEAF: evergreen, up to 40 cm long and 4 cm wide, arching, yellow-green, base yellow-green.

PEDUNCLE: 80 cm, green.

INFLORESCENCE: 25 cm across, over 100 flowers, flat, bud opens on 2 sides.

PEDICEL: green to bronze near the flower.

FLOWERBUD: pale violet-blue.

FLOWER: inside pale violet-blue (91C) with darker midrib (91A), outside pale violet-blue (91C) with midrib slightly darker (91B), horizontal, up to 4 cm long, up to 4 cm across.

NOTE: details supplied by Gary Dunlop.

Agapanthus 'Silver Streak' (Variegated Leaf Group)

SYNONYM: *Agapanthus praecox* subsp. *orientalis* 'Silver Streak'
Agapanthus praecox 'Silver Streak'

ORIGIN: known since 2000.

LEAF: evergreen, variegated.

PEDUNCLE: 50 cm.

FLOWER: violet-blue.

NOTE: details from the Internet [21] and [33].

Agapanthus 'Silver Sword'

ORIGIN: (chance seedling of *A. praecox* subsp. *orientalis*) from Australia, known since 1999.

NOTE: name from Allemand and Pionnat (2001).

Agapanthus silver variegated

ORIGIN: known since 2001 when offered by Merriments Gardens, UK.
LEAF: variegated.
FLOWER: violet-blue.
NOTE: details from the Internet [38].

Agapanthus 'Sky' (Tubular Group)

SYNONYM: *Agapanthus inapertus* subsp. *hollandii* 'Sky' pro parte

ORIGIN: (selection of *A. inapertus* subsp. *hollandii*) from eastern Transvaal. Known since 1987 and still in cultivation. Also offered as seed.
LEAF: deciduous.
PEDUNCLE: 80–140 cm, pale green and glaucous, round.
INFLORESCENCE: 20–30 flowers, drooping.
FLOWERBUD: upright but already hanging downwards before opening, dark violet-blue apex with middle much paler and violet-blue base.
FLOWER: outside pale violet-blue with midrib slightly darker and paler towards base, base a bit green, when out of flower a bit purple, drooping vertically or just slightly projecting, stamens not exserted.
NOTE: the flower colour given in references varies, probably because of confusion with 'Sky Blue'.
ILLUSTRATION: drawing, du Plessis and Duncan (1989); photograph, Duncan (1985 as *A. inapertus* subsp. *hollandii* 'Sky') and Allemand and Pionnat (2001 as *A. inapertus* subsp. *hollandii* var. 'Sky').

Agapanthus 'Sky Blue' (Tubular Group)

SYNONYM: *Agapanthus inapertus* subsp. *hollandii* 'Sky' pro parte
Agapanthus inapertus subsp. *hollandii* 'Sky Blue'

ORIGIN: (selection of *A. inapertus* subsp. *hollandii*) from Lydenburg, eastern Transvaal, introduced by Kirstenbosch National Botanical Garden, South Africa. Known since 1985.
LEAF: deciduous, glaucous.
PEDUNCLE: up to 140 cm, green.
FLOWERBUD: upright, pale violet-blue and paler towards apex and apex normal violet-blue.
FLOWER: very pale violet-blue (97B), stamens not exserted.
ILLUSTRATION: photograph, Duncan (1998 as *A. inapertus* subsp. *hollandii* 'Sky').

Agapanthus 'Sky Rocket' (Tubular Group)

ORIGIN: (an *A. inapertus* hybrid) raised at NCCPG Bicton College, UK, selected by Dick Fulcher in 1993, and still in cultivation.
LEAF: deciduous, 20–65 cm long and 2.5–3 cm wide, upright with upper half arching, pale green and a bit glaucous, leafbase green.
PEDUNCLE: stout, 100–140(–175) cm, normal green and distinctly glaucous, just a bit flat.

INFLORESCENCE: 14 cm across, drooping, up to 70 flowers.

PEDICEL: pale green and purple speckled.

FLOWERBUD: pale violet-blue with a bit of green in the middle and later more coloured, upright but quickly nodding.

FLOWER: inside very pale violet-blue with a purple tint and margin more purple, midrib violet-blue with a purple tint, outside violet-blue (96C) with a purple tint, midrib slightly darker, when out of flower violet-blue with a bit of purple, drooping vertically, tepal segments slightly spreading, 4.8–5 cm long (tube 2.7 cm), 2.3–2.4 cm across, stamens not or just 1–2 exserted, anthers violet becoming black.

NOTE: most details from plants grown by Coen Jansen.

ILLUSTRATION: *color plate.*

Agapanthus 'Sky Star' (Salver Group)

ORIGIN: raised and introduced by Raveningham Gardens, UK, known since 1989, and still in cultivation.

LEAF: more or less evergreen.

PEDUNCLE: 100 cm.

FLOWER: dark violet-blue.

NOTE: said to be mixed up with '**Moonstar**'.

ILLUSTRATION: photograph, Jansen (2002).

Agapanthus 'Slieve Donard' (Salver Group)

SYNONYM: *Agapanthus campanulatus* subsp. *campanulatus* 'Slieve Donard'
Agapanthus campanulatus 'Slieve Donard'
Agapanthus campanulatus 'Slieve Donard Variety'
Agapanthus 'Slieve Donard Variety'

ORIGIN: (probably a selection of *A. campanulatus*) introduced by Slieve Donard Nursery, UK, known since 1987, and still in cultivation. For more details, see *A. campanulatus* 'Nanus'.

LEAF: evergreen, up to 50 cm long and 3 cm wide, arching, pale green and slightly glaucous, base green.

PEDUNCLE: 100 cm, green with purple speckles, round, bending.

INFLORESCENCE: 15 cm across, 40 flowers.

PEDICEL: green heavily speckled purple.

FLOWER: violet-blue, when out of flower purple.

NOTE: details from plants grown by Coen Jansen.

Agapanthus 'Slieve Donard Form' (Funnel Group)

SYNONYM: *Agapanthus praecox* 'Slieve Donard Form'

ORIGIN: sold by Slieve Donard Nursery, UK, named by Gary Dunlop, Ballyrogan Nurseries, UK, known since 1996, and still in cultivation.

LEAF: evergreen.

FLOWER: violet-blue.

NOTE: details supplied by Gary Dunlop.

NOTE: invalid name per the ICNCP-1995, art. 17.15.

Agapanthus 'Slieve Donard Variety' = *A.* **'Slieve Donard'**

NOTE: invalid name per the ICNCP-1995, art. 17.15.

Agapanthus 'Small Dark' (Salver Group)

ORIGIN: ('Blue Dwarf' × *A. campanulatus* subsp. *patens*) raised by Parva Plants, New Zealand, known since 1998, and still in cultivation.
PEDUNCLE: 73 cm.
INFLORESCENCE: 45 flowers, flat.
FLOWER: inside pale violet-blue, midrib violet-blue, stamens not exserted, anthers violet.
NOTE: details from the Internet [2].
NOTE: invalid name per the ICNCP-1995, art. 17.11.

Agapanthus 'Small White'

SYNONYM: *Agapanthus praecox* 'Small White'

ORIGIN: known since 1995, Kirstenbosch National Botanical Garden, South Africa.
NOTE: invalid name per the ICNCP-1995, art. 17.11.

Agapanthus **'Snoopy'** (Variegated Leaf Group)

ORIGIN: known since 1996, Australia.
LEAF: variegated.

Agapanthus 'Snow Baby' = *A.* **'Snowy Baby'**

Agapanthus **'Snowball'** (Funnel Group)

SYNONYM: *Agapanthus praecox* subsp. *orientalis* 'Snowball'

ERROR: 'Snow Ball'

ORIGIN: introduced in New Zealand, known since 1991, and still in cultivation.
LEAF: evergreen.
PEDUNCLE: 30–40(–60) cm.
INFLORESCENCE: 50–70 flowers, globular.
FLOWER: inside pure white with cream midrib, tepals rather wide, stamens slightly exserted.

Agapanthus **'Snow Cloud'** (Funnel Group)

ERROR: 'Snowcloud'

TRADE NAME: FRAGRANT SNOW

ORIGIN: (chance seedling of *A. praecox* subsp. *orientalis*) raised by V. Hooper, Waitara, Taranaki, New Zealand, known since 1997, and still in cultivation.
LEAF: evergreen.
PEDUNCLE: 90–120 cm.
INFLORESCENCE: 300–400 flowers, globular.
FLOWER: on both sides white, horizontal, stamens not or just slightly exserted, anthers yellow.

NOTE: usually with a secondary peduncle. Introduced as being scented.
NOTE: most details from the Internet [2] and some from [36].
NOTE: New Zealand Plant Variety Rights applied for and granted, no. HOM067, by
Lifetech Laboratories Ltd, New Zealand, expires 26 April 2019.
ILLUSTRATION: photograph, Fulcher (2002).

Agapanthus snowdonii Erhardt = *A.* 'Snowdonii'
Erhardt (1997) PPP Index. nom.nud.

Agapanthus 'Snowdonii'

SYNONYM: *Agapanthus snowdonii* Erhardt

ORIGIN: known since 1997, France; no further records.
NOTE: invalid name per the ICNCP-1995, art. 17.9.

Agapanthus 'Snowdrops' (Funnel Group)

ERROR: 'Snowdrop', 'Snow Drop', 'Snow Drops'

ORIGIN: introduced in New Zealand. Known there since 1997, 1998 USA. Still in
cultivation.
LEAF: more or less evergreen, narrow, arching, normal green and slightly glaucous,
base green.
PEDUNCLE: 40–70 cm, green.
INFLORESCENCE: 12 cm across, 20 flowers, flat, bract remains attached.
PEDICEL: pale green.
FLOWERBUD: cream becoming white with midrib cream, rather obtuse, upright.
FLOWER: inside white, outside, white, when out of flower white, horizontal, stamens
not exserted, anthers yellow.
NOTE: some details from plants grown by Joy Creek Nursery.
NOTE: invalid name per the ICNCP-1995, art. 17.13.

Agapanthus 'Snowflake'

ORIGIN: Australia, known since 2001; no further records.

Agapanthus 'Snow Flakes' = **A. 'Stéphanie Charm'**
ERROR: 'Snowflakkes'

Agapanthus 'Snowflower'

ORIGIN: known since 2001, Australia.
PEDUNCLE: 25 cm.
FLOWER: "glistening white."
NOTE: details from the Internet [16].

Agapanthus 'Snow Maiden' (Trumpet Group)

ORIGIN: introduced by A.D. Tomes, UK, known since 1974.
LEAF: deciduous, 20–27.5 cm long and up to 1.2 cm wide, arching, dull green.

PEDUNCLE: 75 cm, normal green.
INFLORESCENCE: 19 cm across, flat.
PEDICEL: normal green with pale brown blush.
FLOWER: white, 4.4 cm long, 3.2 cm across.

Agapanthus 'Snow Princess'

ORIGIN: known since 2001, South Africa.
PEDUNCLE: 30 cm.
FLOWER: white.
NOTE: propagated by tissue culture.

Agapanthus 'Snow Queen' (Funnel Group)

SYNONYM: *Agapanthus orientalis* 'Snow Queen'

ORIGIN: (chance seedling) raised by Fa J. de Jong & Zonen, Aalsmeer, The Nether-
lands. Known since 1963 but probably no longer in cultivation.
FLOWERBUD: cream-yellow.
FLOWER: ivory-white.
NOTE: registered in 1963.
AWARD: GV in 1963.

Agapanthus 'Snowstorm' (Funnel Group)

SYNONYM: *Agapanthus praecox* subsp. *orientalis* 'Snowstorm'
Agapanthus praecox 'Snowstorm'

TRADE NAME: SNOW STORM ex USA

ORIGIN: (chance seedling of *A. praecox* subsp. *orientalis*) raised by R.W. Rother,
Emerald, Victoria, Australia, known since 1995, and still in cultivation.
LEAF: evergreen, green to greenish-yellow.
PEDUNCLE: 75–90 cm.
INFLORESCENCE: 20–40(–60) flowers, more or less flat.
FLOWER: white, horizontal, anthers yellow.
NOTE: most details from the Internet [3], some from [30] and [36].
NOTE: New Zealand Plant Variety Rights applied for and granted, no. HOM050, by
Parva Plants, New Zealand, expires 25 March 2017.
NOTE: European Plant Variety Right applied for and granted, file no. 2000/1529,
grant no. 9529, expires 31 December 2027.
NOTE: U.S. Plant Patent applied for.

Agapanthus 'Snow White'

ORIGIN: known since 1995, South Africa.
LEAF: grey-green.
PEDUNCLE: 30–40 cm.
FLOWER: white.

Agapanthus 'Snowy Baby'

SYNONYM: *Agapanthus* 'Snow Baby'

ORIGIN: known since 1993, UK, and still in cultivation.
LEAF: deciduous.
FLOWER: white.

Agapanthus 'Snowy Eyes'

ORIGIN: known since 2001 when offered by Beeches Nursery, UK.

Agapanthus 'Snowy Owl' (Funnel Group)

ORIGIN: raised by Lewis Palmer, known since 1974, and still in cultivation.
LEAF: probably evergreen, 30–50 cm long and up to 2.5 cm wide, arching, pale glossy green and a bit glaucous, base green.
PEDUNCLE: 70–80 cm, green and slightly glaucous, round.
INFLORESCENCE: 18–20 cm across, 50–70 flowers, globular.
PEDICEL: green with dull purple towards flower.
FLOWERBUD: cream-white with apex very pale purple, upright.
FLOWER: inside white with transparent midrib, outside white, when out of flower more brownish, horizontal, up to 4.5 cm long (tube 1.2 cm long), 4 cm across, stamens slightly exserted, anthers purple-black with orange pollen.
NOTE: details from plants grown at Wisley.
ILLUSTRATION: photograph, Brickell (1996).
AWARD: AM in 1977.

Agapanthus 'Spade' => *A.* 'Spode'

Agapanthus 'Spalding' (Salver Group)

ORIGIN: raised by Kees Duivenvoorde, Beverwijk, The Netherlands, introduced in 1998.
NAME: after the city in England, famous for its many Dutch bulb growers.
PEDUNCLE: 80–90 cm.
PEDICEL: purple.
INFLORESCENCE: 16 cm across.
FLOWER: white, when out of flower white, 2.5 cm long, 4.5 cm across.
NOTE: details supplied by Duivenvoorde.
NOTE: similar to 'Leicester' but differing in the longer peduncle.
NOTE: registered in 1998.

Agapanthus 'Spode'

ERROR: 'Spade'

ORIGIN: introduced by Apple Court, UK, in 1996, still in cultivation.
NAME: a reference to the manufacturer of fine bone china.
LEAF: deciduous.
FLOWER: clear pale violet-blue.

Agapanthus 'Spokes'

SYNONYM: *Agapanthus campanulatus* 'Spokes'

ORIGIN: known since 1997, Gary Dunlop, Ballyrogan Nurseries, UK.
NAME: refers to the flat inflorescence, like the spokes of a wheel.
INFLORESCENCE: few-flowered, flat.
FLOWER: dark violet-blue.
NOTE: details supplied by Gary Dunlop.

Agapanthus 'Starburst' (Funnel Group)

ORIGIN: raised by Gary Dunlop, Ballyrogan Nurseries, UK, named in 1998, and still in cultivaton.
LEAF: evergreen, up to 45 cm long and 3 cm wide, upright, dark green, leafbase green.
PEDUNCLE: 85 cm, green, very sturdy.
INFLORESCENCE: 25 cm across, 70 flowers, globular.
PEDICEL: green with purple towards flower.
FLOWER: inside very pale violet-blue to white at the base, midrib very dark violet-blue, margin violet-blue, outside pale violet-blue with darker midrib and base, when out of flower purple, horizontal to slightly facing downwards, 5 cm long, 4 cm across, stamens not exserted, anthers dark violet with orange pollen.
NOTE: details supplied by Gary Dunlop.
NOTE: nuclear DNA content = 23.9 pg.
ILLUSTRATION: photograph, Snoeijer (1998).

Agapanthus 'Stéphanie' (Salver Group)

ORIGIN: raised and introduced by Ignace van Doorslaer, Belgium, named in 2000, and shown at the first open day of the *Agapanthus* NPC, in Leiden, The Netherlands.
NAME: in honour of a student who worked at the nursery in July 1999.
LEAF: more or less evergreen.
INFLORESCENCE: 13–15 cm across, 80–100 flowers, globular.
PEDICEL: green.
FLOWERBUD: greenish-white, upright.
FLOWER: inside white with midrib slightly darker, outside white, when out of flower white, stamens exserted, anthers black.
NOTE: details from plants grown by van Doorslaer.

Agapanthus 'Stéphanie Charm' (Funnel Group)

SYNONYM: *Agapanthus* 'Snow Flakes'

ORIGIN: (chance seedling of '**Stéphanie**') by Ignace van Doorslaer, Belgium, named in 1999.
LEAF: more or less deciduous, up to 40 cm long and 2.5 cm wide, upright, dark green and glaucous, base green.
PEDUNCLE: 40–60 cm, green and slightly glaucous, round.

INFLORESCENCE: 11–13 cm across, (40–)50–80(–100) flowers, globular, bud opens on 1 side.
PEDICEL: green.
FLOWERBUD: upright, white with yellowish apex.
FLOWER: inside white with midrib slightly transparent, outside white, horizontal, up to 3.5 cm long (tube 1 cm long), 4 cm across, stamens exserted, anthers dark purple.
NOTE: details from plants grown by van Doorslaer.
NOTE: nuclear DNA content = 23.8 pg.
ILLUSTRATION: *color plate.*

Agapanthus 'Stockholm' (Salver Group)

ORIGIN: ('**Blue Triumphator**' × '**Dr Brouwer**') raised by Kees Duivenvoorde, introduced in 2002.
NAME: after the capital of Sweden.
LEAF: deciduous, 20–50 cm long and up to 3.2 cm wide, upright, dark green and glaucous, base green.
PEDUNCLE: 100–130 cm, green and glaucous, round.
INFLORESCENCE: 15–22 cm across, 50–80 flowers, globular.
PEDICEL: green flushed purple.
FLOWERBUD: pale violet-blue with greenish apex, upright.
FLOWER: inside pale violet-blue with margin just slightly darker, midrib violet-blue, outside pale violet-blue with darker midrib, when out of flower purple with dark violet-blue midrib, horizontal, up to 3.7 cm long (tube 1.4 cm long), 4.2–4.4 cm across, stamens slightly exserted, anther violet-blue with yellow pollen.
NOTE: details from plants grown by Duivenvoorde.

Agapanthus 'Stormcloud' ex today's plants = *A.* RUBBISH

NOTE: descriptions published under this name in the USA and New Zealand differ markedly from each other, and plants are widely raised from seed.

Agapanthus '**Stormcloud**' ex Giridlian

ERROR: 'Storm Cloud'
ORIGIN: raised by J.N. Giridlian's Oakhurst Gardens, California, USA, in 1943. The true plant is probably no longer in cultivation.
FLOWER: violet-blue.

Agapanthus 'Storm Cloud' ex Reads Nursery, UK = *A.* '**Purple Cloud**'

NOTE: invalid name per the ICNCP-1995, art. 17.2.

Agapanthus '**Stormcloud Mini**' (Funnel Group)

ORIGIN: (F_2 hybrid of *A. inapertus* [?]) raised by Parva Plants, New Zealand, known since 1998, and still in cultivation.
PEDUNCLE: (65–)100 cm.
INFLORESCENCE: 40–50 flowers, flat.

FLOWER: inside pale violet-blue with slightly darker margin, midrib violet-blue, stamens not exserted, anthers violet.

NOTE: details from the Internet [2].

Agapanthus 'Storms River' (Funnel Group)

SYNONYM: *Agapanthus praecox* subsp. *minimus* 'Storms River'
Agapanthus praecox 'Storms River'

ERROR: 'Storm's River'

ORIGIN: (selection of *A. praecox* subsp. *minimus*) from the Storms River delta, southern Cape. Introduced by Kirstenbosch National Botanical Garden, South Africa. Known since 1987 and still in cultivation. Also offered as seed.

LEAF: evergreen, wide and pale green.

PEDUNCLE: 60–150 cm, green.

INFLORESCENCE: many-flowered but rather open, 80 flowers, more or less flat.

FLOWER: white with pale violet-blue (97D), outside very pale violet-blue-white with darker base, when out of flower purplish, horizontal, stamens exserted, anthers violet.

NOTE: widely propagated by seed and so better to regard this as a group of plants that look similar rather than a proper cultivar.

ILLUSTRATION: drawing, du Plessis and Duncan (1989); photograph, Duncan (1985 as *A. praecox* subsp. *minimus* 'Storms River', 1998 as *A. praecox* subsp. *minimus* 'Storms River').

Agapanthus 'St Pauls Waldenbury'

ORIGIN: raised and introduced by the NCCPG Agapanthus National Collection, UK.

NAME: refers to the royal estate at Windsor, named after the garden of the brother of Queen Elizabeth the Queen Mother, who was former president of the Royal Horticultural Society.

LEAF: deciduous.

PEDUNCLE: 95 cm.

FLOWER: white.

NOTE: some details from the Internet [5].

Agapanthus 'Streamline'

SYNONYM: *Agapanthus africanus* 'Streamline'
Agapanthus praecox subsp. *orientalis* 'Streamline'

ERROR: 'Streamliner'

ORIGIN: introduced by Auckland Botanical Garden, New Zealand, known since 1991.

FLOWER: violet-blue.

NOTE: because of seed propagation, plants differ, and so the description in my 1998 book is excluded here. Several growers already regard it as RUBBISH. In contrast, plants of a clone with small, "grass-like" leaves, propagated by tissue culture, are now offered.

Agapanthus 'Stripes' (Variegated Leaf Group)
> ORIGIN: unknown.
> LEAF: green with yellow margin.
> PEDUNCLE: 50–70 cm.
> FLOWER: "lavender-blue."

Agapanthus 'Summer Clouds'
> ERROR: 'Summer Cloud'
>
> ORIGIN: known since 2001 when offered in the UK.
> PEDUNCLE: 40 cm.
> INFLORESCENCE: 10–20 flowers, flat.
> FLOWER: white.
> NOTE: most details from the Internet [14].

Agapanthus SUMMER GOLD = *A.* 'Hinag'

Agapanthus 'Summer Skies'
> ORIGIN: known since 2001 when offered in the UK.
> PEDUNCLE: 40 cm.
> INFLORESCENCE: 10(–20) flowers, flat.
> FLOWER: pale violet-blue.
> NOTE: most details from the Internet [14].

Agapanthus 'Summer Snow'
> SYNONYM: *Agapanthus* 'White Dwarf' ex Pine Cottage Plants
>
> ORIGIN: in the UK, a few nurseries offer one and the same clone as 'White Dwarf'; Dick Fulcher renamed it so that the clone has a valid name per the ICNCP-1995.
> LEAF: deciduous.
> PEDUNCLE: 50 cm.
> FLOWER: white.
> NOTE: details send by Dick Fulcher.

Agapanthus 'Sunfield' (Trumpet Group)
> SYNONYM: *Agapanthus africanus* 'Sunfield'
>
> ERROR: 'Sunfields'
>
> ORIGIN: introduced by Gebr. J.P. and N.M. Zonneveld, Heemskerk, The Netherlands, in 1987. The plant was given to them as an unnamed seedling. Still in cultivation.
> NAME: English translation of the introducers' surname.
> LEAF: deciduous, 50–60 cm long and 4.5 cm wide, upright, normal green, base green.
> PEDUNCLE: 100 cm, rather stout, green with violet tint, more or less flat.
> INFLORESCENCE: 23 cm across, 50–80 flowers, globular, bud opens on 2 sides.
> PEDICEL: green and dull purple speckled.
> FLOWERBUD: dark violet-blue especially at base, upright.

FLOWER: inside pale violet-blue (93D) but paler towards base, midrib darker (93C), margin with purple tint, outside violet-blue with purple tint, midrib more purple at apex, base darker, when out of flower more dull white-purple, horizontal, 3.5 cm long (tube 1.2 cm long), 3.5 cm across, stamens not exserted, anthers dark violet.
NOTE: details from the plant growing at De Buitenhof, Lisse, The Netherlands.
NOTE: selected for its very late flowering.
NOTE: registered in 1987.
NOTE: nuclear DNA content = 23.8 pg.
ILLUSTRATION: *color plate*; photograph, Snoeijer (2000).

Agapanthus 'Sunfield Tall Pale'

ORIGIN: known since 2001 when offered by Apple Court, UK.
NOTE: name from the Internet [19].

Agapanthus 'Super Star' ex UK (Salver Group)

ORIGIN: raised by Raveningham Gardens, UK, known since 1995, and still in cultivation.
LEAF: deciduous, up to 40 cm long and 2 cm wide, upright, normal green and slightly glaucous, base with purple.
PEDUNCLE: 120–140 cm, green, round.
INFLORESCENCE: 15 cm across, 40 flowers, flat, bud opens on 1 or 2 sides.
PEDICEL: green with pale purple.
FLOWERBUD: pale violet-blue-purple, upright.
FLOWER: inside pale violet-blue (92AB), midrib slightly darker, margin with purple tint, outside pale violet-blue with some purple especially at midrib, when out of flower more purple, horizontal to slightly facing downwards, 3 cm long (tube 1.2 cm long), 3.5 cm across, stamens not exserted, anthers purple.
NOTE: details from plants grown by Coen Jansen.

Agapanthus 'Superstar' ex New Zealand (Funnel Group)

FLOWER: violet-blue with midrib darker.
NOTE: details from the Internet [1].
NOTE: invalid name per the ICNCP-1995, art. 17.2.

Agapanthus 'Supreme' (Funnel Group)

SYNONYM: *Agapanthus praecox* subsp. *minimus* 'Supreme'
ORIGIN: raised by Gary Dunlop, Ballyrogan Nurseries, UK, known since 1998.
LEAF: evergreen.
PEDUNCLE: 100 cm.
INFLORESCENCE: 20 cm across.
FLOWER: pale violet-blue.
NOTE: details supplied by Gary Dunlop.
NOTE: invalid name per the ICNCP-1995, art. 17.11.
NOTE: nuclear DNA content = 25.5 pg.

Agapanthus 'Suzan' (Trumpet Group)

ORIGIN: raised by Kees Duivenvoorde, Beverwijk, The Netherlands, introduced in 1995.
NAME: in honour of the raiser's granddaughter.
LEAF: deciduous, 30–40 cm long and up to 1.8 cm wide, upright, dark green, base green.
PEDUNCLE: 70(–90) cm, green, round and rather sturdy.
INFLORESCENCE: 15–17 cm across, 60–70 flowers, globular, bud opens on 2 sides.
PEDICEL: dull green and heavily speckled purple.
FLOWERBUD: upright, violet-blue with purple tint.
FLOWER: pale violet-blue, margin slightly darker and purple tint, midrib dark violet-blue, outside pale violet-blue with darker midrib and base, when out of flower purple-violet, horizontal, 3.5 cm long (tube 1.2 cm long), 3 cm across, stamens not exserted, anthers dark violet.
NOTE: details from plants grown by Duivenvoorde.
NOTE: registered in 1995.
NOTE: nuclear DNA content = 23.8 pg.
ILLUSTRATION: *color plate.*

Agapanthus 'Swan Lake'

ORIGIN: known since 1996, Australia.

Agapanthus 'Sybil Harton' (Trumpet Group)

ERROR: 'Sybil Hornton'

ORIGIN: raised by Lewis Palmer, known since 1972, and still in cultivation.
LEAF: probably more or less evergreen, 40–50 cm long and 2.3 cm wide, upright, dark green and glaucous, base with purple.
PEDUNCLE: 80–90 cm, green and speckled with dull purple, round.
INFLORESCENCE: 20 cm across, (30–)50–80 flowers, globular.
PEDICEL: green with dull violet-purple towards flower.
FLOWERBUD: dark violet-blue, upright but quickly horizontal.
FLOWER: inside pale violet-blue (91A/92B) and a white base and slightly darker at apex with purple tint, midrib darker (93C), outside violet-blue, midrib slightly darker, base darker violet-blue, when out of flower more purple, horizontal, 3.2 cm long (tube 1.2 cm long), 3 cm across, stamens not or just slightly exserted, anthers violet.
NOTE: details from plants grown at Wisley.
NOTE: flowers tend towards the Salver Group when fully open.
ILLUSTRATION: photograph, Gough (1990–91).
AWARD: FCC in 1977.

Agapanthus 'Sybil Martin'

ORIGIN: raised by D.C. Martin, Havelock North, New Zealand, known since 1991.
NOTE: New Zealand Plant Variety Rights applied for and granted, no. HOM023, by D.C. Martin, Havelock North, New Zealand, expires 14 August 2012.
NOTE: details from the Internet [36].

Agapanthus 'Sylvine' (Funnel Group)

ORIGIN: (chance seedling) raised by Ignace van Doorslaer, Belgium, known since 1997, and still in cultivation.

NAME: in honour of the raiser's daughter.

LEAF: deciduous, up to 40 cm long and 2.5 cm wide, arching, normal green with paler apex, base purple.

PEDUNCLE: 70 cm, green, round.

INFLORESCENCE: 16 cm across, 60–70 flowers, globular, bud opens on 1 side.

PEDICEL: green and heavily flushed violet.

FLOWERBUD: dark violet-blue with dark glossy base, upright.

FLOWER: inside pale violet-blue with margin slightly darker, midrib violet-blue, outside violet-blue with purple tint, midrib dark violet-blue with purple towards apex, when out of flower dark violet-blue with purple base, upright to horizontal, 3.2–3.4 cm long (tube 1.3 cm long), 3.5 cm across, stamens not exserted, anthers dark violet.

NOTE: details from plants grown by van Doorslaer.

NOTE: nuclear DNA content = 23.1 pg.

ILLUSTRATION: *color plate.*

Agapanthus 'Tall Boy' (Tubular Group)

ORIGIN: raised at NCCPG Bicton College, UK, selected by Dick Fulcher in 1993, and still in cultivation.

LEAF: deciduous, 50 cm long and 3 cm wide, upright, normal green, base green.

PEDUNCLE: 150 cm, lower half green and bronze towards inflorescence.

INFLORESCENCE: 10 cm across, 60 flowers, drooping, bud opens on 1 side.

PEDICEL: bronze-purple.

FLOWER: inside pale violet-blue (92B), midrib and margin very dark violet-blue (93A), outside violet-blue (92A), midrib and base very dark violet-blue (93A), drooping vertically, tepal segments slightly spreading, 4 cm long, 2 cm across, stamens not exserted.

NOTE: most details supplied by Gary Dunlop and some by Dick Fulcher.

NOTE: nuclear DNA content = 24.2 pg.

ILLUSTRATION: *color plate.*

Agapanthus 'Tall Double'

SYNONYM: *Agapanthus praecox* 'Tall Double'

ORIGIN: (selection of *A. praecox*) known since 1995, Kirstenbosch National Botanical Garden, South Africa; no further records.

NOTE: invalid name per the ICNCP-1995, art. 17.11.

Agapanthus 'Tall White'

SYNONYM: *Agapanthus praecox* 'Tall White'

ORIGIN: (selection of *A. praecox*) introduced in South Africa, known since 1998 when offered as seed.

PEDUNCLE: 70 cm.

FLOWER: white.
NOTE: invalid name per the ICNCP-1995, art. 17.11.

Agapanthus 'Tandice'

ORIGIN: raised by Tandarra Nurseries Ltd, New Zealand, known since 2001.
NOTE: New Zealand Plant Variety Rights applied for on 26 June 2001, no. HOM135, by Tandarra Nurseries Ltd.
NOTE: details from the Internet [36].

Agapanthus 'Tarka'

ORIGIN: raised by Dick Fulcher, Pine Cottage Plants, UK, named in 1998, and still in cultivation.
NAME: after the lead character in Henry Williamson's 1927 novel, *Tarka the Otter*.
LEAF: evergreen, up to 60 cm long and 3.5 cm wide.
PEDUNCLE: 90–110 cm, dark green speckled with dark violet.
INFLORESCENCE: 17 cm across, more or less flat.
PEDICEL: green with dark violet speckles.
FLOWERBUD: violet-blue (91A).
FLOWER: pale violet (85B).
NOTE: similar to '**Lilac Time**', but slightly late in flower, September into early October in the UK.
NOTE: details supplied by Dick Fulcher.

Agapanthus 'Tenshi' (Funnel Group)

ORIGIN: raised and introduced in Japan, known since 1999.
INFLORESCENCE: flat.
FLOWER: white, stamens exserted, anthers yellow.

Agapanthus 'The Giant'

ORIGIN: known since 1997, New Zealand, when offered as seed.

Agapanthus 'Thinkerbell' => *A.* '**Tinkerbell**'

Agapanthus thomsonii Erhardt = *A.* 'Thomsonii'

Erhardt (1997) PPP Index. nom.nud.

Agapanthus 'Thomsonii'

SYNONYM: *Agapanthus thomsonii* Erhardt
ORIGIN: known since 1997, France; no further records.
NOTE: invalid name per the ICNCP-1995, art. 17.9.

Agapanthus 'Tigerleaf' (Variegated Leaf Group)

SYNONYM: *Agapanthus praecox* subsp. *orientalis* 'Tigerleaf'
ERROR: 'Tiger Leaf'

ORIGIN: (selection of *A. praecox* subsp. *orientalis*) introduced by Hugh Redgrove, New Zealand. Known since 1991 and still in cultivation.
LEAF: evergreen, with wide yellow margin.
FLOWER: violet-blue.

Agapanthus 'Timaru'

SYNONYM: *Agapanthus* 'Imaru'

ERROR: 'Timary'

ORIGIN: introduced in New Zealand, known since 2001 when offered in the UK.
NAME: after the province in New Zealand.
LEAF: evergreen.
PEDUNCLE: 75 cm.
FLOWER: violet-blue.
NOTE: most details supplied by Beeches Nursery, UK.

Agapanthus 'Tinkerbell' (Variegated Leaf Group)

SYNONYM: *Agapanthus* 'Peter Pan Variegated' [?]
Agapanthus praecox subsp. *minimus* 'Tinkerbell'
Agapanthus praecox 'Tinkerbell'
Agapanthus 'Tinkerbelle Variegated'

ERROR: 'Thinkerbell', 'Tinker Bell', 'Tinkerbelle', 'Tinker Belle'

ORIGIN: (sport from **'Peter Pan'**) known since 1991, New Zealand, and still in cultivation.
NAME: after the popular character in children's literature.
LEAF: evergreen, up to 30 cm long and 1 cm wide, flat on the soil, pale green with thin yellow stripes and broad yellow margin, base cream.
PEDUNCLE: 40–50 cm.
FLOWER: violet-blue.
NOTE: widely grown and usually offered as "slow growing," probably to give the impression that the plant is difficult for the nursery to propagate and so priced higher than other cultivars. In my experience, it is a very easy grower; I have grown plants for at least six years now and have divided them many times to give away to friends. As with many other variegated cultivars, it hardly flowers; my own plants have never flowered (the label that sometimes accompanies retail plants, with a photograph showing a plant covered with flowers, is most likely a composite). Since **'Peter Pan'** is widely propagated by seed worldwide, it is more likely that **'Tinkerbell'** is a mutant rather than a sport.
NOTE: some details from the Internet [3].
NOTE: some plants sold as 'Tinkerbell' are actually **'Argenteus Vittatus'**.
NOTE: the plant offered as **'Peter Pan Variegated'** is probably the same.
NOTE: nuclear DNA content = 25 pg.
ILLUSTRATION: *color plate*; photograph, Hirose and Yokoi (1998), Snoeijer (1998, 1999), and van Dijk (2002).

Agapanthus 'Tinkerbelle Variegated' = *A.* 'Tinkerbell'

Agapanthus 'Titan' (Funnel Group)

SYNONYM: *Agapanthus praecox* 'Titan'

ORIGIN: introduced by Gary Dunlop, Ballyrogan Nurseries, UK, known since 1999.
NAME: after Saturn's largest moon, which was discovered by Huygens in 1655.
LEAF: evergreen, up to 50 cm long and 4 cm wide, arching, normal green, base green.
PEDUNCLE: 110 cm, green.
INFLORESCENCE: 25 cm across, over 100 flowers, globular, bud opens on 2 sides.
PEDICEL: green strongly flushed violet.
FLOWER: inside very pale violet-blue and slightly darker margin (92B), midrib dark violet-blue (93B), outside pale violet-blue (92B) with darker midrib and base (93B), when out of flower purple, horizontal, up to 5 cm long, up to 5.5 cm across, stamens exserted, anthers violet with yellow pollen.
NOTE: details supplied by Gary Dunlop.
NOTE: nuclear DNA content = 25.1 pg.

Agapanthus 'Tom Thumb'

ORIGIN: known since 1996, Australia.

Agapanthus 'Torbay'

SYNONYM: *Agapanthus umbellatus* 'Torbay'

ORIGIN: from Bert Hopwood. Introduced by J.C. Archibald and Eric Smith, Buckshaw Gardens, UK, around 1983 and still in cultivation.
LEAF: deciduous.
PEDUNCLE: 80–120 cm.
FLOWER: dark violet-blue.

Agapanthus 'Tresco' (Funnel Group)

SYNONYM: *Agapanthus* 'Tresco Select'

ORIGIN: probably from Abbey Gardens, Isles of Scilly, UK. Known since 2001 when offered in the UK.
LEAF: evergreen, up to 3 cm wide.
INFLORESCENCE: "large open heads."
FLOWER: "very widely flared opening almost flat with narrow, round tipped tepals almost recurving at the tips and very gappy, sky blue with deeper stripe."
NOTE: details supplied by Beeches Nursery and some from the Internet [12].

Agapanthus 'Tresco Select' = *A.* 'Tresco'

NOTE: invalid name per the ICNCP-1995, art. 17.16.

Agapanthus 'Trudy' (Funnel Group)

SYNONYM: *Agapanthus orientalis* 'Trudy'
ERROR: 'Trudi'

ORIGIN: (selection of *A. praecox*) raised in South Africa, introduced in the UK by L. Maurice Mason, King's Lynn, in the mid 1950s. Still in cultivation.
LEAF: evergreen, up to 75 cm long and 5 cm wide.
PEDUNCLE: up to 200 cm.
INFLORESCENCE: 40(–50) cm across, 100–150 flowers, globular.
PEDICEL: up to 12 cm long.
FLOWER: inside very pale violet-blue with darker midrib (92B), outside pale violet-blue with violet-blue midrib and base, horizontal, up to 6 cm long, stamens not exserted.
ILLUSTRATION: photograph, Fulcher (2002).
AWARD: AM in 1957.

Agapanthus Trudy Seedlings = *A.* RUBBISH

Agapanthus tuberosus L. ex P.DC. = *A. africanus* (L.) Hoffmanns. subsp. *africanus*

L. ex P.DC. (1802) Redouté Liliacées.

Agapanthus 'Twilight' (Funnel Group)
ORIGIN: introduced by Gary Dunlop, Ballyrogan Nurseries, UK, known since 2000.
LEAF: deciduous, slightly glaucous.
FLOWER: "silvery-blue."
NOTE: details supplied by Gary Dunlop.
NOTE: nuclear DNA content = 21.9 pg.

Agapanthus 'Ultramarine' (Salver Group)
    SYNONYM: *Agapanthus campanulatus* subsp. *patens* 'Ultramarine'
    Agapanthus campanulatus 'Ultramarine'

ORIGIN: (selection of *A. campanulatus* subsp. *patens*) raised and introduced by Messrs Treseders' Nurseries Ltd, Truro, Cornwall, known since 1972, and still in cultivation.
LEAF: deciduous, up to 30 cm long and 1.5 cm wide, upright, very dark green and glaucous.
PEDUNCLE: 50 cm, dark green.
INFLORESCENCE: 9–12.5 cm across.
FLOWER: violet-blue (93B) but paler at the base and throat white, midrib darker violet-blue (93A), 2.5 cm long, 2.5 cm across.
AWARD: HC in 1977.

Agapanthus 'Umbellatum Albus'
ORIGIN: Japan, known since 2001 when offered by Komoriya Nursery Ltd.
LEAF: evergreen.
PEDUNCLE: 120 cm.
FLOWER: pure white.
NOTE: details from the Internet [25].
NOTE: invalid name per the ICNCP-1995, art. 17.9 and 17.11.

Agapanthus 'Umbellatum Blue'

    ORIGIN: Japan, known since 2001 when offered by Komoriya Nursery Ltd.
    LEAF: evergreen.
    PEDUNCLE: 120 cm.
    FLOWER: pale purple-violet.
    NOTE: details from the Internet [25].
    NOTE: invalid name per the ICNCP-1995, art. 17.9 and 17.11.

Agapanthus umbellatus L'Hér. =

    = pro parte = ***A. africanus*** (L.) Hoffmanns. subsp. ***africanus***
    = pro parte = ***A. praecox*** subsp. ***orientalis*** F.M. Leight.
    L'Hér. (1788) Sertum Anglicum, 17.
    NOTE: in the past, plants offered under this name were expected to flower in violet-blue, and those flowering white were labelled *A. umbellatus albus*.
    NOTE: this name has been used for all manner of plants. In literature, it refers to the plants listed above. In reality, the name refers to a many different kinds of living plants. Thus, if a nursery offers a plant under this name, it is better to buy another plant or—better yet—turn around, run away, and never come back.

      Unfortunately, nurseries buy plant labels from wholesale companies, who only print a few different kinds of labels. A plant that arrives at the nursery or garden centre with a correct cultivar name might be given a general label, something like *A. africanus* "blue," or *A. umbellatus* "white." If a nursery does not make the effort to label the plant correctly but just sticks a general label in the pot, it is better to follow the advice that concluded the last paragraph. Also, do not spend your money on any book that recommends *A. umbellatus* as the best choice for your garden.

Agapanthus umbellatus Redouté = ***A. africanus*** (L.) Hoffmanns. subsp. ***africanus***

    Redouté (1813) Redouté Liliacées, 69.
    NOTE: this plate is reproduced in Mallary, Waltermire, and Levin (1986).

Agapanthus umbellatus Redouté = ***A. praecox*** subsp. ***orientalis*** F.M. Leight

    Redouté (1813) Redouté Liliacées, 403.
    NOTE: this plate is reproduced in Mallary, Waltermire, and Levin (1986).

Agapanthus umbellatus var. *albidus* L.H. Bailey = ***A. praecox*** 'Albiflorus'

    L.H. Bailey (1914) Cyclopedia of Horticulture.

Agapanthus umbellatus var. *albidus* Besant = ***A.*** 'Umbellatus Albus'

    Besant (1903) Flora and Sylva, 1.
    Bonstedt (1931) Pareys Blumengärtnerei.

Agapanthus umbellatus var. *albidus* Numa Schneider = ***A. praecox*** 'Albiflorus'

    Numa Schneider (1911) Revue Horticole.

Agapanthus umbellatus var. *albiflorus* Hend. ex Boom = *A. praecox* 'Albiflorus'
Hend. ex Boom (1950) Flora der gekweekte, kruidachtige gewassen.

Agapanthus umbellatus var. *albo-lilacinus* Krelage = *A.* 'Albo-lilacinus'
Krelage (1888) catalogue.

Agapanthus umbellatus var. *albo-monstrosus* Krelage = *A.* 'Albo-monstrosus'
Krelage (1888) catalogue.

Agapanthus umbellatus var. *albus* hort. =
= pro parte = *A. praecox* 'Albiflorus'
= pro parte = *A.* 'Umbellatus Albus'

Agapanthus umbellatus var. *angustifolius* Redouté ex Roem. & Schult. =
A. praecox Willd. ex F.M. Leight.
Roem. & Schult. (1830) Systema vegetabilium.

Agapanthus umbellatus var. *argenteus vittatus* van Tubergen = *A.* 'Argenteus Vittatus'
van Tubergen (1926) Catalogue

Agapanthus umbellatus var. *atricoeruleus* Bonstedt = *A.* 'Atrocaeruleus'
Bonstedt (1931) Pareys Blumengärtnerei.

Agapanthus umbellatus var. *atrocaeruleus* Leichtlin = *A.* 'Atrocaeruleus'
Leichtlin (1880) catalogue.

Agapanthus umbellatus var. *aureis vittatus* van Tubergen = *A.* 'Aureovittatus'
van Tubergen (1936) catalogue.

Agapanthus umbellatus var. *aureus* G. Nicholson = *A.* 'Aureovittatus'
G. Nicholson (1892) Dictionnaire pratique d'Horticulture et de Jardinage.

Agapanthus umbellatus var. *candidus* Baines = *A.* 'Candidus'
Baines (1885) Greenhouse & Stove Plants.

Agapanthus umbellatus var. *caulescens* A. Worsley = *A. caulescens* Sprenger
A. Worsley (1913) J. Roy. Hort. Soc.

Agapanthus umbellatus var. *excelsa* Lemoine = *A.* 'Excelsus'
Lemoine (1878) catalogue.

Agapanthus umbellatus var. *excelsus* Leichtlin = *A.* 'Excelsus'
Leichtlin (1880) catalogue.
van Tubergen (1926) catalogue.

Agapanthus umbellatus var. *flor. albidis* Roem. & Schult. (1830) Systema
vegetabilium. nom.nud.

Agapanthus umbellatus var. *fl. albis* Mater = **A. *praecox*** 'Albiflorus'
J. Mater & Fils (1892) catalogue.

Agapanthus umbellatus var. *fl. monst.* Mater = **A. 'Montrosus'**
J. Mater & Fils (1892) catalogue.

Agapanthus umbellatus var. *flore pleno* Lemoine = **A. 'Flore Pleno'**
Lemoine (1880) catalogue.
E.-A. Carrière (1880) Revue Horticole.
van Tubergen (1936) catalogue.

Agapanthus umbellatus var. *foliis albo-vittatis* Lemoine = **A. 'Argenteus Vittatus'**
Lemoine (1875) catalogue.

Agapanthus umbellatus var. *foliis argenteis vittatis* Boom = **A. 'Argenteus Vittatus'**
Boom (1975) Flora der gekweekte, kruidachtige gewassen. nom.nud.

Agapanthus umbellatus var. *foliis aureis variegatis* Krelage = **A. 'Aureovittatus'**
Krelage (1891) Weekblad voor Bloembollencultuur.

Agapanthus umbellatus var. *foliis aureo-vittatus* Lemoine = **A. 'Aureovittatus'**
Lemoine (1875) catalogue.

Agapanthus umbellatus var. *fol. variegatis* Roem. & Schult. (1830) Systema
vegetabilium. nom.nud.

Agapanthus umbellatus var. *foliis variegatis* Boom = **A. 'Argenteus Vittatus'**
Boom (1950) Flora der gekweekte, kruidachtige gewassen.

Agapanthus umbellatus var. *formosus* Mater = **A. 'Formosus'**
J. Mater & Fils (1892) catalogue.

Agapanthus umbellatus var. *giganteus* Lemoine = **A. 'Giganteus'**
Lemoine (1909) catalogue.

Agapanthus umbellatus var. *globosus* Lemoine = **A. 'Globusus'**
Lemoine (1909) catalogue.

Agapanthus umbellatus var. *insignis* Thomas = **A. 'Insignis'**
Thomas (1990) Perennial Garden Plants. nom.nud.

Agapanthus umbellatus var. *intermedius* van Tubergen = *A.* 'Intermedius'
van Tubergen (1920) catalogue.

Agapanthus umbellatus var. *latifolius* Red.Lil ex Roem. & Schult. = *A. africanus*
(L.) Hoffmanns. subsp. *africanus*
Roem. & Schult. (1830) Systema vegetabilium.

Agapanthus umbellatus var. *latifolius* Voss ex Bonstedt = *A.* 'Latifolius'
Voss ex Bonstedt (1931) Parey Blumengärtnerei.

Agapanthus umbellatus var. *leichtlinii* Baker = *A.* 'Leichtlinii'
Baker (1878) Gardeners Chronicle.

Agapanthus umbellatus var. *lilacinus* Krelage = *A.* 'Lilacinus'
Krelage (1888) catalogue.

Agapanthus umbellatus var. *major* Leichtlin = *A.* 'Major'
Leichtlin (1873) catalogue.

Agapanthus umbellatus var. *maximum* Edwards ex Thomas = *A. caulescens*
Sprenger
Thomas (1990) Perennial Garden Plants. nom.nud.

Agapanthus umbellatus var. *maximum* 'Aureovittatus' = *A.* 'Aureovittatus'

Agapanthus umbellatus var. *maximus* Lindl. = *A.* 'Maximus'
Lindl. (1843) Edward's Bot. Reg. Vol. 29. 7.

Agapanthus umbellatus var. *maximus albus* Lemoine = *A.* 'Maximus Albus'
Lemoine (1909) catalogue.
van Tubergen (1926) catalogue.

Agapanthus umbellatus var. *maximus* 'Krelagei' = *A.* 'Krelagei'

Agapanthus umbellatus var. *minimus* Lindl. = *A. praecox* subsp. *minimus*
(Lindl.) F.M. Leight.
Lindl. (1823) Bot. Reg. 699.

Agapanthus umbellatus var. *minor* DC. ex Redouté = *A. africanus* (L.)
Hoffmanns. subsp. *africanus*
DC. ex Redouté (1813) Redouté Liliacées.

Agapanthus umbellatus var. *monstrosus* A. Worsley = *A.* 'Monstrosus'
A. Worsley (1913) J. Roy. Hort. Soc.

Agapanthus umbellatus var. *mooreanus* G. Nicholson = *A.* 'Mooreanus'
  G. Nicholson (1892) Dictionnaire pratique d'Horticulture et de Jardinage.
  Synge (1986) Dictionary of Gardening. nom.nud.

Agapanthus umbellatus var. *multiflorus* Baker = *A.* 'Multiflorus'
  Baker (1897) Flora Capensis VI.
  Voss ex Bonstedt (1931) Pareys Blumengärtnerei.

Agapanthus umbellatus var. *pallidus* Krelage = *A.* 'Pallidus'
  Krelage (1888) catalogue.

Agapanthus umbellatus var. *plenus* Bonstedt = *A.* 'Flore Pleno'
  Bonstedt (1931) Pareys Blumengärtnerei.

Agapanthus umbellatus var. *praecox* Baker = *A. praecox* subsp. *minimus* (Lindl.)
  F.M. Leight.
  Baker (1897) Flora Capensis VI.

Agapanthus umbellatus var. *repens* A. Worsley = *A.* 'Repens'
  A. Worsley (1913) J. Roy. Hort. Soc.

Agapanthus umbellatus var. *saundersonianus* Bonstedt = *A.* 'Saundersonianus'
  Bonstedt (1931) Pareys Blumengärtnerei.
  ERROR: var. *saundersianus*

Agapanthus umbellatus var. *variegata* Schauenberg = *A.* 'Argenteus Vittatus'
  Schauenberg (1964) Les Plantes Bulbeuses.

Agapanthus umbellatus var. *variegatus* G. Nicholson = *A.* 'Argenteus Vittatus'
  G. Nicholson (1892) Dictionnaire pratique d'Horticulture et de Jardinage.

Agapanthus umbellatus var. *variegatus falcatus* A. Worsley = *A.* 'Variegatus Falcatus'
  A. Worsley (1913) J. Roy. Hort. Soc.

Agapanthus umbellatus var. *weillighi* van Tubergen = *A.* 'Weillighii'
  van Tubergen (1916) catalogue.

Agapanthus umbellatus 'Albus' = *A.* 'Umbellatus Albus'

Agapanthus umbellatus 'A. Worsley' = *A.* 'A. Worsley'

Agapanthus umbellatus 'Blue Giant' = *A.* 'Blue Giant'

Agapanthus umbellatus 'Blue Globe' = *A.* 'Blue Globe'

Agapanthus umbellatus 'Blue Queen' = *A.* 'Blue Queen'

Agapanthus umbellatus 'Blue Ribbon' = *A.* 'Blue Ribbon'

Agapanthus umbellatus 'Blue Triumphator' = *A.* 'Blue Triumphator'

Agapanthus umbellatus 'Bressingham Blue' = *A.* 'Bressingham Blue'

Agapanthus umbellatus 'Dnjepr' = *A.* 'Dnjepr'

Agapanthus umbellatus 'Donau' = *A.* 'Donau'

Agapanthus umbellatus 'Headbourne' = *A.* RUBBISH

Agapanthus umbellatus 'Headbourne Hybrids' = *A.* RUBBISH

Agapanthus umbellatus 'Isis' = *A.* 'Isis'

Agapanthus umbellatus 'Isleworth Blue' = *A.* 'Isleworth Blue'

Agapanthus umbellatus 'Johanna Gärtner' = *A.* 'Johanna Gärtner'

Agapanthus umbellatus 'Krelagei' = *A.* 'Krelagei'

Agapanthus umbellatus 'Majestic' = *A.* 'Majestic'

Agapanthus umbellatus 'Maximus' = *A.* 'Maximus'

Agapanthus umbellatus 'Minor' = *A. africanus* (L.) Hoffmanns. subsp. *africanus*

Agapanthus umbellatus 'Mooreanus' = *A.* 'Mooreanus'

Agapanthus umbellatus 'Polar Ice' = *A.* 'Polar Ice'

Agapanthus umbellatus 'Profusion' = *A.* 'Profusion'

Agapanthus umbellatus 'Torbay' = *A.* 'Torbay'

Agapanthus umbellatus 'Underway' = *A.* RUBBISH

Agapanthus umbellatus 'A. Worsley' = *A.* 'A. Worsley'

Agapanthus umbellatus 'Wolga' = *A.* 'Wolga'

Agapanthus 'Umbellatus Albidus' = *A.* 'Umbellatus Albus'
    NOTE: invalid name per the ICNCP-1995, art. 17.9.

Agapanthus 'Umbellatus Albus' (Trumpet Group)
    SYNONYM: *Agapanthus africanus* subsp. *umbellatus* var. *albidus* H.R. Wehrh.
    Agapanthus africanus 'Albidus' pro parte

Agapanthus africanus 'Albus' pro parte
Agapanthus 'Maximus Albus' pro parte
Agapanthus praecox 'Umbellatus Albus'
Agapanthus umbellatus var. *albidus* Besant
Agapanthus umbellatus var. *albus* hort. pro parte
Agapanthus umbellatus 'Albus'
Agapanthus 'Umbellatus Albidus'

ORIGIN: most likely Dutch. Known since 1888 and still widely grown, but usually under different names.

LEAF: deciduous, rather dark green, 20–50 cm long and 1.5–2.5 cm wide, upright but later arching, green and slightly glaucous, base purple.

PEDUNCLE: 80–100 cm, green but towards inflorescence flushed with purple, round, some forms have straight peduncles but most forms tend to bend especially when not grown in an open space.

INFLORESCENCE: 15 cm across, (20)30–50(–80) flowers, usually with pagoda fasciation, more or less globular, bud opens on 2 sides.

PEDICEL: purple.

FLOWERBUD: greenish-white with pale purple apex, upright but quickly horizontal.

FLOWER: white (155AB) with transparent midrib, outside white with pale purple (65AD), midrib near apex, when out of flower more brownish with pale purple apex, horizontal, 2.5–3.3 cm long (tube 0.9–1.3 cm long), 3 cm across, stamens not exserted, anthers brown.

NOTE: usually with a second flowering.

NOTE: details taken from plants growing at different nurseries.

NOTE: plants grown under *A. africanus* 'Albus' usually belong to this cultivar.

NOTE: seed-propagated and so better to regard this as a group of plants that look similar rather than a proper cultivar. Most seed offered under this name belongs to *A. praecox* 'Albiflorus'.

NOTE: nuclear DNA content = 23.2 pg.

ILLUSTRATION: *color plates*; drawing, Gillissen (1982); photograph, Kostelijk (1986), Vermeulen (1996 as *A. africanus* 'Albidus'), Scott (1997 as *A. africanus* 'Albus'), and Snoeijer (1998, 2000 also as *A. praecox* 'Umbellatus Albus').

AWARD: the plant that received an FCC in 1879 as *A. umbellatus albus* probably refers to *A. praecox* 'Albiflorus'.

Agapanthus umbelliferus Poir. = **A. africanus** (L.) Hoffmanns. subsp. *africanus*
Poir. (1810) Encl. Meth. Bot. Suppl. 1.

Agapanthus 'Underway' = *A.* RUBBISH
ORIGIN: rejected and/or surplus chance seedlings from '**Norman Hadden**' are sold as 'Underway'. Eventually introduced by Mrs June Towe, UK, known since 1991.
NAME: after the nursery of the late Norman Hadden, Porlock, UK.

Agapanthus 'Vague Bleue'

ORIGIN: raised by J.-Y. Poiroux, Ets Horticole, France, in 2000.
FLOWER: violet-blue with darker midrib.
NOTE: invalid name per the ICNCP-1995, art. 17.11.

Agapanthus **'Valerie Finnis'**

ORIGIN: known since 2001 when grown by Ets Horticole, France.

Agapanthus **'Vans White'** (Funnel Group)

ORIGIN: known since 2001 when offered by Magnolia Gardens Nursery, USA.
LEAF: evergreen, arching, dark green.
PEDUNCLE: 80 cm, green.
INFLORESCENCE: "large," 100 flowers, globular.
PEDICEL: green.
FLOWER: white on both sides, when out of flower white, horizontal, stamens exserted, anthers yellow.
NOTE: details from the Internet [23].

Agapanthus **'Variegated Baby Blue'** (Variegated Leaf Group)

ORIGIN: known since 2001 from Australia.
LEAF: "striped in cream."
NOTE: details from the Internet [26].

Agapanthus **'Variegated Wilken'** (Variegated Leaf Group)

ORIGIN: known since 2001.
LEAF: variegated.
NOTE: name from the Internet [19].

Agapanthus variegatus Steud. = *A. africanus* (L.) Hoffmanns. subsp. *africanus*
Steud. (1840) Nomencl. ed. 2.

Agapanthus variegatus Numa Schneider (1911) Revue Horticole. nom.nud.

'Variegatus' => *Agapanthus africanus* 'Variegatus'

'Variegatus' => *Agapanthus campanulatus* 'Variegatus' = *A.* **'Beth Chatto'**

'Variegatus' => *Agapanthus orientalis* 'Variegatus'

'Variegatus' => *Agapanthus praecox* subsp. *minimus* 'Variegatus'

'Variegatus' =>*Agapanthus praecox* subsp. *orientalis* 'Variegatus'

'Variegatus' => *Agapanthus praecox* subsp. *praecox* 'Variegatus'

'Variegatus' => *Agapanthus praecox* 'Variegatus'

Agapanthus 'Variegatus Falcatus' (Variegated Leaf Group)

SYNONYM: *Agapanthus orientalis* var. *variegatus falcatus* Synge
Agapanthus umbellatus var. *variegatus falcatus* A. Worsley

ORIGIN: cultivated. Known since 1913, UK, and still referred to in 1986, but probably no longer in cultivation.
LEAF: evergreen, shaped like a sickle, variegated.

Agapanthus Ventnor Hybrids => see note under *A*. RUBBISH

ORIGIN: offered as seed by Ventnor Botanic Garden, Isle of Wight, UK, in 1999.

Agapanthus Verwood Dorset => see note under *A*. RUBBISH

ORIGIN: mixture selected by John Gallagher, Dorset, UK, introduced as a seedling-grown strain by Heronswood Nursery, Washington, USA, known since 1998, and still offered.
FLOWER: "rich blue."
NOTE: some details from the Internet [4].

Agapanthus 'Victoria' (Funnel Group)

ORIGIN: raised by Lewis Palmer, known since 1972, and still in cultivation.
NAME: after an aristocratic lady.
LEAF: more or less evergreen, 30–40 cm long and 2.3 cm wide, arching, normal green and glaucous, base green.
PEDUNCLE: 40–60 cm, green, flat.
INFLORESCENCE: 20 cm across, globular.
PEDICEL: yellowish-green.
FLOWERBUD: cream coloured especially at base and apex, upright but quickly nodding.
FLOWER: inside white, midrib transparent, outside white, when out of flower white with brownish-purple midrib, horizontal, 3.5 cm long (tube 1 cm long), 3.5–4.4 cm across, stamens slightly exserted, anthers black.
NOTE: most details from plants at Wisley.
AWARD: HC in 1977.

Agapanthus 'Violetta' (Trumpet Group)

ORIGIN: raised by Gary Dunlop, Ballyrogan Nurseries, UK, and introduced in 1996.
LEAF: deciduous, up to 25 cm long and 2.5 cm wide, upright but apex bended, normal green and slightly glaucous, base green.
PEDUNCLE: 70 cm, green.
INFLORESCENCE: 12.5 cm across, 35 flowers, flat, bud opens on 2 sides.
PEDICEL: purple-green.
FLOWERBUD: dark violet-blue, upright.
FLOWER: on both sides pale violet (85B) with darker midrib (88A), outside with a dark base, 3 cm long, 3 cm across, stamens not exserted and remarkably short, anthers dark violet.

NOTE: details supplied by Gary Dunlop.
NOTE: nuclear DNA content = 22.7 pg.
ILLUSTRATION: *color plate*.

Agapanthus 'Violet Tips' (Funnel Group)

ORIGIN: introduced by Mrs D. Palmer, known since 1974.
LEAF: more or less evergreen, up to 30 cm long and 4 cm wide, arching, normal to dark glossy, green.
PEDUNCLE: 75 cm, normal green.
INFLORESCENCE: 20 cm across, globular.
PEDICEL: dark green heavily flushed purple.
FLOWER: inside violet-blue (97A/96C), margin darker (94B), midrib dark violet (86A), upright to horizontal, 3.2 cm long, 4.4 cm across.

Agapanthus 'Virginia' (Funnel Group)

SYNONYM: *Agapanthus* 'Virgineus'

ORIGIN: raised by Kees Duivenvoorde, Beverwijk, The Netherlands, introduced in 2000.
NAME: after the state of Virginia, USA.
LEAF: evergreen, 30–40 cm long and 3–4 cm wide, upright with upper half arching, dark green, base green.
PEDUNCLE: 40–60(–80) cm, green, flat.
INFLORESCENCE: 16–18 cm across, 40–60(–80) flowers, more or less flat, bud opens on 1 side.
PEDICEL: pale green to very pale green towards flowers.
FLOWERBUD: white also in the very early stage, upright but later horizontal to slightly nodding.
FLOWER: inside white, midrib hardly visible and white (not transparent), outside white including the base, when out of flower usually falling off, horizontal to slightly nodding, 4.5–4.7 cm long (tube 1.1 cm long), 5 cm across, stamens exserted, anthers yellow, usually no fruit.
NOTE: details from plants grown by Duivenvoorde.
NOTE: nuclear DNA content = 25.2 pg.
ILLUSTRATION: *color plate*; photograph, van Dijk (2002).

Agapanthus 'Virgineus' = A. 'Virginia'

'Vittatus' => Agapanthus praecox 'Vittatus'

Agapanthus 'Volendam' (Salver Group)

ORIGIN: raised by Kees Duivenvoorde, introduced in 2001.
NAME: after the village in The Netherlands.
LEAF: deciduous, upright, normal green.
PEDUNCLE: 80 cm.
INFLORESCENCE: 15 cm, 30–40 flowers, flat.

PEDICEL: green.

FLOWERBUD: white with cream apex, upright but quickly horizontal.

FLOWER: inside white, outside white with slightly darker base, when out of flower white becoming pale brown, horizontal, stamens exserted, anthers yellow becoming brown.

NOTE: details from plants grown by Duivenvoorde.

Agapanthus 'Waga' (Trumpet Group)

ORIGIN: raised by Th. P.W. de Groot, Hillegom, The Netherlands, introduced by Maas & van Stein, also of Hillegom, introduced in 2001.

NAME: Dutch spelling of the Vaga River.

LEAF: deciduous, up to 45 cm long and 3.3 cm wide, upright, dark green, base green.

PEDUNCLE: 80 cm, normal to pale green, flat.

INFLORESCENCE: (15–)22 cm across, 40 flowers, flat, bud opens on 1 side.

PEDICEL: green, slightly flushed purple towards flower.

FLOWERBUD: very pale violet-blue with midrib and base slightly darker, upright but quickly nodding.

FLOWER: 8–12 tepals, distinctly spathulate, inside very pale violet-blue (92D), midrib violet-blue (92A), outside very pale violet-blue (92D), midrib slightly darker (92B) with a hint of purple, base violet-blue (92B) with a bit of purple and green, when out of flower purple with small violet-blue base, horizontal, 3.8–4 cm long (tube 1.6 cm long), 3.6–4 cm across, stamens 6–12, not exserted, anthers greenish-brown.

NOTE: registered in 2001.

NOTE: details from plants grown by Maas & van Stein.

ILLUSTRATION: *color plate*; photograph, van Dijk (2002).

Agapanthus walshii L. Bol. = *A. africanus* subsp. *walshii* (L. Bol.) Zonn. & G.D. Duncan

L. Bol. (1920) Ann. Bol. Herb. Vol. III, 14.

Agapanthus 'Washfield' (Trumpet Group)

FLOWER: white with midrib pale purple, anthers not exserted, black.

ILLUSTRATION: photograph, Jansen (2002).

Agapanthus 'Wavy Navy'

ORIGIN: known since 1990 when offered as seed. Still in cultivation, offered both as seed and as plant.

Agapanthus 'Weaver' (Funnel Group)

SYNONYM: *Agapanthus praecox* subsp. *orientalis* 'Weaver'

ORIGIN: (selection of *A. praecox* subsp. *orientalis*) introduced from South Africa. Known since 1991 and still in cultivation. Also offered as seed.

LEAF: evergreen, up to 50 cm long and 5 cm wide, upright but lower ones arching, normal green, leafbase green.

PEDUNCLE: 100–120 cm, green, round.

INFLORESCENCE: 30 cm across, 50 flowers, globular, bud opens on 1 side.

PEDICEL: green and slightly purple speckled to purplish towards flowers.

FLOWERBUD: pale violet-blue-green with bit darker base, upright.

FLOWER: inside pale violet-blue (97B) with margin slightly darker and purple (97A), midrib slightly darker violet-blue, outside pale violet-blue (97A) with margin a bit darker and with purple, base violet-blue (92A), 5 cm long (tube 1.8 cm long), 4–5 cm across, stamens not exserted, anthers violet with orange pollen, slightly fragrant.

NOTE: details from plant obtained from Bulbes d'Opale, France.

NOTE: nuclear DNA content = 24.5 pg.

ILLUSTRATION: *color plate.*

Agapanthus 'Weaver Lineata'

SYNONYM: *Agapanthus praecox* subsp. *orientalis* 'Weaver Lineata'

ORIGIN: known since 2001 when grown by Ets Horticole, France.

FLOWER: pale violet-blue with darker midrib.

NOTE: invalid name per the ICNCP-1995, art. 17.9.

Agapanthus 'Wedding Bells'

ORIGIN: raised by J.N. Giridlian's Oakhurst Gardens, California, USA, in 1949. Still offered by them in 1962 but probably no longer in cultivation. The description in their 1962 catalogue reads, "An unusually beautiful and outstanding variety. It is a superior plant in every way and there is nothing like it on the market. The 4½-ft. spikes arise from robust plants. The flowers are bell shaped and pendent and form large heads of pure white umbrella shaped umbels seven inches across."

Agapanthus 'Wedgwood' = A. 'Wedgwood Blue'

Agapanthus 'Wedgwood Blue' (Salver Group)

SYNONYM: *Agapanthus campanulatus* subsp. *campanulatus* 'Wedgwood Blue'
Agapanthus campanulatus 'Wedgwood Blue'
Agapanthus 'Wedgwood'

ERROR: 'Wedgewood Blue'

ORIGIN: (selection of *A. campanulatus*) raised by Gary Dunlop, Ballyrogan Nurseries, UK, introduced in 1995, and still in cultivation.

LEAF: deciduous, up to 35 cm long and 1.5 cm wide, arching, normal green and slightly glaucous, base green.

PEDUNCLE: 65 cm, green.

INFLORESCENCE: 10 cm across, up to 30 flowers, bud opens on 2 sides.

PEDICEL: green.

FLOWER: pale violet-blue (97B) on both sides, horizontal, up to 2.5 cm long, 2 cm across.

NOTE: details supplied by Gary Dunlop.

Agapanthus weillighii Leichtlin = *A.* 'Weillighii'

Leichtlin (1901) catalogue.

Agapanthus weillighii albus van Tubergen = *A.* 'Weillighii Albus'

van Tubergen (1956) catalogue.

Agapanthus 'Weillighii' (Tubular Group)

SYNONYM: *Agapanthus africanus* subsp. *umbellatus* var. *weillighii* H.R. Wehrh.
Agapanthus inapertus Beauv. ex Sealy pro parte
Agapanthus umbellatus var. *weillighi* van Tubergen
Agapanthus weillighii Leichtlin

ORIGIN: (probably a selection of *A. inapertus* subsp. *pendulus*) known in cultivation since 1898, when Max Leichtlin in Baden-Baden, Germany, sent plants to van Tubergen, The Netherlands. Van Tubergen offered the plant in 1913 and as recently as 1950; it was no longer listed in 1954, but van Tubergen did supply plants to the 1974–75 Wisley trial, and from Wisley, plants were sent back to Holland for the Aalsmeer trial in 1978. As to whether or not this plant remains in cultivation, a large plant, similar in appearance and still growing at Battleston Hill, might be it (see color plate and also "Trials" in chapter 1).

NAME: in honour of German explorer Weilligh, who collected the rootstock on a tour of inspection in Swaziland. A friend of Weilligh sent the rootstock to Max Leichtlin.

LEAF: deciduous, 5–8 per shoot, from a short leek-like stem, 24–55 cm long and 1.5–2.5 cm wide, upright to slightly arching, green and glaucous.

PEDUNCLE: 50–120(–150) cm, pale green with purple and slightly glaucous.

INFLORESCENCE: up to 12 cm across.

PEDICEL: 1–2 cm long, green with grey-purple flush.

FLOWER: inside pale violet-blue to almost white, margin and midrib darker violet-blue (94B), outside violet-blue with darker base, drooping vertically, (3–)4.4–4.8 cm long (tube 1.6 cm long), 2–2.5 cm across, stamens slightly longer than the flower, anthers yellow.

NOTE: the name *A. weillighii* is always referred to as being published by van Tubergen, but in fact van Tubergen published the name as *A. umbellatus* var. *weillighi* at least until the year 1926.

NOTE: a good description and drawing by Sealy (1940–42) can be found in *Curtis's Botanical Magazine*, t.9621, published as *A. inapertus*. The description clearly states, "The material from which this plate was prepared was kindly sent to us by Mr. Besant from the Glasnevin Botanic Garden, where the plants were grown under the name *A.* Weillighii. . . . The plants figured here certainly agree with Beauverd's description in all points except one—the exception being that in our plant the style is only just exserted from the corolla, whereas Beauverd describes and figures it as markedly exserted."

NOTE: Leighton's 1965 monograph refers the name to *A. inapertus* subsp. *pendulus* as a synonym. But, as I have not yet come across a reference that 'Weillighii' was seed-raised, I am convinced that pieces of the rootstock of this particular clone were sent around Europe. Therefore I accept this clone as a cultivar and not as a synonym of *A. inapertus* subsp. *pendulus*. If 'Weillighii' is a synonym of *A. inapertus* subsp. *pendulus*, the value of naming cultivars within *Agapanthus* is nil.

ILLUSTRATION: *color plates*; drawing, Sealy (1940–42 as *A. inapertus* pro parte), reproduced in Snoeijer (1998).

AWARD: AM in 1913.

Agapanthus 'Weillighii Albus' (Tubular Group)

SYNONYM: *Agapanthus weillighii albus* van Tubergen

ORIGIN: known since 1956 when offered by van Tubergen, The Netherlands, still offered by them in 1959. Probably no longer in cultivation.

FLOWER: "pure white."

Agapanthus 'Wendy' (Salver Group)

SYNONYM: *Agapanthus campanulatus* subsp. *campanulatus* 'Wendy'
Agapanthus campanulatus 'Wendy'

ORIGIN: (selection of *A. campanulatus*) raised by Gary Dunlop, Ballyrogan Nurseries, UK, introduced in 1995, and still in cultivation.

NAME: chosen as a counterpart to 'Peter Pan'.

LEAF: deciduous, up to 20 cm long and 1.2 cm wide, more or less upright, pale green and slightly glaucous, base with purple.

PEDUNCLE: 40–45 cm, green but with purple towards inflorescence.

INFLORESCENCE: 10 cm across, 45 flowers, bud opens on 2 sides.

PEDICEL: purple.

FLOWER: white, outside flecked purple, horizontal, 2 cm long, 2.5 cm across.

NOTE: details supplied by Gary Dunlop.

NOTE: nuclear DNA content = 22.1 pg.

Agapanthus 'White' (Tubular Group)

SYNONYM: *Agapanthus inapertus* subsp. *inapertus* 'White'
Agapanthus inapertus subsp. *inapertus* white
Agapanthus inapertus 'White'

ORIGIN: from eastern and northern Transvaal. Introduced by Kirstenbosch National Botanical Garden, South Africa. Known since 1980 and still in cultivation.

LEAF: deciduous, upright, glaucous, green.

PEDUNCLE: 120–140 cm, green.

INFLORESCENCE: 30–40 flowers, drooping.

PEDICEL: green.

FLOWERBUD: greenish-white, upright but drooping before opening.

FLOWER: white (155B), drooping but just not vertically, apex not or just slightly spreading, stamens not exserted, anthers yellow.

NOTE: invalid name per the ICNCP-1995, art. 17.11.

ILLUSTRATION: *color plate*; photograph, Duncan (1985 as *A. inapertus* subsp. *inapertus* 'White', 1998 as *A. inapertus* subsp. *inapertus* 'White').

Agapanthus white = *A.* RUBBISH

Agapanthus 'White Beauty' (Trumpet Group)

SYNONYM: *Agapanthus* 'White Superior' ex Reintjes

ORIGIN: selection from a parcel of plants bought as white-flowering by cut flower grower Reintjes, Veulen, The Netherlands, in about 1970. Reintjes himself changed the cultivar's name in 2001, so that it would be valid according to the ICNCP-1995. Still in cultivation.

LEAF: deciduous, up to 40 cm long and 2.5 cm wide, upright, normal glossy green, base green.

PEDUNCLE: 70–90 cm long, green and slightly speckled pale purple, more or less flat.

INFLORESCENCE: 18 cm across, 60–80 flowers, flat.

PEDICEL: dull purple-green.

FLOWERBUD: greenish-white with a bit of violet-purple at apex, upright.

FLOWER: inside white, thin midrib more or less transparent, outside white with the three outer lobes with purple or violet-purple and the inner lobes sometimes with violet-purple midrib, when out of flower almost pale purple coloured, up to 4.3 cm long (tube 1.2 cm long), 3.5–3.8 cm across, stamens not exserted, anthers purple becoming black.

NOTE: details from plants grown by Reintjes.

NOTE: nuclear DNA content = 24 pg.

ILLUSTRATION: *color plate*.

Agapanthus 'White Christmas', *A.* 'White Xmas' (Funnel Group)

ORIGIN: (probably a selection of *A. praecox* subsp. *orientalis*) introduced from South Africa. Known since 1993 and still in cultivation.

LEAF: evergreen.

PEDUNCLE: 100–150 cm.

INFLORESCENCE: 20 cm across.

FLOWER: pure white.

Agapanthus 'White Classic' (Funnel Group)

ORIGIN: raised by Haden Tebb, Mutare, Zimbabwe, known since 2001 when registered by Oudendijk Import B.V., De Kwakel, The Netherlands.

PEDUNCLE: glossy green with paler stripes, flat.

INFLORESCENCE: up to 12 cm across, 40 flowers, flat.

FLOWER: inside white, outside white with pale greenish base, horizontal, 3–4 cm long, 3–4 cm across, anthers yellow.

NOTE: details from the Internet [18].

Agapanthus 'White Dwarf' = *A*. RUBBISH

> NOTE: invalid name per the ICNCP-1995, art. 17.11.
> NOTE: some plants sold as 'White Dwarf' are actually '**Lady Moore**'.

Agapanthus 'White Dwarf' ex Pine Cottage Plants = *A*. '**Summer Snow**'

> NOTE: invalid name per the ICNCP-1995, art. 17.11.

Agapanthus White Dwarf Hybrids = *A*. RUBBISH.

> NOTE: widely propagated by seed and, accordingly, extremely variable. It is not even
> possible to regard this as a group of plants that look similar; unfortunately, nurseries
> tend to offer selections as 'Dwarf White' or 'White Dwarf' simply because they
> bought seed labelled as such.

Agapanthus 'White Form' = *A*. RUBBISH

> ORIGIN: according to the catalogue, different kinds of white-flowering *Agapanthus*
> are offered by Thompson & Morgan as seed. Known since 1997, UK.
> NOTE: invalid name per the ICNCP-1995, art. 17.11 and 17.15.

Agapanthus 'White Giant'

> ORIGIN: known since 1955, as Alan Bloom (1991) writes: "The only white-flowered
> *Agapanthus* I grew at that time was *Agapanthus* '**White Giant**' which I had obtained
> from the Continent. At 1.2 m it was quite a giant, but I found it rather shy to flower
> profusely as well as being ungainly." Still in cultivation.

Agapanthus 'White Heaven' (Funnel Group)

> ORIGIN: raised by C.J. de Jong & A.Ph.M. Rijnbeek en Zoon B.V., Boskoop, The
> Netherlands, introduced in 1999.
> LEAF: evergreen, up to 60 cm long and 3.5–5 cm wide, upright but nicely arched,
> glossy green, base green.
> PEDUNCLE: 70–80 cm, green and slightly glaucous, flat.
> INFLORESCENCE: 20–24 cm across, 50–80 flowers, globular.
> PEDICEL: green, usually with several fasciations within an inflorescence.
> FLOWERBUD: white with base pale green-white, upright but quickly horizontal.
> FLOWER: usually 8 or 10 tepals, inside white with midrib slightly transparent, outside
> white with base slightly darker white, when out of flower white, horizontal to slightly
> nodding but within an inflorescence usually a few upright flowers, 4.5–5 cm long
> (tube 1.3 cm long), 5 cm across, stamens not or just 1–2 exserted, anthers yellow
> becoming brown, green fruit.
> NOTE: most flowers within an inflorescence have 8 or 10 tepals; only a few will have
> 6 tepals.
> NOTE: European Plant Variety Right applied for and granted, file no. 1999/0781,
> grant no. 7376, expires 31 December 2026.
> NOTE: details from plants grown by Rijnbeek.
> ILLUSTRATION: *color plate*.
> AWARD: silver medal at Plantarium, Boskoop, The Netherlands, in 2003.

Agapanthus 'White Hope' (Salver Group)

> SYNONYM: *Agapanthus campanulatus* 'White Hope'

ORIGIN: (selection of *A. campanulatus*) raised by Gary Dunlop, Ballyrogan Nurseries, UK, known since 1998.
LEAF: deciduous.
INFLORESCENCE: "much fuller than *Agapanthus campanulatus* 'Albidus'."
FLOWER: white.
NOTE: details supplied by Gary Dunlop.

Agapanthus 'White Ice' (Funnel Group)

> SYNONYM: *Agapanthus orientalis* 'White Ice'

ORIGIN: introduced in New Zealand, known since 1997, and still in cultivation.
LEAF: evergreen, arching, glossy green.
PEDUNCLE: 75–100 cm, green.
INFLORESCENCE: 18 cm across, 20–30 flowers, globular.
PEDICEL: green.
FLOWERBUD: white with slightly darker base.
FLOWER: inside white, outside white, when out of flower white, horizontal, stamens exserted, anthers yellow with yellow pollen, no fruit.
NOTE: details from plants grown at Wisley and by Duivenvoorde.

Agapanthus 'White Queen'

ORIGIN: known since 1961 when shown by Fa J. de Jong & Zonen, Aalsmeer, The Netherlands. Probably no longer in cultivation.
FLOWER: white.
AWARD: GV in 1961.

Agapanthus 'White Ribbon' = *A.* 'Ruban Blanc'

Agapanthus 'White Smile' (Funnel Group)

> SYNONYM: *Agapanthus praecox* 'White Smile'

ORIGIN: introduced by Maas & van Stein, Hillegom, The Netherlands, and named in 1996. Still in cultivation.
LEAF: deciduous, 40–50 cm long and up to 2.5 cm wide, upright, pale green, base pale green.
PEDUNCLE: 80 cm, green with purple towards inflorescence, flat.
INFLORESCENCE: 16 cm across, 40–50 flowers, flat, bud opens on 1 side.
PEDICEL: purple with green at the base.
FLOWERBUD: cream with pale dull purple apex, upright but quickly nodding.
FLOWER: inside white with thin transparent midrib, outside white with pale purple on the tepals facing the sun and midrib slightly darker purple, when out of flower purple, horizontal to slightly nodding, 3.7 cm long (tube 1 cm long), 4–4.5 cm across, stamens slightly exserted, anthers dull violet-yellow becoming brownish, fruit green flushed purple.

NOTE: details from plants grown by Maas & van Stein.
NOTE: nuclear DNA content = 24.4 pg.
ILLUSTRATION: *color plate*; photograph, Snoeijer (1998).

Agapanthus 'White Star' (Salver Group)

ORIGIN: raised by Raveningham Gardens, UK, known since 1989, and still in cultivation.
LEAF: deciduous, up to 30 cm long and 2 cm wide, upright, normal green and glaucous, base purple.
PEDUNCLE: 60–70 cm, green, round.
INFLORESCENCE: 10 cm across, 25 flowers, flat, bud opens on 2 sides.
PEDICEL: purple.
FLOWERBUD: white with apex pale purple, upright.
FLOWER: inside white, midrib transparent, outside white, when out of flower purple, horizontal, 2 cm long (tube 1 cm long), 2 cm across, stamens not exserted, anthers purple.
NOTE: details from plants grown by Coen Jansen.
ILLUSTRATION: photograph, Jansen (2002).

Agapanthus 'White Starlet' (Salver Group)

SYNONYM: *Agapanthus campanulatus* 'White Starlet'
ORIGIN: raised by Raveningham Gardens, UK, known since 1989, and still in cultivation.
LEAF: deciduous.
PEDUNCLE: 60 cm.
FLOWER: white.

Agapanthus 'White Superior' ex Bristol Botanic Garden (Funnel Group)

ORIGIN: known since 1997, when offered as seed by the University Botanic Garden, Bristol, UK, through the international seed exchange between botanic gardens. Still in cultivation and widely offered in the UK.
PEDUNCLE: 80–140 cm, purplish.
INFLORESCENCE: 40–50 flowers, more or less flat.
PEDICEL: green flushed purple.
FLOWERBUD: upright, cream with purplish apex.
FLOWER: on both sides white, when out of flower with purple, horizontal to slightly nodding, stamens exserted, anthers orange-brown.
NOTE: details from plants grown by the late Lewis Hart, Hadleigh, Suffolk, UK.
NOTE: invalid name per the ICNCP-1995, art. 17.11.

Agapanthus 'White Superior' ex Reintjes = *A.* 'White Beauty'

NOTE: invalid name per the ICNCP-1995, art. 17.2 and 17.11.

Agapanthus 'White Superior' ex Snoeijer

NOTE: I published this name in the *Agapanthus* Newsletter but without a description, so the name published by Bristol Botanic Garden has priority.

Agapanthus 'White Triumphator'

SYNONYM: *Agapanthus campanulatus* 'White Triumphator'

ORIGIN: offered by Cotswold Garden Flowers, UK, in 1999 and still in cultivation.
LEAF: deciduous.
PEDUNCLE: 130 cm.
FLOWER: white.
NOTE: details from the Internet [39].

Agapanthus 'White Umbrella'

ORIGIN: known since 1995, UK, and still in cultivation.
INFLORESCENCE: usually with pagoda fasciation.
FLOWER: white.

Agapanthus 'White Wave'

ORIGIN: offered as seed.
NOTE: name from the Internet [32].

Agapanthus 'White Xmas' => *A.* 'White Christmas'

Agapanthus 'Whitney' (Funnel Group)

ORIGIN: raised by C.H.A. van Eijk, Nootdorp, The Netherlands. Known since 1999 when Kwekersrecht (plant variety right) was applied for by A.C. van Wijk, Rotterdam, The Netherlands.
LEAF: more or less evergreen, 30–35 cm long and 1.5–1.7 cm wide, arching, dark green, base green.
PEDUNCLE: 40–50 cm, green, round.
INFLORESCENCE: 15 cm across, 20–30 flowers, flat, bud opens on 1 side, bract remains attached.
PEDICEL: green.
FLOWERBUD: white with yellow-greenish apex, upright.
FLOWER: inside white with transparent midrib, outside white, when out of flower white, horizontal, up to 4.2 cm long (tube 1.5 cm long), 4.5 cm across, stamens slightly exserted, anthers yellow.
NOTE: European Plant Variety Right applied for and granted, file no. 2002/0190, grant no. 10694, expires 31 December 2028.
NOTE: Kwekersrecht (plant variety right) applied for and granted, The Netherlands, no. AGP3.
NOTE: details from plants offered in The Netherlands in 2001.
NOTE: nuclear DNA content = 25.1 pg.
ILLUSTRATION: *color plate.*

Agapanthus 'Wholesome' (Trumpet Group)

ORIGIN: raised by Gary Dunlop, Ballyrogan Nurseries, UK, named in 1998.
INFLORESCENCE: 18 cm across, globular.
FLOWER: inside pale violet-blue with darker midrib, outside similar with darker base, when out of flower more purple, stamens shorter than the flower.
ILLUSTRATION: photograph, Snoeijer (1998).

Agapanthus 'Willy Bik'

ORIGIN: raised by Maas & van Stein, Hillegom, The Netherlands, known since 1983. Probably no longer in cultivation.
PEDUNCLE: 65 cm.
FLOWERBUD: violet-blue.
FLOWER: inside violet-blue (91C) with darker midrib (92A), outside violet-blue (85C) with darker midrib (90C).
NOTE: registered in 1983.

Agapanthus 'Windlebrooke' (Salver Group)

ERROR: 'Windelbrook', 'Windelbrook'

ORIGIN: raised by The Crown Estate, Windsor, UK, introduced in 1995, and still in cultivation.
NAME: after a location near Windsor.
LEAF: deciduous, up to 15 cm long and 1.4 cm wide, upright, normal green, base purple.
PEDUNCLE: 30–40 cm, green with purple tint towards inflorescence, round.
INFLORESCENCE: 8–9 cm across, 20–30 flowers, bud opens on 1 side.
PEDICEL: green with violet towards flower.
FLOWERBUD: dark violet-blue, upright.
FLOWER: inside dark violet-blue (95BC), midrib slightly darker (95A), margin with purple tint, outside dark violet-blue, base slightly darker, when out of flower more purple, horizontal, 2.5 cm long (tube 1 cm long), 3 cm across.
NOTE: details from plants grown at Beth Chatto Gardens.

Agapanthus 'Windsor Castle' (Trumpet Group)

ORIGIN: raised by The Crown Estate, Windsor, UK, known since 1986, and still in cultivation.
NAME: after the royal estate near London.
LEAF: more or less evergreen, 30–40 cm long and 1.8 cm wide, arching, pale green, base green.
PEDUNCLE: 120–150 cm, green with purple, rather weak and therefore usually arching, round.
INFLORESCENCE: 20 cm across, 40–80 flowers, globular.
PEDICEL: dull violet-purple.
FLOWERBUD: dark violet-blue, upright.
FLOWER: inside violet-blue (96B), midrib darker (93A), margin with purple tint,

outside dark violet-blue, midrib and base slightly darker, when out of flower more purple, horizontal, 3.2 cm long (tube 1.2 cm long), 3 cm across, stamens not exserted.

NOTE: details from plants grown at various nurseries.

NOTE: nuclear DNA content = 22.7 pg.

ILLUSTRATION: *color plate.*

Agapanthus 'Windsor Grey' (Trumpet Group)

SYNONYM: *Agapanthus* 'Grey'

ORIGIN: raised by The Crown Estate, Windsor, UK. Introduced in 1995, still in cultivation.

NAME: a reference both to the royal estate and the flower colour.

LEAF: more or less evergreen, up to 70 cm long and 4 cm wide, arching, normal green, base purple.

PEDUNCLE: 100–130 cm, green and glaucous, rather sturdy, round.

INFLORESCENCE: 19–22 cm across, 70–100 flowers, more or less flat but when 100 flowers then more or less globular.

PEDICEL: dark green and just slightly flushed purple.

FLOWERBUD: very pale blue-white with greenish base, upright.

FLOWER: inside very pale violet-blue to white with margin very pale violet-blue (91D), midrib pale violet-blue, transparent with a slight purple tint, outside very pale violet-blue to white with margin very pale violet-blue, midrib transparent, base greenish because the young fruit is visible, when out of flower purple-white with violet-blue midrib, upright to horizontal to slightly facing downwards, up to 4.2 cm long (tube 1.4 cm long), 2.6 cm across, stamens not exserted, anthers violet-blue with yellow pollen becoming black.

NOTE: most details from plants grown by van Doorslaer.

NOTE: very similar to 'Rosemary', but in general the flowers of **'Windsor Grey'** are slightly darker and with a larger inflorescence with more flowers.

NOTE: nuclear DNA content = 24.2 pg.

ILLUSTRATION: *color plate*; photograph, Warren (1995), Wray (1998a), Farger (1999 as *A.* 'Grey'), Dunlop (2000), Fulcher (2000), and Jansen (2002).

Agapanthus 'Winsome' (Trumpet Group)

ORIGIN: raised by Gary Dunlop, Ballyrogan Nurseries, UK, named in 1998.

LEAF: deciduous, up to 44 cm long and 2.5 cm wide, upright, normal green, leafbase green.

PEDUNCLE: 60 cm, green.

INFLORESCENCE: 8–11 cm across, 100 flowers.

PEDICEL: green flushed purple towards flower.

FLOWER: on both sides very pale violet-blue, midrib violet-blue (94A), margin pale violet-blue (94D), horizontal to slightly facing downwards, 4.5 cm long, 3.5 cm across.

NOTE: details supplied by Gary Dunlop.

NOTE: nuclear DNA content = 24.2 pg.

Agapanthus 'Winterdwarf'

ORIGIN: (selection of 'Peter Pan') known since 2001.
PEDUNCLE: 30–40 cm.
FLOWER: dark violet-blue.

Agapanthus 'Winter Sky' (Funnel Group)

ORIGIN: raised at NCCPG Bicton College, UK, selected by Dick Fulcher in 1993, and still in cultivation.
LEAF: evergreen.
PEDUNCLE: 90 cm.
FLOWER: "very pale blue."
NOTE: details supplied by Dick Fulcher.

Agapanthus 'Wolga' (Trumpet Group)

SYNONYM: *Agapanthus africanus* 'Wolga'
Agapanthus umbellatus 'Wolga'

ORIGIN: (chance seedling) raised by W. Schoehuys, Uitgeest, The Netherlands. The plant was grown as "Blauw 800" by Gebroeders van Buggenum, named 'Wolga' in 1979. Still in cultivation.
NAME: Dutch spelling of the Volga River.
LEAF: deciduous, up to 40 cm long and 2 cm wide, upright but later a bit spreading, pale green and slightly glaucous, base green.
PEDUNCLE: 100 cm, green and glaucous, flat.
INFLORESCENCE: 18–20 cm across, 20–40 flowers, globular.
PEDICEL: green speckled purple.
FLOWERBUD: violet-blue with darker veins, a bit green in the middle, and base dark glossy violet-blue, upright but quickly horizontal.
FLOWER: inside very pale violet-blue (92C) with a purple tint, midrib darker (93C), margin violet-blue (92B) with purple tint, outside pale violet-blue (92B) with purple tint, midrib violet-blue (94A) and rather wide, darker violet-blue (94A) base, when out of flower purple, horizontal to slightly nodding, 3.5–4 cm long (tube 1.7 cm long), 3.3 cm across, stamens not or just 1 exserted, anthers brown.
NOTE: details from plants grown by Duivenvoorde.
NOTE: registered in 1979.
NOTE: nuclear DNA content = 24.3 pg.
ILLUSTRATION: *color plate.*
AWARD: GV in 1979.

Agapanthus 'Wolkberg' (Tubular Group)

SYNONYM: *Agapanthus inapertus* subsp. *intermedius* 'Wolkberg' pro parte

ORIGIN: (selection of *A. inapertus* subsp. *intermedius*) from Wolkberg Peak, northeast Transvaal, introduced by Kirstenbosch National Botanical Garden, South Africa. Known since 1989. Also offered as seed.
LEAF: deciduous.

PEDUNCLE: 100–150 cm.

INFLORESCENCE: "rather small."

FLOWER: clear violet-blue (96C), hanging downwards.

NOTE: two different cultivars are grown under this name; see next description.

Agapanthus 'Wolkberg' (Salver Group)

SYNONYM: *Agapanthus campanulatus* 'Wolkberg'
Agapanthus inapertus subsp. *intermedius* 'Wolkberg' pro parte

ORIGIN: unknown, see previous description; the mix-up probably started in South Africa.

LEAF: deciduous, 45 cm long and 2 cm wide, upright, normal green, base green.

PEDUNCLE: 110 cm, green.

INFLORESCENCE: 13 cm across, 80 flowers, bud opens on 1 side.

PEDICEL: green to purple towards flower.

FLOWER: inside rather pale violet-blue (92C) with midrib and margin slightly darker (92B), outside violet-blue (92A) with dark violet-blue base (93B), horizontal, 2 cm long, 3 cm across.

NOTE: details supplied by Gary Dunlop.

NOTE: invalid name per the ICNCP-1995, art. 17.2.

ILLUSTRATION: photograph, Duncan (1998 as *A. inapertus* subsp. *intermedius* 'Wolkberg').

Agapanthus 'Woodcote Paleface'

ORIGIN: (selection from the same seedbatch as **'Charlie Morrell'**) raised by Brian Hiley, Wallington, Surrey, UK, introduced in 1997, and still in cultivation.

NAME: refers to the location of the nursery at Little Woodcote Estate and the flower colour.

LEAF: evergreen.

PEDUNCLE: 80 cm.

FLOWER: white with midrib very pale violet-blue.

NOTE: details supplied by Brian Hiley.

Agapanthus 'Yellow Tips' (Salver Group)

ORIGIN: raised at NCCPG Bicton College, UK, selected by Dick Fulcher in 1993, and still in cultivation.

LEAF: deciduous.

PEDUNCLE: 85 cm.

FLOWER: "white with yellow tips," anthers yellow.

NOTE: details supplied by Dick Fulcher and some from the Internet [5].

Agapanthus 'Yves Klein' (Trumpet Group)

ORIGIN: raised by Gary Dunlop, Ballyrogan Nurseries, UK, named in 1998.

NAME: in honour of French artist Yves Klein (1928–1962), with special reference to his monochrome period; in 1957 he started to use only blue, and since then his name has become synonymous with the colour cobalt blue.

LEAF: deciduous, up to 30 cm long and 1.5 cm wide, arching, pale green, leafbase purple.

PEDUNCLE: 70 cm, pale green.

INFLORESCENCE: 15 cm across, 50 flowers.

PEDICEL: purple.

FLOWERBUD: very dark violet-blue, upright but quickly horizontal.

FLOWER: inside violet-blue with purple tint, midrib and margin darker, outside dark violet-blue, horizontal to slightly facing downwards, 2 cm long, 2.5 cm across, anthers shorter than the flower.

NOTE: details supplied by Gary Dunlop.

ILLUSTRATION: photograph, Snoeijer (1998).

Agapanthus 'Zella Thomas' (Salver Group)

ERROR: 'Zelah Thomas', 'Zela Thomas'

ORIGIN: raised by Mrs A.F. George, introduced by Hydon Nurseries, UK, known since 1972, and still in cultivation.

LEAF: deciduous, 30–40 cm long and 2.3 cm wide, upright, normal green, base with purple.

PEDUNCLE: 80 cm, green and glaucous, round.

INFLORESCENCE: 13 cm across, 40 flowers, globular, bud opens on 1 side.

PEDICEL: dull violet with purple tint.

FLOWERBUD: dark violet-blue, upright.

FLOWER: inside violet-blue, midrib darker (95C/96A), margin darker (95C/96C) with purple tint, outside dark violet-blue, midrib and base slightly darker, when out of flower distinctly purple, horizontal, 2.8 cm long (tube 1.1 cm long), 3 cm across.

NOTE: details from plants grown at Hydon Nurseries.

NOTE: seed-propagated plants grown in other gardens and nurseries differ from the plants growing at Hydon Nurseries and should be referred to as RUBBISH.

ILLUSTRATION: photograph, Snoeijer (1998).

AWARD: FCC in 1977.

Crinum (Amaryllidaceae) [c. 120 species, c. 75 cultivars]

Crinum africanum L. = *Agapanthus africanus* (L.) Hoffmanns. subsp. *africanus*
L. (1753) Species Plantarum, ed. 1, 292.

Mauhlia Dahl = *Agapanthus* L'Hér.
Dahl (1787) Obs. Bot. Syst. Linne, 25.

Mauhlia africana Dahl = *Agapanthus africanus* (L.) Hoffmanns. subsp. *africanus*
Dahl (1787) Obs. Bot. Syst. Veg. 26.

Mauhlia linearis Thunb. = ***Agapanthus africanus*** (L.) Hoffmanns. subsp. ***africanus***

Thunb. (1781) Nov. Gen., III.
Thunb. (1794) Prod. Pl. Cap., 60.

Mauhlia umbellata Thunb. ex Roem. & Schult. = ***Agapanthus africanus*** (L.) Hoffmanns. subsp. ***africanus***

Roem. & Schult. (1830) Systema vegetabilium.

Polyanthes L. (Agavaceae) [c. 10 species, 1 cultivar]

Polyanthes Mill. = ***Agapanthus africanus*** (L.) Hoffmanns. subsp. ***africanus***

Mill. (1760) Gard. Dict. 210.

Tulbaghia L. (Alliaceae) [22 species, 8 cultivars]

Tulbaghia africana (L.) Kuntze = ***Agapanthus africanus*** (L.) Hoffmanns. subsp. ***africanus***

Kuntze (1893) Revisio Generum Plantarum.

Tulbaghia africana var. *heisteri* (Fabric.) Kuntze = ***Agapanthus africanus*** (L.) Hoffmanns. subsp. ***africanus***

Kuntze (1893) Revisio Generum Plantarum.

Tulbaghia africana var. *minor* (Lodd.) Kuntze = ***Agapanthus africanus*** (L.) Hoffmanns. subsp. ***africanus***

Kuntze (1893) Revisio Generum Plantarum.

Tulbaghia africana var. *praecox* (Willd.) Kuntze = ***Agapanthus praecox*** Willd. ex F.M. Leight.

Kuntze (1893) Revisio Generum Plantarum.

Tulbaghia heisteri Fabric. = ***Agapanthus africanus*** (L.) Hoffmanns. subsp. ***africanus***

Fabric. (1759) Enum. Pl. Helmstad.

Chapter 6

Cultivation

It seems impossible to influence how abundantly a certain plant will flower from year to year, but it is important, whether grown in the soil or as a potplant, that the plant be placed in a warm and sunny spot. This will also be better for the flowerstalk (peduncle): all peduncles (except for those of *Agapanthus inapertus*, which will be upright regardless) grow towards the light. If you grow the plant in too much shade, you always end up with bending peduncles. Some shade is preferable if the site is very exposed and warm; in such a case, you simply have to accept that the peduncles will bend forwards.

Agapanthus will grow in any soil, be it peat or heavy clay—it actually does not matter much. Even the pH appears to be of no importance. Do be sure potted plants have drainage and a heavier soil; besides better feeding the plant, this last helps ensure that the plant is not blown over with every breeze. When a peat-based potting soil is used (or indeed any light potting soil), a brick at the bottom of the pot will give some stability.

When grown outside in the garden, soil must be prepared to give the plant drainage during winter; add grit, especially in peat and clay soil. In sandy soil, add compost to give the plant enough moisture during summer.

The plant looks very pretty in a pot or other container. The pot can be placed somewhere out of sight while the plant grows and brought into a prominent spot when flowers develop; in some cultivars the leaves are ornamental as well. The best-flowering plants are those that remain in the same container for several years; it is not necessary to repot every year.

Plants that are grown in the same pot for several years need to be checked to avoid the roots' breaking the (probably expensive) pot. When possible, grow the plant in a plastic pot to avoid the soil's drying out during summer. A large pot is best, as this allows the plant to be grown for several years in the same pot but also prevents the plant's being blown over when in full leaf.

Pot-grown *Agapanthus* should be kept frost-free during the winter. If during winter the outside temperatures rise above freezing, open the greenhouse windows for ventilation; this keeps the leaves of evergreen plants from rotting. Deciduous plants will start to regrow from late winter onwards. With fresh air and full light the young shoots will grow normally; when too warm and lacking light the young shoots will become too weak and flop over.

Feeding

Plants need feeding during the growing season. Well-known Dutch *Agapanthus* grower Kees Duivenvoorde prescribes a feeding for nurseries who grow their stock in the field: after cleaning the winter cover, feed with cow manure 10-4-8, followed by a fertilizer 7-14-28 at 7 kg per 100 m^2. In late summer, apply the same fertilizer but half the quantity.

The home gardener can apply some dried manure once in early spring as a soil topping, either to potted plants or those in the garden; later, a liquid feeding is better until flowering starts. During flowering the plant will need the fertilizer 7-14-28 once, as this will help it develop new flowerbuds for next season; this fertilizer is available through plant shops and garden centres in small packets of tomato and other vegetable fertilizers.

Hardy or Not Hardy?

This question is a good start for a fight between two plantsmen or nurseries, as frost resistance differs from species to species and from cultivar to cultivar. Many stories circulate; one is that frost resistance depends on the width of the leaves: the smaller the leaf, the more frost-resistant the plant. This is nonsense. It all depends on the garden or nursery situation, the protection afforded by other plants or buildings, the soil, the weather, the protection material, and so forth—which is why cultivars should not be billed as hardy by nurseries and garden centres. If a plant does not survive at a particular place in the garden, try it some meters further on, if possible.

When the soil is wet or waterlogged in winter, it is better to grow your plants in pots and store them frost-free during winter. *Agapanthus* needs lots of water during its growing season but needs to be kept almost dry in winter, especially those cultivars that are deciduous.

Materials used as a covering in winter for protection should be placed in late autumn or early winter, depending on the weather. As soon as winter is over (meaning that long periods of frost are no longer expected), this covering must be removed. The only problem is late-night frosts, which can harm the young sprouting shoots. Such frosts lead to leaf damage and a slow start of the plant; however, they seem not to have any effect on flowering, other than that it can be somewhat later than normal. If the covering is removed too late, the young shoots can grow through the material and be harmed; and as they are also more weak than those growing without cover, such young shoots are more vulnerable to night frosts.

In Holland, straw is the material preferred by growers for winter protection, 200 kg per 100 m2. If a harsh winter is expected, an extra layer of black polythene plastic is used over the straw. For the garden, any dry, dead plant material, such as leaves or the branches from the Christmas tree, can be used.

But to answer the question: *Agapanthus* is not hardy. To make a more international statement: evergreen plants are hardy to zone 10, deciduous plants are hardy to zone 7, with winter protection.

Why Doesn't My Plant Flower?

This is probably the most frequently asked question concerning *Agapanthus* plants in cultivation. New flowerbuds for the next flowering season are developed during flowering or directly after, so before the resting period. In winter, low temperatures are necessary. Plants grown outside in gardens usually get their cold treatment naturally; plants grown in pots, especially deciduous plants, should be kept outdoors as long as possible.

Pot-grown plants should be kept under a shelter to avoid rainfall. Evergreen plants can resist temperatures just above freezing, especially when they are stored in light; deciduous plants can endure a couple of nights of temperatures just below freezing with no trouble. When deciduous plants are overwintered in too-high temperatures, the peduncle will not emerge. For evergreen plants, high winter temperatures usually lead to early flowering, up to two months earlier than normal, and floppy peduncles that need staking.

As to how to influence the making of a new inflorescence, I have no direct answer. Most likely there is a relationship between the condition of the plant (healthy, compost, soils, feeding, etc.) and temperature. The intensity of light is another part of the equation, meaning that if a pot-grown plant is put in a darker spot after flowering, there is little chance that the plant will develop a new inflorescence for next season.

Most *Agapanthus* growers in Holland are situated near the coast, in between our world-famous bulb fields. The light is intense, the land is flat and open, without trees, houses, or other obstructions. Grown in these conditions, a good cultivar produces about 50–80 peduncles per m2 after the second year of planting (Consulentschap 1987).

Propagation

By seed

Agapanthus is easy to grow from seed but does not come true from seed. Cultivars should, therefore, always be propagated vegetatively.

After flowering, a small fruit will grow, which will be green (and in many cultivars stained with purple or violet) for a long time. As the seed in the fruit starts to ripen, the fruit colour changes to pale brown. At this stage the fruit can be harvested and can be left to ripen indoors. The fruit will split open on three sides to release the seed. Store the seed (a paper bag is best) in a frost-free place, as the seed is not frost-resistant.

Seed can be sown in early spring in a mixture of potting soil and sand. Do not cover the seed but cover the pot with a transparent plastic bag to keep the moisture inside. Some heat (15–18°C/59–64°F) will help germination but is not really necessary. After 3–4 weeks the seed will germinate. *Agapanthus* being a monocot, a grass-like cotyledon appears first, usually with the seed coat on top. The first true, somewhat wider leaf will grow quickly afterwards. If possible use a larger pot so that the seedlings can grow on for the first year without pricking out. Seedlings of deciduous plants can be evergreen the first winter.

It will take up to three years after germination before the first flowers can be expected.

As far as I could discover, plants are not harmed by producing seeds and will flower normally next year.

By division

All cultivars should be propagated vegetatively, preferably by division. When buying a cultivar you should be convinced the plant is propagated this way. If the nursery cannot guarantee you that the plant is vegetatively propagated, it is better to choose another cultivar or, perhaps wiser, go to another nursery. The best nurseries know how their plants are propagated and will have put this on the label; honest nurseries are open with their information and note in their catalogue whether the plants are raised from seed or propagated by division.

Plants at a garden centre have been grown by suppliers; it will be hard to know whether these plants are seed-raised. A very easy characteristic to use as a control is the colour of the leafbase. If plants offered under any one cultivar name have different coloured leafbases—one green, another purple—then the plants are mixed. Another possibility is to see whether the plants offered are of the same size. If they are, they are from seed, as plants propagated by division yield very variably sized plants. Also, similar sized plants growing nicely in the middle of the pot are most likely from seed; divided plants will vary in size and therefore will grow anywhere in the pot.

Plant division demands attention. Plants must be carefully handled, not just dug up and split with a spade through the middle; too many wounds are made in the wrong place thus. The best way is to clean the roots with water; then, using a sharp knife, cut the rootstock into several parts, yielding only one or just a few wounds. Immediately after dividing, the parts should be potted up or planted in the garden. The best time for division is during the growing season, as active roots will give the best results. The growing season lasts roughly from early spring until mid autumn. The very best time for division and/or replanting is directly after the flowering period, when the shoots are developing the new flowerbuds; plants will then have enough time before winter to make new roots in the generally warm soil.

Old rootstocks can be cut in small pieces, with resting buds present on each; if these are then potted up and put directly into a greenhouse, they will usually make shoots without any problem.

Contrary to the advice just given, nurseries that grow *Agapanthus* on a large scale, for mail-order, divide in winter in order to have indoor work and then harvest the plants in late autumn.

Micropropagation of *Agapanthus* is increasingly common, especially for difficult-to-divide cultivars like 'Purple Cloud'. The problem for gardeners is that when offered, micropropagated plants look similar to seedlings: all plantlets are of a similar age and shape, nicely potted in the middle of the pot. Nurseries should clearly identify tissue-cultured plants for their customers.

Micropropagation companies usually claim their plants are 100% true, without any mutants. But one nursery informed me that 3–5% of their micropropagated plants were unstable, a percentage they considered too high, and so this nursery has returned to reliable division.

Pests and Diseases

Most *Agapanthus* in cultivation are infected with viruses, apparent on the leaves, which will have paler stripes. As far as could be determined, virus-infected plants will live as long as virus-free plants but tend to lose their abundance of flowering after several years. Allemand and Pionnat (2001) refer to several different viruses, arabis mosaic virus, cucumber mosaic virus, and odontoglossum ring spot virus among them. The main vector is man himself: by using infected tools, he transfers the virus from one plant to another. In general, newly introduced cultivars are virus-free.

Especially during flowering, red stripes on the leaves and peduncle may appear, caused by the fungus *Botrytis*. Affected flowers might be misformed. The fungus thrives in warm, damp weather.

When leaves die from the apex during growing season, they might have been attacked by the fungus *Macrophomina agapanthi*. When infected from the base, brown spots appear, which may eventually cover the whole leaf.

Environmental factors too can cause leaves to turn yellow or brown. Also, the leaves of some cultivars will be yellow early in the year, when starting to develop; and other cultivars start dying off quickly in late summer. All this has nothing to do with fungi infections.

Phytophthora causes drying of the leaves from the base. Infected rootstock dies quickly, by rotting followed by bacterial infection. When the flowers are infected, they too will dry out.

Fusarium moniliforme var. *subglutinans*, known since 1973 from Italy on flowers, causes small sunken spots that are pinkish of colour and either round or long. The fungus might also appear on the leaves but usually without much damage.

In warm summers, red spider mites and thrips might be a problem; they usually house beneath the leaves and are therefore hard to destroy. Mealybugs, scale, and aphids also might appear, under the leaves but especially in the inflorescence. Young shoots in early spring are a delicacy for snails and slugs, but the plant usually recovers easily and quickly. Many different hoverflies will visit the flowers, but these do no harm, of course; they mainly collect pollen.

Another problem, in some cultivars, is the weak peduncle, or, as you wish, the too-large inflorescence. All such peduncles will need staking, which does not look nice. Fortunately, many new cultivars have strong peduncles.

Fasciations

Some cultivars produce two peduncles per shoot instead of the normal single peduncle; this second peduncle is usually shorter, with fewer flowers, and seems cultivar-restricted. Another, rather rare, fasciation is the elongation of the peduncle through the inflorescence; this pagoda growth, which usually appears in evergreen cultivars that are transplanted, also seems cultivar-restricted. Accordingly, flowers might appear with more than the normal six tepals.

Most fasciations in an inflorescence occur as one or more internodes within the bostryx elongates. In extreme forms, elongated internodes might appear within several bostryces, which gives a strange effect.

Some cultivars will have their stamens changed into tepal-like staminodes (double flowers). These staminodes are the same size as the tepals and have the same colour (or are perhaps slightly paler). Double-flowering cultivars do not open well.

Other cultivars have flowers with extra tepals (semi-double) together with the normal range of stamens. In extreme forms, there will be some extra stamens as well. The flowers open well and still keep their shape according to the cultivar group. This semi-double flowering also seems to be cultivar-restricted.

Rarely two peduncles are grown together, forming a strange fasciation. And finally, in the fasciation called "hens and chickens," a cluster of flowers might appear just below the main inflorescence or even halfway along the peduncle or more rarely at the base.

Appendix

Breeders/Introducers and Their Cultivars

Apple Court, UK: 'Apple Court', 'Penny Slade', 'Spode'

Blooms of Bressingham, UK: 'Bressingham Blue', 'Bressingham Bounty', 'Bressingham White', 'Isis'

Botanical Garden Auckland, New Zealand: 'Sea Foam', 'Sea Mist', 'Sea Spray', 'Streamline'

Cape Seed & Bulbs, South Africa: 'Admiral's Cascade', 'Buddy Blue', 'Double Diamond'

The Crown Estate, Windsor, UK: 'Balmoral', 'Ben Hope', 'Birkhall', 'Buckingham Palace', 'Castle of Mey', 'Clarence House', 'Glamis Castle', 'Loch Hope', 'Princess Margaret', 'Queen Mother', 'Royal Blue', 'Royal Lodge', 'Sandringham', 'Silver Jubilee', 'Windlebrook', 'Windsor Castle', 'Windsor Grey'

Ignace van Doorslaer, Belgium: 'Charlotte', 'Stéphanie', 'Stéphanie Charm', 'Sylvine'

Kees Duivenvoorde, The Netherlands: 'Aberdeen', 'Amsterdam', 'Black Beauty', 'Bristol', 'Cambridge', 'Catharina', 'City of Lincoln', 'Columba', 'Debbie', 'Dr Brouwer', 'Duivenbrugge Blue', 'Duivenbrugge White', 'Edinburgh', 'Elisabeth', 'Goldfinger', 'Helsinki', 'Holbeach', 'Johanna', 'Jolanda', 'Kopenhagen', 'Leicester', 'Marcus', 'Marianne', 'Mariètte', 'Martine', 'Nottingham', 'Oslo', 'Parijs', 'Pinchbeck', 'Prinses Marilène', 'Rotterdam', 'Spalding', 'Stockholm', 'Suzan', 'Virginia', 'Volendam'

Don Duncan, USA: 'Blue Danube', 'Prolific Blue', 'Prolific White'

Gary Dunlop, UK: 'Adonis', 'Aphrodite', 'Atlas', 'Ballyrogan', 'Bangor Blue', 'Blue Cascade', 'Blue Companion', 'Blue Formality', 'Blue Mercury', 'Bright Eyes', 'Colossus', 'Cyan', 'Density', 'Fafner', 'Fasolt', 'Formality', 'Fulsome', 'Helen', 'Innocence', 'Latent Blue', 'Magnifico', 'Mount Stewart', 'Nyx', 'Oxbridge', 'Oxford Blue', 'Patent Blue', 'Plas Merdyn Blue', 'Plas Merdyn White', 'Plenitude', 'Premier', 'Rotunda', 'Royale', 'Silver Sceptre', 'Slieve Donard Form', 'Spokes', 'Starburst', 'Supreme', 'Titan', 'Twilight', 'Violetta', 'Wedgwood Blue', 'Wendy', 'White Hope', 'Wholesome', 'Winsome', 'Yves Klein'

C.H.A. van Eijk, The Netherlands: 'Atlantic Ocean', 'Bianca Perla', 'Pacific Ocean'

Dick Fulcher, UK: 'Angela', 'Autumn Mist', 'Beatrice', 'Becky', 'Bicton Bell', 'Bicton Bride', 'Blue Gown', 'Blue Ice', 'Blue Steel', 'Blue Stripe', 'Blue Velvet', 'Cool Blue', 'Dorothy Kate', 'Far Horizon', 'Gem', 'Harvest Blue', 'Jodie', 'Kirsty', 'Lavender Girl', 'Liam's Lilac', 'Lilac Bells', 'Lilac Time', 'Loch Hope Variegated', 'Lorna', 'Lost Horizon', 'Mercury', 'Nikki', 'Pride of Bicton', 'Silver Mist', 'Sky Rocket', 'Summer Snow', 'Tall Boy', 'Tarka', 'Winter Sky', 'Yellow Tips'

Hundertmark/Hooijman, The Netherlands: 'Corinne', 'Marike'

V.J. Hooper, New Zealand: 'Blue Brush', 'Snow Cloud'

Kirstenbosch National Botanical Garden, South Africa: 'Adelaide', 'Graskop', 'Hardingsdale', 'Lydenburg', 'Mount Thomas', 'Politique', 'Sky Blue', 'Storms River', 'White', 'Wolkberg'

Hans Kramer, The Netherlands: 'Graskopje', 'Meibont', 'Septemberhemel'

Los Angeles State and County Arboretum, USA: 'Elaine', 'Ellamae', 'Mood Indigo'

Fa J. de Jong & Zonen; Schoehuys; Th. P.W. de Groot; Maas & van Stein, The Netherlands: 'Aalsmeer's Glorie', 'Blue Perfection', 'Dnjepr', 'Donau', 'Duná', 'Emba', 'Glacier Stream', 'Ice Lolly', 'Kama', 'Lena', 'Newa', 'Pinocchio', 'Polar Ice', 'Rhone', 'Snow Queen', 'Waga', 'White Smile', 'Willy Bik', 'Wolga'

J.N. Giridlian's Oakhurst Gardens, USA: 'Albus Select', 'Dwarf White', 'Jeanette Dean', 'My Joy', 'Peter Pan', 'Stormcloud', 'Wedding Bells'

Lewis Palmer, The Grange, Headbourne Worthy, UK: 'African Moon', 'Alice Gloucester', 'Anthea', 'Blue Bird', 'Blue Peter', 'Cherry Holley', 'Crystal', 'Delft', 'Diana', 'Dorothy Palmer', 'Dutch Tiles', 'Elizabeth Salisbury', 'Enchanting', 'Eve', 'Joyce', 'June', 'Kirstenbosch', 'Lady Grey', 'Lady Wimborne', 'Luly', 'Margaret Wakehurst', 'Molly Howick', 'Mystery', 'Penelope Palmer', 'Rosemary', 'Roy', 'Saint Michael', 'Snowy Owl', 'Sybil Harton', 'Victoria', 'Violet Tips'

J.-Y. Poiroux, Ets Horticole, France: 'Beauregard', 'Ile d'Yeu', 'Les Barges', 'Vague Bleue'

Raveningham Gardens, UK: 'Arctic Star', 'Bethlehem Star', 'Blue Star', 'Cedric Morris', 'Dawn Star', 'Evening Star', 'Ice Blue Star', 'Midnight Star', 'Moonstar', 'Morning Star', 'Sky Star', 'Super Star' ex UK, 'White Star', 'White Starlet'

C.J. de Jong & A.Ph.M. Rijnbeek en Zoon B.V., Boskoop, The Netherlands: 'Blue Heaven', 'White Heaven'

Eric B. Smith, UK: 'Blue Moon', 'Torbay'

Haden Tebb, Zimbabwe: 'Blue Eyes', 'White Classic'

van der Zwet, The Netherlands: 'Amethyst', 'Blauwe Valk', 'Blauwe Wimpel', 'Blue Penant', 'Josephine' ex Holland, 'Moira'

References

Literature

Pierre **Allemand** and Jean-Claude **Pionnat** (2001) L'agapanthe. Botanique, physiologie, pathologie et culture pour la fleur coupée. Association Nationale des Structures d'Expérimentation et de Démonstration en Horticulture / Institut National de la Recherche Agronomique, Paris. ASTREDHOR, INRA Editions, 44 Reu d'Alesia, 75682 Paris cedex 14, France.

American Nurseryman Editor (2002) Perennials. In: American Nurseryman, June, December.

Susyn **Andrews** and Christopher **Brickell** (1999) Does the true *Agapanthus africanus* 'Albus' exist in cultivation any more? Notes from the RHS Nomenclature Panel: 1. In: The New Plantsman.

The **Angiosperm Phylogeny Group** (1998) An ordinal classification for the families of flowering plants. Ann. Missouri Bot. Gard. 85:531–553. 1998.

Anne and Peter **Ashley** (1993) The Canadian Plant Sourcebook. 1992/93 Edition. Peter Ashley, Ottawa.

———— (1996) The Canadian Plant Sourcebook. 1996/97 Edition. Peter Ashley, Ottawa.

Staff of the L.H. **Bailey** Hortorium, Cornell University (1977) Hortus Third. A Concise Dictionary of Plants Cultivated in the United States and Canada. Macmillan, New York.

Thomas **Baines** (1885) Greenhouse and Stove Plants. John Murray, London, UK.

A. **Batten** and H. **Bokelmann** (1966) Wild Flowers of the Eastern Cape Province. Books of Africa (Pty.) Ltd, Cape Town.

Gustave **Beauverd** (1910) *Agapanthus inapertus* sp. nov. Et revision des espèces et variétés du genre *Agapanthus*. In: Bulletin de la Société botanique de Genève.

John William **Besant** (1903) The Blue African Lily. In: Flora and Sylva, 1.

De **Bloemisterij** [editors] (1999) *Agapanthus* als kuipplant goed voor bloemenafzet. In: De Bloemisterij, 37.

Alan **Bloom** (1968) Alan Bloom's Selected Garden Plants. Jarrold and Sons Ltd, Norwich.

——— (1991) Alan Bloom's Hardy Perennials. B.T. Batsford, London.

J. **Bond** (1978) *Agapanthus* trial. In: J. Roy. Hort. Soc.

Pauline **Bond** (1984) Plants of the Cape Flora. A Descriptive Catalogue. In: J. South African Bot. Suppl. Vol. 13.

C. **Bonstedt** (1931) Pareys Blumengärtnerei. Beschreibung, Kultur und Verwendung der gesamten Gärtnerisch en Schmuckpflanzen.

Dr B.K. **Boom** and Dr J.D. **Ruys** (1950) Flora der gekweekte, kruidachtige gewassen. H. Veenman & Zonen, Wageningen.

Dr B.K. **Boom** (1975) Flora der gekweekte, kruidachtige gewassen. H. Veenman & Zonen, Wageningen.

Johs. de **Breuk** (1892) Vergadering der Vaste Commissiën op Woensdag 12 Oct. j.l. ter beoordeeling van nieuwe bloemen en planten. In: Weekblad voor Bloembollencultuur.

Christopher **Brickell** and Fay **Sharman** (1986) The Vanishing Garden. John Murray.

Christopher **Brickell** [editor in chief] (1996) The Royal Horticultural Society A-Z Encyclopedia of Garden Plants. Dorling Kindersley Limited, London.

E.-A. **Carrière** (1880) Agapanthe a fleurs doubles. In: Revue Horticole.

——— (1882) Prolification et transformation des fleurs d'Agapanthe. In: Revue Horticole.

Beth **Chatto** (1985) The Dry Garden. J.M. Dent & Sons Ltd, London.

——— (1989) The Green Tapestry. Simon and Schuster, London.

Gordon **Cheers** [editor] (1997) Botanica. Random House Australia Pty Ltd.

Ruth Rogers **Clausen** and Nicolas H. **Ekstrom** (1989) Perennials for American Gardens. Random House, New York.

Consulentschap in algemene dienst voor de bloemisterij & Proefstation voor de bloemisterij te Aalsmeer & Proefstation voor de tuinbouw onder glas te Naaldwijk (1987) Teelt van Zomerbloemen, buiten en onder glas. Geheel herziene en uitgebreide druk van de voormalige delen I en II. November.

Francoise and Jean-Pierre **Cordier** (1993) 25.000 Plantes. Ou et comment les acheter? Societe Nationale d'Horticulture de France. La Maison Rustique, Paris.

M. **Courtenay-Latimer** and G.G. **Smith** (1967) The Flowering Plants of the Tsitsikma Forest and Coastal National Park. National Parks Board of the Republic of South Africa.

L.B. **Creasey** (1939) *Agapanthus africanus*, Hoffmgg., and *A. orientalis*, Leighton. In: The Gardeners' Chronicle.

CropLink (1997) CropStart - An Introduction to *Agapanthus* Production. 1st Edition September 1997. CropLink (N.Z.) Ltd, 111 Pt Wells Rd, R D 6, Warkworth, New Zealand.

W. **Curtis** (1800) *Agapanthus umbellatus*. African Agapanthus, or Blue Lily. In: The Botanical Magazine, t.500.

R.M.T. **Dahlgren**, H.T. **Clifford**, and P.F. **Yeo** (1985) The Families of the Monocotyledons. Structure, Evolution and Taxonomy.

Brian **Davis** and Brian **Knapp** (1992) Know Your Common Plant Names. MDA Publications, Newbury, England.

Department of Nature Conservation (1967) Some Protected Wild flowers of the Cape Province. Department of Nature Conservation of the Cape Provincial Administration.

Hanneke van **Dijk** (1996) TuinenReisgids. Midden- en Oost-Engeland. Gottmer, Haarlem.

———— (1996a) TuinenReisgids. Noord-Engeland en Schotland. Gottmer, Haarlem.

———— (1996b) TuinenReisgids. Zuidwest-Engeland en Wales. Gottmer, Haarlem.

———— (1997) Borderplanten Encyclopedie. Rebo International, Lisse.

———— (2002) De Nederlandse Planten Collectie van *Agapanthus*. In: Tuin & Landschap 19.

Hanneke van **Dijk** and Wim **Snoeijer** (2001) Nederlandse Planten Collecties. Op bezoek bij verzamelaars van planten. Tuinenreisgids. Gottmer, Haarlem.

Richard L. **Doutt** (1994) Cape Bulbs. Timber Press, Portland, Oregon.

Graham **Duncan** (1983) The white form of *Agapanthus walshii* L. Bol. In: Veld & Flora, March.

———— (1985) *Agapanthus* species: their potential . . . . In: Veld & Flora, December.

———— (1993) *Agapanthus dyeri*, Plate 2062 Transvaal. In: The Flowering Plants of Africa. National Botanical Institute, South Africa.

———— (1998) Grow *Agapanthus*. Kirstenbosch Gardening Series. A guide to the species, cultivation and propagation of the genus *Agapanthus*. Nat. Bot. Inst., Kirstenbosch, South Africa.

———— (1999) Grow Clivias. Kirstenbosch Gardening Series. A guide to the species, cultivation and propagation of the genus *Clivia*. Nat. Bot. Inst., Kirstenbosch, South Africa.

Gary **Dunlop** (2000) Plant Profile. Singing the blues. In: Gardens Illustrated.

R.A. **Dyer** (1966) *Agapanthus praecox* subsp. *orientalis* forma, Plates 1476 and 1477. In: The Flowering Plants of Africa, Botanical Research Institute, South Africa.

———— (1966a) *Agapanthus campanulatus* subsp. *patens*, Plate 1478. In: The Flowering Plants of Africa, Botanical Research Institute, South Africa.

———— (1966b) *Agapanthus inapertus* subsp. *inapertus*, Plate 1479. In: The Flowering Plants of Africa, Botanical Research Institute, South Africa.

———— (1966c) *Agapanthus inapertus* subsp. *pendulus*, Plate 1480. In: The Flowering Plants of Africa, Botanical Research Institute, South Africa.

S. **Edwards** et al (1821) The Botanical Register, t.699.

Anne and Walter **Erhardt** (1995) PPP Index. Pflanzen. Pflanzeneinkaufsführer für Europa. Eugen Ulmer, Stuttgart.

———— (1997) PPP Index. Pflanzen. Pflanzeneinkaufsführer für Europa. 3 Auflage. Eugen Ulmer, Stuttgart.

———— (2000) Pflanzen gesucht? Der große Einkaufsführer für Deutschland, Österreich und die Schweiz. 50000 Arten und Sorten. 4. Auflage. Eugen Ulmer, Stuttgart.

Yves **Farger** (1999) *Agapanthus*, sinds eeuwen geloofd en geroofd. In: De Tuinen van EDEN, lente/zomer.

Michael F. **Fay** and Mark W. **Chase** (1996) Resurrection of Themidaceae for the *Brodiaea* alliance, and recircumscription of Alliaceae, Amaryllidaceae and Aga-panthoideae. In: Taxon 45, August.

Dick **Fulcher** (2000) From Africa with love. In: The Garden.

———— (2002) *Agapanthus* and other plants. Pine Cottage Plants [including the catalogue]. Pine Cottage, Fourways, Devon, England.

Meg **Gaddum** (1997) New Zealand Plant Finder. David Bateman.

Hans **Ganslmeier** and Kurt **Henseler** (1985) Schnittstauden. Verlag Eugen Ulmer, Stuttgart.

Gardeners' Chronicle Editor (1905) *Agapanthus umbellatus globosus*. In: The Gardeners' Chronicle.

A.J.M. **Gillissen** (1980) Sortiments onderzoek van het geslacht *Agapanthus* L'Héritier. Thesis, Department of Taxonomy of Cultivated Plants, Wageningen.

———— (1982) Aspecten uit onderzoek *Agapanthus* sortiment. In: Vakblad voor de Bloemisterij, 22.

Peter **Goldblatt** (2000) Wildflowers of the Fairest Cape. ABC Press.

G. **Gough** (1990–91) *Agapanthus*. In: Focus on Plants. Thompson & Morgan, winter vol. 5, no. 1.

———— (1991) Blue African Lilies. In: Focus on Plants. Thompson & Morgan, spring vol. 5, no. 2.

Henk **Griffioen** (1996) Tirion Vaste Planten Gids. B.V. Uitgeversmaatschappij Tirion, Baarn.

Miles **Hadfield**, Robert **Harling**, and Leonie **Highton** (1980) British Gardeners. A Biographical Dictionary. A. Zwemmer Ltd, London.

Sarah **Hart** (1994) Planten vinder voor de lage landen. Uitgeverij Terra, Zutphen.

———— (1995) Planten vinder voor de lage landen. Editie '95–'96. Uitgeverij Terra, Zutphen.

———— (1997) Planten vinder voor de lage landen. Editie '97–'98. Uitgeverij Terra, Zutphen.

Roy **Hay** [consultant editor] and Kenneth A. Beckett [technical adviser] (1979) Reader's Digest Encyclopaedia of Garden Plants and Flowers. The Reader's Digest Association Limited, London.

R. **Hegnauer** (1963) Chemotaxonomie der Pflanzen. Eine Übersicht über die Verbreitung und die systematische Bedeutung der Pflanzenstoffe, Band 2. Birkhäuser Verlag Basel und Stuttgart. Birkhäuser verlag, Basel und Stuttgart.

———— (1986) Chemotaxonomie der Pflanzen. Eine Übersicht über die Verbreitung und die systematische Bedeutung der Pflanzenstoffe, Band 7. Birkhäuser Verlag Basel und Stuttgart. Birkhäuser verlag, Basel-Boston-Stuttgart.

O.M. **Hilliard** and B.L. **Burtt** (1987) The Botany of the Southern Natal Drakensberg. National Botanic Gardens.

Craig **Hilton-Taylor** (1996) Red Data List of Southern African Plants. National Botanical Institut, Pretoria.

Yoshimichi **Hirose** and Masato **Yokoi** (1998) Variegated Plants in Color. Varie Nine Ltd, Iwakuni, Japan.

———— (2001) Variegated Plants in Color. Vol. 2. Varie Nine Ltd, Iwakuni, Japan.

Ian **Hodgson** [editor] (1998) NEWS, Wisley Flower Show. In: The Garden, September.

F.E. **Hulme** and S. **Hibberd** (1907) Familiar Garden Flower. Cassell & Company, London.

D.R. **Hunt** (1972) *Agapanthus caulescens* ssp. *gracilis*. Liliaceae. In: Curtis's Botanical Magazine, t.632 (N.S.).

A. **Huxley** [editor-in-chief], M. **Griffiths** [editor] and M. **Levy** [managing editor] (1992) The New Royal Horticultural Society Dictionary of Gardening. Macmillan Press Limited, London.

Richard T. **Isaacson** [editor] (1993) The Andersen Horticultural Library's Source List of Plants and Seeds. Minnesota Landscape Arboretum.

———— (1996) The Andersen Horticultural Library's Source List of Plants and Seeds. Minnesota Landscape Arboretum.

———— (2000) The Andersen Horticultural Library's Source List of Plants and Seeds. Minnesota Landscape Arboretum.

Coen **Jansen** (2002) *Agapanthus*. In: De Tuin *Exclusief*, nummer 9.

Mary Maythma **Kidd** (1950) Wild flowers of the Cape Peninsula. Geoffrey Cumberlege, Oxford University Press.

Kirstenbosch National Botanical Garden (1996) Collection data, genus *Agapanthus*. Printed 23 December 1996.

Max **Kolb** and J.E. **Weiss** [editors] (1882) Neue und empfehlenswerte Pflanzen. In: Dr. Neubert's Deutsches Garten-Magazin. XXXV.

Koninklijke Algemeene Vereeniging voor Bloembollencultuur KAVB [redactie] (1996) Keuring. Royale gladiolen- en *Agapanthus*keuring. In: Bloembollencultuur nr 17.

Satoshi **Komoriya** (1998) *Agapanthus* chapter in: Popular garden flowers of perennial plants. Shufu-to-seikatsusha, Japan. (text in Japanese)

Harold **Koopowitz** (2002) Clivias. Timber Press, Portland, Oregon.

P.J. **Kostelijk** (1986) *Agapanthus* de afrikaanse lelie. In: Bulletin van de Botanische tuinen Wageningen, nr. 17.

Hans **Kramer** (1998) Alles over *Agapanthus*. In: Groei & Bloei, Juli.

K. **Krause** (1930) Liliaceae. In: A. Engler, Die Natürlichen Pflanzenfamilien, band 15a.

Carolo Sigismundo **Kunth** (1843) Enumeratio Plantarum. Stutgardiae et Tubingae.

Otto **Kuntze** (1893) Revisio Generum Plantarum. Plantarum Exoticarum Pars III. Berlin.

Roy **Lancaster** (2000) Cally Gardens. In: The Garden.

Frances M. **Leighton** (1939) Some changes in Nomenclature II. *Agapanthus africanus* (L.) Hoffmgg. In: J. South African Bot. Vol. 5, Part 2.

———— (1965) The Genus *Agapanthus* L'Héritier. In: J. South African Bot., Suppl. Vol. IV.

O.A. **Leistner** (2000) Seed plants of southern Africa: families and genera. In: Strelitzia 10, National Botanical Institut, Pretoria.

Cytha **Letty** (1962) Wild Flowers of the Transvaal. Trustees Wild Flowers of the Transvaal Book Fund. Division of Botany, Department of Agriculture, Pretoria.

T.K. **Lowrey** and S. **Wright** (1987) The Flora of the Witwatersrand. Volume I: The Monocotyledonae. Witwatersrand University Press, Johannesburg, South Africa.

D.J. **Mabberley** (1997) The Plant-book. A portable dictionary of the vascular plants. 2d ed. Cambridge University Press.

Eric B. **Maliehe** (1997) Medicinal Plants and Herbs of Lesotho. Mafeteng Development Project, Lesotho.

Peter and Frances **Mallary**, Joan **Waltermire**, and Linney **Levin** (1986) A Redouté Treasury. 468 Watercolours from Les Liliacées of Pierre-Joseph Redouté.

Rudolf **Marloth** (1915) The Flora of South Africa, with synoptical tables of the genera of the higher plants. Volume IV, Monocotyledons. Darter Bros. & Co., Cape Town.

Yvonne **Matthews** (1988–89) Lilies and Their Relatives in Cornwall. In: Lilies and Related Plants.

Directie Tuinbouw van het **Ministerie** van Landbouw en Visserij (1963) Tuinbouwgids.

Dietrich **Mueller-Doblies** (1980) Notes on the inflorescence of *Agapanthus*. In: Plant Life, The Amaryllis Year Book, vol. 37, no. 1.

National Council for the Conservation of Plants and Gardens NCCPG (1991) The Pink Sheet. A list of rare and endangered garden plants.

G. **Nicholson** (1892) Dictionnaire pratique d'Horticulture et de jardinage. Librairie Agricole, Paris.

W. **Nieuman** and D. **Smit** (1987) Afrikaanse lelie of liefdesbloem. In: Groei & Bloei.

Trevor **Nottle** (1996) Gardens of the Sun. Godwit Press, Auckland, New Zealand.

Jo **Onderstall** (1984) South African Wild Flower Guide 4. Transvaal Lowveld and Escarpment including the Kruger National Park. Botanical Society of South Africa.

L. **Palmer** (1954) The Genus *Agapanthus*. In: J. Roy. Hort. Soc.

——— (1967) Hardy *Agapanthus* as a plant for the outdoor garden. In: Journal of the Horticultural Society.

Tessa **Paul** and Daphne **Ledward** (1990) New flowers. Cassell Publishers Ltd, London.

R.O. **Pearse** (1978) Mountain splendour. Wild flowers of the Drakensberg. Howard Timmins (Pty) Ltd, Cape Town.

Ch. **Penninck** (1906) L'*Agapanthus insignis*. In: Revue de l'Horticulture Belge et Étrangère recueil mensuel illustré.

Chris **Philip** and Tony **Lord** (1987) The Plant Finder. Headmain Ltd for the Hardy Plant Society.

——— (1989) The Plant Finder. 1989–90 ed. Moorland Publishing Co. Ltd, Ashbourne.

——— (1990) The Plant Finder. 1990–91 ed. Moorland Publishing Co. Ltd, Ashbourne.

———— (1993) The Plant Finder. 1993–94 ed. Moorland Publishing Co. Ltd, Ashbourne.

———— (1994) The Plant Finder. 1994–95 ed. Moorland Publishing Co. Ltd, Ashbourne.

———— (1995) The RHS Plant Finder. 1995–96 ed. Moorland Publishing Co. Ltd, Ashbourne.

———— (1996) The RHS Plant Finder. 1996–97 ed. Moorland Publishing Co. Ltd, Ashbourne.

———— (1997) The RHS Plant Finder. 1997–98. Dorling Kindersley, London.

———— (1998) The RHS Plant Finder. 1998–99. Dorling Kindersley, London.

———— (1999) The RHS Plant Finder. 1999–2000. Dorling Kindersley, London.

———— (2000) The RHS Plant Finder. 2000–01. Dorling Kindersley, London.

———— (2001) The RHS Plant Finder. 2001–02. Dorling Kindersley, London.

———— (2002) The RHS Plant Finder. 2002–03. Dorling Kindersley, London.

———— (2003) The RHS Plant Finder. 2003–04. Dorling Kindersley, London.

R. **Phillips** and M. **Rix** (1991) Perennials. Vol. 2, late perennials. Pan Books, Ltd, London.

Kristo **Pienaar** (1987) A–Z of garden flowers in South Africa. C. Struik Publishers, Cape Town.

Karen **Platt** (1996) The Seed Search 1997. Karen Platt, Sheffield, UK.

———— (1997) The Seed Search. Karen Platt, Sheffield, UK.

———— (1998) The Seed Search. Karen Platt, Sheffield, UK.

N. du **Plessis** and G. **Duncan** (1989) Bulbous Plants of Southern Africa. Tafelberg, Cape Town, South Africa.

I.B. **Pole Evans** (1921) *Agapanthus umbellatus*, Plate 1. In: The Flowering Plants of South Africa. The Speciality Press of South Africa Ltd, Johannesburg.

Elsa **Pooley** (1998) A Field Guide to Wild Flowers Kwazulu-Natal and the Eastern Region. Natal Flora Publications Trust c/o Natal Herbarium, Durban.

Nori and Sandra **Pope** (1999) Combineer op kleur. Planten voor de eigentijdse tuin. Terra.

Tome **Premier** (1828) Herbier de L'Amateur de fleurs. Bruxelles, Ve P.J. de Mat.

Bob **Purnell** (1999) Out of Africa. Plant Answers. In: Garden Answers.

Hugh **Redgrove** [editor] (1991) An Illustrated Handbook of Bulbs and Perennials. Godwit Press, Auckland, New Zealand.

Ann **Reilly** (1978) Park's Success with Seeds. Geo. W. Park Seed Co., Greenwood, South Carolina.

E. **Retief** and P.P.J. **Herman** (1997) Plants of the northern provinces of South Africa: keys and diagnostic characters. In: Strelitzia, 6. National Botanical Institut, Pretoria.

Elsie Garrett **Rice** and Robert Harold **Compton** (1950) Wild flowers of the Cape of Good Hope. The Botanical Society of South Africa, Kirstenbosch, South Africa.

Martyn and Alison **Rix** (1989) Wisley, The Royal Horticultural Society's Garden.

Roemer and J.A. **Schultes** (1830) Systema vegetabilium, vol. VII, part II, Stuttgarditiae.

J.P. **Rourke** (1973) *Agapanthus walshii*, Plate 1675. In: The Flowering Plants of Africa, Botanical Research Institute, South Africa.

Royal Horticultural Society [John Weathers (Assistant Secretary)] (1893) Plants, et c., certificated by the Society from 1859 to 1893.

————— (1950) Some Good Garden Plants. Plants that received the Award of Garden Merit, 1922–1944.

————— (1977) Wisley Trials. In: Proceedings of the Royal Horticultural Society.

————— (1994) Award of Garden Merit Plants.

————— (1998) Wisley Flower Show. In: The Garden, September.

————— (1999) Spice of life. Hampton Court review. In: The Garden, September.

Wilhelm **Schacht** and Alfred **Fessler** (1990) Die Freiland-Schmuckstauden. Handbuch und Lexikon der winterharten Gartenstauden. Begründet von Leo Jelitto und Wilhelm Schacht.

Paul **Schauenberg** (1964) Les Plantes Bulbeuses. Delachaux & Niestlé, Neuchatel, Swiss.

Numa **Schneider** (1911) L'*Agapanthus umbellatus* et ses variétés. In: Revue Horticole.

Justine **Scott-Macuab** [editor] (1997) Reader's Digest New Encyclopedia of Garden Plants. Reader's Digest Association Limited, London.

J.R. **Sealy** (1940–42) *Agapanthus inapertus*. Liliaceae. In: Curtis's Botanical Magazine, t.9621.

W.G. **Sheat** and Gerald **Schofield** (1995) Complete Gardening in Southern Africa. Struik Publishers (Pty) Ltd, Cape Town.

Christine **Skelmersdale** (2001) *Agapanthus*: a very personal appraisal. In: Hortus, no. 58.

Wim **Snoeijer** (1995) *Agapanthus*. In: De Parel, bericht van de Oranjerievereniging.

————— (1996) *Agapanthus* Newsletter. LACDR Division of Pharmacognosy.

————— (1997) *Agapanthus* Newsletter. LACDR Division of Pharmacognosy.

————— (1998) *Agapanthus*. A review. Wim Snoeijer, Gouda.

————— (1999) Er is meer in *Agapanthus* ... Uitbundige Afrikaanse lelies. In: Bloemen & Planten, augustus.

————— (2000) Immergrüne und laubabwerfende *Agapanthus*. In: Gartenpraxis Nr. 7.

Carl **Sprenger** (1901) *Agapanthus caulescens* n. sp. In: Gartenflora, 50.

Patrick M. **Synge** (1986) The Royal Horticultural Society, Dictionary of Gardening. 2d ed. Oxford at the Clarendon Press.

————— [editor] (1987) The Royal Horticultural Society, Supplement to the Dictionary of Gardening. Oxford at the Clarendon Press.

Vive **Täckholm** and Mohammed **Drar** (1954) Flora of Egypt, Vol.III. Cairo University Press.

W.T. **Thiselton-Dyer** [editor] (1896–97) Flora Capensis: being a Systematic Description of the Plants of the Cape Colony, Caffraria and Port Natal (and neighbouring territories). L. Reeve & Co. London.

Graham Stuart **Thomas** (1990) Perennial Garden Plants or the Modern Florilegium. 3d ed. J.M. Dent, London.

P. **Trehane** [editor] (1995) International Code of Nomenclature for Cultivated Plants - 1995. Quarterjack Publishing, Wimborne, UK.

W.B. **Turrill** (1960) *Agapanthus patens*. Liliaceae. In: Curtis's Botanical Magazine, t.380 (N.S.).

Nico **Vermeulen** (1996) Kuipplanten encyclopedie. R & B, Lisse.

Arie in't **Veld** (2001) KAVB-Bloemenkeuring. *Agapanthus* domineert de keuringszaal. In: Vakwerk.

The IUCN Species Survival Commission, Kerry S. **Walter**, and Harriet J. **Gillett** [editors], compiled by The World Conservation Monitoring Centre (1998) 1997 IUCN Red List of Threatened Plants. IUCN, Gland, Switzerland and Cambridge, UK.

Helen **Warren** (1995) Out of Africa. Collecting for the Nation. In: Amateur Gardening.

H.R. **Wehrhahn** (1931) Die Gartenstauden. Beschreibung der in Mitteleuropa kultivierten und winterharten Schmuch- und Blütenstauden mit Analytischen bestimmungstabellen. Verlag von Paul Parey in Berlin.

Theodorus van der **Wiel** (1996) Bloemenkeuring. Gladiolen en *Agapanthus* maken de dienst uit. In: Vakwerk.

——— (1998) KAVB-Bloemenkeuring. C. Duivenvoorde introduceert *Agapanthus* 'Prinses Marilène'. In: Vakwerk.

——— (1999) KAVB-Bloemenkeuring. C. Duivenvoorde zet *Agapanthus* in Lisse neer. In: Vakwerk.

——— (2000) KAVB-Bloemenkeuring. Duivenvoorde zet *Agapanthus* in Lisse neer. In: Vakwerk.

Anja van de **Wiel** (2001) Bloeiverlating *Agapanthus*. Praktijkonderzoek Plant & Omgeving, Praktijkonderzoek Bloemisterij en Glasgroente, Dr Droesenweg 5, 5964 NC Horst, The Netherlands.

D.O. **Wijnands** (1983) The Botany of the Commelins. A.A. Balkema, Rotterdam.

J.C. **Willis** [revised by H.K. Airy **Shaw**] (1988) A Dictionary of the Flowering Plants and Ferns.

Dr L. **Wittmack** (1901) *Agapanthus caulescens* Sprenger, Plate 1487. In: Gartenflora, 50.

A. **Worsley** (1913) The genus *Agapanthus*, with a description of *A. inapertus*. In: J. Roy. Hort. Soc.

Nicholas **Wray** (1995) Grow something different. Success with Unusual Plants. BBC Books, London.

——— (1998) Index Seminum Anno 1997 collectorum. University Botanic Garden, Bristol, UK.

——— (1998a) *Agapanthus*. A place in the sun. In: Gardeners' World, July.

Ben-Erik van **Wyk**, Bosch van **Oudtshoorn**, and Nigel **Gericke** (2000) Medicinal Plants of South Africa. Briza Publications, Pretoria, South Africa.

Braam van **Wyk** (2000) A Photographic Guide to Wild Flowers of South Africa. Struik Publishers (Pty) Ltd, Cape Town.

B.J.M. **Zonneveld** and G.D. **Duncan** (2003) Taxonomic implications of genome size and pollen color and vitality for species of *Agapanthus* L'Héritier (Agapanthaceae). In: Plant Syst. Evol. 241.

Shelly van **Zyl** [house editor] (1984) Wild Flowers. South Africa in Colour. Centaur (Pty) Ltd, Cape Town.

Internet
[1] www.bulbsociety.com
[2] www.vanplant.co.nz
[3] www.pga.com.au
[4] www.heronswood.com
[5] members.xoom.com
[6] www.horticopia.com
[7] www.biofleur.com
[8] www.aaronscanna-amaryllis.com
[9] www.smgrowers.com
[10] www.sgaravatti.net/ita
[11] www.gaboriau.com
[12] www.beechesnursery.co.uk
[13] www.ces.ncsu.edu
[14] www.new-worldplants.com
[15] *Web site defunct*
[16] www.norgates.com.au
[17] http://parft.uspto.gov
[18] www.plantscope.nl
[19] www.members.tripod.com/~Hatch_L/agapchek.html
[20] www.montereybaynsy.com
[21] www.smgrowers.com
[22] www.plantdelights.com
[23] www.magnoliagardensnursery.com
[24] www.lambley.com.au
[25] www.komoriya.co.jp
[26] www.possumpages.com.au
[27] www.capitalgardens.co.uk
[28] www.kwekersrecht.nl
[29] www.waysidegardens.com
[30] www.monrovia.com
[31] www.tytyga.com
[32] www.bulbmania.com
[32] www.smgrowers.com
[33] www.agier.net
[34] www.garden-nz.co.nz
[35] www.cpvo.fr [European Plant Variety Right]
[36] www.pvr.govt.nz [New Zealand Plant Variety Rights]
[37] www.nurseriesonline.com.au
[38] www.merriments.co.uk
[39] www.cgf.net

Catalogues, seed and price lists, etc.

Belgium
Ignace van Doorslaer, Melle-Gontrode (1997, 1997 and collection list, 1999, 2001, 2002 and collection list, 2003 and collection list)

France
B&T World Seeds, Olonzac (1998)
Bulbes d'Opale, Buysscheure (1995, 1996, 1997 collection list)
Lemoine, Nancy (1875, 1876, 1877, 1878, 1909, 1910, 1911)
Ets Horticole, Sophie and Jean-Yves Poiroux (2001)

Germany
Jelitto Staudensamen GmbH, Schwarmstedt (1996)
Max Leichtlin, Baden-Baden (1873, 1880, 1882, 1883, 1884, 1885, 1887, 1888, 1889, 1893, 1895, 1896, 1897, 1898, 1900, 1901, 1902, 1903, 1904, 1905, 1906)

Japan
Sakata (2001)
Takii, Kyoto (1999, 2001)

New Zealand
Kiwi Callas New Zealand, New Lynn, Auckland (1997)
Liners Plants NZ Limited, Hobsonville, Whenuapai (2001)

The Netherlands
Coen Jansen, Dalfsen (1996, 1998)
De Bloemenhoek, De Bilt (1994)
De Hessenhof, Ede (1994, 2002)
Hobaho Intermediairs, Veiling en bemiddeling siergewassen (1995)
Kieft Seeds Holland, Venhuizen (2000)
E.H. Krelage & Zoon, Haarlem (1888, 1894, 1897, 1906, 1920)
Maas & van Stein, Hillegom (1989)
J. Mater & Fils, Leiden (1892)
Rijnbeek en Zoon, Boskoop (1994)
van Tubergen, Haarlem (1914, 1916, 1920, 1925, 1926, 1933, 1936, 1937, 1938, 1939, 1940, 1946, 1950, 1954, 1956, 1965, 1967, 1968, 1970, 1973)
Verberghe Bloembollen, Zwanenburg (2001, 2002)
Victoria Seeds, Hilversum (1995)
Van Vliet New Plants, Boskoop (2001)
Rita van der Zalm, Noordwijk (2001, 2002, 2003)

South Africa
Microprop, Groot Drakenstein (2001)

United Kingdom

Apple Court, Lymington
Ballyrogan Nurseries, Ballyrogan, Newtownards, County Down (1995)
The Beth Chatto Gardens Ltd, Elmstead Market, Essex (1995, 1999, 2001)
Bressingham Gardens, Diss, Norfolk (1993)
Bristol University Botanic Garden, Bristol (1997)
B&T Associates, Fiddington, Somerset (1990)
Burncoose & South Down Nurseries, Redruth
Chiltern Seeds, Ulverston, Cumbria (1996)
Duncan & Davies Ltd, Highleigh Nurseries, Sidlesham, West Sussex (1996)
Goldbrook Plants, Hoxne, Eye, Suffolk (1995)
Great Dixter Nurseries, Northiam, Sussex (1987)
Monksilver Nursery, Cottenham (1991)
National Council for the Conservation of Plants and Gardens NCCPG,
    Agapanthus National Collection Bicton College of Agriculture (1994)
National Council for the Conservation of Plants and Gardens NCCPG,
    Agapanthus National Collection (1997)
Pine Cottage Plants (Dick Fulcher), Fourways, Eggesford, Devon (2000, 2001)
Raveningham Gardens, Norwich, Norfolk (1994)
R.D. Plants, Tytherleigh, Axminster, East Devon (1995)
Reads Nursey, Hales Hall, Loddon, Norfolk (1990, 1993, 1995, 1996)
Rowden Gardens, Brentor, Devon (1995)
Thompson & Morgan, Ipswich, Suffolk (1987, 1995, 1996, 1998, 1999)
Ulverscroft Grange Nursery, Markfield
Washfield Nursery, Hawkhurst, Kent (1995)
Waterwheel Nursery, Bully Hole Bottom, Gwent (1994)

United States

Joy Creek Nursery, Scappoose, Oregon (1998)
J.N. Giridlian's Oakhurst Gardens, Arcadia, California (1962)
Heronswood Nursery, Kingston, Washington (2000, 2001, 2002)
Plant Delights Nursery, Raleigh, North Carolina (2002)
Wayside Gardens, Hodges, South Carolina (1993, 1995)
White Flower Farm, Litchfield, Connecticut (1983)

South Africa

The Botanical Society of South Africa/Die Botaniese Vereniging van Suid-Afrika
    (1997)
Kirstenbosch, National Botanical Institute (1996, 1997)
Silverhill Seeds, Kenilworth (1993, 1995, 1996, 1997, 1998)

Index

umbellatus 'Profusion' see 'Profusion' 221, 261

umbellatus 'Torbay' see 'Torbay' 254, 261

umbellatus 'Underway' see RUBBISH 231, 261

umbellatus 'A. Worsley' see 'A. Worsley' 261

umbellatus 'Wolga' see 'Wolga' 261, 277

'Umbellatus Albidus' see 'Umbellatus Albus' 261, 262

'Umbellatus Albus' 25, 27, 33, 45, 51, 66, 69, 79, 122, 183, 220, 256, 257, 260, 261

umbelliferus see *africanus* subsp. *africanus* 65, 262

'Underway' see RUBBISH 231, 262

'Vague Bleue' 263, 288

'Valerie Finnis' 263

'Vans White' 44, 263

'Variegated Baby Blue' 48, 263

'Variegated Wilken' 48, 263

variegatus see *africanus* subsp. *africanus* 65, 263

'Variegatus' 263

'Variegatus Falcatus' 48, 49, 199, 260, 264

Ventnor Hybrids see RUBBISH 264

Verwood Dorset see RUBBISH 264

'Victoria' 44, 264, 288

'Violetta' 26, 33, 46, 264, 287

'Violet Tips' 45, 265, 288

'Virginia' 29, 33, 44, 52, 265, 287

'Virgineus' see 'Virginia' 265

'Vittatus' 265

'Volendam' 46, 265, 287

'Waga' 46, 57, 266, 288

walshii see *africanus* subsp. *walshii* 20, 21, 23, 67, 266

'Washfield' 45, 266

'Wavy Navy' 266

'Weaver' 28, 33, 45, 215, 266

'Weaver Lineata' 215, 267

'Wedding Bells' 267, 288

'Wedgwood' see 'Wedgwood Blue' 267

'Wedgwood Blue' 47, 111, 114, 267, 287

weillighii see 'Weillighii' 160, 268

weillighii albus see 'Weillighii Albus' 268, 269

'Weillighii' 10, 48, 67, 157, 260, 268

'Weillighii Albus' 48, 269

'Wendy' 26, 33, 46, 111, 114, 269, 287

'White' 48, 50, 154, 155, 157, 269, 288

white see RUBBISH 231

'White Beauty' 28, 33, 45, 50, 270

'White Christmas', 'White Xmas' 44, 270, 274

'White Classic' 44, 270, 288

'White Dwarf' see RUBBISH 170, 231, 271

'White Dwarf' ex Pine Cottage Plants see 'Summer Snow' 248, 271

White Dwarf Hybrids see RUBBISH 231, 271

'White Form' see RUBBISH 231, 271

'White Giant' 271

'White Heaven' 44, 52, 53, 271, 288

'White Hope' 46, 114, 272, 287

'White Ice' 44, 200, 272

'White Queen' 272

'White Ribbon' see 'Ruban Blanc' 230, 272

'White Smile' 28, 33, 44, 51, 220, 272, 288

'White Star' 46, 53, 273, 288

'White Starlet' 46, 114, 273, 288

'White Superior' ex Bristol Botanic Garden 44, 273

'White Superior' ex Reintjes see 'White Beauty' 270, 273

'White Superior' ex Snoeijer 274

'White Triumphator' 114, 274

'White Umbrella' 274

'White Wave' 274

'White Xmas' see 'White Christmas' 270, 274

'Whitney' 29, 33, 44, 52, 274

'Wholesome' 46, 275, 287

'Willy Bik' 275, 288

'Windlebrook' 47, 275, 287

'Windsor Castle' 26, 33, 46, 275, 287

'Windsor Grey' 28, 33, 46, 55, 148, 276, 287

'Winsome' 28, 33, 46, 276, 287

'Winterdwarf' 277

'Winter Sky' 277, 288

'Wolga' 28, 33, 46, 54, 71, 133, 168, 261, 277, 288

'Wolkberg' (Tubular Group) 48, 155, 277, 288

'Wolkberg' (Salver Group) 47, 114, 156, 278

'Woodcote Paleface' 118, 278